THE MAJULI ISLAND

THE MAJULI ISLAND

Society, Economy and Culture

D. NATH

Maulana Abul Kalam Azad Institute of Asian Studies, Kolkata

ANSHAH Anshah Publishing House

Price: Rs. 995 US $50.00

ISBN: 978-81-8364-056-5

First Published in India in 2009

The Majuli Island: Society, Economy and Culture

Published by:
ANSHAH PUBLISHING HOUSE
Delhi
Sales Office: 115-A, Vikas Marg, Shakarpur, Delhi-110092 (India)
Tel. : 9810522367, 22500954

Dedicated to the memory of
my late parents

Kanlara Nath Muktiyar
and
Pramila Muktiyar

Foreword

Majuli, a subdivision of the Jorhat district in Assam (India) and situated between 26°-25' and 27°-12' North latitude and 93°-39' and 94°-35' East longitude, is well known as one of the largest river islands in the world that immensely deserve the glory of a global heritage site for its unique scenic beauty and the cultural creativity of the indigenous communities that the island has nurtured since antiquity. Located close to the junctions where the rivers Dihing, Dikhou and Subansiri confluence into the mighty Brahmaputra, the size of the island was estimated towards the end of the eighteenth century by John Peter Wade to be 160 miles in length and 60 miles in width (160 × 60 = 960 sq. miles). A. J. Moffat Mills found the area to be 2,82,165 acres in 1853, while B. C. Allen mentioned it be 485 square miles in 1901. That the area sharply depleted in the second half of the twentieth century due to wanton erosions is understood from the records of the Revenue Department of the Government of Assam which recorded the total area of the island to be 1,246 sq kms in 1950, 924 sq. kms in 1971, 875 sq. kms in 1997 and 480 sq. kms in 2001. On the other hand, the population grew from 31,219 in 1901 to 1,53,362 in 2001. The majority of the inhabitants in the island are the followers of *eka sarania dharma* or the neo-vaisnavite religion propounded by the great saint Srimanta Sankaradeva who was the apostle of the *Bhakti* movement in mediaeval Assam and the founder of the *Satra* system that happens to be a unique socio-cultural and religious institution in the Brahmaputra Valley. Three of the well known *Satras*, namely, Auniati, Garamur and Kamalabari, are situated in Majuli and the social and cultural processes in the island are by and large oriented towards these *Satras*. Although the immigrations and settlements of the other communities over the centuries have significantly affected the demographic complexion in almost all parts of the valley, the Majuli Island is almost an island of the traditional Assamese life and culture. The indigenous art and crafts, the music and dance forms, and the food and dress habits of the indigenous Assamese have considerably survived the stresses and strains of time and circumstances in Majuli. Nevertheless, the life in the island is as vibrant and as dynamic as elsewhere in the valley. The modern educational institutions and other modern amenities reached the island due to the efforts of the government and the *Satras* as well as the enlightened leaders of the society. Some of the well known educationists, litterateurs, artists and scholars of Assam hailed from Majuli. The harmonious coexistence and the spontaneous blending of tradition and modernity is something that may not escape the experience of even the occasional visitors to the island.

Professor Dambarudhar Nath's *Majuli Island* (*Assam*): *Society, Economy and Culture* that emerges from the report of a project sponsored by the Maulana Abul Kalam Azad Institute of Asian Studies, Kolkata and the Department of Culture, Ministry of Tourism, Government of India, is indeed a full length monograph on the fascinating island that happens to be a pride of the Northeast and the entire country. The study reflects on the geography, geology and antiquity of Majuli, its ecology and environment, society, economy, polity and cultural life, the *Satras* and their socio-cultural role, and the history of the island from earliest times to the twentieth century. Besides his lifelong experience as a native of the island, the author has been gathering data for many years for comprehensively profiling the land and the people—life and conditions—of Majuli. His work is sure to be acclaimed as a well researched and scholarly presentation of the society, economy and culture of Majuli with a concern for the place and its inhabitants. The problems of the environmentally threatened island, besides its serene atmosphere and the achievements of its inhabitants, are scripted by the author to focus on what make Majuli so unique. I have no doubt that many will like to visit Majuli to see the things for themselves after reading the book.

(J. B. Bhattacharjee)
Chairman, Institute of Northeast India Studies, Kolkata &
Ex-Vice Chancellor, Assam University, Silchar

Preface

The present work is the result of a persistent desire that preoccupied me for the last three decades since at least the late seventies of the last century when I first felt an obligation to make a systematic reflection on my native place—the Majuli island of the Brahmaputra which distinguishes itself both geographically and culturally. As a matter of fact, I began with an ordinary article on its historical geography and social formation in the *Post-Graduate Journal* of Dibrugarh University for the year 1975, perhaps the next specific writing on the island after Benudhar Sarma's "*Luitar Sonta*", later published in his *Buranjir Sanphura* incorporated in his *Rachanawali* (ed. Ajit Kumar Sarma) in the year 1987. His writing was, however, not warranted by his innate desire, nor that was aimed at understanding the entity of the world's largest river-made island; but it was simply to record a tradition that speaks about the changes of the courses of the largest river of Assam (the Brahmaputra).

Two important factors attracted me towards the study of the island's history- one, its integrated society shaped by geography and religion; and two, its distinguished culture formed and designed by the Satras to which, so many people of the state are attached. To this I must add another factor: I was born and brought up there, at least my upbringing was amidst the nature of the solitary island during my formative years. I still cherish that memory with a nostalgia in the core of my heart; and I feel a kind of attachment to its topographical and social atmosphere.

Often, I feel, I should have started with Majuli in my early research career; there was enough scope for that. But my watertight academic specialization and some other accompanying factors compelled me to do otherwise. Then there was the question of professional advances, and I had to follow the course for my career. And when I traced out some time for my preserved subject to look into, I felt, it was by then quite late. Fortunately, the esteemed Maulana Abul Kalam Azad Institute of Asian Studies, Kolkata, under the Directorship of Dr. Mahavir Singh, came to feel my pulse, and I was granted this research project. In this case I remember with respect the help and suggestions offered by late A. K. Rai, who was then an executive member of the MAKAIAS, a renowned scholar by his own merit, and a member of Indian Foreign Service; and his daughter Reshmi Dasgupta who was in journalism, but who did her best to get the proposal approved at the Ministry. A. K. Rai is now no more. But his support for fulfilling my desire to do something good to the people of the North East still occupies my mind.

The present work is the result of this project on the Majuli Island. Two major questions have been addressed here: one is concerning its geographical identity-its distinction as a river-made island, and the other is its heritage character arising out of its geographical identity and religious distinction. The address has been made through an attempt at understanding of certain socio-economic and cultural aspects of the people on one hand, and its geographical antiquity and topographical conditions on the other.

The project was started from January, 2004. It was a two and a half year project to be completed by the middle of 2006. But it was not a work on a society which could be investigated in all times. Majuli island being cut off from the mainland by vast watermass all around, and it being subject to flood almost for the half of the year, field investigations could not be done in all the times. This was more so when flood seasons lengthen, and insurgency occupies the mind and movement of the society. *Bandh* due to killings and other causes, had made my work sufficiently slow for which I had to request the MAKAIAS authority many times to consider further extension. On the way, the two research assistants dropped themselves from the service to join their jobs elsewhere. To this must I add the poverty of power supply from which this University suffers regularly so that often I had to spend the whole day, or days together, without work. All this had made my work much delayed. I must thank the MAKAIAS authority for allowing me extended times to make amends for that delay.

I am indebted to the two Research Assistants, particularly to Sri Debajyoti Khataniar, who supplied me necessary materials as and when I needed them from the field. I am also grateful to all the individuals, Government Departments and institutions of Majuli which accorded their cooperation and help in the process of my completing the work. In this regard, I must sincerely remember the cooperation of Garamuriya *Satradhikara* Harideva Goswami, Auniatiya *Satradhikara* Dr. Pitambaradeva Goswami, Natun Kamalabariya *Satradhikara* Narayan Chandra Goswami, Uttar Kamalabariya *Satradhikara* Janardandeva Goswami, noted educationist of Majuli Bagaram Nath, Prof. K. C. Bora, Prof. R. P. Deori, Prof. D. Doley and Prof. J. N. Sarma of Dibrugarh University, Jagat Bora, Sri Rajib Lochan Pegu, MLA, Majuli, Hiteswar Bora, Ghana Kanta Nath, my friends Mrs. Arati Bora of the History Department of Majuli College, Mrs. Minati Saikia of Garamur

Pitambardeva High School, Rajen Bora of the Economics Department, Majuli College, Prof. Himadri Banerjee of Jadavpur University, Kolkata, Sri Manik Bora, a noted writer from Majuli, and all the Government Departments stationed at Majuli, and above all, all respondents from whom I have taken so much information in the process of completing this work.

Prof. Kulendu Pathak, the last Vice Chancellor of Dibrugarh University, had offered every kind of cooperation in my work. It was he without whose encouragement and cooperation the working out of the report would not have been possible. Equally, I would like to offer my thanks to Dr. K.K. Deka, the then Registrar and present Vice-Chancellor of the University, for all kinds of his official help and cooperation in carrying out the project. It is certainly my sincere duty to acknowledge my thanks to my wife Dr. Jahnabi Gogoi Nath, Professor and Head of the Department of History, Dibrugarh University, who offered all sorts of help and inspiration in completing the work. I must acknowledge that in most of the problems which I have experienced in the course of the work, she was the only person who encouraged me to face them, and helped me in solving them out. To this category of supporting people who offered to inspire me in more than one way, is Mr. Chandan Kumar Sarma, my junior colleague in the Department of History, without whose help a few books would have remained untouched in the process of preparing the report, which were of immense significance. Last but not, of course the least, I must acknowledge my thanks to my elder brother Sri Punaram Nath, Head Master, Jakaibowa Kalia M.E. School, Majuli, and my younger brother Sri Gunamani Nath, Vice-Principal, Garamur Pitambardeva College, Majuli, for their help in collecting data and for their constant inspiration in completing the work. In this group of constant inspirants are my two children—Mauman and Iman who exerted much pressure on me to swiftly complete the work. Equally I am grateful to Prof. H. Goswami of the Economics Department, Dibrugarh University, who has very carefully gone through some portions of the work scrutinizing their contents and compitions. I would also record my thanks to Sri Hemanta Kumar Nath, my cousin, and a lecturer of English, Sibsagar College, Jaysagar, for carefully looking at the draft. My thanks are also due to Sri Bidyut Chutiya who has typed out the work.

Place: Dibrugarh, Assam

Date: 30-10-2008

D. Nath

Contents

APPENDICES

Abbreviations

ADB : *Ahomar Din* by H.Barbarua

HAG : *A History of Assam* by E.A. Gait

ABSM : *Asam Buranji otained from the family of Sukumar Mahanta*

ASBS : *Auniati Satrar Buranji* by T.N.Sarma

DAB : *Deodhai Asam Buranji*

MDPH : *Mahapurush Shrimat Dharmacharyya Pitambardev* by Gangadhar Hazarika

GCK : *Guru Charit Katha* (ed.) M. Neog

KGC : *Katha Guru Charit* (ed.) U. C. Lekharu

SAB : *Satsari Asam Buranji*

SHTN : *Sankaradeva And His Times* by M.Neog

TB : *Tungkhungiya Buranji*

1

Introduction

Like few other places of India the Majuli Island in Assam is also a geographically and culturally known place with all its pride of past heritage and rich culture. A river-made island, Majuli is the largest of its kind over the world; and it is also the place of numerous Vaishnava monasteries of Assam called *Satra* that include the most well-known ones of the state. Naturally, its society also has some inherent features of its own, which are reflected in all aspects of its culture, although for an ordinary observer, its demography, economy, polity and culture may appear no different from those of the places like Jorhat, Sivasagar, Dibrugarh, Nagaon, Tezpur, Guwahati, Goalpara, or for that matter, any other place of the state. It is not unlikely for some others to contend that the island is populated by the same people as found in other places of the state, and that they are members of the same culture as their brethrens elsewhere. The most significant aspect of similarity they may see is in that all indigenous people here who have inhabited the island since at least the middle ages, inherit the same history and heritage as people in other parts of the state. To such viewers, topographically too, the island may not be much different from other parts of the country. For, Majuli nourishes the same soil pattern and topography and, therefore, agriculture and economy as any other riverine belt of the state; and its inhabitants live in the same pattern of houses, eat same food and use same dress and ornaments. Thus Majuli presents, according to them, a part of the whole system of the society. But this does not speak the entire truth about the island and its people, and their culture and society.

GEOGRAPHY

Majuli is, first, a river-made island, a water-locked inhabited zone; and, second, it is known as a land of the Satra which has made its life and culture distinguished from other societies. Being an island cut off from the mainland, its inhabitants had no free contact with the mainstream society in early times, nor the mainstream had such contact with it. It is sometimes said that most of the old generation people, born and brought up in the island, did not even cross the Brahmaputra to see the other banks of the great river during their life time. This was the situation till at least the sixties and seventies of the last century. The present investigator was informed by a few illiterate women of the island that they had never been to Jorhat, the nearest town on the other side of the Brahmaputra, the last capital of the Ahom state in the monarchical days. Crossing of the large river in boats before introduction of the steamer services during the British rule was so difficult and discouraging that only a few persons dared to cross the river for purposes unavoidable, who used to offer some *puja* or prayer and give feast to the neighbours before starting their journey as if that was their farewell function. Even today, hardly any village woman of old generation dare cross the great river without offering a prayer and some amount of *dakshina* to that large river and go out to the cities unless required by reasons of health. As a result, till a few decades ago rural Majuli presented the picture of a medieval society. Old beliefs and superstitions and blind support to whatever was preached by the religious *gurus* had kept it an unchanging, stagnant society. At the close of the 19th century, B.C. Allen, recorded that an 'old-world air' pervades the entire island[1] indicating that no sense of modernism till that time prevailed over the people.

Majuli being surrounded by water on all sides was a secluded site even before it took the form of a concrete island. It was then a kind of protected sanctuary sheltering varieties of wild animals—elephants, tigers, rhinoceros and others, and many migratory birds. During the middle ages, this topographical situation was taken advantage of by the rulers of the land who sometimes used it as a hunting ground,[2] sometimes, as a war camp,[3] and sometimes as a place for exiles or punishment.[4]

VAISHNAVISM

The fact stated above does not, however, explain the total distinction of the island. Being perhaps a part of the ancient kingdom of Kamarupa as testified by various legends, and in later times, of the Chutiya and the Bhuyan territories,[5] Majuli was always an inhabited area although its population density was certainly very thin.[6] Nakul Chandra Bhuyan, in his *Bara Bhuyanr Chamu Buranji*, has stated that after the main stream of the Brahmaputra had shifted to the course of the Dihing,[6(a)] many villages on the mouth of the Dihing in its right bank became part of the Majuli island.[7] It was here that Sankaradeva (1449-1568), the chief Vaishnava preacher and social reformer of the 15th-16th century Assam, first established his Satra at a place called Belaguri Dhuwahat and proselytized Madhavdeva (1498-1596), chief among his disciples, in the first quarter of the sixteenth century.[8] This historical background consequently opened the way for the next chapter of the growth of Neo-Vaishnavism there in the second half of the 17th century. Taking inspiration from this fact, and from the fact that the place was (and still is) isolated enough to accommodate the revolting Vaishnava spirit, the Ahom kings of Assam who ruled the state for about six hundred years beginning with the first part of the 13th century A.D., made it the home of the Vaishnava preachers by a royal decree so that all preachers would have their place in the island.[9] Thus, Majuli became a land of the religious preachers and of their monasteries called Satras. Since then a large number of the monasteries had been established either through the king or through personal endeavour of the preachers. It is said that once there were about hundred such Satras in Majuli. Thus in course of time, Majuli became a place of the Vaishnava monasteries and the Vaishnava *gurus,* and therefore, a pilgrim's place to be properly called the 'Vatican of Hinduism'.[10] It was from this fact, that the island came to be called as '*Etaka Mahantar Than*'.[11]

The Satras were, and still are, the most influential socio-cultural organizations of the land, and every person—old or young, belong to one or the other of the Satras.[12] Members from non-Hindu and tribal families too are here under the stamp of the Satra culture which has shaped not only their moral life, but also their material culture. The Vaishnava monasteries are the centres of all sorts of arts and crafts, music and dance, and other forms of performing arts, such as theatrical performance called *bhaona*. Dances cultivated in the Satras called *Satriya Nritya*, form the classical Assamese dance forms. Similarly, songs called *bargeet*, composed by Sankaradeva and his disciple Madhavdeva respectively, form the most distinguished class of Assamese classical song. It is to be noted that being the land of the Vaishnava monasteries, and isolated from the mainland urban society, people of the island developed peculiar behavioural patterns—simplicity of living, contented, and receptive in nature. Indeed, they form a distinct social unit with distinct value system that deserves to be noted.

POPULATION—COMPLEX

Being an isolated zone[13] with abundance of unoccupied land, Majuli provided shelter to all immigrants coming from all around since the middle ages, particularly from its northern border accross the Suvansiri river. Originating on the northern hills, this river has served as a migration route since ancient times; and it was through this river route that a section of the hill tribes now known as Mising (earlier *Miri*) came down and settled in the northern and northeastern part of the island.[14] It was from the north again, that large flocks of fugitives from erstwhile East Pakistan migrated to the island and settled in its periphery. Known earlier as *Silathiya* (Sylhetty) they now form a good segment of its population.[15]

Demographically, the society of the island presents a diversified complex, beginning with the tribes to the highly acculturated Brahmans and the Kayasthas. Among the tribes the most numerous are the Misings, earlier known as *Miri*. They form, according to the last census report, 34 per cent of the total population of the island. Other tribes include the Deoris and the Kacharis who together with the Misings form 43 per cent of the total strength, while the Scheduled Caste population forms about 15 per cent. According to the census of 1901, the density of population in the island was 24 per sq. km., which has reached the mark of 362 in 2001, which is higher than the state average of 340.[15(a)] According to the same census report, it has a population of 1,53,400 souls consisting of 79,481 males and 73,919 females, their ratio being 930:1000.[16] The society of the island could be seen also in terms of various linguistic and religious groups. There are Bengali, Marwari, Bihari (Deswali), Nepali, and a few Muslims. Thus the society of the island attracts much attention in so far as its varieties and distinguishing nature is concerned. One important aspect of their system is that despite all differences among themselves the people belong to a culture that is distinguished by what is called as *Majulial*—simplicity in behaviour and spirituality in living.

ECONOMY

Geographical location and topographic condition have much to do with the island's economy. Being surrounded by water on all sides, the land was once prone to recurring floods which were, of course, a regular source of fertility of the soil. Crops, therefore, regularly and abundantly grew here.[17] But, due to its geographical condition, cultivation of summer rice called *ahu*, and the long variety called *bao* are still popular than wet rice called *sali*. Among the cash crops, mustard and varieties of pulses are abundantly produced. But as flood also is a strong threat to agriculture, winter crop has now become more popular here than summer crop which is uncertain in nature. There is no industrial work worth the name. Boat building has been, however, a known craft here since early times. Similarly, pottery has been still a widely practised craft of a section of its people as the riverbank soil found a few feet below the surface, is its best source. Thus, both boat and pottery form a part of its river-borne trade commodities since early times. Fishing is a profession of a significant section of the people in the island. But many other traditional professions are slowly dying for want of innovation and competence.

There are a few semi-urban centers in Majuli; but no town as such. In recent years small townships are slowly emerging at Kamalabari and Garamur. Barring these two places, the entire Majuli is considered as rural area, and is treated as a *char*.[17(a)]

LOCATION AND EXTENT

Believed to be the largest river made island in the world,[18] Majuli, a sub-division of the Jorhat District of Assam today, is situated between 26°-25/ and 27°-12/ North Latitude and 93°-39/ and 94°-35/ East Longitude. Situated at 85 meters above the mean sea level; on the north of this island flows the old stream of the Brahmaputra—the *Luit* or the *Luhit Suti* with a thin stream of water at present and sparsely located reservoirs of water here and there creating numerous *chaporis* in its course. Its eastern part is called *Kherkatiya Suti* and the western part is *Suvansiri* (also spell as Subansiri). This part called *Suvansiri* is named after the river Suvansiri which is a tributary of the Brahmaputra (Luhit), and which, coming down from the northern hills, has fallen to the great river almost at the middle point of the island. Since the source of the *Luhit Suti* at its junction with the Brahmaputra through the *Kherkatiya Suti* has now been blocked by the Government of Assam by building a gigantic embankment across it,[19] this part, till it conjugates with the Suvansiri river, is now dead leaving the latter to flow alone over the old course of the Luhit covering the part to the west from its confluence. On the south of the island flows the Brahmaputra proper which was once the course of the Dihing and Dikhow combined. Thus, the two extreme ends of the island—east and west, are marked by the bifurcation and unification respectively of the two channels of the same great river.

That Majuli has been a large island ever since is evident from the beginning of its known history. Muhammad Cazim, for example, the biographer of emperor Aurangzeb (1658-1707), has stated that it was about 50 *kosh* in length[20] which is equivalent to 100 miles. In the last decade of the 18th century the British officer Ensign Wood, who was assigned the duty of surveying the Brahmaputra and preparing a report on Assam for the Company Government when he accompanied Captain Thomas Welsh to Assam in 1792 to quell the Moamariya disturbances,[21] has recorded that the island ended at Kajalimukh, in Nagoan (southern mouth of the Kalang) comprising roughly 130 miles in direct line up to Tekelipotarmukh in the east where the Brahmaputra divides itself into two branches, the Luit or Brahmaputra and the Dihing.[22] As published in the map prepared by Arrowsmith and Company in London in 1814 on the basis of data collected by Ensign Wood, J.P. Wade and others, it was recorded as 'a very large island'[23].

Dr. J.P. Wade, who also accompanied Captain Welsh to Assam as a military surgeon in 1792, on the basis of his personal experience collected from the Assamese people, and on his own observation, has stated that at the close of the 18th century the island was about 160 miles in length and 60 miles in breadth in the maximum.[24] He wrote, "Above Coliaburh, and opposite to Banfangh, the two great streams called the Dehingh and Looicheh, formed by the principal branches of the Berhampooter, form a junction and again assume the name of the last. The interval from Banfangh on the west to Baignman on the east, is occupied by the great island, called by preeminence Majuli; one hundred and sixty miles are calculated as the length, and sixty miles as the utmost breadth of the third division of Assam."[25] Wade's calculation was based on the presumption that a man in those days and in such topographic conditions, could traverse on foot about 20 miles a day.[26] He has further stated that the island was then covering the territory extending over the region from Banfang/Zoontiaran, a place about 40 miles above Kaliabar, in the west, to Baignman in the east. To be more specific, he further says, "The larger, and more rapid stream, named the Dehingh, takes its course to the southward, and passing Soonai, Deoorgown, and other celebrated places, turns to the westward, and joins the Looicheh opposite to Zoontiaran, about forty miles above Coliabur. Poolarghaut, on the southern, and Phogaderagown on the noprthern bank, are near the junction of these rivers. ...Ten miles above Coliabur, and a little below Soolalphat, the Berhampooter discharges a considerable branch to the southward, through Coliabur, Korungi, Nagown, Bebizia, Pait-burra-cossari, Jevointia, Dimurooa, Maiyungh, and Kawjuli, where it resumes its connection with the Berhampooter at Kawjulimook, about twenty miles above Goahawtee, after performing a semi-circular course of one hundred and sixty miles or more, and returning in a northerly and westerly direction."[27]

Thus, all early British writers while referring to Majuli after him, termed it as a "great/large island"; and in cases where they themselves took some kind of survey, they specified it in their own terminologies and concepts. For example, in the beginning of the 19th century, Francis Hamilton has recorded that "This island is said to be $7^3/^4$ days journey by land in length, and from one half to three fourths of a day's journey in width, the former we may call 30 miles in a direct line, and the width may be from ten to fifteen miles."[28] Similarly, A.J. Moffatt Mills, the Judge of the Sadar Dewani Adalat, Calcutta (Kolkata), who visited Assam in 1853, has reported that at that time the area of the Majuli island covered some

2,82,165 acres of land of which 7446 acres only paid rent.[29] Similarly, B. C. Allen while compiling the *Gazetteer of Eastern Bengal and Assam*, wrote in 1905 that Majuli island covered an area of 485 square miles, its western extremity being at the mouth of the Dhansiri river.[30]

There is no doubt that once Majuli island covered a large tract of land. Records show that in the beginning of the 20th century it covered $^{2}/_{3}$ of the total area of the Jorhat subdivision of the then Sibsagar District.[31] But, the island has been always prone to erosion since inception with consequent result of gradual reduction of its territorial extent. This is not only evidenced by large-scale migration of its inhabitants to other parts of the state, it has also been testified by growing population density in the island. As found in the state government revenue records, its area which was some 1246 square kilometers in 1950, was reduced to 924 square kilometers in 1971. It was further reduced to 875 square kilometers in 1997, and 480 square kilometers in 2001.[32] It is stated by the older generation there that erosion has become more rampant and a havoc to the island since the 1950 great earthquake. Even at the time of preparation of this work, erosion of the island has been going on posing a threat to the Bengenaati Satra and its neighbourhood.

ANTIQUITY

The history of the creation of this island is shrouded in obscurity. Neither the date nor the record of the event of creation of this island has been available to us at present. However, on the basis of certain geographical evidences and literary accounts, it may be presumed that Majuli took its island shape at least before the 13th century A.D., before Sukapha's coming to the Brahmaputra valley in the year 1228.

Existence of an island between the Dihing river (combined with a stream of the Brahmaputra or Luit) and the Brahmaputra (the old stream Luit) at least as early as the 13th century A.D. can be known from the early Assamese chronicles. It has been mentioned in one of such chronicles that Sukapha, the founder of the Ahom state in Assam in the early 13th century, had followed the course of the Dihing river down the Patkai up to the Luit or Brahmaputra through which he sailed down and arrived at a place called Habung. Here at Habung he stayed for three years; but finding that the place was low-lying and affected by regular flood, he sailed further downstream (the Luit) and arrived at the mouth of the Dikhow river through which he sailed upstream and arrived at Sangtak near Charaideo within the area covered by the present Sivasagar district of Assam.[33] This geographical narration of the chronicle gives us a picture whereby it can be presumed that the mouth of the Dikhow at that time was not very far from Sangtak, and that Habung was lying on the Brahmaputra a little to the west from the mouth of the Dihing, but contiguous to the mouth of the Dikhow. This mouth of the Dikhow river was certainly not the one at Kaliabar in Nagaon as known from the local tradition which states that at one time Dikhow had an independent course with the Brahmaputra till it empties itself into the great river at Kaliabar.[34] For it is not presumable in the then geographical context to think that Sukapha, sailed upstream the Dikhow from Kaliabar to Charaideo. Nor this mouth can be somewhere further east from Kaliabar on the northern branch of the Brahmaputra (called Luit) beyond the territory covered by the Majuli island. There is no record to show that the Dikhow had ever joined the old Brahmaputra on the north across the Majuli island. In that case there would have been a running stream (of the Tuni river) joining the Brahmaputra with the Luit across the island. The location of Habung and its nature of being a regularly flood affected region is to be noted in this regard. It appears to us that Habung at that time either included the region covered by the Majuli island, or the island itself was called Habung, a word which is derived from Bodo root meaning low lying and extensive flood-affected region, a name that points to the area of Majuli.[35] It is interesting to note that while narrating Sukapha's route from Patkai to Charaideo through the courses of the Dihing, the Brahmaputra and the Dikhow the chronicler did not mention the name Majuli, although it was certain that he was sure to arrive at the mouth of the Dikhow only after passing over a part of this island region.

Another chronicle, containing the geographical narration of the campaign of the Koch king Naranarayan (1540-1587) against the Ahom kingdom in 1562, has stated that Chilarai, the Koch general, had halted first at Dikhowmukh, and from there, he deputed one Lathuna Karji, his deputy, to proceed upstream through the Luit and then downstream through the Dihing to arrive at the mouth of the Dilih,[36] a tributary of the Dikhow.[37] This geographical scenario indicates the existence of an island located between the Luit on the north and the Dihing on the south which were forming the eastern extremity of the island through their junction. It also speaks of two mouths (*mukh*) of the Dikhow (one forming the western extremity of the Majuli island, while the other lying on the Dihing on the south of Majuli which was nearer to Gargaon. Thus, it was possible for a person to sail upstream the Luit (on the north) and then downstream the Dihing (on the south) and reach the mouth of Dikhow on the way. Therefore, it can perhaps be contended on the basis of this chronicle that from Narayanpur onwards the fleet of Naranarayan followed the course of the Luit flowing on the north of Majuli and reached its eastern extremity from where it turned westward downstream the Dihing and arrived at the mouth of the Dikhow. This further indicates that by that time the eastern border of the Majuli island was almost demarcated by the channel of the Dihing which has left its old mouth and has fallen into the course of the Dikhow that finally emptied into the Brahmaputra at Solalphat near Mahura about 40 miles to the east of Kaliabar by creating an almost a straight course.[38] As a matter of fact, another Assamese chronicle has referred to the island in the Brahmaputra very much distinctly as 'Luitar Majuli.' It has been stated therein that the Koch king Naranarayan had made his camp at Majuli, and it was there at the camp, that he received the tributes and presents from the Ahom king Sukhampha *alias* Khora Raja (1548-1563) who was defeated in the war.[39] In another such early chronicles also it has been stated that during his campaign, Naranarayan built a road (the *Gohain Kamala Ali*) from Koch Behar up to Narayanpur on the north, from where he sailed upstream the Luit and reached Chinatoli at Habung and made his camp at Juriya.[40] The name Chinatoli is well-known in the northeastern part of Majuli near Ratanpur. While Habung indicates a larger area, Chinatoli is a historic village of Majuli; and Juriya might have meant the junction of the two large rivers, for it is also recorded in the same chronicle that the Koch army then crossed the Dihing and reached the Ahom capital at Charaideo (through the Dikhow).[41] The crossing of the Dihing by the Koch soldiers at the point of the mouth of the Dikhow to arrive at Charaideo, when their king was encamping at Majuli, is important, for this information clarifies that by that time the Dihing was taking its southern course through the Dikhow, a process which had created the Majuli island. There is still another chronicle in original Tai, which mentions that the Koch army under Naranarayan and Chilarai advanced up to Narayanpur on the north and then crossing the Luit entered Majuli. " The Koch king entered into our country and stopped in Majuli. Chaopha Sukham ordered Chao Phru Phrang Ikhek to go to the Koch king to negotiate peace with an offer of two gold vessels, two silver vessels and a large silver jar. Chao Ikhek came to the Koch king who was in Majuli and offered him those things."[42] The Koch king received them along with the hostages at the turn of the *Dariya jan* (*dariya janar kokh*).[43] It appears that the Koch forces divided themselves into two parts at Narayanpur, one was a fleet under the command of Chilarai, while the other was a land force under the command of king Naranarayan.[44]

The next reference to the island by name (*Majali*) is found in another chronicle where it is stated that king Pratap Singha (1603-1641) built an embankment connecting the northern and the southern borders of his kingdom called *Meragarh* in Majuli, *Choatalar* Garh on the north bank, and *Lahdoi* and *Kotoha Garh* on the south bank.[45] But the most distinctive mention of the island is made by Muhammad Cazim, the biographer of emperor Aurangzeb, who, on the information supplied to him by the soldiers accompanying Mir Jumla to Assam, has mentioned the island as existing between the rivers Dihing and the Brahmaputra. In his language "To the northward is the plain of Khata (Tibet/Chia), that has been before mentioned as the place from whence the Brahmaputra issues, which is afterwards fed by several rivers that flow from the southern mountains of Assam. The principal of these is the Dhonce (Dihing), which has before occurred in this history. It joins that broad river at the village Luckeigereh (Lakhaugarh). Between these rivers is an island well inhabited, and in an excellent state of tillage..... extending to the distance of about fifty cos,"[46] equal to 100 miles. It is interesting that Cazim not only recorded that there was an island between the Brahmaputra and the Dihing, but he has also recorded its length.[47] Significant aspect about this information is that it was supplied to him by soldiers accompanying Mir Jumla to Assam in 1662 who had direct experience about the physical geography of this region.

Towards the second half of the 18th century we get a different account from a more serious observer. It was in the year 1792-94 that a serious internal commotion in the state[48] invited the British intervention, and Captain Welsh of the Bengal army, had to launch a campaign to the state to quell the internal disorders.[49] He was accompanied by a group of experts including Dr. John Peter Wade, a medical surgeon, and Colonel Ensign Wood. Wade has mentioned this island as Majuli, and gives an estimate of its measurement on the basis of information supplied to him by the people and on his own observation.[50]

Thus, the large island located between the Brahmaputra and the Dihing, has been known since at least the 13th century onwards. It is not known by what name it was called at that time. But it appears from contemporary geographical narrations as recorded in the early Assamese chronicles that it was perhaps called by the name Habung. The simple reason for such a contention is that after crossing the Patkai, Sukapha is recorded to have followed the course of the river Dihing downwards till he arrived at the Luit or Brahmaputra. Then he followed the Brahmaputra downstream to arrive at Habung. Being affected by regular flood, he is stated to have left Habung and sailing down stream the Brahmaputra he arrived at the mouth of the Dikhow wherefrom he sailed upstream that river and reached Charaideo.[51] This geographical picture indicates that Habung was no other than Majuli, a part of which falls in between the mouths of the Dihing and the Dikhow, or at least, Majuli formed a part of it. That this contention has some ground can also be understood in the light of its morphology. As we have stated above, Habung is a Bodo word meaning a low-lying flood prone area.[52] This fact justifies Majuli's identification with Habung as it is a low-lying and flood-prone area. It is to be noted that Majuli and its neighbourhood was once ruled by the Chutiyas who belong to the Bodos.[53]

It is difficult to ascertain when did the name *Majuli* first came to be used replacing the word Habung, if at all, it was so called. But there is confirmed evidence to show that the first mention of the term *Majuli* to mean that island of the Brahmaputra, was made at least before the mid-16th century A.D. In an old Assamese chronicle the compound word—*Luitar Majuli* (literally, island of the Luit/Brahmaputra) was used as early as 1562 to mean the island.[54] Consequently, that *Luitar Majuli* became simply 'Majuli' indicating the conversion of a terminology to a nomenclature. So, in some other chronicles the island is very clearly mentioned by the name Majuli.[55] The present author, however, believed that the island was called *Majali* prior to its taking a complete island form, which, then it was believed, took place long after the 16th century.[56] Some others even went to the extent of explaining the formation of the word (*Majali*) as *maj*+*ali* i.e. a road lying in between: *maj* means middle/in between, and *ali* means road[57] although it might be known that in Assamese there is no provision for conjugation of words (*sandhi*). There is no doubt that the word *Majali* sometimes occurs in some of the literary and epigraphic records along with the name Majuli. But these mentions are not only casual, but also indicative of being a substitute of the term Majuli. We find how even as late as the 19th century *Majuli* and *Majali* were synonymously used to mean the same island. Thus in Kasinath Tamuli Phukan's *Asam Buranji Puthi* (1844) we find the term *Majali*,[58] and in Harakanta Barua Sadaramin's *Asam Buranji* (c. 1870-1880) as *Majoli*, and Maniram Dewan's Buranji Vivek Ratna as *Majali* [59] while Hiteswar Barbarua in his work has used the word *Majali*.[60] Further, in a land grant inscription of the Bengenaati Satra recording grant of land to the Satra in Majuli in the year 1699 *Sak* (1777 A.D.) we find both the terms—*Majuli* and *Majali*. Interestingly, this inscription adds a third term—*Majali* to mean the same island.[61] It is interesting to note that the term *Majali* and *Majuli* were used in the early chronicles indiscriminately to mean any island in the Brahmaputra. For example, the *Asam Buranji* obtained from the family of Sukumar Mahanta, which is one of the earliest pieces of the Assamese chronicles, has mentioned that the Mughal forces were fought by the Ahom army in the year 1634 at the *Majulir bali* (sandy shore of the island) at Agiathuti in Guwahati.[62] This Majuli of the chronicle is simply an island in the Brahmaputra. It is far more interesting to note that the same chronicle mentions both the terms—*Majali* and *Majuli* to mean the same island in a different context.[63] Similarly, in the *Satsari Asam Buranji* and the *Deodhai Asam Buranji*, two of such early chronicles, we find both the terms—*Majuli* and *Majali* or *Mojali*—all casually used to mean the island.[64] Thus, *Majali, Majali, Mojali* or *Majoli* can be some of the corrupt forms of the name Majuli. There is, therefore, no denying the fact that *Majali, Majali, Mojali* or *Majoli* are some of the local or individual uses only on part of the copiers, or writers of the chronicles or of the epigraphs. They do not indicate certain geographical stages of the island at its formation process. As a result, the word *Majali* which was earlier used by the present author and by some others to mean the land mass lying between the Dihing-Dikhow combined and the Luit, i.e. the strip of peninsular land extending from the southern mainland like a gourd that finally formed Majuli, has perhaps no standing.[65] It is significant that no British record dealing with the geography and topography of this region beginning at least with the 18th century has mentioned the island by any other name than Majuli (written, of course, with different spellings). Existing evidences, make it clear that the term *Majuli* to specifically mean the great island, emerged during the 16th century, more specifically, in the mid-16th century when Assamese language slowly became popular in the official circle of the Ahom state. It is to be noted that when Suhungmung *alias* Dihingiya Raja conquered Panbari across the Luit to the west of Majuli, he conquered Habung, a name which we have identified with a place that included Majuli, on the way, in the year 1512, and subjugated its Bhuyans.[66] But, when Naranarayan, the Koch king, invaded the Ahom kingdom in the year 1562, he encamped at the Majuli island (but not referred to it as Habung) of the Brahmaputra and received tributes from the Ahom king at the turning of the *Dariya jan*,[67] a dead river channel, a part of which is still inside the Majuli island.[68] Thus, the years from 1512-1562 were significant in the history of the island in so far the development of its name (*Majuli*) is concerned.

TRACING THE GEOGRAPHICAL BACKGROUND

Some Presumptions

On the basis of traditions it was once believed that the island was created due to extensive siltation by the Brahmaputra at its bottom.[69] Researches done on the subject, however, have shown that the island was created due mainly to the geological causes leading consequently to the changes of the courses of the two rivers—Dihing and the Brahmaputra. The time and the process of creation of the island are, however, still remaining hypothetical.

According to traditions prevalent among the Assamese people, once (in unknown ancient times) the Dikhow had an independent course running almost parallel to the course of the Brahmaputra till it met that great river at Kajalimukh in Nagaon.[70] At that time Disang, Dikhow, Jhanji and Dhansiri were Dikhow's tributaries; and Dihing was falling into the Brahmaputra 'further east'.[71] In between the courses lay a long and a narrow strip of land extending from the southern landmass with almost all characters of an isolated island.[72]

In course of time (that too is not known when), the junction of the Dihing with the Brahmaputra, slowly dried due possibly to some geological process and consequent siltation in its mouth leading the course of the river to divert towards Dekhow.[73] It is presumable that there might have been already some connecting but peripheral or dead channel, or depression in the span of the landmass lying between the Dihing and the Dikhow which had facilitated Dihing's diversion towards the latter river. As a result of this turn a strong and a large volume of water began to pass through the course of the Dikhow making its course almost straight and parallel to the course of the Brahmaputra. This strong flow of water fell into the Brahmaputra at Lakhaw, about forty miles above Kaliabar in Nagaon leaving a part of Dikhow's old course beyond Lakhaw to fall into the Brahmaputra at Kajalimukh.[74] According to the traditions that left out part of the Dikhow beyond Lakhaw is the Kalang river of Nagaon.[75] As a result of the straightening of the course of the Dikhow, another curve of that river, resembling the circumference of a bow was left out on its right bank within what later came to be known as Majuli. This part of the Dikhow, according to the same tradition, is the Tuni river of the great island.[76] Lieutenant Wilcox, therefore, while collecting the tradition about the creation of the island, has stated that once "the Dihing did not disembogue itself where it does now into the Brahmaputra, but turning to the south-east received the Disang, and Dikho, the Jazi, and Disai river, and was discharged into the great river near Mahura."[77] It is possible that curves and channels of the Dikhow river creating and running around some smaller islands in its course facilitated the water mass of the Dihing river to flow straight through them from Majuli downwards as happened when the latter river first diverted itself to embrace the Dikhow leaving its old mouth.[77(a)] Thus, at this time, as pointed out by Sir Edward Gait, the Brahmaputra "flowed down the course of what is now called the Lohit river, along the north of the Majuli island, while the Dihing followed the present channel of the Brahmaputra to the south of it, and, after receiving the waters of the Disang and the Dikhu, united with the Brahmaputra at its western extremity."[78] *Thus, the land mass now encircled by the Brahmaputra on the north, and the Dihing-Dikhow combined on the south took shape of an island in its most embryonic form with the half-dead mouth of the Dihing demarcating its eastern extremity.* This historic event must have happened at least before the 13th century A.D. when Sukapha, the founder of the Ahom state in Assam, had arrived in the Brahmaputra valley. The narration of Sukapha's travel through the Dihing-Brahmaputra-Dikhow streams towards Charaideo as recorded in the early Assamese chronicles, and as stated above, is indicative of such a conclusion.

Dikhow, now being embraced by the Dihing with its enormous volume of water, came to be called as Dihing, and the former became one of its major tributaries. As a result, when in the middle of the 17th century the big Satras were established in Majuli, the biographical works of the *Satradhikaras* have mentioned them to have been established on the south of the Brahmaputra.[79] There was, however, a small stream of water that had been maintaining the connection between the Dihing-and the Brahmaputra through the former river's old mouth which could still then be topographically very much distinguished. This stream was perennial, periodical or occasional; and, as could be presumed, had been living during the summer.

Be that as it may, the landmass lying between the two large and long streams of water now took the shape of an island—*chapori*, variously called in Assamese as *Luitar Majuli, Majuli, Majali, Mojali, Majoli*, or *Majuli chapori,* etc. all meaning a piece of land encircled by river waters,[80] although the extreme eastern boundary was till then very much flexible, not well-demarcated. In the Assamese dictionary therefore, *Majali* is called an adjective of Majuli and is defined simply as a landmass encircled by water.[81] In the chronicles, inscriptions and the biographical literature, therefore, while describing any event of later times where the island was associated, all the terms were found to have been used indiscriminately to mean the same place according to the practice of the writers or copiers.[82] This clearly shows that the landmass that formed *Majali* or *Majuli* was possibly not known at that time by the name *Majuli* or *Majali*; for had it been so called, Sukapha's chronicler must have mentioned it by name as he had done in other cases, and, as he must have passed a part of it to arrive at the mouth of the Dikhow.[83] After this geographical developments both Dikhow and the Dihing had two confluences—one each at the places of their merger, and the other—first at Kajalimukh in Nagaon, and then subsequently at Solalphat or Lakhaugarh near Mahuramukh where the two jointly emptied into the Brahmaputra.[84]

The final stage was extraordinary; and it reflects nature's secret power to create and destroy. The major channel of the Brahmaputra then flowing on the north might have faced natural blockade in its course by its own

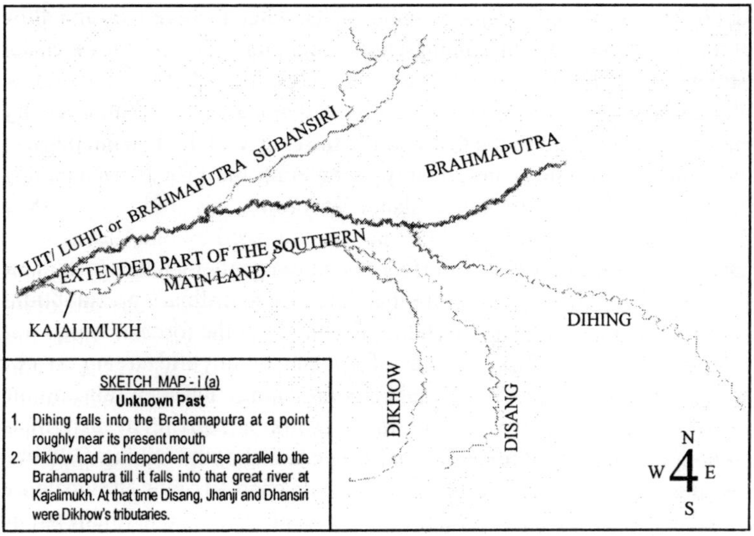
LUIT/ LUHIT or BRAHMAPUTRA SUBANSIRI
BRAHMAPUTRA
EXTENDED PART OF THE SOUTHERN MAIN LAND.
KAJALIMUKH
DIHING
DIKHOW
DISANG
N
W E
S
SKETCH MAP - I (a)
Unknown Past
1. Dihing falls into the Brahamaputra at a point roughly near its present mouth
2. Dikhow had an independent course parallel to the Brahamaputra till it falls into that great river at Kajalimukh. At that time Disang, Jhanji and Dhansiri were Dikhow's tributaries.

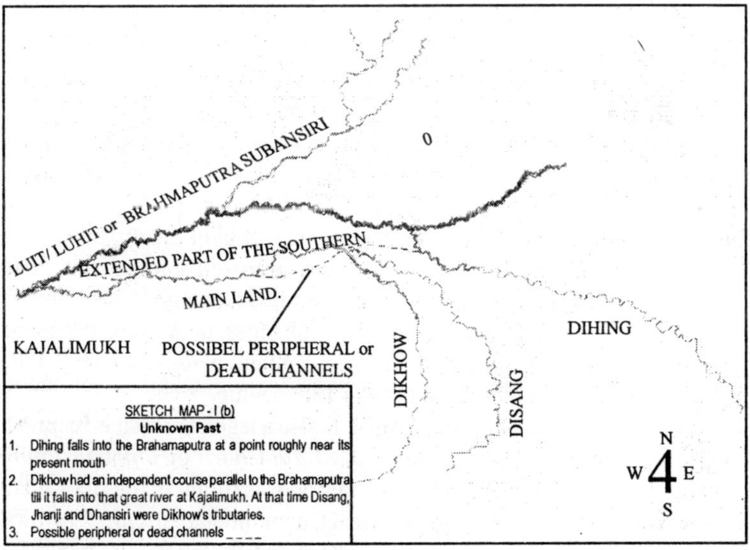
LUIT/ LUHIT or BRAHMAPUTRA SUBANSIRI
EXTENDED PART OF THE SOUTHERN
MAIN LAND.
KAJALIMUKH
POSSIBEL PERIPHERAL or DEAD CHANNELS
DIHING
DIKHOW
DISANG
N
W E
S
SKETCH MAP - I (b)
Unknown Past
1. Dihing falls into the Brahamaputra at a point roughly near its present mouth
2. Dikhow had an independent course parallel to the Brahamaputra till it falls into that great river at Kajalimukh. At that time Disang, Jhanji and Dhansiri were Dikhow's tributaries.
3. Possible peripheral or dead channels ____

deposition leading a major volume of its water to divert to and flow through the courses of the Dihing-Dikhow combined through the perennial stream at the dying mouth of the Dihing. Traditions have it that a great flood which occurred in the Dihing river in the year 1735, or half a century before that date, led to the diversion of the course of the Brahmaputra to fall into the Dihing, consequently completing the process of creating Majuli as a well-demarcated island. Recording this tradition in 1825 Lieutenant Wilcox has stated that he was informed by one Bagadamara Barphukan and some well-informed Assamese gentlemen that in the year 1735 or about fifty years before that date (all on ordinary presumption) there was a great flood in the Dihing/Dihong river the force of which was so great that by breaking one side of its bank the forceful stream created a new channel of the Dihing (called Noa-Dihing) and then fell into the Brahmaputra for which the latter took a southern turn near Tekelipotarmukh and joined the existing channel of the Dihing-Dikhow-Disang combined.[85] After this event the main channel of the Brahmaputra flowing on the north of Majuli, slowly died. This event finalized the process shaping the land mass into a well-demarcated island, distinctly cut off from the mainland, making it gradually larger in the coming years with the addition of almost the entire dead bed area of the great river lying in the north.

Thus, as recorded by Wilcox, "the great river from near Silani Mur to Sisi, flowed in a bed which still continues to fill in the rains, though it is of diminished size to the north of the present channel. It is called the Buri Suti, or Suti Lohit. The Buri Lohit, since this singular division of its former supply of water, has become of so little consequence that above the junction of the Subansiri, it is barely navigable in the dry season."[86] On the basis of traditions handed down from old generations, also supported by historical evidence of major earthquakes and floods bringing in astounding natural and geographical changes in Assam, it can be presumed that this great and significant event took place sometime in the last part of the 17th or early part of the 18th century.[86(a)]

About the creation of the island there is also a legend, which is recorded in a work of the late 18the century called *Adi Charit* or *Bhuyanr Puthi*. According to this legend, king Arimatta who was ruling in the Biswanath region within the present Sunitpur district, committed patricide for which he was to go for penance and make gifts to the Brahmans to amend for his sinful act. He approached many Brahmans including Lord Jagannath and the Bhagirathi Ganga. But all refused to accept his gift. Finding no way he approached the river Ganga in the form of Dikhow and sank into it his one hundred and seven boats laden with gold and silver and committed suicide by drowning. But Dikhow too rejected the gift and abandoned it by creating a large pool within it and placing all gold, silver and gems there. The news of the king's death reached Brahmaputra who was his son-in-law. Brahmaputra then rushed to Ratanpur, the capital, and buried all its gold, silver and gems under a heap of sands, and changed its course by bifurcating itself into two streams at the head of the heap. This heap of sands thereafter became the famous island Majuli with Ratanpur within it as a city of gems.[87] This name Ratanpur is still applied to a place in the extreme northeastern extremity of the Majuli island although the original place with that name had been eroded by the Brahmaputra long time before. The legend possibly has no significance in understanding the history of the creation of the island. It is, however, indicative of the fact that the Majuli island was created due to siltation and the changes of the courses of the rivers Dikhow and the Brahmaputra. It is to be noted that the legend forecasts that in the middle of the Kali age, the northern branch (Luhit) will take its course with the southern one, and Brahmaputra himself will uncover the buried Ratanpur city by eroding the heap of sand again.[88] The work called *Adi Charit* or *Bhuyanr Puthi* which relates the story, is in fact, an attempt to construct a history of the Bhuyans by some member of the (Kalita/Kayartha/Kath) Bhuyans themselves[89] who were ruling over the Majuli area in the early middle age including Ratanpur, a place believed to be named after the Chutiya king Ratnadhvajpal(1210-1250 A.D.).[90] Construction of the legend may therefore be an attempt on their part to rechristen the name of the city rejecting the Chutiya (tribal) identity, if it was at all named after their king.

There is no doubt that the final stage was materialized through the sudden shift of the course of the Brahmaputra through the dead channel of the Dihing. Suspecting that a single flood in the Dihong could not have altered the entire state of the geographical situation, Lieutenant Wilcox has stated: "Judging from this wild story as a specimen, it might be inferred, that the Assamese account of the singular rise of the Dihong in 1735 (?) is not well authenticated. Not only, however, have we the evidence of their histories for this fact, but sufficient proof exists in the great alterations in the state of the rivers which then occurred…The Abors and the Miris ought to be in possession of all the facts relative to this occurrence, as they were the first observers of it, and the latter tribe having their village on the east bank of the Dihong in the plains desolated by it; but they deny all knowledge of these remarkable circumstances…. The Abors gave a reason for the rise of the Dihong; but they did not speak confidently; they thought it was occasioned, by the river having suddenly penetrated, at a sharp turning, the earthy barrier opposed to it, or overturned a ledge of rocks. That this enormous body of water having so

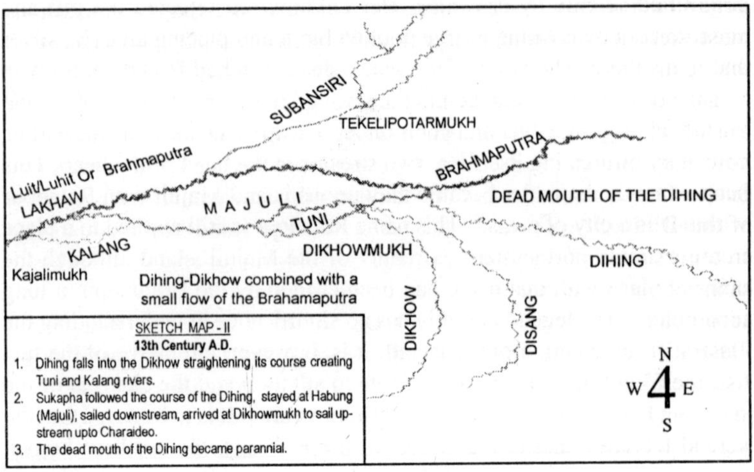

SKETCH MAP - II
13th Century A.D.

1. Dihing falls into the Dikhow straightening its course creating Tuni and Kalang rivers.
2. Sukapha followed the course of the Dihing, stayed at Habung (Majuli), sailed downstream, arrived at Dikhowmukh to sail up-stream upto Charaideo.
3. The dead mouth of the Dihing became parannial.

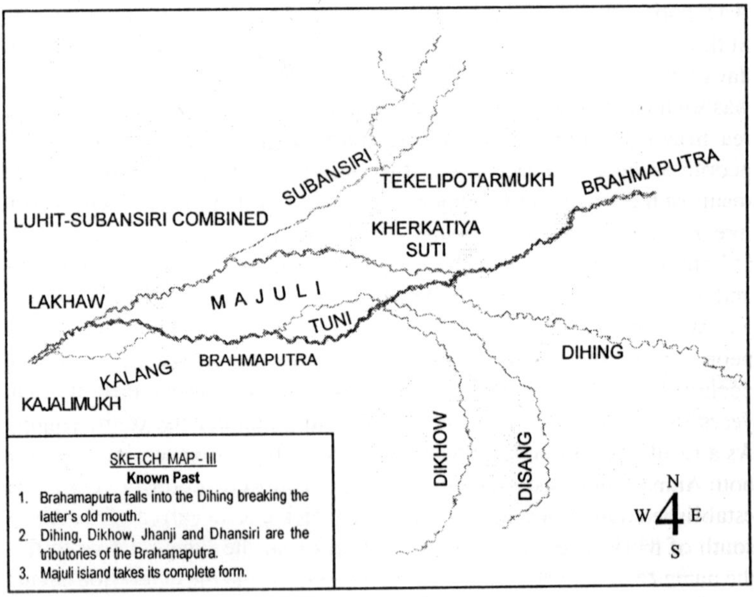

SKETCH MAP - III
Known Past

1. Brahamaputra falls into the Dihing breaking the latter's old mouth.
2. Dihing, Dikhow, Jhanji and Dhansiri are the tributories of the Brahamaputra.
3. Majuli island takes its complete form.

large a fall in that part of its course southward through the Abor mountains must exert an extraordinary force cannot be doubted".[91] But what created that 'extraordinary force'?

Decades ago, we presumed that the situation which compelled Dihing to shift its mouth from the Brahmaputra to Dikhow, the same situation now made Brahmaputra divert its course from the line of the Kherkatiya Suti to the course of the Dihing-Dikhow combined widening the old mouth of the Dihing.[91(a)] There is no doubt that large flood was essential for creating such changes in the existing geographical set up. But flood alone cannot bring about such changes unless earthquakes of higher magnitude accompany the flood. The earthquakes of 1897 and 1950 give ample illustrations for that. Interestingly, however, there is no reference in the Assamese chronicles to any earthquake of higher magnitude that occurred in Assam in the year 1735. But they refer to two great earthquakes which were also accompanied by floods of higher magnitude about half a century before that date. The chronicle called *Tungkhungiya Buranji* has mentioned that in the years 1613 and 1618 *Saka,* i.e. in 1691 and 1696 A.D. two great floods overflowed the state. According to this chronicle, in the year 1691 there occurred two great floods within a span of three days time when the entire state was submerged in flood, and its height was such that the level of water reached up to the third stage of the ladder reaching the platform of the king's palace at Gargaon.[92] Termed by the people as *Sanka* and *Sankini,*[93] it is recorded in the chronicle that as a result of the flood and earthquake that occurred in the year 1696 fishes like *magur* and *kawai* at Sadiya in the neighbourhood of the Dihang and Dibong rivers came out from their deep holes, mountains broke down, and great rifts occurred in the earth's surface leading to the burst of sand and water.[94] If, according to the tradition kept alive by the Assamese people, it is believed that the shift of the course of the Brahmaputra occurred about half a century before 1735, then it were the floods of the years 1691 and 1696 that resulted in the final shaping of the Majuli island. As a result, all biographical works written at the Satras have stated that both Auniati and Dakhinpat, the two most well-known Satras of Majuli, established sometimes in the mid-17th century, were established on the south of the Brahmaputra.[95] Contemporary records have mentioned that the name *Dakhinpat* means a settlement area (*pat*) in the south.[96] It is to be noted that even though the four years, 1691-1696, were the turning points in finalising the process of creation of the Majuli island, the entire process took some time, at least after the flood, to complete its creation process—dying out of the old channel of the Brahmaputra and making of its old bed into a landmass attached to the mainland Majuli on its north.

Thus, the process of creation of this historic island testifies to the fact that the island was born not by siltation alone, but that a major part of it was formed with a sliced out portion of landmass lying once to the south of the old Brahmaputra, i.e. Luit. This character of the island—an amalgam of sand (siltation) and clay (hard soil of the south) is still apparent there; although most part of its south-eastern territories consisting originally of the sliced out land mass being gradually washed away by erosion, almost the entire remaining part presents the bed of a dead river course with layers of sands and sediments, buried reeds and with innumerable ponds and dead river channels criss-crossing each other.

ECOLOGY AND ENVIRONMENT

Physical Feature

As the formation process indicates, the island has been once marked by a large number of dead river channels, ponds and marshes.[97] Dr. J. P. Wade at the close of the 18th century had noted that the territory covered by the name Majuli was criss-crossed by numerous river channels making it a cluster of islands. Even at present an acute observer will notice numerous and scattered dead river channels covered by village sites and agricultural fields. It was so distinct geographically that Dr. Wade has called Majuli the third division of Assam. He says, "Assam was divided by the Brahmaputra into three grand divisions, called Outrecole or Outre parh, (north bank), Deccancole, or Decccanparh, and the Majuli, a large island".[98] He has further stated that Majuli was intersected, in several places, by channels of communication between the Dihing and the Luhit (Luit, old Brahmaputra); which in actual sense, converted it into a 'cluster of islands.' In addition to these subdivisions, numerous smaller islands ranged along its whole length, all formed by various branches of the great river. He, however, clearly stated that 'these smaller islands were not included in the general appellation of Majuli, but were indiscriminately called *Chapori*; or small islands. Some of these were 'always overflowed in the season of inundation, others occasionally only.'[99] He then mentions a number of such *chaporis*, such as Rupei Chapoori, Runga Chapoori, Haludiati, Buragohain Chapoori, and a number of other distinct territories with specific and extended areas, such as Haludiati, Tamoolbari, Ghoria, Auneati, Baignauti, Comolabarri, Cowpotia, Poritia, Decanpat, Goromoor and Pohmara.[100] Dr. Wade, however, confessed that a "considerable part of Majuli, probably one fourth, remained unnoticed.[101]

The *chaporis* mentioned by Wade have now either fallen to erosion or else have come under human settlement. Almost half of the island towards west from Ahataguri onwards have been seceded by criss-crossing of the channels, and a separate zone called Dhodang Chapori has come into being. This zone is physically attached to Dergaon on the south bank although for all practical purposes, it is considered as a part of the Majuli. Similarly, most part of its southeastern zone have fallen to erosion,[102] and many known villages are shifting either to other parts of the island or have shifted to outside. Noted among those villages were the villages of Lahkar Gaon, the Salmara Gaon, the Meragarh Gaon, the Salmara Kumar Gaon, Ratanpur area and so forth. On the northern side, of course, old *chaporis* which were once full of reeds and jungles, and were shelters of many wild animals and birds, have come under human settlements. It is on this area of the island that most of the Mising villages are now located. One of such *chaporis* earlier known by the name Yogi Pathar Chapori, which was till early sixties a natural sanctuary of varieties of birds and wild animals, has now become a large inhabited area. It is to be noted that among others, there is a large village with more than five hundred population belonging to the East-Bengal Hindu immigrants locally known as *Silathiyas* (Sylhetty). Called by the name Manik Chapori village at present, this village was started by one or two settlers in the midst of the jungles in the late fifties when one had to cross a large channel of the old Brahmaputra from the mainland to arrive at the *chapori*,[103] and compromise with its wild animals including densely populated tiger families. Many other such large *chaporis* on the northern side of the island which once spread over extensive tracts throughout its length could now no longer be seen, nor even heard of. For a minute observer, however, this part of the Majuli island still bears the stamp of its creation history.

Majuli island can be divided into two broad divisions—outer and inner. Most river bank sides are made of sandy soil and prone to recurring floods. This region consists of the outlying *chaporis* and the lands lying outside the embankments, which is suitable for winter cultivation like pulses, mustard, vegetables and for making poultry and cattle farms. Almost all the buffalo rearing areas are within this part of Majuli. It is in this region that the ferry-ghats are located and which are inhabited by a major part of the tribal population. This part of the island form the outer area. The inner division too is made of sandy soil, but it has a thick layer of fertile crust made of black soil. It is this region which shelters the villages, Satras, schools and colleges, towns, administrative corners, and above all, the permanent agricultural fields. It is surrounded by high embankments all around, and it is this region which is drastically affected by break of embankments during the flood. The area lying inside the embankments can be divided into swamps (*bil /doba /pukhuri)*, and habitable and cultivable areas. While *bil* or *dobas* are used mostly for fishing, habitable areas provide for men's habitation (*bari*) and agriculture.

Majuli can also be divided into two broad divisions as far as its soil type is concerned. As we have stated earlier, a major part of the island was formed with a sliced out portion of the southern landmass. The rest was by the siltation and by the addition of the dead bed of the Luhit (Luit/Brahmaputra). The sliced out part has formed its southern belt mainly. Thus, one finds here both hard soil—*alatiya mati* and sandy soil—*bali-mati*. A part of this hard soil is used by the potters to make pottery. It is called *kumar-mati,* i.e. soil used by the potters. This class of soil is available in the south-eastern part of the island.

Rivers, Channels, Swamps, and Ponds (*Sota* or *Suti*, *Bil* or *Jan*, *Doba* or *Dubi* etc.)

Till half a century ago Majuli was a land of numerous dead river channels, most of them converted into ponds or *bils*. Their number was certainly enormous during the initial years of its (Majuli) creation; but gradually this number decreased due mainly to the topographical changes and dying out of many of them, and (then) their conversion to agricultural fields. According to an estimation made by the *Survey of India* there were at least 49 named river channels (dead and alive) and 112 swamps and wetlands in 1917. This number decreased to 50 in 1966-1972. It is to be noted that according to the same estimation, the total forest area of the island was 22.19 per cent in 1917 which decreased to 1.02 per cent in 1966-72.[104] Now, there is no forest, or jungle, even the *bils* and swamps have decreased to a much smaller number.[105] This topographical condition has given it a distinct ecology and a structure of economy. As we shall see in a subsequent chapter (Chapter-on Economy), the *bils* and dead river channels once provided flourishing breeding ground for fishes in the island which gave it a distinguished character as a land of fishes and scenic beauty.

There is no river as such inside the island. The only river is the Tuni. Originating from the Brahmaputra at the northeastern part, it flows through the island to fall into that great river again on its southeast. As we have mentioned elsewhere, it is a cut off part of the river Dikhow which once had a long course running almost parallel to the Brahmaputra.[106] In fact, this was the only flowing river that acted as drainage in the island. But, recently the river has been blocked at the Patiya Gaon village by building a large embankment across the river by the villagers thinking that it will block incoming of flood water from the Brahmaputra. But, what has happened after the blockade is horrible; all lands on its banks which once were good cultivable zones for winter crops, have now been submerged under water for a long time creating an artificial lake due to the land-locked water mass which would otherwise have passed into the

Brahmaputra sweeping all garbage from all around. Similarly, the old channel of the Brahmaputra called Kherkatia Suti which separated Majuli from the north bank creating an island, has also been blocked by the E & D Department, Government of Assam, in 1979 by building a large embankment across the channel at its extreme eastern point where it originates from the present Brahmaputra. As a result, Majuli has lost not only a great drainage channel on its north, but what is galling is that it has also to lose its identity as an island, the largest of its kind, and unique in its character of being made by a river. Thus Majuli's identity as a river-made island has now been questioned in certain quarters.

Climate

Like any other place of Assam, Majuli falls within the tropical zone being located within 26°-25/ and 27°-12/ North Latitude and 93°-39/ and 94°-35/ East Longitude. But encircled all around by the great water bodies, it possesses a moderate climate, cold from November to February, pleasant in mid-September to October and March-April, and summer in May to mid-September. A cool breeze always submerges it on the river sides, and it is not so rare also in the centre. Muhammad Cazim while recording about it has stated that the island "contains a spacious, clear, and a pleasant country."[107] Similarly, the account of Shihabuddin Talish about the climatic condition of Assam also applies equally to the island. He says : "The climate of the inhabited and lonely places on the banks of the Brahmaputra suits natives and strangers alike. But at a distance from the river, the climate agrees with the natives, while it ranks poison to foreigners. It rains for eight months (in the year); and even the four months of the winter are not (altogether) free from rain"[108] Thus, being situated amidst the two great rivers, its climate was pleasant and suitable for all people including the outsiders.

The same sort of climate prevailed over the island during the British. Francis Hamilton writing in 1808 has recorded it to be a very fine island. John MCosh writing in the year 1837 has recorded about the climate of Assam as follows:

> Assam is quite uninfluenced by the changes of the monsoon; the wind blows from east or north-east for more than nine months in the year, and seldom from any other direction for more than a few days at a time. At the commencement of the rains it more frequently blows from the west than at other seasons; these westerly winds are always hotter and more unpleasant than the easterly, and are as unwelcome as the east winds in the Upper Provinces during the hot winds. There is a greater equality of temperature whether during the 24 hours or throughout the year, than it is general throughout India. The hot

weather is much more moderate and endurable; there are no "hot winds", and a *tattie* is unknown. The nights are cool and refreshing, and a *pankhah* is seldom put in motion. It must be allowed that the cold weather is not so cold and bracing as in Upper India. During November, December, January, and February, intense fogs prevail, impenetrable to the sun's rays till eleven and twelve o'clock. March, April, and even May are the most agreeable months in the year, and during that season, Assam has better advantage than most provinces. So cool and congenial is the temperature during April that warm clothing is then not agreeable."[109]

Record of M'Cosh that "long continuance of the rains, together with the heavy fog, renders the atmosphere extremely damp,"[110] has no longer hold good now. As per data available, maximum temperature in Majuli today remains between 30°-34° Celsius in summer, and minimum 10°-12° in winter; its humidity being as high as 80 per cent. Summer is a season of heavy rain, annual average being 200-250 inches.[111] It sets in beginning with April and continue till first part of September. With sandy top layer one significant aspect of the island's physical feature is the absence of forests and jungles, and due to population growth and urbanization, winter and the dry seasons here as a whole are marked by clouds of dust-smoke which makes movement quite unpleasant and difficult.

Flora and Fauna

Being made fertile by flood and rain, the soil of the island has been suitable for growing varieties of herbs, trees and crops. Assamese chronicles have made few references to its topographic conditions. Being contiguous to and identifiable with Habung,[112] Majuli and its contiguous region on the north were always affected by flood. Sukapha is recorded to have left Habung for recurring flood.[113] King Pratap Singha (1603-1641) built large embankments to prevent havoc of flood here. King Gaurinath Singha (1781-1795) spent much time in Majuli while chasing game birds and animals.[114] Muhammad Cazim while recording about it has stated that "the cultivated tract is bounded by thick forest, which harbours elephants, and where these animals may be caught, as well as in four or five other forests of Assam. If there be occasion for them, five or six hundred elephants may be procured in a year."[115]

While recording about the general condition of Assam in the mid-17th century, Shihabuddin Talish has noted as follows:

> The trees of its hills and plains are exceedingly tall, thick and strong. Its streams are deep and wide, and both those that contains pools and those that do not, are beyond the range of numbering. Many kinds of

arduous fruits and herbs of Bengal and Hindusthan grow in Assam. We saw here certain variety of flowers and fruits, both wild and cultivated, which are not to be met with elsewhere in the whole of India. .....Large high spirited and well-proportioned elephants abound in the hills and jungle. The deer, elk, nilgau, fighting ram and partridge are plentiful."[116]

The middle age scenario continued till the beginning of the last century as testified by the office records. At the close of the 18th century, Dr. John Peter Wade has noted that Majuli being regularly inundated, is possessed of a stratum of rich soil above a deep layer of sand, and often clay.'[117] A century later the *Gazetteer of Eastern Bengal and Assam* (1905), recorded at the close of the 19th century that Majuli "contains numerous streams, lakes, and patches of tree forest covered with beautiful cane brake; and the general effect is very picturesque."[118] Stretch of green grass and forests and large *chaporis* provided for rearing herds of cattle, especially buffalo and cow and sheltered folks of wild animals. In another context, the *Gazetteer* recorded that Majuli 'presents a very different appearance. The land lies low, the population is comparatively sparse, and extensive tracts are covered with high grass jungle and forest, which is rendered particularly beautiful by the luxuriant growth of the creeping cane."[119]

Once full of jungles and forests, and shelter of enormous wild animals and birds, Majuli has, however, gradually lost its forest resources. It is interesting to note that while ¼th part of the island was still undiscovered till 1800 A.D.[120] due to its impenetrable topographic conditions, its forest cover has since been reduced to insignificance.[121] Even a few decades ago, Majuli was a land of forests and jungles, and large boats capable of bearing loads of enormous quantity and size could be built from a single trunk.[122] During the middle ages Majuli provided the Ahom state with a few boat-making factories (*naosali*/naosal) at Salmora, Auniati, especially Saraibari and a few other places.[123] Baloram Nath who hailed from village Baraguri in northeastern part of upper Majuli, and who studied in the Majuli Auniati Hemchandra High School (at Kamalabari) in the thirties of the last century, has noted his experience by saying that in those days it was awesome to go to the school hostel located at Kamalabari, a distance of about 20 kilometers from his village, due to thick forests and jungles that covered the path and sheltered wild animals.[124] There was no road as such, and one had to move amidst jungles full of tigers and wild buffaloes.[125] A dense forest wooded with Urium, Autenga, Azar, Koroi, and other valuable trees stretched over the region surrounding two large ponds called *Batamari* and *Solmari bil* created long back by the dead river channels.[126] Pitambardeva Goswami, *Satradhikara* of Garamur Satra (1885-1962), was to devote most part of his daily life in hunting tigers in the neighbourhood for the safety of the cows and the villagers.[127] The present author experienced in his childhood (during the early sixties) how moving to and fro in the evening in the village was not at all safe because of frequent roaming of wild animals. It was quite enjoyable to hear a tiger's roar, jackel's evening cry, and regular rhythms produced by flocks of birds called *haikali* and *dauk* coming from amidst the jungles covering the *chaporis* across the river channels. Remembering his early days in the early decades of the last century, Tarun Chandra Pamegam one of the early educated persons from among the Mising tribe of Majuli, has recorded as follow:

> Till that time most of its areas were covered with the forests, jungles and ponds, and grazing lands with high grass jungles. The forests were full of trees such as *uriam*, *koroi* and *ejar*. There were large number of fruit trees from where men and the birds had eaten fruits in their own way. The forests were known by various names such as Barbari, Dhekiajan, Paikpara, Chakarpeti, etc. At that time Majuli was thinly populated and the land was the abode of wild animals. Although there was no scope for catching elephants through *mela chikar* or *kheda chikar*, there were herds of wild elephants roaming hither and thither in search of food. During this time cultivators used to build elevated tents on the branches of the large and long trees and lit lamps to ward off the wild elephants which came to eat the paddy from the field. Some times even rhinoceros were also appearing in its jungles. I remember, one of such rhinos was killed by the people near Kamalabari about the mid thirties of the last century. Rhino hunters were not penalysed which was due possibly to the fact that Majuli being situated far away and cut off from the district headquarters, no body came to know about it. ...The forests of the island were also the roaming ground of herds of wild buffaloes. Among the wild animals tigers were the most numerous in the forests of the island.[128]

This picture is no longer there in Majuli now, and by early seventies, its forest cover was reduced to just 1.02 per cent only.[129] And now, except the peripheral *chaporis* with thinly covered *birina* reeds, no jungle or animal herds are to be seen there, although in the months of December-January mustard crop with yellow flowers still covers the field up to the extreme horizon. In February and March, villages look ablaze with the blooming flowers of *simalu*, *palash* and *modar* trees. And in winter like early times, some flocks of migratory birds still try to make here a heaven of their sports.[130]

With river channels, marshes, swamps and ponds Majuli was till recent years a land of fishes. Indeed, it was known for both fish and milk. It is a folk saying that if men had not eaten fish, the fish would have eaten them (men) here. It is stated by the elderly generation in Majuli that during the 1950 earthquake, men could not move around due to the rotten smell of volumes of fishes that got scattered over the fields and grazings.[131] Majuli, however, does not present such a picture of availability of fish today.[132]

THE STUDY

Scope and Objective

The scope of the work is confined to the study of the Majuli island in its historical perspective. It includes study of its social, cultural and economic aspects in the past and in the present. The objective is to unearth the distinguished features of the society in the island and the extent and nature of changes it has experienced through the ages. Attempt has been made to understand its cultural heritage and its present status.

Literature Survey

There is no existing research work on Majuli in humanities and social sciences. There are however, a few works on the Satras: T. N. Sarma's *Auniati Satrar Buranji* (Assamese, 1975), Benudhar Sharma's *Dakhinpat Satra* (Assamese, 1977), Gangadhar Hazarika's *Mahapurush Dharamacharaya Sri Srimat Pitambardeva Goswami* (Assamese, 2 vols. 1924, 1964), Narayan Chandra Goswami's *Satra Sanskritir Swarna Rekha* (1987), Dr. Pitambardeva Goswami's *Satriya Utsavar Parichoy aru Tatparyya* (2001), and the present author's *Adhunikatar Unmeshat Shri Shri Auniati Satra* (Assamese, 2004). But they are all on certain individual Satras only; even those by Narayan Chandra Goswami and Dr. Pitambardeva Goswami are mainly about Kamalabari and Auniati Satra respectively. And Gangadhar Hazarika's work too is a biography of a *Satradhikara*. Moreover, except the one by the present author, most other works are not based on proper historical methodology and interpretation. Another work on the economy of the island is the *Income Expenditure and Savings in Rural India* (1985) by K.C. Bora. But this is strictly a work on 'behavioural relationships between income, expenditure, savings and investment in the rural areas of Assam' for which a few villages from Majuli were taken as model study. Besides, there are two other edited works on the Majuli island; one edited by K. C. Kalita, and the other by P. K. Mahanta. But they are merely collection of some unsystematically arranged articles attempting on some fragmentary aspects, mainly on the Satras of Majuli. They not only fail to be a systematic study, but they are also devoid of any methodology. At the same time, the one edited by

FIG. 1.1 MIGRATORY BIRDS VISITING MAJULI

P. K. Mahanta is but a form of conglomeration of some illogically arranged emotional writings where the editor has presented them in his own cut-and-paste methods.

There are however, a few articles on the historical geography of Majuli. The first one, titled 'Brahmaputrar Sonta" by Benudhar Sharma, was published in 1987 in his collected work (Vol. II) where the author without reference to any source has attempted to record the change of the course of the Dihing and the Brahmaputra. Long time after, in 1993, the present author wrote his paper titled "Luitar Majuli Majuli Dvip: Iyar Sristi aru Aitihasik Avasthan" which the organizing committee for the 14th session of the North East India History Association, held at Jorhat, had published in its *Souvenir*. This paper is, in fact, the first attempt to make a scientific study of socio-geographical and cultural history of the island. This was followed by J.N. Sarma's paper titled "Origin and Some Geomorphological Changes of Majuli Island of the Brahmaputra River in Assam, India" which was published in the journal *Geomorphology* (Vol. 60, pp. 1-19) in 2004. The paper deals with certain geomorphological aspects about the island. Recently, the present author has published a few research papers on the Satras of Majuli and their role in the social change and development of Assam. These include *Satras in Colonial Assam: Their Response to the Emerging Socio-Political Issues* (published by the ICHR, Regional Centre, Guwahati, 2007), *Social Change in Rural Assam in the 20th Century: A Study of the Majuli Island* (*Proceedings of the Indian History Congress*, 66th Session, Visva-Bharati, Santiniketan, 2005-2006), and *Preparation and Preservation of Manuscript—A Dead Tradition in the Vaishnava Monasteries of Assam* (published in the *Proceedings of the North East India History Association*, 25th Session, Shillong, 2004).

Thus Majuli despite its long history and heritage, still awaits a proper historical study. It is expected that the present work will open a new chapter inaugurating the study of history and culture of the island, and of such societies elsewhere.

Methodology

Materials for writing the present work have been collected from various sources which can be broadly divided into (a) literary-cum-historical and (b) field report and personal observation. Thus the present study is based on both empirical and historical methodology. Extensive field work was done in the nook and corner of the island to collect materials on the basis of direct investigation and observation.

There are more than 210 cadastral villages in Majuli at the time of our field investigation. They are distributed in two blocks—Majuli Development Block and Ujani Majuli Development Block comprising of twenty Gaon-Panchayats. We have surveyed 33 villages, 15.71 per cent of the total, for our investigation selected on certain parameters, such as geographical distribution, administrative distribution, class and caste distribution, and on the basis by religion, economy and education. Thus, the villages under survey are distributed over all regions of the island and represent all communities inhabiting it. Well-devised questionnaires were prepared and distributed among certain families of a village consisting of not less than 15 per cent of the population. These families were selected on the basis of certain criteria, such as education, economy, family status, location and so forth. Investigators visiting the families supplied the questionnaires to the head of the family and filled up the answer sheets by noting them down right at their place. In some other cases, written responses were collected. The Principal Investigator frequently visited the field and supervised the system and, if necessary, himself noted down or tried to find out the answers to certain queries. The latter also visited the libraries for purpose of verification of data so collected, or to collect new and additional data. Collected data were then assimilated and verified, and used as per requirement. Some of the data thus collected and used in the report are placed in the appendices. Historical data used in the present work include all literary sources, epigraphic records, Government and non-government documents, biographical works, foreign travelers' accounts, chronicles, diaries and letters and so forth. Indeed, the work being historical, most part of the work is based on these data used in the pattern of historical analysis.

Most literary materials are taken from early Assamese chronicles (*buranjis*), biographical works (*charit puthis*), Persian chronicles (in English translations), British records including reports, gazetteers, census records and accounts, archival records, modern Assamese literature, and oral traditions prevalent among the people of the Majuli island. Assamese chronicles are used for understanding of the geographical formation of the island, and for study of its socio-economic and cultural base. The biographical literature are used for the same purpose. It is to be noted that some of the later biographical works written on the life and works of the *Satradhikaras* of the Vaishnava monasteries (*Satra*) of the island, are useful not only to investigate the socio-cultural aspects of the 18th—19th century society, but they are also useful to understand political history of the island, more particularly, to understand the relationship between religion and politics, or relation of the Satras with the politics of the state. We have one modern biography of a *Satradhikara* (Pitambardeva Goswami of Garamur Satra), called *Mahapurush Sri Srimat Dharmacharyya Pitambardeva Goswami* (by Gangadhar Hazarika), which is not only most exhaustive, but also authentic to understand 20th century socio-cultural history of the island as it contains most of the documents recording the events of the time. Many original records which are difficult to procure at present, are quoted from this work. Similarly, a good number of biographical works composed in the Satras of Majuli supply material for the period of the British rule in Assam. Most modern literature used in the report include works of Tarun Chandra Pamegam, Pitambardeva Goswami, Tirthanath Sarma, Benudhar Sarma, and those of the present author.

The work important groups of literature include the records, accounts, and reports of the British administrators. Mention may be made of Horace Hayman's *Documents Illustrative of the Burmese Wars* (for Ensign Wood's map and survey report, published in 1827), Dr. J.P. Wade's *A Geographical Sketch of Assam* -1800, Captain Welsh's *Report*,1793, (incorporated in Mackenzie's *Report on the Eastern Frontier of British India*), reports left by Neufville and Lieutenant Wilcox (in the *Asiatic Researches*), Francis Buchanon Hamilton's *An Account of Assam* (1808), John M'Cosh's *Topography of Assam* (1837), William Robinson's *A Descriptive Account of Assam* (1841), A.J. Moffatt Mills' *Report on the Province of Assam* (1853), W.W. Hunter's *A Statistical Account of Assam* (1872), Gait and other's *Report on the Census of India*, 1891, B.C. Allen et.al.'s *Gazetteer of Eastern Bengal and Assam* (1905), and E.A. Gait's *A History of Assam* (1905).

The work has been prepared in historical perspective, and due care has been taken to make interpretations rational and scientific.

END NOTES

1. B.C. Allen et. al., *Gazetteer of Bengal and North East India* (earlier *Provincial Gazetteer of India: Eastern Bengal and Assam,* 1905), Reprint, New Delhi, 1979, (Reproduced, 2001), p. 159.
2. See the *Tungkhungiya Buranji* (ed.) S.K. Bhuyan, Reprint, Guwahati, 1964, p. 93 (abbreviated as TB).
3. See *Deodhai Asam Buranji*, (ed) S.K. Bhuyan, Reprint, Guwahati, 1990, p. 47 (abbreviated as DAB).
4. Assamese chronicles refer to the exile of the second queen of the Ahom king Tyaokhamthi (1380-1389) in Habung on the Brahmaputra where she was given shelter by a Brahman family. It was here that she gave birth to Sudangpha *alias* Bamuni Konwar, who ascended the throne in 1397 after the death of his father. See, DAB, p. 11; also E.A. Gait, *A History of Assam*, 2nd edition Reprint, Gauhati, 1981, p. 82 (abbreviated as HAG).
5. This has been discussed in Chapter VI of this work. Also see B. Sharma, *Dakhinpat Satra*, Guwahati, 1977, p. 7; K.L. Barua, *Early History of Kamarupa*, Gauhati, 1966, p. 181.
6. Dr. J.P. Wade in his *A Geographical Sketch of Assam, 1800 A.D.*, (incorporated in his *An Account of Assam*, ed. B. Sharma, North Lakhimpur, 1927) has stated that till the close of the 18th century about 1/4th part of the island remained undiscovered and uninhabited. See p. 32. The *Gazetteer* of Allen *et. al.* (pp. 159, 572) has mentioned that at the beginning of the 20th century there were only 35,000 inhabitants in the island.

6(a). This aspect has been discussed later. See *infra*, pp. 19ff.

7. Golaghat, 1961, p. 47.
8. M. Neog, *Sankaradeva and His Times: Early History .of the Vaishnava Faith and Movement in Assam*, Gauhati, 1965, p. 110 (henceforth abbreviated as SHTN).
9. HAG, p. 171; D. Nath, 'Satra and Social Change in Majuli,' in *Jyotirgamaya* (a commemorative .volume published on the occasion of the 350th anniversary of the Garamur Satra, Majuli, April, 2007), ed. D. Saikia, Garamur, 2007, pp. 127ff.
10. See D. Nath, 'Majuli-Eti Aitihasik Parichay' in K. C. Kalita (ed.), *Majuli*, Guwahati, 2001, p. 11.
11. This has been discussed in Chapter-V of this work.
12. D. Nath, 'Satras in Colonial Assam—Their Response to the Emerging Socio-Political Issues', occasional lecture no.5, ICHR, Guwahati, 2007, pp. 6ff; Audrey Cantlie, *The Assamese*, London, 1984, p. 152; Anil Raichaudhury, 'Nava Vaishnav Satrar Artha-Samajik Dis: Eti Samikshya' in S. Barman *et.al.* (ed.) *Amalendu Guha Abhinanda Grantha*, Guwahati, 2005, pp. 26ff
13. Technically, Majuli has now no longer been an island, isolated and cut off from the mainland society being open to all sorts of contact with the

outside world. As an attractive place of tourist interest, Majuli receives few thousand tourists from all over the world annually, and lakh of visitors every year who go there to participate in various religious festivals. It is stated that the Auniati Satra *P<u>a</u>ln<u>a</u>m* held in the month of October/November, and the Garamur Satra *R<u>a</u>s* festival, held immediately after the *P<u>a</u>ln<u>a</u>m*, together attract few lakh people from outside. Thus, the island has now no longer been a virgin place for the outside visitors; nor its culture has been so secluded as we some times presume it to be.

14. See Chapter-II of this work, pp. 56f

15. They have mainly settled in the *ch<u>a</u>pori* lands where native people have little or no entry. Some of them have also settled in the neighbourhood of some of the township areas. Milanpur in Garamur and Manikpur nearby, are two such villages surveyed for the present work.

15(a). Growing density of population in Majuli is mainly due to its erosion problem leading to the contraction of its territory. This has been discussed in Chapter-II of this work. See pp. 97f

16. *Census of India, Assam, Majuli*, 2001; K.C. Bora, 'Economic Profile of Majuli', a paper presented at the state level Seminar, held on 26 March, 2004, at the Auniati (Branch) Satra, Teok, on the subject "Majuli Island—Erosion and Protection" (Ms).

17. *Gazetteer* by Allen et. al., p. 159.

17(a). K. C. Bora, *loc cit.*, (Ms.), Majuli is now treated under the *Char* Area Development Plan, Government. of Assam. Also see R. Kerim, 'Majulik Char Bulato Uchitne?', *The Dainik Janambhumi*, 28th Feb., 2005.

18. The belief that Majuli is the largest river-made island in the world has now been challenged. It is stated that there are even larger such islands elsewhere in the world. But there is a difference between the other river-islands and the Majuli which is the only inhabited and fresh water island of its kind. See D. Nath, '*Luitar Majuli-Majuli Dvip: Iyar Sristi aru Aitihasik Avasthan*', in the *Souvenir* published from Jothat on the occasion of the XIV annual conference of the North East India History Association (NEIHA), 1993, p. 81. It is interesting to note that Dr. J. P. Wade has called it 'a great island', while Francis Hamilton (*An Account of Assam* (1808), 3rd print, Gauhati, 1987, p. 26) calls it to be 'a very large island.'

19. The embankment was built in 1978 by the E & D Department, Government. of Assam, which completely blocked the river. See Illustration

20. *Alamgirnamah* by Muhammed Cazim translated (English) in the *Asiatic Researches*, Vol II, 2nd edition, New Delhi, p. 132.

21. Francis Hamilton, *An Account of Assam*, (ed.) S. K. Bhuyan, 2nd edn., Guwahati, 1963 p. 27; S. K. Bhuya, *Anglo-Assamese Relations*, Gauhati, 1948, p. 519.

22. Hamilton, *op cit.*, p. 26.

23. Ibid, p. 27: S.K. Bhuyan, op. cit., p. 519

24. *A Geographical Sketch of Assam, op cit.*, p. 32. Wade's record about its breath is not perhaps correct. For, it is neither supported by any other

record subsequent to Wade, nor by the present geography of the island, nor by the width of the Brahamaputra flowing on the south of Majuli. The span of the Brahmaputra together with the entire breadth of the island does not make even half of that measure today. It appears that it was sixteen in stead of sixty; and probability is that it was a typing error.

25. Ibid.
26. Ibid.
27. Ibid, p. 31.
28. op cit, pp. 26f.
29. *Report on the Province of Assam* (1853), 2nd edition, Gauhati, 1984, p. 504.
30. Allen *et. al. Gazetteer*, p. 159.
31. Ibid, p. 583.
32. cf. J.N. Sarma, 'Origin and Geographical Changes of Majuli Island of the Brahmaputra River in Assam, India', presented in a state-level seminar held on 26 March, 2004, at the Auniati Satra, Teok, on the subject 'Majuli Island—Its Erosion and Protection'. Also J. N. Sarma and K. Phukan, 'Origin and Geographical Changes of Majuli Island of the Brahmaputra River in Assam, India', in *Geomorphology 60 (2004) 1-19*, p. abstract.
33. DAB, p. 8.
34. HAG, p. 133.
35. In Bodo *h<u>a</u>* means extensive land, and *bung* means affected regularly by flood. According to R. M. Nath, Habung 'extended to the west up to the Subansiri river and included the present North Lakhimpur sub-division and a portion of Majuli—the richest paddy growing area—which the Bodos called H<u>a</u>bung or vast land (*H<u>a</u>*-land, *B<u>a</u>ng*—plenty, vast). The kingdom was called H<u>a</u>b<u>a</u>ng or H<u>a</u>bung, and the people were generally known as Kaltas or Kalitas." See *The Background of Assamese Culture*, Shillong, 1948, p. 6.
36. *Satsari Asam Buranji*, (ed.) S. K. Bhuyan, 2nd edition, Guwahati, 1964, p. 72 (henceforth abbreviated as SAB).
37. The Dilih has its source at the Naga hills, and when Wade had recorded in 1800 A.D, it fell into the Dikhow about four miles above its present mouth. See Wade, *A Geographical Sketch of Assam*, p. 24.
38. *Infra*, p. 19.
39. DAB, p. 47.
40. *Asam Buranji* obtained from the family of Sukumar Mahanta, (ed.) S. K. Bhuyan, 3rd edition, 1988, p. 32 (henceforth abbreviated as ABSM)
41. Ibid, p. 33; Although Suhungmung is better known as Dihingiya Raja for his building a new capital city at Bakata on the Dihing, (See HAG, p. 86), Charaideo always remained the first capital
42. *Ahom Buranji*, (Tr.) G. C. Barua, Reprint, Guwahati, 1985, p. 87
43. Ibid.
44. It appears that Dikhow had by that time three mouths, one at the present

place where the Dihing had merged into it, one at Lakhau near Solalphat near Mahuramukh where it emptied into the Luit (Luhit) or Brahmaputra along with the Dihing, and the other at Kajalimukh at Kaliabar in Nagaon. This contention has also been supported by local traditions and historical evidence. Gait has stated that at one time "according to native traditions, the Dikhow had an independent course as far as Kajalimukh, part of which still survives in the Majuli as the Tuni river, and (a) part in Nowgong, as the Kallang" (cf. HAG, p. 133). This condition was there till the early 19th century. Standing on the eastern extremity of Majuli, Ensign Wood says in 1825, "On the right bank is the Mojoulee, or island formed by the two branches of the river, which, separating at this point (at the eastern extremity), unite at Solal Paat, near Maura Mookh; on it are also found remains of villages, of which Ruttunpore alone is thinly populated." Cf. H. H. Wilson, *Documents Illustrative of the Burmese War*, London, 1827, Appendix, p. ii.

45. *Asam Buranji Sar* by Kasinath Tamuli Phukan, (ed.) P. C. Chaudhury, 4th print, Guwahati, 1991, p. 40
46. Cf. *Asiatic Researches*, Vol. II, *op cit*, p. 131.
47. Ibid.
48. In the year 1769 there occurred a rebellion in the Ahom kingdom caused by the Moran tribe who dethroned the reigning king and occupied the throne for a time being. The rebellion soon spread like a wild fire all through the state and took the form of a civil war with involvement of almost all classes of people. As the Morans were also called *Matak*, this rebellion was also called '*Matak Bidroh*'. The rebellion ended in the year 1805 along with the grant of an autonomous state for the Mataks with present Tinsukia as its headquarter. For a comprehensive account of this rebellion, see M. Neog, *Socio-Political Events in Assam leading to the Militancy of the Mayamariya Vaishnavas*, New Delhi, 1982; also A. Guha, *Vaishnav Badar para Moamariya Bidroholoi*, Guwahati, 1993. See also Chapter-VI of this work., pp. 273ff.
49. See S.K. Bhuyan, *Anglo Assamese Relations*, Guwahati, 1949, pp300ff.
50. Ibid, p. 579; Wade, *A Geographical Sketch of Assam*, *op cit.*, p. 32.
51. DAB, p. 8
52. See fn. 35 above
53. R. Endle, *The Kacharis*, Reprint, Delhi, 1979, pp. 1ff
54. DAB, p. 47
55. *Ahom Buranji*, p. 87
56. D. Nath, NEIHA Souvenir, 1993, loc. cit, also see D. Nath, 'Majuli—Eti Aitihasik Parichay', and D. Goswami, ' Majulir Bhu-Prakritik Parichay', in K. C. Kalita, *op cit.*, pp. 1ff and pp. 23ff
57. D. Goswami, 'Majulir bhu-Prakritik Parichay', ibid, pp. 26f
58. See p. 27
59. *Asam Buranji*, *op cit.*, p. 40; *Buranji Vivek Ratna* by Maniram Dewan Barbhandar Barua, (ed) N. Saikia, Dibrugarh, 2002, p. 26.
60. ADB, pp. 68, 128,143

61. See the *Bengenaati Satrar Bhumidan aru Paikar Nibandhanar tamar Pholi,* in M. Neog (comp. & ed), *Prachya Sasanawali*, Guwahati, 1974, Ins. No.82
62. ABSM, p. 58
63. Ibid. p. 5 7
64. DAB, p. 47; SAB, p. 23.
65. D. Nath, in K. C. Kalita, *op cit.*, p. 6; Goswami, in K. C. Kalita, *op cit.*, p. 24; D. Phukan, 'Majulir Jana-Gathani aru Samajik Paribesh', a paper presented in a state level seminar organized jointly by the Archaeological Survey of India, New Delhi, and the Ministry of Culture, Government of Assam, at the Srimanta Sankaradeva Kalakshetra Society, Guwahati, on 15-16 June, 2005. It is interesting to note that the term *Majali* was perhaps used also to mean the best convenient/central place communicable and reachable from all directions. At least this is what the author of the *Auniati Satrar Buranji* has stated. See, ASBS, p. 224
66. HAG, p. 86.
67. ABSM, p. 33; DAB, p. 47.
68. It lies on the Kamalabari-Garamur-Jengrai Road. Also see J. N. Sarma and K. Phukan, *Geomorphology, loc cit.*
69. D. Nath, NEIHA *Souvenir, loc cit.*, p. 133.
70. HAG, p. 133.
71. Ibid.
72. See D. Nath, NEIHA *Souvenir*, loc. cit, pp. 82f. Also see Sketch Map—1
73. Ibid; HAG, p. 133; also see See Sketch Map-2.
74. Ibid.
75. Ibid.
76. Ibid.
77. Cf. *Asiatic Researches*, vol. XVII, p. 320.

77(a). See Sketch Map-I (a).

78. HAG, p133.
79. *etekese Auniati nama satra kahe,*
dakhine Dihinga nadi mahabege bahe
mahadeva daula nadi sikule achay.
Keshavdev Charit,

cf. ASBS, p123fn. (tr. Therefore, it is called Auniati. The Dihing flows fast on the south, with the Siva Mahadeva temple standing on the other side.)

namata dakhinapata buli sabe kahe
uttarata mahanadi Brahmaputra bahe
Banamalidev Charit,

cf. B. Sharma, *Dakhinpat Satra*, Guwahati, 1977, p. 6 (tr. It is called Dakhinpat by all. For, on the north flows the Brahmaputra)

80. D.Nath, in K. C. Kalita, *op cit.*, p. 6.
81. *Hemkosh*, p. 805. The attempt to define the name *Majuli* as 'store house of the love of the mother, or 'the place of the goddess Lakshmi'—*ma*—Lakshmi, *juli*—store, (See B. K. Barua, *Asamiya Bhasha aru Sanskriti*, p. 89) is simply emotional and fabricated.

82. Here I have modified my earlier contention that the 'term *Majali* must have preceded the word *Majuli* to mean the same strip of land.' See D. Nath, K. C. Kalita, *op cit.*, p. 6 and also NEIHA *Souvenir*, 1993, *loc. cit.*
83. See sketch map 2; also see fn. 13 above.
84. D. Nath, in K.C. Kalita, *op cit.*, p. 4.
85. *Asiatic Researches*, Vol. XVII, pp. 320f; B. Sharma, *Benudhar Sarma Rachanawali* (*Buranjir Saphura*), Guwahati, 1987, p. 334.
86. Cf. *Asiatic Researches*, *op cit.*, p. 320.
86(a). D. Nath, NEIHA *Souvenir, loc cit.*, pp. 81ff.
87. *Adicharit* (Ms.), pp. 200-300.
88. Ibid, pp. 293-296.
89. See SHTN, p. 29.
90. See Chapter-VI, p. 270.
91. *Asiatic Researches*, XVII, pp. 326f.
91(a). D. Nath, NEIHA *Souvenir*, *loc. cit.*
92. TB, p. 25.
93. Ibid.
94. Ibid, p. 28.
95. Cf. *Keshavdev Charit*. See fn. 79 above.
96. *Dakhinpat Satra*, *op cit.*, pp. 5f.
97. Despite many topographical changes in the past centuries, there are still a part of those marshes, ponds and river channels. See Appendix—V.
98. *A Geographical Sketch of Assam*, *op cit.*, p. 3.
99. Ibid., p. 32.
100. Ibid., pp. 32f.
101. Ibid, p. 33.
102. See Sketch Map showing bank-line between 1917-2001 in Chapter III.
103. See illustration.
104. *Survey of India Reports*, 1917, 1966-72; cf. J. N. Sarma, 'Origin and Geographical Changes of Majuli Island ... etc', (Ms.), *loc cit.*
105. Also see Appendix-V
106. *Supra*, fn. 44.
107. Cf. *Asiatic Researches,* Vol. II, *op cit.*, p. 130.
108. Cf. Ms, DHAS, Transcript No.300 *Assam and the Ahoms in 1600 A.D.*— being a Portion of Shihabuddin Talish's *Fathiya-I-Ibriya*, translated into English by Sir Jadunath Sarkar, and published in the *Journal of Bihar and Orissa Research Society*, Vol. I, Part-II, December, 1915; cf. HAG, 41.
109. *Topography of Assam* (1837), Reprint, Delhi, 1986, *op cit.*, p. 0.
110. *op cit.*, p. 72.
111. information obtained fro SDO (civil) Office, Majuli.
112. See above fn. 35.
113. DAB, p. 8; ABSM, p. 6; *Ahom Buranji*, (tr. G.C. Baruah), p. 46; Wade, *An Account of Assam*, *op cit.*, pp. 17f.
114. TB, p. 93.
115. *op cit.*, p. 131.
116. Cf. HAG, pp. 142f.

117. *A Geographical Sketch of Assam*, *op cit.*, p. 32.
118. p. 159.
119. p. 572.
120. Wade, *A Geographical Sketch of Assam, op cit.*, p. 33.
121. See fns. 104, 105 above.
122. U.N. Gohain, *Assam Under the Ahoms*, 2nd edition, Guwahati, 1992, p. 127.
123. ADB, p. 552; Wade, *An Account of Assam*, *op cit.*, (Introduction), p. xxxv.
124. *B. Nath, Aranye Aranye Garaki,* North Lakhimpur, 1995, pp. 10ff
125. Ibid.
126. Ibid; T.C. Pamegam, *Tarun Chandra Pamegam Rachanawali* (2 Vols.), Vol. II, (comp. & ed.) B. Kagyung, Guwahati, 2005, pp. 38ff
127. G.D. Hazarika, *Mahapurush Sri Srimat Dharmacharaya Pitambardeva Goswami,* 2 Vols. combined, Titabar, 1964, pp. 131ff (henceforth abbreviated as MDPH), pp. 131f
128. T.C. Pamegam, *Tarun Chandra Pamegam Rachanawali*, II, *op cit.*, pp. 46f
129. J.N. Sarma, *loc cit.*
130. See illustration.
131. Information collected from the living memory of the old generation people of the island.
132. T.C. Pamegam, *Tarun Chandra Pamegam Rachanawali*, II, *op cit.*, pp. 47ff.

2

Society

Majuli Island, according to the report of the last census (2001), is the homeland of 1,53,400 people consisting of both castes and tribes, and pursuing various religious beliefs including animism, although its major religious belief is Vaishnavism of the order of Srimanta Sankaradeva (1449-1568). Out of them 68,198 belong to the Scheduled Tribe communities and 21,479 to the Scheduled caste communities.

Among the non-tribal Assamese communities, the most numerous are the Kalitas enlisted as an agricultural caste in the early census reports.[1] Their total strength in Majuli is not known for certain as no numerical estimate of the community has been maintained in the census records as is done in case of Scheduled Tribes and Scheduled Castes. But there is no doubt that the Kalitas are one of the most early groups of settlers of the Majuli island. Unlike other places of Assam, we find in Majuli only a few sub-sections of the Kalitas, such as the *Bar Kalita*, *Saru Kalita* and the *Kumar Kalita*. Some other sub-sections found elsewhere, like *Dhoba Kalita*, *Kamar Kalita*, *Not Kalita*, *Sonari Kalita*, *Teli Kalita* and *Mali Kalita*, are strikingly absent. The Tantis, who were classed in the census reports of colonial times among the weavers castes along with Yogi or Katani[2] however, have started claiming themselves as Kalita. There is a village in Majuli of these people specifically introduced as Pahumara Tanti Gaon within the Ujani Majuli Development Block. Similarly, many members of the Koch caste also have started claiming themselves as Kalita wherever possible. As a result, the Kalitas par excellence have begun to call themselves as *Bar Kalita* (big Kalita) to retain a distinction between them and the upcoming communities claiming the Kalita status.

The Bar Kalitas like to maintain reservations in their social relationship with other communities, particularly with those whom they consider to have belonged to an inferior rank. This relationship they maintain even with the *Saru* and the *Kumar Kalitas* whom they consider as inferiors.[3] The Kumar Kalitas are also enlisted into the Other Backward Classes. In fact, most individuals using the surname '*Kalita*' in Majuli belong to the category of this Kumar Kalita caste; the rest are from the Koches or from the Keots. The Kumar Kalitas used to inhabit in the past in the southeastern part of the island on the bank of the Brahmaputra where the soil, suitable for making pottery with which they were associated, was available. But the havoc of erosion caused by the Brahmaputra has been always and largely felt in those areas, and the Kumar Kalitas had to shift from their ancestral place to take shelter either on the nearby embankments, or in the interior areas of the island, or migrate to some places outside Majuli.[4] As a result, most of the displaced Kumar Kalitas lost their traditional professions of pottery to engage in other vocations. It is here that many of them have slowly registered themselves as the Bar Kalitas, and with education and service, and improved economic status they have formed a new group of the Bar Kalitas, increasing their number.

Like the Kumars, some of the Koches also have started to write titles like Kalita, Dutta, Saikia, etc. and claim Kalita status. During our field investigation it was found that a few families who were earlier enlisted as Koch, now claim themselves as Kalita. An example of such a case was found at a village under survey in which case the head of the family claimed that he is a Kalita although he was known as a Koch a few years ago. Thus, as elsewhere, the Kalitas are a composite caste in Majuli with a considerable fraction being from among the ethnic, but Sanskritised communities of the land. This shows that a desire for mobility to obtain a higher social status have governed the psyche in the island. It is to be noted that here some men desire higher status in the social hierarchy but would like to be contented with a tribal status for gaining political and economic opportunities. This was particularly noted in case of the Koches and the Chuliyan who demand a tribal status, but who would not like to relinquish a higher social status at the same time. Thus while in medieval times caste mark was used in Assam for identity of a man and his economic status, at present caste is used for both identity and opportunity. In this connection assumption of surnames supposedly bearing higher social status by members of so many communities has become a common phenomenon today. Even, while retaining the same caste mark, one prefers to shift from a minor 'Bora' to a major 'Phukan.'

The (Bar) Kalitas are socially most powerful in Majuli as in other part of the state and occupy higher status in the society. They hold important jobs in the monastic Satras and enjoy the highest social status next to the Brahmins, and are economically more advanced than other communities. Most contractors and business-men, and job holders in Majuli belong to them. They are one of the most orthodox communities being concerned with maintenance of their superior status. Villages of the Kalitas are found in almost all parts of the island.

The next numerous caste might be the Koch who forms a greater part of the population of the island. It is difficult to presume their strength as many of them would like to enroll themselves as Kalita hiding their identity as Koch.[5] The Koch belong to one of the aboriginal tribes of the Brahmaputra Valley. They are found in all parts of Assam although they are concentrated in the lower Assam districts of Kamrupa and Goalpara, and the adjoining parts of West Bengal—Koch Behar, Jalpaiguri and the foothills of Bhutan.[6] It is not known for certain when did the Koch people come to settle in the island. It is, however, reasonable to suppose that they first came to this part of Assam during the invasion of the Ahom state by their king Naranarayan (1540-1587) in the year 1562. For we know for certain that king Naranarayan made his camp at the Majuli island during his campaign against the Ahom state in that year.[7] It is also stated that the Koch forces occupied the territories up to Narayanpur on the north of the Brahmaputra in the western border of Majuli, and in the treaty concluded between the Ahom and the Koch king that followed, this territorial occupation was ratified as conquered.[8] Supposing that the Koches came to Majuli in the middle of the 16th century, we cannot but note that till that time members of the community were in their tribal habits and culture. The *Darrang Raj Vamsavali*, a genealogical work of the Koch kings, for example, has recorded that the Koch soldiers had protested against king Naranarayan's worship of the god Siva with Brahmanical rituals; and Naranarayan had to arrange for his worship according to their own tribal rites in order to appease and conciliate the revolting soldiers.[9] It is therefore presumable that the Koches in Majuli and its neighbouring areas were Brahmanised in later times, most probably in the late 17th century and early 18th century when many Satras grew here and proselytized its people. The Brahmanisation, however, was so complete that the Koch today occupy a status next to the Kalitas, at least in Majuli; and being considered eligible to be members of the monastic institution they share a major part of the Satra culture. The attempt to identify themselves with the Kalitas had faced a set-back in Majuli when the Koches (in fact, the Koch Rajvansis of Goalpara) were granted by the state Government in 1996 Scheduled Tribe (Plains) status. For, finding this new (tribal) status to be more effective to get political advantage, a major part of the caste Kalita (who assumed that status through mobility) shifted to the Koch identity; and this had created some social instability in the caste-concerned villages of the island. It was often heard that in some of the villages with mixed population, rifts occured on the line of caste, and demands were raised for separation of their common prayer halls which they all shared in common earlier.[10] Be that as it may, the

Koches are the next advanced group of people among the castes and tribes of Majuli.

The Nath or Yogi (miss-spelt Jugi) of Majuli earlier called as *Katani* might occupy the next status so far as their population strength is concerned. According to a recent estimation, their number exceeds 20,000 in Majuli.[11] They are spread over 20 odd villages located in the middle and the southeastern part of the island.

Most people in Assam know much less about the people called by the name '*Natha*', 'the least known community' of the state as reported in the research publication of the *Anthropological Survey of India.*[12] But, they are a very ancient community of Assam. Developed from the later phases of the Buddhist fraternity of early Assam,[13] the Saiva-Yogi cult of Matshyendranatha and Gorakshanatha is at the root of the creation of this religious community who are said to have led the movement for religious reform by Hinduisation of the Buddhist sect.[14] Known as the *Natha*, this cult therefore presented a mixture of both Buddhist and Saiva-Yoga systems. In early Kamarupa, the cult received much patronage from the Pala rulers as it did in Bengal.[15] It was perhaps under their patronage that its preachers, known generally as *Siddhas,* created the earliest specimen of vernacular literature in the form of a devotional/religious songs called *charya pada* and *doha*.[16] But, it was because of their relationship with Buddhism that the Nathas had to lose their social and economic status in the orthodox Brahmanical society as was the case during the Sena rulers of Bengal who were ardent supporters of Brahminism. This had happened in Assam during the 14th-15th centuries and at the time of the Neo-Vaishnavite movement when Brahmin writers and the Vaishnava preachers with the support of the royalty condemned any religion that was heretical. It was because of this decline in their social and economic status that their profession of silk rearing and spinning too began to be looked down upon by others in later periods.[16(a)]

Although it is not known by what name these people were identified in the ancient times or in the early middle ages, there is evidence to show that some of them were called *Katani* for their professional craft of spinning silk thread and rearing silk worm.[17] While *Jugi* is a wrong substitute of *Yogi* that was derived from their sect of Yoga, *Katani* stands for spinning of silk (*pat*—mulberry) thread. Be that as it may, the religious sect of Goraksha-Matsyendra spread among the masses as early as the early middle ages, its preachers proselytized people by both the methods of establishing monasteries (Satras)[18] and initiating people from place to place. Condemned perhaps as *bauddhamatiya* (i.e. belonging to the Buddhism) and *tatakiya* (mystic) by the Vishnava saints of Assam[19] due to their Buddhist leanings, those preachers were mobilizing in Majuli converting peoples of different castes when Sankaradeva was at Dhuwahat.[20] From what has been known from the *Charit Puthis*, it has come to light that the *Bauddhamatiyas* faced a tartar in the Vaishnava *gurus*[21] who either uprooted their sect for good, or compelled its members to hide themselves away from their contact consequently leading to the conversion of the believers to Vaishnavism.[22] Thus, the Yogi or Katanis in Majuli became a part of the overall Vaishnava system as early as the 16th century. A significant point in this regard is that being a part of the religious sect, the Nath people are not homogeneous racially; even in Majuli, they present different ethnological traits. And therefore, it is not correct to opine that Naths of Majuli are the same people as the Nathas of other parts of Assam, and that they originated in the same place.[23]

Whatever that may be, till the colonial rule, the Nathas in Majuli, and as such in any place of Upper Assam, did not identify themselves as *Nath* as they did not have anything of their *Natha* religion. During the colonial period, particularly towards the close of the 19th century, as a result of the communal resurgence, such as those led by the Ahoms, the Kaivartas and the spinning mill-owners of East Bengal—the latter belonged to the Nathas—there was an attempt to unify all its members into a pan-Assam-Bengal community by forming the *Assam-Bengal Yogi Sanmilan* in 1911 and publishing a monthly journal *Yogi Sakha* in 1905.[24] Accordingly, the movement for assumption of the surname 'Nath' and putting on the sacred thread in imitation of Lord Siva also came to Assam from Bengal. Maguram Neog Muktiyar of Jogi Gaon (Bangaon), who was one of the pioneers of modern education among his community men, was the leader of the movement in Majuli. It was in course of the movement that these people in Majuli first took up the communal title 'Nath' for their surname in the early decades of the 20th century replacing the earlier one 'Katani' or any title granted by the Ahom state, and assumed sacred thread (*upabit/ lagun dharan*) in the forties of the last century to claim *Siva gotra*.[25] This event was a turning point in the history of social relationship of this community, for it was immediately following this movement that all villages of this community were directed by the central committee (of the *Assam Bengal Yogi Sanmilani*) to boycott Brahmin priests who till that time used to officiate at their rituals and ceremonies. As a result, there was uproar among other communities against assumption of their sacred thread and boycott of the Brahmin priests, and even among themselves schisms erupted.[26] Finally, however, it was at the instance of Pitambardeva Goswami (1885-1962), the *Satradhikara* of Garamur Satra, that the problem subsided. Today all people of this caste in Majuli use to put on sacred thread, and enjoy a better social status than it was before.

As explained, the Nathas in Majuli maintain no trace of their traditional religion nor any reason to have it. During the Neo-Vaishnavite movement, as we have stated above, many of the Natha *gurus,* who are still engaged in proselytizing act making an attempt to spread the cult in upper Assam, came into conflict with Sankaradeva when he was at Belaguri Dhuwahat in Majuli.[27] Such of the preachers who carried on their work in the post-Sankaradeva times, too, were also dispersed in religious discourses by their Vaishnava counterparts. As a result, all attempts to preach finally came to an end. Today they are all orthodox Vaishnavas in their beliefs and practices except perhaps their identity as 'Nath' or 'Natha.' They are now disciples of this or that Satra and a part of the culture called by the name Vaishnava culture. Economically, most of them are not well-to-do; but educationally some of their villages like Rangachahi are well advanced. They also occupy a fairly high social status in the society.

The Nathas are an agricultural community in Majuli. Their traditional craft of producing silk is no longer their vocation today. As reported by Ms. Labanya Nath of Sonariati village near Rangachahi, who is an M.A. in History, most members today dislike the old profession as it is considered a profession of low status in the society and unprofitable.

Of the other notable castes are the Chutiyas. They are concentrated in the northeastern part of the island centering round Ratanpur, the traditional name for the capital city of the Chutiya king Ratnadhvajpal.[28] As we have stated earlier, Majuli once formed a part of the Chutiya kingdom, and some remains of the times of the Chutiya state are still to be seen on the northeast at Dhakuwakhana accross the Bahmaputra.[29] Belonging to the greater Mongoloid tribes, the Chutiyas belong to the Bodos, and are akin to the Morans and the Kacharis.[30] In early times they had their tribal gods and goddesses whom they worshipped with tribal rites and made sacrifices. It is said that they were the worshippers of the goddess *Kechaikhati* at Sadiya, and the Deoris were their priests. They had also their own tribal language which is at present spoken by the Deoris.[31] But after they had formed their state in the pre-Ahom period, the Chutiya royal house, the aristocracy and the nobility were brought under Brahminism, and they left their tribal belief and culture for good. As a result, they are considered as the earliest of the tribes to have converted to Brahminism discarding much of their tribal culture.[32] The Chutiyas are now ardent followers of Brahminism maintaining all sorts of rituals and practices and social customs. Presently, however, the Chutiyas are rising to revert to their ethnic identity as the Koches. They have started a movement under their organization called *All Assam Chutiya Sanmilan.* They have also got their history written as a documentary evidence[33] in support of their movement.

Most Chutiyas were earlier artisan people working in gold, iron and bamboo.[34]

The Kaivartas, earlier called *Dom* in Assam, form another of the numerous castes in the island's population. According to Risley, they present a distinctly intermediate one 'equally removed from the extreme types of Aryan and Dravidian races found in Bengal.'[35] They are included among the Scheduled Castes, who, according to the estimation of the year 2001, form 21,479 souls. In the beginning of the last century a movement was started by the Kaivartas for their social uplift when they demanded replacement of the term *Dom* for the honourable word *Kaivarta*, a Sanskrit word meaning people who live on water, i.e. by boating and fishing.[36] Their movement was supported by Pitambardeva Goswami, the powerful *Satradhikara* of Garamur Satra, against all sorts of opposition from the orthodox religious heads of the time.[37] Their demand was also supported by Lakshminath Bezbaroa, one of the founder fathers of modern Assamese literature, and the most known satirist, in his journal *Banhi*.[38] Consequently, in 1914 their demand was conceded, and they came to be known as *Kaivarta*.[39] The Kaivartas are found in almost all places of Majuli living in their own exclusive villages. Some of their known villages are at Salmara, Sensowa, Kamalabari, Garamur, Kharjan, Nagargaon, Dhekiajuli, Kakarikata, Chilakala, Dakhinpat, and so forth. The present study has included surveying of a few of their villages, such as Kharjan, Natun Kamalabariya, Sensowa, Salmara and Dakhinpat.

It is not known for certain as to the time of beginning of their settlement in the island. As the Kaivartas belong to the early group of settlers of the region, there is no doubt that they belong to the early generation of its inhabitants. It is also not improbable to suppose that they formed a part of its population along with other artisan peoples, like the Yogi Katanis or Naths, Khanikar Chutiyas and so forth during the early monarchical days. There are historical evidences that Aniruddhadeva (1553-1626), the founder of the Mayamara sect of Vaishnavism of Assam, proselytized some of them here in Majuli itself at the beginning of the 17th century. Following him, his sons and brothers also had made their centres of proselytisation among those people later.[40] As a matter of fact, Majuli has now a fraction of the Kaivartas called by the name Matak, a term, said to have been derived from two Assamese compounds—*mat* and *ek*, meaning—opinion one (*mat* = opinion, *ek* = one).[41] The Kaivartas including the Matak Kaivartas are a section of the poor and backward peoples of the island. They are listed as Scheduled Caste who form 19,278 souls in the island according to the Census of 1991, and 21, 479 according to the census of 2001. A very few families of the caste in Majuli have been able to up-stare the ladder of economic progress backed by education and capital. As a whole more than 90 per cent of them live from hand to mouth. The decline of the fishing business in Majuli and scarcity of agricultural land for cultivation[42] are the main reasons for poor economic status of the Kaivartas of Majuli. The present study shows that the average land possession among them per family is 3 *bigha̲*. Thus there is sharp classification among them with a microscopic few in the higher echelon of the economy, while the rest in the lowest of the ladder.

Of the other indigenous castes who are enlisted among the Scheduled Castes, are the Baniyas (earlier called *Hadis*) traditionally associated with sweeping work.[42(a)] It is possible that they were engaged in sweeping during the early times; but those in Majuli today who are concentrated in one or two villages, such as Jorbil in middle Majuli, are cultivators by profession. They are a little better in their economy and education than the Kaivartas.

The Keots form another caste among the peoples of Majuli. Scholars believe that they belong to the Dravidians to which group the Kaivartas belong too.[43] Indeed, the term 'Kaivarta' is the Sanskritised form of the *Prakrit* word 'Kevatta', *Keot*.[44] The Keots had two divisions—*Halowa* or *Haloi Keot* and *Jalowa* or *Jaloi Keot*; the former adopts cultivation, while the latter lives on fishing.[45] Thus, Keots and the Kaivartas are stated to have belonged to the same stock. In Majuli, however, all Keots are cultivators, and they have a better economy than the Kaivartas. In fact, the Keots hold a higher social status, and can become resident inmates of any Satra.[46]

The Brahmins (of different clans) are an early group of inhabitants of the island. Early records speak of the Habung area to be a habitat of the Brahmins. Known as 'Habungiya Bamun' they formed a distinct class among the Brahmins of the state.[47] It is not known when did the Brahmins first make their settlements in the island. But there is possibly no doubt that they were those pioneers who brought the Brahmanical religion first to this part of the Brahmaputra valley. Assamese chronicles mention that it was here in one of the Brahmin families that the fugitive queen of king Tyaokhamthi (1380-1389) was given shelter when she was set adrift by the ministers on a raft on the Brahmaputra where she gave birth to a son who subsequently became the king, with the popular title *Bamuni Konwar*.[48] It was since the rule of this king, therefore, that Brahmanical religion entered the royal palace of the Ahoms.[49] Being alredy well-established, the Brahmins in Majuli did not like to see Sankaradeva's proselytizing its people to *Bhakti* religion. So, they alleged before the king (Suhungmung *alias* Dihingiya Raja) that Sankaradeva had destroyed the society by polluting the established religious systems.[50] These Brahmins again fought the army of the Koch king Naranarayan by sitting on the bullocks in the year 1562 during their invasion of the Ahom kingdom.[51] It is stated that during this war many non-Brahmins also put on the sacred thread and smeared their forehead with *chandan,* and thus disguising themselves as Brahmins joined the actual Brahmin force. These disguised soldiers, however, never resumed their original caste, even after the war was over.[52] During the rule of Rudra Singha (1696-1714) Majuli was made a colony of the Brahmins and the Kayasthas by establishing numerous Satras and making them their (Satras') *adhikaras*.[53] Thus, Brahmins in Majuli are a very early group of settlers.

The Brahmins, however, like in any other place of the state, form a minor group in Majuli; but they occupy the highest social and economic position. None but a Brahmin (or a Kayastha) can be a *Satradhikara*. In the royal Satras, even the *Bhagavati* or the reader of the *Bhagavata* is also a Brahmin. The priest called *pujari* who performs the worship of the idol is always a Brahmin.[54] There is no such village to be properly termed as a Brahmin village;[55] but the people of this caste are found everywhere, mostly in the Satras and in the villages inhabited by the caste Hindu people, or, by the people whom they consider touchable. No Brahmin family is to be found in the tribal villages, or villages peopled by members of the so-called low castes. They are educationally advanced and culturally forward. In the service sector too they have better advantage than any other community. A few *Satradhikaras* because of their religious authority over mass of the people, exercise much political power as some of them had done in the middle ages.[56] It is interesting to note that no MLA or MP from the Majuli Assembly constituency or the Lakhimpur Parliamentary constituency to which Majuli till now belongs, have ever participated in any election without seeking the blessings of the principal *Satradhikaras* of Majuli.[57]

The Sut or *Sutkuliya*, also called *Bariya* in earlier times,[58] form another community in Majuli of significant population strength. There are a number of villages belonging to this caste. In the traditional outlook of the caste-ridden villagers the *Sut* or *Sutkuliyas* rank low in the social hierarchy, and the term *Bariya* had been used to despise them.[59] is pointed out for that as a means of defence. It was because of such derogatory social outlook towards the caste that in the beginning of the 20th century there was a movement among this community for its upward mobility whereby they demanded the replacement of the word *Bariya* by the word Sut. Accordingly, a long battle had to be fought against the orthodoxy of the caste Hindus, particularly the *Satradhikaras*. Finally, however, at the initiative of the then *Garamuriya Satradhikara* Pitambardeva Goswami (1885-1962) the word *Bariya* was substituted in Government records with the more respectable word *Sut*.[60] The Suts are agriculturists and profess same business as other neighbours. In our field investigation three villages inhabited by them are included, and it was found that literacy percentage among their women was not lower than the average of the other castes.

The Ahoms are the most numerous community in Upper Assam. They are a composite caste in Assam today formed with members of almost all castes and communities. The forefathers of the Ahoms, however, came to this part of the state from upper Burma bordering China in the early 13th century A.D. under their leader prince Chaolung Sukapha, who formed a state in this part of the country. As the number of the Ahoms was small enough to successfully combat the situation here, Sukapha laid the principle of Ahomization and assimilation of the other local tribes in order to increase their strength.[61] Thus along with the growth of their state their population strength also grew; but for all practical purposes Sibsagar remained the cradle of their power. In Majuli there are two Ahom villages—Ratanpur Lahan Gaon and Chaorekia, both are located in the extreme southeastern part of the island bordering Brahmaputra. There is no record to know about the time of settlement of these two villages when the whole island is populated by the non-Ahoms. It is presumable that they are there since the days of the Ahom rule in Assam (1228-1826) which may be traced as far back as Sukapha's arrival at Habung.[62] Be that as it may, being minority in Majuli, the people of these two villages are developing the overall Vaishnava character which govern the people of the island at large. These characteristics are to be noted in their social behaviour, food and dress habit and, above all, in their cultural pattern. This is particularly to be seen in their rituals and functions associated with birth and death; but they always perform their marriage ceremony in the *chaklang* system.[63] Unlike Ahoms of other parts of the state the *Ratanpuriyas* and the *Chaorekias* in Majuli do not celebrate the Ahom festival of *Me-dam Me-phi*.[64] They perform *nam-kirtan* (congregation prayer), and *bhaona*, and like any other caste of the island, burn the dead and observe 11 days *brat* (fastine or purificatory rites). While carrying on field investigation in the Chaorekia village, it was, however, found that all families selected for investigation belonged to the *paka* Ahom division—the group which is habituated to the traditional Ahom culture of regularly preparing *sanj/rah* or *rahi,* i.e. rice beer and using it for ritual purposes. They are the only people in the island who often rear *muga* (silk) worm and produce muga silk thread and weave cloth.

The rest of the population belong to the Scheduled Tribes formed by the Mising, the Deori and the Kachari. The Misings earlier called *Miri*, who form about 37 per cent of the total population strength in Majuli, are the best advanced of the tribes in the island. With 57,760 population according to the census of 2001, they form 84 per cent of the total tribal strength. They are found over almost the entire island, although they are concentrated in its northern belt, Jengraimukh in northeastern Majuli being their cradle. Its hinterland consists of Daphalakata, Jakaibowa, Rangachahi Miri, Ratanpur, Kalitapar, Patharichuk, Chitadarchuk, Phutuki Chapori, Baraguri, Naganachuk, Bargaya, Dhapak, Baralimara and so forth.

It is not possible to trace exactly the history of migration of the Misings in the Majuli island. But it is almost certain that they did not inhabit this area long before, at least before the early 19th century. Assamese chronicles do not testify to their settlement in the island till at least the close of the 18th century. Shihabuddin Talish, the official Mughal historian who accompanied Mir Jumla to Assam in his campaign during 1662, and who had one of his army camps at the Majuli island, has noted that the Miri Misimis dwelt on the hills "which lie on the east of Assam on the *Uttarkul* side at a distance of eleven days' journey from Garhgaon. Silver, copper and tin are also obtained in the hills of the same tribes."[65] Similarly, Muhammad Cazim, the biographer of emperor Aurangzeb, has noted that "Asam which lies to the north-east of Bengal, is divided into two parts by the river Brahmaputra, that flows from Khata. The northern portion is called Uttarcul, and the southern Dachincul. Uttarcul begins at Gowahatty, which is the boundary of his Majesty's territorial possessions, and terminates in mountains inhabited by a tribe called Meeri Michimi."[66] But there was possibly no doubt that they occupied the northern bank of the Luhit river (northern branch of the Brahmaputra) by the beginning of the 19th century. Early British writers have left ample evidence to that effect. For example, writing in the thirties of the 19th century, John M'Cosh has stated that they "occupy that strip of alluvial land along the northern bank of the Brahmaputra, from the large island Majuli to the river Dihong, the northern branch of the Brahmaputra; and are bounded on the north by the hill country of the Abors. Till of late years, this district was deserted on account of the ravages of the Abors; but on our affording them protection, the original inhabitants returned. The land is still very thinly populated, and the only cultivation is along the banks of the great river. Their head village is Motgong"[67] Similarly, William Robinson in his *A Descriptive Account of Assam* (1840) has noted that the cradle of the Miris "appears to be the low hills on the north' " from where they have spread out into the plains at the foot of the hills and emigrated in the large numbers throughout Upper Assam."[68] According to him, it was the subordination of the powerful Abors (Adis) who considered the Miris (Misings) as their dependents, that the Miris left for the plains in order to escape their wrath.[69] In the plains they received sympathy of the British who had strained relations with the Abors and thus became settlers of the plains.[70] As for their settlement, Robinson has noted that they had some villages on the banks of the Dihong river of which the Matgong is the principal village.[71] "Till late years, their territories were almost deserted on account of the ravages of their formidable neighbours—the Abors. Their vicinity continues to act as a great drawback upon the Miris."[72] This shows very clearly that the Misings (Miris) were by and large the hill dwellers till the coming of the British to Assam. The policy of the latter being one of subjugation of the hill tribes, they welcomed the Misings who were evacuated from their homeland on the hills by the Abors (Adis) who were inimical with the British. Welcoming the Misings therefore was a strategic policy on part of the British, for by this way it became comparatively easy to subjugate the Abors. Robinson has frankly confessed: "The Miris are by no means so jealous of British influence as most of the neighbouring tribes, and as a better acquaintance with them would lead to a free intercourse, and to the extension of the trade between them and the natives of the plains, and thus be of mutual advantage to both parties, it is hoped government will shortly avail themselves of such means as will best insure these advantages; and probably none would better answer the purpose than a friendly embassy."[73]

The *(A)Statistical Account of Assam* prepared by W. W. Hunter has recorded that in the year 1871 the Miris in Sivasagar district numbered 6862 out of a total population of 296589[74] forming 2.31 per cent of the total strength of the district. There is no doubt that this number might have included the Misings of Majuli also, if there was any, besides those living in the other parts of the district. And if this is the case, then the Misings might have begun to settle in the island towards the middle of the 19th century; but till almost the last quarter of the 19th century their strength remained insignificant. An understanding of the distribution system of their settlement in the island indicates that the first area of their settlement was somewhere in the northeastern region bordering Suvansiri and the Kherkatia Suti.

The Misings are an agriculturalist community in Majuli. They cultivate mainly *a̲hu* and *ba̲o* rice. Initially, they were accustomed to living on the outskirts of the jungles opening new lands every two/three years for shifting cultivation. W. Robinson has stated that "The Miris are an industrious race, and partial to living in the skirts of the forests, clearing new ground, which they cultivate for a year or two, and then moving off to another place, when the soil is exhausted."[75] In the same style, the *Statistical Account of Assam* has recorded in 1871-1872 that the Miris "are very industrious, and in Sibsagar generally live along the banks of the rivers, which they cultivate. They may be classed as nomadic

FIG. 2.1: A MISING VILLAGE ON THE BANK OF THE BRAHMAPUTRA

FIG. 2.2: SKETCH OF A TIPICAL MISING VILLAGE DRAWN BY A DUTCH ARCHITECT RENE KOLKMAN

FIG. 2.3: POTTERS TRAVEL FROM VILLAGE TO VILLAGE SELLING POTS OF DIFFERENT SIZES

agriculturists, seldom staying in one place for more than four or five years, but moving away to a fresh locality as soon as the soil of their fields becomes exhausted".[76] Their chief cultivation then consisted of *ahu* rice, "grown along the banks of the rivers, yams of different sorts, Indian corn, chilies, plantains, ginger, melons and pumpkins."[77]

The Mising carried their hill culture till they came to the island, so much so that many of them till the early part of the 20th century did not know the Assamese language, and the male members used bow and arrow for hunting and defence. But during the last one hundred years the Mising have undergone significant changes in their socio-economic life. Almost all of them are now used to Assamese language besides their tribal tongue, have acquainted themselves to the Brahmanical way of life, changed their dress and ornaments, and above all, have adapted to the habit of settled agriculture and habitation.[78] They have now changed their food habits, and have adapted to the life-styles of the plains.[79] In some advantageous places, such as, Jengraimukh and Phulani, they are also accustomed to transplanted *sali* variety of paddy, although till a few decades ago they were shifting from one place to another in search of agricultural fields; and since the *chapori* lands were then abundantly available in the region, it was not difficult to pursue their tribal traditions and habits. But opening up of all lands irrespective of the *chaporis* and the riverine belts for cultivation and habitation due mainly to the growth of population, has now left no scope for them to follow their traditional shifting systems. As a result, they are, irrespective of their locations, now settled cultivators and village dwellers in Majuli.

The Misings are recorded to have cultivated a great deal of opium in early times which they used to barter for grain with the Assamese.[80] They also cultivated cotton to a large extent, and manufactured cotton rugs which were peculiar to themselves. They also rear a great number of pigs and poultry, and live comparatively in a very expensive style.[81]

The Misings have eight sub-ethnic and social divisions, such as *Chayengiya*, *Mayengiya*, *Ayengiya*, *Tayu-Taye*, *Pagar*, *Dambuk*, *Chamaguriya* and *Tamar*. Again, within these social divisions there are numerous clans, such as Doley, Pegu, Kuli, Nara, Payeng, Kumbang etc.[81(a)] In Majuli, not all these are found; but the *Mayengiyas* and the *Chayengiyas*, perhaps, the early comers and the late comers, predominate.[82] In education and economy, the *Chayengiyas,* also known as *Chutiya Miri,* are more advanced than the *Mayengiyas* because of the obvious reason of their early settlement in the valley and holding of better quality lands suitable for almost all kinds of agriculture. Jengraimukh is the cradle of the *Chayengiyas*, and almost all MLAs from Majuli elected so far belong to this clan.

The Kacharis are one of the most well-known aboriginal tribes of Assam. Known by different names, they belong to the great Bodo race. The Kacharis of the plains of Assam have lost their original tribal language, although most of their brethrens on the hills still speak their own dialect.[82(a)] According to the Assamese chronicles, the Kacharis who had earlier formed their state in the plains of Upper Assam, left for Cachar after the land was occupied by the Ahoms.[83] Thus the tribe who once formed a state and was a major community of Upper Assam, became minority here. According to the Census of the year 1871,[84] there were 15,320 Kacharis in the entire district of Sibsagar which formed about 5.16 per cent of the total population strength of the District.

In Majuli there is only one village inhabited by the Kachari people. It is called Sonowal Kachari Gaon after the name of the clan to which they belong. This village is situated on the extreme southeastern border of the island on the bank of the Brahmaputra. The Sonowal Kachari Gaon has been included into the list of our surveyed villages.

The Deoris form another significant tribal population group of the island. There are three villages inhabited by the Deoris. They are Majar Deori Gaon, Sriram Deori Gaon (it has two divisions—Sriram Dori and Sriram Deori Pam), and Deori Pam Gaon. Out of them two villages—Sriram Deori and the Majar Deori—were surveyed. According to the last census report, the Deoris form less than 2 per cent of the total population of the island, and a little less than 4 per cent of the total tribal strength. Said to be a remnant of the Chutiya priestly class,[85] they have four social divisions—Dibangiya, Tengapaniya, Bargaya and Patargaya.

The main occupation of the Deoris of Majuli is agriculture. They cultivate rice of *ahu*, *bao* and *sali* varieties, various kinds of pulses (such as *mati*, *mug*, *arahar*, pea), and wheat, garlic and vegetables. The Deoris have comparatively larger amount of land. During our field survey in the island it was found that the average land holding per family among the Deoris in the two villages is 26 *bigha* approximately.

Unlike the Mising, the Deori women play a subordinate role in the family. Although they participate in all family business equally with men, and sometimes take part in village politics, go to the schools and colleges, manage poultry farm, weave clothes and wear all sorts of modern dress and ornaments, there is no record of any widow remarriage among them as against the Misings among whom it is not unknown, nor independence in the pursuits of economic life. In the total apparatus of the village too there are indications of changes towards modernity. Most significant of all these is that one can hardly see a joint family system among them at present as it was in early times. They are now significantly inclined towards

Assamese Vaishnavite culture, such as performing *bhaona* in the village. Even in their dresses and ornaments changes are noted.

While the above is the list of the indigenous inhabitants of the island, there are immigrant settlers coming from other parts of the country. They include the Bengalis, the Marwaris, the Biharis/Deswalis, and the Telis. Recently, some immigrant Muslims also have had their settlement in the island. The Bengalis live in camp like settlements which the Assamese people call *chuburi*. In Majuli, however, we find certain compact villages of these people besides such settlements. These villages, formed in imitation of the local people, are Barhola Bengali, Milanpur, Nayabazar, Garamur Bengali, Madhupur Bengali, Kharjanpar Bengali, Manik Chapori and others. They are scattered all over the island, particularly in the township or in the distant peripheral areas. Their major occupation is business—in milk, fish or grocery. Most of them belong to the Scheduled Castes.

Bengalis of Majuli are the immigrants from erstwhile East Bengal, East Pakistan (presently Bangladesh). They are all Hindu by religion. It was immediately before Independence, and during the decade immediately following it, that these people came and began to settle in the peripheral *char* and jungle areas. The present writer remembers how in his childhood days in the late fifties and early sixties of the last century, isolated settlements of these people speaking a language which was termed by the indigenous people as *Silethiya/Silotiya* (Sylhetty), could be detected amidst the jungles of the Yogi Pathar *Chapori* beyond a dead channel of the old Brahmaputra (Luhit) near Garamur. It gradually came to light that some people of outside origin had made their settlements there and used to trade in *muri*, *ladu*, milk and so forth. At that time there were ample cultivable lands at the hands of the local people, and there was no concern about such influx and occupation of lands, and no body suspected it as a beginning of a historical process. This *chapori* now is an open agricultural land stretching over an extensive area where the extreme end touches the horizon; and the Bengali village grown out of this zygote has now become one of the most affluent villages of the greater Majuli island. It is named Manik Chapori, after the name of the man called Manik Das who had founded it. The topography of the Majuli island provided them with ample opportunities to trade in milk and fish, and to pursue agriculture.

There are two villages of the Nepali community in Majuli. They are Sriram Devottar Nepali Gaon, and the Karkichuk Nepali Gaon—both are located in upper Majuli in the suburb of Jengraimukh and Phulani township with a tentative population of about 350 people. In our field survey the former village has been included. The two Nepali villages grew in the post-Independence period. It is possible that taking advantage of the open grazing lands suitable for growing cattle farms some of the immigrant Nepalis settled here coming from the north bank through Dhakuwakhana-Ratanpur-Jengraimukh route. The Nepalis are Hindu and celebrate all major Hindu festivals including the *Durga Puja*[86] called by them as *Donchei*. Other such celebrations include *Nag Panchami*, *Raksha Bandhan* (called *Janai Punai*), *Tij*, *Tihar*, and *Makar Sankranti*.

The Nepalis settling in Majuli are mainly agriculturists. Some of them maintain herds of cows and sell milk. Most of them have small area of land. In our field investigation in the Sriram Devottar Nepali Gaon, it was found that the average land holding per family was about 7 *bigha*. There were 3 service holders and 1 business-man having a grocery shop. The rest are either cultivators working on share cropping basis, or else wage earners.

The Muslims (also called *Goriya*) form a small hamlet in the heart of the island in the vicinity of the Kamalabari township. It is called Barhola Muslim Gaon. It is not known how and when the Muslims came to the island and formed a settlement there. According to some of the local inhabitants, one person came in the past and acted as personal washerman of the Auniati *Satradhikara*. But it is doubtful if the *Satradhikara*, known for his orthodoxy, took a Muslim person as his personal washerman. According to another source, the first person went to Majuli for trade—buying cattle in Majuli and selling them in other parts of the state. There is still another information which states that the first Muslim came to Kamalabari as a tailor. The two latter informations appear more acceptable as trade in cattle in Majuli was once entirely done by some Muslim traders from outside; and it is not impossible that one of those traders settled down there shifting his business to a settled form. Again, it is informed that the first tailor in Kamalabari was one Phalu Miyan, a Muslim,[87] who started his business in the first half of the 20th century.[88] Even the oldest photo studio in Kamalabari belongs to one of their families. A few members of this community still export dry fish from there to outside. It is possible that the founder of the Muslim hamlet in the heart of the township was a businessman who came and settled here from outside in pre-Independence time. They are still alien to the local situation. Their alien nature is reflected in the nature of their settlement in a low-lying swampy place, in having no cultivable land, and more particularly, in the use of some alien mode of speech in their family communications.

At the time of our survey in the winter of 2005, there were twelve households in the hemlet having, on an average, 8 members each; 3 members on an average more than any other Hindu individual family.

Located in a low-lying marshy place (*hola* in Assamese) in a part of the dried bed of the Tuni river under the Tuni river bridge, Barhola is the only settlement area of this religious community in the Vaishnavite island. The largest household of the families is that of Dulal Ahmed where there were 24 members—13 male and 11 female. They belonged to the Sunni sect of Islam. Being economically sound, the family had bought some land in the neighbouring areas. At the time of our investigation, it had 4 *puras* of cultivable land where they used to cultivate rice, potato, garlic, onion and varieties of vegetables with traditional methods and technologies.

Dulal Ahmed's household is interesting in some other ways. His brother has married a Mising girl from Jengraimukh, and has converted her to Islam. Similarly, one Phukan Ali has married a Hindu Bengali girl from the same place, and Abul Ahmed has married a Kaivarta girl from Kharichakhowa area. Similarly, the elder sister of Aju Ahmed has been married to a person (Mising) of the village Bargaya. And this is the method by which they have developed the process of maintaining social connections with the rest of the society. Members of Dulal Ahmed's family also know Mising language which is the major tribal language spoken by the people of the island. Interestingly, at the absence of a mosque in Majuli, Dulal's family use to offer prayer and read the *Quran* in his family prayer house called *punja gana* and celebrate festivals like *Id*, *Muharram*, *Sabebarat*, *Ramzan*, and other festivals and rituals. The meaning of the term *punja-gana* could not be ascertained; but the word *punja* might have been derived from the Hindu word *puja*, meaning worship/sacrifice. The fact that with maintenance of all Islamic culture they have tried to increase their number by means of other than the normal process, shows that the Barhola settlement will some day or other try to assert their identity as a settled village claiming historicity, and like any minority community living in an alien context, would try to secure its guarantee by increasing their members and supporters. At least that would have impact on the island's heritage character.

The smallest family in the village has two members while the next smallest has four. Thus the family of Habibur Rahman has two, and that of Nurul Hussain has four. The smallest land holding is 1 *katha* in a family. Thus, Aju Khan and Isa Khan's families have 1 *katha* of land each; but they have ten members altogether. It is observed that barring the young members, almost all senior members spoke in broken Assamese resembling the accent of an East Bengali. It is reported that most senior members of the village know Urdu. In Majuli there is neither Urdu teaching school, nor Urdu speaking people which fact indicates outside origin of the Muslims of Majuli. It is reported that a *Janab* usually visits the settlement during

Ramzan to teach Urdu to the young members. The household of Dulal Ahmed had at that time 24 members including 11 female and 13 male, and as reported, Urdu was the household language of communication among the senior members. It is interesting to note that there were as many as 24 members in a family, which is therefore exceedingly larger than any average family found in Majuli. On investigation it was found that the family consisted of sons, daughters, sons-in-law, and daughters-in-law, and grandchildren. The fact that they do not send away their daughters after their marriage to the household of the sons-in-law, but keep them at home along with the sons-in-law, shows that Dulal and other of his type are trying to increase their strength to ensure their safety in a supposedly alien social atmosphere.

CASTE-CLASS DIVISIONS—CLASSIFICATION OF THE MAJULI SOCIETY

The society of Majuli is composed of both caste and tribe. While the caste fraction is composed of the Brahmins, Kalitas and other Brahmanised communities assuming caste rank, the tribe consists of the Mising, the Deori, and the Kachari elements. Thus society in Majuli consists of two distinct divisions—caste and tribe. The Bengalis, Marwaris, Biharis, Nepalis, and the Muslims come under the caste hierarchy.

Being based on the caste system social hierarchy in Majuli is always dominated by the Brahmins followed by the Kalitas. Villages were largely formed on the basis of the caste. This is still to be found in the village system of the island. For example, some villages are there which are inhabited by the Misings alone, while some others by the Kaivarta or Hadis, or by the Nath or Yogi or Katanis. Similarly, in some villages there are only Sut or the Deori. The only mix villages are to be found among the Kalita, Koch and Keots. Brahmins have no village; they inhabit either in the Satras, or in the villages of other people or in the township areas.

Inter village relationship was earlier determined by caste relationships. There was no social communication between a Kalita village and a non-Kalita village, or between the Katani village and a Kalita or Kaivarta village, or between a Kaivarta village and a Brahmin settlement, or between a Kumar Kalita village and a Koch or Keot village except perhaps on matters of business or economy. Inter-caste marriage or inter-caste dining was a taboo. A Brahmin refused to accept even a piece of betel-nut from the hand of a non-Brahmin or Sudra particularly from those belonging to the low social status. Smilarly, a Kalita refused to accept *mah-prasad* from the hands of a *Katani* or Nath-Yogi man, or from the hand of a Sut or a Koch man. This distance is slowly disappearing among the people after Independence, particularly during the last few decades as a result of the growing education among the masses and frequent communication with the world outside. When asked, Megha Medhi of Kharjan Kaivarta village, has told about his association with Garamur Satra. Punaram Nath of Puranibari village also told us that there is no caste prejudice in the present society as it was in early times. It is interesting to note that of late, quite a good number of individuals have inter-caste marriages, and Satras now play a second fiddle in this regard in comparision to what they did in early times. During our field investigation it was found that inter-caste marriage in Majuli is gradually being accepted by the society. At least every village and every community has now examples of it.

Thus, Inter-caste marriage which was once presented by the Satras as sinful in the minds of the people, has now become an accepted system. All castes beginning with the Brahmins to the Muslims and tribes are becoming used to inter-caste marriage. Analysing the cases in our hand it is found that economic background of the families, particularly that of the boy, derived specially from his education and service, has been of much consideration in the settlement of any inter-caste marriage. And as Majuli has now been largely opened to the outside world along with the demand of the visiting tourists, and as there are symptoms of internal urge for socialisation, inter-caste marriage is expected to be much popular in the society in the future.

Besides caste-tribe composition, people of Majuli can also be seen in terms of rich and poor. Being a non-industrial land, Majuli mainly depends on agriculture and Government or semi-Government services. In early times, when population was small and agricultural land ample with natural fertility of the soil, people of the island had a self-sufficient economy. But in modern times, especially after Independence, when education began to grow among a section of the fortunate, and schools and colleges also grew, a service-holding class slowly emerged which could earn sufficient cash to spend for luxury and comfort. It is to be noted that teachers in Majuli serving in Government or provincialised colleges or schools, lead a comfortable life with money power at hand to purchase and employ labourers to cultivate on their behalf. As a result, barring a few who can spend money for maintenance of living standard, for education and sophistication, like the contractors and the service holders, teachers are the next affluent class with conserved money and a secured granary. As against this, growth of population and consequent scarcity of cultivable land accompanied by loss of soil fertility due to building of large embankments preventing flood had heavily acted upon the economy of the agriculturists. In Majuli, therefore, cultivators consisting of more than 80 per cent of the people form the poor class.

In the post-Independence period, building of roads and embankments, and school, college and office constructions became a feature of the Majuli development projects. As a result, a class of contractors—their number being very few and confined mostly to the advanced section of the society, has emerged which handles a good amount of cash. Gradually supply of various materials—building materials and edibles, from nearby Jorhat town also came into the hands of this contractor class. Thus a rich class of contractors came into being which began to distinguish the local *Majulial* society. It is this rich affluent class that has a strong role in the society—in its economy, polity, administration, and even culture. Naturally background for a class-divided society was formed with the teachers, employees and contractors on one side, and the marginal cultivators on the other side. The proportion is heavier towards the cultivators.

FOOD

Like in any other place of Assam, rice forms the staple food of the people in the island. Almost all, excepting the Marwaris and the *adhikaras* of the monastic Satras, are fond of fish. Meat is not as popular as fish is, as killing of animals by men of a certain age is still considered prohibitive as per custom ordained by religion governed by the Satras.[89] Earlier most people used to consume rice from what they had produced; and buying rice from the market was considered derogatory and unfortunate (*kulakshaniya*).[90] Nor any body was willing to sell rice in the market as the act was considered unlawful in the society. It was the custom of the people here to keep the rice with straw stored in the storehouse called *bharal*. Some people whose produce was more than sufficient to be preserved in the store, often separated them from the straw and put them in some bamboo baskets called *mer* or *duli,* or kept them in some small stores made for that purpose called *guti bharal*. It is to be noted that at one time, the villagers counted the number of stores along with number of cows and buffaloes possessed by a family to assess its economy. This was particularly unavoidable when the status of the family was to be ascertained for purposes of cementing some marriage alliance or for bestowing headship of the village (*gaonburha*).

Two types of rice, boiled and raw, called respectively as *ukhuwa* and *aroi* were once known to the villagers. *Aroi* is a kind of rice husked from the dried grains (unboiled) and is normally used for ritual purposes then called *prasadar chaul*. It is also used to feed the invited guests in any ritual functions. This kind is not usually consumed by the ordinary peasants as it is not economic. The affluent families, however, took *aroi* rice in their daily meals too as they could produce enough for both consumption and ritual purpose. The term *ukhuwa* means boiled. Boiled rice was usually consumed by the villagers as, on one hand, it was economic, and on the other, it could be preserved for the times of emergency, such as summer or rainy days. We have reference to the effect that Sankaradeva had made provisions for *ukhuwa* rice for emergency purposes while he was at Belaguri Dhuwahat in Majuli.[91] Being economic, the boiled rice is still popular among the villagers who run their families on what they produce from their own resources. The boiled rice, however, is not used in the ritual purposes..

Aroi rice is used to prepare rice powder called *pithaguri*. Particularly, the rice from the *sali* variety is used to make rice powder with which they make different kinds of cakes on the occasions of the *Bihu* and other social functions. Rice powder is also used for ritual functions, such as marriage, worship—*puja*, and some other social functions. Rice powder is largely used in the villages and the Satras to make a kind of powder balls called *mithoi*. They prepare two varieties of powder balls, *paka mithoi* and *kecha mithoi*; the former is made with dried rice powder mixed up with boiled jaggery, while the latter is made of undried powder with un-boiled jaggery. The *paka mithois* are very popular among the *bhakats* of the Satras, and in most cases, the *Satradhikaras* send them to far-flung areas as *naivedyas* (offerings) to his disciples.

There are three varieties of rice in the main produced in the island—*ahu*, *bao* and *sali*. The land once being unprotected by bund from the havoc of the flood of the Brahmaputra, most people used to cultivate *ahu* and *bao* rice only. *Ahu* is sown in winter and reaped in summer. Its corn is red in colour. Rarely there is a kind which has white corn. The one which is white is called *bar dhan*. While the red variety is mostly used as consumption rice, the white variety is normally used for ritual purposes. The *bao* is a summer crop. It is sown broadcast during the months of March and April and is reaped during November-December. Its corn is red although some varieties of the *bao* crop, such as the *rangali* or *kokuwa*, have white rice. Like the *ahu* variety, red *bao* is used for consumption, while the white variety is normally used for ritual purpose. Being prone to recurring flood, *sali* or the transplanted varieties were rare in the past, when there was no embankment to protect from flood. There are, however, certain localities, such as Rangachahi, Bangaon, Jengraimukh, where some amount of *sali* crop is grown. The *salis* form consumption rice for those who produce it or who could afford to consume it as it is costlier. Thus, despite there being a universality in the consumption of rice, it varied in quality from place to place on certain conditions, such as availability of suitable land to grow them and the economic ability of the family to consume.

Besides the two principal meals, one in the morning and the other in the evening, tiffin and breakfast are also made from rice. The Bengali community prepare *muri* and *akhoi* from boiled rice by a frying process, while the Assamese prepare *chira* by the process of boiling, frying and pressing. *Chira* is still the most prestigious item of tiffin used by all sections of the people, and is popular during the festival days of the *Bihus*, *bhaonas* and marriages. Some special kind of *sali* rice is needed to make *chira*, and since *sali* variety has slowly become rare, home-made *chira* is now mostly confined to the well-to-do families alone who can afford to grow the kind, or who can purchase it from neighbouring areas of Lakhimpur. All others buy *chira* from the Marwari shops during the *Bihu*, or on the occasions of marriage, or any such socio-religious functions. Another special kind of tiffin is made from the same kind of *sali* rice. It is called *komal chaul*. Rice is boiled to a certain degree and then dried in the sun so that it dries in a single day, for it is said that rice boiled for that purpose if not dried in a day, the tiffin made out of it becomes harder and thus not of better quality. The process of boiling and drying the rice for both *chira* and *komal chaul* is serious and done with utmost care.[91(a)]

It is believed that if the boiled rice in the time of drying gets touched by a way-man, a dog, or a crow, it becomes unusable. It is particularly maintained when rice is boiled by the *bhakats* of the Satras, or for the purpose of using them in any ritual or religious functions. As a result, a person sits by the side of the boiled rice with a bow and an arrow at hand to ward off the unwanted contacts. It is therefore noticed that rice boiled and dried for making *chira*, *sandah* (a coarse flour made from parched rice) or *komal chaul* are put to dry in a secluded place, and a stranger is not allowed to go nearby. *Bhakats* of the *Nika Sanghati* Satras[92] are more particular about it. *Chakowa* and *bara* varieties of rice are considered suitable for making *chira* and *komal chaul*. The latter variety is the only one to make varieties of *pitha*. Poor people who do not afford to have *bara* or other kind of soft rice, would go without *chira* or *komal chaul*, and those who would have no *bara* rice would have a course variety of cake (*pitha*) often called *bhurukia pitha* which can be made from the powder of any variety of rice.

Fish forms one of the major items of the diet for all classes of the families except the *adhikaras* of the monastic Satras and the Marwaris. Majuli's geographical location has endowed it with enormous potentialities for availability of fish in its rivers and ponds. We have mentioned elsewhere[93] that there are still a large number of *bils* paying revenue to the state as fisheries. It is traditionally believed that once villagers were afraid of fish which created terror in the eye of the villagers who went to catch them in the ponds in the winter. It is also stated by the members of the older generation that even during the 1950 earthquake fishes splashed over to the fields, and people could not move there for the repugnant smell coming from those dead fishes. The present author remembers how in his childhood days, small fishes were rejected in the villages for big ones. This aspect has been discussed in another occasion; it is sufficient to mention here that fish forms the most known and popular component in the dish of the villagers of the island. But here too some restrictions of peculiar kind are to be noted. It was a custom of the non-tribal people to avoid certain kind of fish, such as *sal*, *singi*, *nadani*, *neriya*, and *mirika*. Nor was it a custom with them to sell fish except the Kaivartas. But, during our field investigation, it was found that such restrictions are now no longer maintained. There are men who eat all those kinds of fishes, and some who sell them. When asked Sri Kanpai Das of (*na*) Kamalabariya Gaon on the Kamalabari-Jengraimukh road[94] reported that he sells every kind of fish in the villages where once only particular types were sold. *Singi* is now a popular kind among the educated class as it is a fatless fish and is normally prescribed by the Doctors for the patients. The root of this change is to be searched in the nature or extent of availability of fish in the island. The scarcity of fish accompanied by unemployment problem which has curtailed men's purchasing power, is a strong factor under the change.[95] It is interesting to note that the land which was once so well known for availability of fish, is now importing *chalani* fish from outside; during one of my visits to the island during 10-13 June, 2005, I found there was no local fish at all in all the daily fish markets at Garamur and Kamalabari. It has been reported that poor villagers having no power to purchase, have to go without fish for days and months together as they had neither the opportunity to catch fish nor the ability to buy them from the market.

Fish is also used in the ritual functions, such as in giving feast to the people in the marriage receptions, performing ritual functions in the family, doing *sakam* (family religious function) to propitiate different gods and goddesses and so forth. The *barali* and the *sol* fishes are particularly used for some ritual purposes. Priests and astrologers prescribe certain forms of feast for recovery of men from certain form of diseases, such as *bagabhage chaul khuwua* (feast with white rice and *barali* fish) or *kola/ ronga bhage chaul khuwua* (feast with red rice and sol fish). Such types of feasts are still known to the villages of the island. But feast with tortoise meat has now become obsolete.

People are accustomed to eating fish in different ways. In the past, during the good harvesting days, in the months of September-November, when the rivers dried up and ponds subsided, numerous varieties of fishes, both big and small, became available, villagers used to eat them in different ways. First and formost method was to make curry of different sorts, such as *adkhariya, tenga, kharani charchari, tenga charchari, kharikat diya* (a process whereby small fishes are pinned into a long bamboo pin and then dried in the fire place till it becomes edible), *pitika, patat diya* (a process by which small fishes such as the *moa* or the *pona* or the tender new born fishes are put to fire by making a roll in the soft plantain leaf), *pora* (burnt fish), *bhaja* (fried) etc. "But, most new generation members are ignorant of those items", lamented Sri Bagaram Nath, one of the senior-most citizen of the Rangachahi area, and a noted educationist of Majuli. "It is due to swift decline in the availability of fish and drying up of the rivers and the ponds, and growth of population and consequent impact on the environments"—he said. It was due to easy availability of fish in the island in the past that men here paid little heed to other components of diet, such as milk and ghee, for which early British officers had noted that "milk is very little used by the mass of the people."[96] The remark made by S.N. Sarma that Robinson's statement does not stand good because "Assamese ceremony and festival could not be conceived of without milk, curd and milk preparations,"[97] therefore cannot hold good as the daily food habit and food culture is different from occasional and ritual habits. In another context we have discussed the place of milk and curd among the present dietary systems of the people of the island, and we have found that milk was once abundantly found in the island and was used for all ritual and ceremonious functions. But milk as a regular item of diet could not compete with fish. Sarma's stand therefore was limited to the orthodox section of the Brahmin society alone who perhaps do not form more than 2-3 per cent of the total population strength in the island. Even then it is too orthodox a statement. For men in the Majuli island, irrespective of caste and creed, run more after fish than after milk.

Meat was not very popular among the villagers, and it is still playing the second fiddle among the items of diet. Among the meat used in the families, the most known is the meat of the pigeons, and rarely that of ducks. Rearing of pigeon, duck and goat is still despised in Majuli as irreligious.[98] Of other kinds, the old generation is acquainted with those of *kacha* (tortoise), *harin* (deer), *banariya hanh* (migratory swan), *darikala* (a kind of wild bird), *kukuha* (a kind of bird that resides in the jungles of reeds) and *dauk* (a small bird living in the jungle of the neighbourhood). During the last few decades, flocks of a kind of migratory bird called *k<u>a</u>m char<u>a</u>i* were killed and eaten. This bird is known to the people since past and it is a subject of folk song of the people of the island.[99] The aphorisms of Dak[100] were applied in all their essence while preparing the meat curry. Chicken is popular among the tribal population. As they use to rear them at home, chicken and the tribal communities were once identified as the two faces of the same coin. But this was totally prohibited among the non-tribal societies. Similarly, pork was popular in the tribal society, while it was prohibitive in the other. This state of food habit has now been changed. Chicken has now become popular among all classes of the people irrespective of caste and tribe affiliation. Pork too has good markets in the island. This, however, does not mean that the use of chicken and pork have become universal; their use as an item of the dish is still limited to tribal communities in the main, and the urban, young and service holding section only of the non-tribal society. Village doors are still formally closed for them, particularly for the older and illiterate generation.

During our field investigation we found that markets are growing for selling meat in places such as Kamalabari, Garamur, Bangaon, Rangachahi, Jengraimukh, and Balichapori in western Majuli besides some sub-urban villages. For example, pork meat is sold at Phutuki *Ch<u>a</u>pori* and at Chitadarchuk Mising village near Garamur, Sonapur, Sumoimari, Dhapak Mising village near Kamalabari, Barpamua and Phulani chariali near Jengraimukh, and some other villages in between, such as Jakaibowa, Kalitapar, etc. In the weekly markets at Phulani held on every Friday, at Kaliagaon every Wednesday, at Kalitapar every Sunday, at Jakaibowa every Saturday, and in lower Majuli at Borunchuk on every Wednesday pork meat is sold at an average rate of Rs.80.00 per kilogram.[101]

Fish being the popular item of the dish, villagers of the island in the past used to have an item of fish always. It was then that they had normally two items only as their food—fish curry and rice. They had also enough pulses to meet the need of the whole year. Particular reference may be made to a kind called *m<u>a</u>ti m<u>a</u>h* (*Phaseolus radiatus*)[102] with which they prepared their *d<u>a</u>l* for food. They also produced mug called magu *m<u>a</u>h* (Phaseolus mungo) which they largely used to offer on ritual occasions, particularly on the occasions of the village and family rituals and functions. There was still another kind called *Kalam<u>a</u>h* or *khech<u>a</u>ri* (*Lathyrus sativus*). People used to grind them to make powder, which were then made into small balls called *pitik<u>a</u>* mixed with chilly and used as a component of diet. The production of this variety is now gradually getting discouraged as it has been publicised that this variety is not very good for health. But a different variety, they call *matar mah*, i.e. pea, have occupied the cultivators' mind as it could be cultivated during the winter and can also be collected in the same season. This has become popular due to the *Green Revolution* programme encouraged by the Department of Agriculture. One of the significant contributions of the *Green Revolution* in the Majuli island is the production of wheat about which we have discussed elsewhere.[103] Most villagers of the island now cultivate wheat and thereby try to manage the need of the family of its demand for rice for at least the dry months of scarcity. It is to be mentioned here that production of rice to meet the needs for the whole year is often not sufficient as the flood and erosion cause heavy damage to the crops. As a matter of fact, poor villagers unable to meet both ends with whatever rice they produce, exert for producing wheat which has no risk of being damaged by flood. The only notable concern in this regard is that being novice in the art of preparing items of food from wheat, the villagers make cakes of a form and size that does not resemble those normally known to the people in other parts of the country. Still, with potato (*aluguti*) *bhaji* and *ruti pitha* these wretched villagers are now contented enough to steer through the days of scarcity.

Salt was unknown in rural Assamese society till at least the close of the middle ages; people used an alkaline preparation called *khar* or *kharani* as its substitute. A kind of herb grown on water called *puni*, leaves of the fig tree and barks of plantains were used for the purpose.[103(a)] The practice of preparing *khar* by this method is still popular among the villagers of the island. It was because of this culture of consumption of *khar* as a substitute of salt, that people of Assam were once ridiculed by the outsiders as *Kharkhowa Asamiya*, and society of Majuli formed a part of it.

Of the easily available natural products, the popular were *betgaj* (cane-shoots), *pachala* (plantain shoot), *kharicha* (bamboo shoot), *naltenga* (a kind of wild creeper with souring taste), *dhekia* (edible fern), *kochu/ banariya kochu* (arum leaf and root). They are still popular among the villagers, although their availability has been drastically reduced due to reduction of the jungles and the *chapori* lands. Geographical and topographic conditions of the island have largely conditioned the growth of the vegetables. Fertile lands of the island once favoured growth of every kind of vegetables such as potato, chilly, cabbage, cauliflower, brinjal, other kinds of leafy vegetables, etc. It was however noted that vegetables for earning cash such as cabbage or cauliflower have been grown on a large scale only recently when markets for such vegetables emerged in the island during the later part of the British rule and early part of the post-Independence period.

Modern process of preservation was not known to the villagers till today. An attempt has however been made to build one at Jengraimukh.[103(b)]

They have a traditional system of preservation of certain items of food, such as salt, jaggery (*gur*), potato, garlic, onion and seeds of rice, mustard and different kinds of pulses, such as *mati mah* and *mug mah*. They use to pack up the rice seeds and salt in bamboo baskets called *tom* and put them on the ceilings or lintels of the houses. Other items such as mustard and pulses or rice, they preserve in large baskets called *duli* and *mer* made of bamboo. Potatoes and some vegetables, such as gourd and pumpkins, are also preserved on the ceiling of the house. And it is from here that they use to take some amount when necessary, particularly during the flood season when scarcity prevails. The tribal communities have a special preservation system. They dry the fishes in the sun during winter and preserve them for the future. The Misings have a special kind of preservation system of fishes. They grind the dry fishes with some medicinal herbs and put them inside bamboo tubes and keep them airtight for use in future. They call it *namsing*.[104]

Beliefs Associated with Food

Largely governed by the Satra codes, people of Majuli have certain beliefs associated with food preparation, food offering and food distribution. Fasting has been a rule on th , days of *ausi* (the day of the conjunction of the sun and the moon) and *ekadasi* (eleventh day of the lunar half of the month) and on the days of the death of the parents and the saints. Similarly, some people used to fast on Saturdays and Tuesdays as a custom. It was once a hard and fast rule that a girl was not to be allowed to cook if she was in the pre-marital but post-puberty stage. Nor a married woman was allowed to do the job unless she was ordained to certain degree of initiation called *saran*, *bhajan* and *katha-batara lowa*.[105] Taking of food was largely controlled by caste affiliation. A man normally took food from the hands of a member of his own caste; and if necessary, also from the hand of a senior member of a so-called superior caste. Thus when it was cooked by a Brahmin, food was taken almost by all. This is particularly noticed among the illiterate and elderly village folk, and among the inmates of the Satras. There were instances when a person was made socially outcast if he had taken food from the hand of a person who belonged to another caste considered inferior to him, or when he took food cooked by a junior member having still to undergo ordinances. It has been pointed out that even among the members of the same family food taking had been restricted to certain conditions. Influence of caste and superstitions, however, do not apply in case of the tribal society. A Mising, for example, shall take cooked food from any non-tribal family.

Another aspect of belief associated with the cooked food is that all appliances used to cook food are considered as personification of some gods and goddesses. For example, the pot (*choru*) where the rice is boiled is treated as the God Vishnu, the stick—*taru* or *heta* (a kind of long spoon) used to shuffle the items is treated as Brahma, the pitcher called *lota* used to carry water to pour into the hearth is treated as Lakshmi and so forth.[106] These beliefs had no scientific base, but these lessons are preached by the *gurus* to make them believe that they had attained a certain degree of initiation, and that therefore, they were senior class among the villagers. It is significant that in the traditional society of the Majuli island, it has been a custom that every one should take bath after going for extrication (*bahir phura*) and before going to take the lunch. It is still a custom that a person must take bath as many times as he/she goes to extrication. Taking bath is a must before taking the major meal in the day. This is, of course, not hard and fast in the tribal society. In the common feasts, it is a custom that a distributor called *deori-bilaniya* should cover his mouth with a clean towel called *gamocha*, and he is not to wear any shirt except a piece of cloth called *chadar* to cover his body behind the *dhuti* or the waist cloth. This practice has its own meaning and utility for the society for reason of hygiene. Often women distributors are also appointed for distribution among women participants (*bhakat*, feminine—*bhakatani*). In either case no one, *bhakat* or *deori-bilaniya*, is allowed to put on shoes inside the ritual zone, in the individual's house, or in the common prayer hall called *namghar*. It is to be noted that the selection of the distributor is also conditioned by certain rules, such as family background, degree of ordinance, health and character. No person with a record of ill health and infectious diseases, and having a record of immoral character, or who are childless (barren) is selected for the job of the distributor.

In personal life a man has to maintain certain code of conduct in matters of food. It will be better if Dr. P. D. Goswami, *Satradhikara* of the Auniati Satra, is quoted here: "In the Satriya system one is to sit on the ground and take food by keeping silence. It is a special rule in the Satras that at the time of eating food one is never to look hither and thither. One is always to take one's food by just looking down to the plate of the food. There is a proverb which says—give food to the wise he will concentrate on his dish, but a fool will look left and right before he takes his food. One is not to go away from the dish before finishing the food; if one does so, it is not suggestive that he should go back and take from the same plate. Taking curd in the evening and keeping it in the bell-metal and brass vessels are prohibitive........ gourds like *jatilao* and *komora* should not be cut into pieces in the middle; and when a plantain shoot (*pachala*) is cut, it should be brought inside by covering it with its leaf. A plantain leaf should not be taken in full inside the house. After food, one is to walk for some time and take betel-nut and leaf."[107] These are equally applied in the conduct of the villagers in Majuli also.

DRESSES AND WEARS OF THE PEOPLE

Traditional Dress

Dress and ornaments of the people of the island do not differ from those of the other Assamese people. Ordinarily, the dress of man consisted of a *churiya* or a *dhuti* (waist cloth of a metre breath and two to three metre length), a *cha̲dar* (a wrapper cloth), and a *gamocha̲* (napkin). The *Guru Charit Katha*, a biographical work of the Vaishnava saints of medieval Assam, mentions how Sankaradeva, while he was at Belaguri Dhuwahat in Majuli, used to keep his *churiya̲* and the *gamocha̲* at the roof of the house at the time of his taking bath before he had a bath room constructed for him by Madhavdeva.[108] Assamese chronicles mention that during that time every family was to weave clothes to meet its own requirements failing which the state imposed penalties. In continuation of this medieval tradition, some families till recent decades used to make their essential clothes at their family looms. This habit of weaving cloths to meet the minimum of their needs consisting of a *cha̲dar* (a piece of cotton cloth to cover the body) for both men and women, and a *mekhela̲* (women's waist cloth) and a *riha̲* (a long piece of cloth used to cover the upper part of the women's body) consisted of the usual wear in almost every average family in the society. It was a tradition in the society that every family must produce necessary clothes at home, and girls must know how to weave. A girl who lacks that skill of weaving was, therefore, hardly preferred for marriage. She was despised as *thupori*. At present, however, this old fashion could be seen only among the old generation inhabitants. All modern dresses and wears have come to the society of the island as in any other part of the state. And this is known when Kanmai, wife of Gangadhar of (Meruwabari) Jogi Gaon, who once used to make a better part of her living by weaving clothes for others, says that her weaving loom is now no longer in use as it was before. Similar is the answer of Neelakshi of Puranibari village who happened to be an expert weaver, but who has now no time to go to the loom because of her Government job. Availability of cheaper variety of clothes in the market for various kinds of uses has made the strongest blow on this cottage industry which once was unavoidable in the rural society of the island.

Among the male section of the people, the celibate inmates of the Satra are a distinct class by themselves in their dress and movements. They, both young and the old, have to put on a *dhuti* or *churiya̲* wide enough to cover up to the ankle, a *cha̲dar* of either cotton or silk, if old, a *pag* or *paguri*, keep long and twisted hair (called *khopa*), and *chandan* on the forehead. The *adhikara* of the Satra puts on silk cloth, *chandan* and beautifully designed *paguri*.[109] The *adhikara* always keeps long hair. It is a medieval custom of the Assamese society when keeping long hair was considered a symbol of dignity and aristocracy, and no one except the inmates of the Satra and a few dignitaries from the high castes, were allowed by the state to keep it.[110]

Tribal Dress

Tribal dresses are essentially distinguished with colourful design and craftsmanship. It is not known what sort of clothes the Misings, or for that matter, the Deoris and Kacharis of the Majuli island used to put on at the beginning of their settlement in the island. It is presumable, however, that clothes of the Misings did not differ much from their hill brothers with whom their (Misings) ancestors lived together for centuries.[111] It was originally the custom of the Misings, like any other community of the state, to produce whatever amount of clothes they needed to put on. Assamese chronicles have recorded that they used to grow cotton in the hills and from the cotton thus produced, they made in their family looms necessary clothes for the family. As cultivation of cotton in the island was not possible due to inundation, most cottons were earlier imported from the north bank. Mising women put on a waist cloth resembling *mekhela* of other women called *gapa*, and another piece on the upper part of their body called *gare*.[112] Married women used a third piece of cloth called *loutum* or *gero* on the waist as a special cover of the middle part of the body.[113] Now a days this piece has been replaced by a piece with new design called *cheg-raug*. They use a long piece of cloth called *ribi* by which they bind their child with the body of their mother. A similar piece called *gacheng* woven with colourful threads they use to put on in the festival days. Waist clothes of the Mising women are particularly noteworthy. They bear floral works sometimes over the whole piece, and sometimes over the lower part. Girls put on flowers of various kinds on the hair-knot during the festive days.[114]

Winter garments consisted of a special kind called *gadu* or *mirijim* made of cotton produced at home or purchased from the market, the latter process being popular today. A standard *mirijim* is about seven cubits long and two and a half cubit broad. Its manufacturing process is time-consuming, and weaving out a piece took about three to six months on average for a weaver woman. It is also heavy, as heavy as five to ten kilograms. Woven in their family loom of a special kind, *mirijim* is a special feature of the tribal heritage of Majuli. It is used collectively by all members of a family together during the winter night. While writing in the seventies of the last century, T. C. Pamegam, the noted thinker and writer of the Mising community, has stated that an average piece of *mirijim* could fetch as much as Rs. 500.00.[115] *Mirijim* is still woven in some families, although mostly for purposes of sale or exhibition. It has become unpopular among most of the educated and economically affluent families as the need of the warm clothes is filled up by the modern-day, often imported, blankets available in the markets. The breakdown of the tribal social and economic structure in the recent decades has been another cause of growing unpopularity of the *mirijims*.

Mising women of the Majuli island and its adjoining areas on the north bank, from Dhakuakhana to the the Suvansiri delta, used to rear a kind of silk worm called *eri*. It is not known for certain when did the Misings first started rearing the *eri* worms. It is, however, certain that they possibly did not bring the culture from their hill abodes. On the other hand, *eri* culture was popular among the villagers of Assam in the middle ages like the culture of the *pa̱t* (mulberry) and *muga̱* (amber colour silk). A Mising *eri cha̱dar* is about four to five cubits long and from three to three and a half cubits broad. It is woven by the women in their family loom from the thread they produce from the *eri* cocoon. It is to be noted that unlike the *mirijim*, *eri cha̱dars* are retaining considerable popularity among the Misings as well as among the non-Misings due to their warmth, handiness and commercial value. For *eri* cloth is now treated with respect as a piece of cultural heritage of the tribe. It is interesting to note that *eri chadar* made by the women of the Jengraimukh and Dhakuakhana area of Assam draws attention of people all over the world, and is the best of its kind in the state. Today, *eri cha̱dars* are produced on commercial lines and are sold in the market and also exported to outside. In the rural market, said Phanidhar Tahu, Principal of UMK College, Ratanpur, Majuli, whose wife is an expert weaver, a good *eri cha̱dars* fetches Rs. 500 to Rs.1000 at present. But, as far as popular use is concerned, a Mising girl or an aged woman are more impressed by a sweater or a Kashmiri shawl today than by an *eri cha̱dars* or a home made warm cloth, and by a *sa̱ri* than a traditional waist cloth.[116] Growth of urban centres and availability of varieties of machine-made, cheap, warm and woollen cloth, and more particularly, the gradual growth of purchasing power of the Mising community has knocked a blow to the handicraft. In the past, Mising male dress was different from the male dress of the non-tribal counterparts of the society. It was a piece of cloth, black or red, that was used as waist-cloth. The body was usually naked except the part to be covered by the waist cloth. Growth of education and literacy and purchasing power among the Misings have changed their old habit. Mising men are now accustomed with all sorts of modern wears including shoes and varieties of warm cloths.

Like the Misings, all other tribes like the Sonowal Kacharis and the Deoris have their own traditional tribal dresses which are always colourful and hand-made. The Deori traditional dresses include *hoku* (*dhuti*), *beche* (*gamocha̱*), *igu* (*mekhela̱*), *jakachiba̱* (a piece of thin cloth wrapped in the waist above the *mekhela̱-igu*), and *gathigi* (head wear). Similarly, the Kacharis too have their own tribal wears amidst modern sophistication.

POSITION OF WOMEN

In any society position of women depends upon their rate of literacy and strength of economy.[117] In Majuli, as in any traditional society in India, women literacy and employment was almost nil till after Independence. In 1920 when Keshabram Bora, a worthy son of Majuli, graduated from Cotton College in Science, and started the first High School in Majuli in 1924 (now Majuli Auniati Hemchandra High School), there were no literate women to send their daughters to the school.[118] Similarly, when Dehiram Nath of Jogi (Yogi) Gaon (Puranibari), took his First Division Normal Third Year Certificate in 1926, there was no women in his village who could read and write.[119] This tradition continued till almost after Independence. When asked, Bagaram Nath, an M.A., a retired Head Master of Rangachahi T.N.High School, and a pioneer in growth of modern education in post-Independence Majuli, replied that when he passed his Matriculation Examination in First Division in 1954, there was no woman in his village Rangachahi who could put her signature. Similar was the situation almost over entire Majuli. Needless to speak about the Mising or any tribal community; even Bangaon, Salmara, Kamalabari and Garamur, the advanced places in the island, passed through the same situation.

Traditional outlook of men towards women, and the role of the Satras which considered women as unworthy of cultivating religion and literature,[120] had great impact on the status of women in the society. Monastic Satras in the past did neither allow women to enter its prayer halls (*na̱mghar*), nor any of them were allowed to be a residential devotee—nun (*bhakatani*). The Hindu marriage rituals of making the bride a kind of slave of her husband by its own marriage rituals (*sa̱t pa̱ke ba̱dha̱*) is to be noted in this regard. In this connection the observation of the American Baptist missionaries is to be noted.

> Hindu is never seen to treat his wife with familiarity or fondness...The supreme duty of a wife is to obey her husband...the husband is God to the wife...therefore he should be the chief object of worship; after her husband's death, he is to be the object that she must worship...His will and authority are permanent to any law human or divine.[121]

FIG. 2.4: VILLAGE MISING WOMAN AT WORK

There was the practice of child marriage among the Brahmans, and early marriage among all other castes.[122] They were never to move openly or alone, or exchange things as traders, or move without the permission of the husband or the senior of the family, or without a companion. Nor they were allowed to enter the Satra *namghar* and participate in the schedule of religious work of the village.[123] In this regard the American Baptists have mentioned:

> "Again the daughters have no choice in the matter of choosing their husbands. Marriages are contracted by the father....But they seldom see each other until the age of 12 or 13 when according to Hindu custom the son may claim his wife. She is married and taken to husband's *zenana* often much against the wishes. She knows little of him and he of her. The husband buys his wife as he does a beast of burden and regards her in the pretty much the same light. If the wife be of high birth, she is little else than her husband's prisoner...If she is a person of low caste she at once becomes the wife and drudge."[124]

In the orthodox traditional Hindu society in Majuli, position of women was not much different from that of their counterparts in other places of the state.

Growth of education and employment among women in Majuli is considerably a late development. Even now no woman from Majuli has been in the professional and administrative jobs, such as in the profession of a doctor, engineer, lawyer, and civil administrative officers. The first ever woman graduate (in Arts) Anima Hazarika took her degree only in 1965, the woman science graduate Minati Saikia in 1973, and woman

Post-Graduate Arati Bora in 1975.[125] But the women of Majuli are now school and college goers, service and job holders, traders, artists and so forth, although the number of such women is small. In our investigation, it was found that only 2.24 per cent of the women in Majuli are service holders, and a very insignificant part of them are engaged in business.[126] Interestingly, women literacy has grown tremendously during the last few decades of the post-Independence period. In the Puranibari village, where there was not a single literate woman in the year 1926, women literacy rate has risen to 63 per cent today, and in Rangachahi to 75 per cent.[127] Unfortunately, women employment at present in the Puranibari village is 2.24 per cent, and in Rangachahi it is 5 per cent.[128] Similar is the rate of women employment in many other villages.

This is however not the total picture of status of women in Majuli. Modernization of the outlook of the *Satradhikaras*, and growth of education among women, have had impact on some other aspects—they have now begun to respond to the situations with a sense of dignity and strength. They are also given comfortable status by the Satras. Pitambardeva Goswami of Garamur Satra who, for the first time, allowed women to participate in the religious and cultural functions of his Satra, broke their age-old bondage.[129] It is a significant step forward in the field of women empowerment in Majuli. It was he again who for the first time permitted them to participate in the stage performance in the year 1950.[130] Pitambardeva Goswami opened the door for a new status for women in Majuli. Women in Majuli today have their organization to fight for their rights.[130(a)]

Comparatively, however, position of the tribal and Scheduled Caste women was and still is higher than those of the caste society. A Mising woman in the past not only cultivated in the field along with men by using the plough, but also maintained poultry farm, engaged in fishing in the river, brought up children and went to the market for shopping. But the literacy rate was almost nil among them then. We have illustration from at least one such Mising village which is still lagging much behind their neighbours. Thus, in the Kalitapar Mising village there were only 1 graduate (in Arts), and 5 Higher Secondary School passed members in 2004. There was no woman who passed School Certificate Examination. Simple literacy (ability to read and write the name) too is limited to the school going children alone. But they participate almost equally with men in all sorts of family and social work. And the bridegroom party is still to bear much the same way the burden of the bride price in the Kalitapar village. Similarly, a Kaivarta woman in the past had openly moved in the streets, in the market places, and exchanged articles by barter system by traveling from house to house. Known as *pohari*, they were once the major agency of carrying messages from one village to another.

Gradually however, an adverse scenario is being noted even in the tribal societies of Majuli. It is interesting to note that while growth of education raises the status of women everywhere in the country, in Majuli growth of education among the tribal communities has made them imitate the life-styles of their non-tribal Hindu counterparts who are naturally submissive to their husbands and to the superiors of the family or of the village.[131] Along with the growth of education they have developed a dislike to go to the field, or maintain a poultry farm as their illiterate part does. When asked, Miss Basabi Pegu, who is an M.A. student in Dibrugarh University, and who hails from the Barpamua village under Ujani Majuli Development Block, has replied that being a University goer she feels it shameful to go for the manual works in the field. She has also left the habit of keeping a poultry farm as she did in her childhood or like her mother who is an illiterate village woman. She has further informed that she prefers an arranged marriage for herself and (would like to) offer feast to the invitees on the occasion like that done by her friends in the neighbouring non-Mising villages. Mising or a Deori or a Kachari married and educated woman, therefore, for all practical purposes, now attires herself like her non-tribal Assamese Hindu counterparts, such as using vermilion, laying prostrate before the superiors on ceremonial days and so forth. Thus, arranged marriage governed by social, religious and constitutional laws, has slowly replaced the early forms of elopement. And this is, interestingly, one of the reasons for decline of their status. Widow remarriage which was once known to the society among the Misings and Deoris, has now slowly become unpopular. Economically too they have lost their earlier independence. No educated Mising woman today goes to plough or to the nearby river for fishing, or would like to maintain a poultry farm of their own. Thus modernity has also a reverse impact on the status of tribal woman.

HEALTH AND FAMILY PLANNING

Majuli, as reported by the early writers, had been always a good health station in the region. It was neither very hot nor very cold being subject to a continuous cool breeze blowing all around the year. "The climate of this part of the Brahmaputra", says Shihabuddin Talish, "suits natives and strangers alike. But at a distance from the river, though the climate agrees with the natives, it ranks poison to foreigners..... In the cold weather the diseases of cold and moisture affect foreigners with greater severity than the natives, while in summer excessive secretion of the bile grasps foreigners more violently than natives. The people of this country are free from certain fatal and loathsome diseases—such as leprosy, white leprosy, elephantiasis, cutaneous, goiter and hydrocoele—which prevail in Bengal. They are also immune from many other lingering maladies."[132] Although Shihabuddin's account is based on his observation on the state of the Ahoms in general, it is equally applicable in case of Majuli. Even today, Shihabuddin's observation applies well to understanding the condition of Majuli although some of his observations such as absence of goiter is not applicable in case of the island. It is to be noted that people suffering from this disease in Majuli is even now not very insignificant.

Writing about the scenario in Assam in the mid-19th century, William Robinson has recorded that (i) dysentery was common to the natives of Assam; 'it carried off more victims than almost all the other diseases put together.' 'Upon the whole, the poorer classes seem to be greatest sufferers from dysentery. The prevalence of the diseases, and the great mortality occasioned by it, may be accounted for in the deficiency of food and proper clothing, the use of putrid fish, indigestible fruits and vegetables, bad water procured from stagnant pools in the vicinity of their dwellings.... and, were there no other cause, poverty alone, from its distressing influence on both body and mind, would render them liable to all the diseases usually arising from debility."(ii) asthma is common in Upper Assam, (iii) scorbutus is frequently seen among the lower classes, (iv) "venereal complaints and gonorrhea are prevalent at all stations. The natives say the former disease became common soon after the Burmese invasion", (v) "Sporadic cases of cholera frequently occur; on an average it has hithertho appeared epidemically, every fourth year. Thus, the years 1825, 1829,1833, 1835 and 1838 it created havoc almost in all parts of the state".[133] He has however stated that despite such diseases, 'Europeans usually enjoy very excellent health.'[134]

The above description still applies well to the state of health of the people in Majuli, although some of the major diseases are now no longer seen, such as cholera or small pox, gonorrhea or any other such diseases. It is heard from the old generation people that at one time cholera destroyed village after village; and men used to believe that it was created by a goddess. Similarly, small pox was also considered as a goddess called *bar ai* whom they used to worship and treat in their own ways. There is still a class of song called *ai sitala* or *ainam*. Similarly, many other diseases of malignant nature, or of similar effect such as tetanus were believed to be creation of spirits or ghosts. As pointed out by Robinson, many of the diseases were due to poverty and ignorance of the people, and due to use of dirty water and unhygienic condition. The biographical work called *Guru Charit Katha* has recorded that Madhavdeva had to make a toilet house at Belaguri Dhuwahat for Sankaradeva when he noticed that the *guru* was having no system for that purpose.[135] As far as the records go, this is the first ever reference to any toilet and a bath room built for anybody in Majuli. Traditions have recorded that even Vamsigopaldeva is believed to be happy with Majuli which had sufficient open and sunny shore for doing all washing works in the morning. This system of using open or grazing fields for extrication (*bahir phura*) purpose was popular among some of the people in Majuli till recent years, particularly among the lower classes of the society.

In the colonial period, gradually the sense of hygiene grew among the people. Modern medicine now began to pour in, and at least the richer section of the society could avail themselves of this advantage. At the close of the 19th century, a hospital was established at Kamalabari.[136] And this was the beginning of the modern practices of medicine and treatment in the Majuli island.

According to the Departmental report, there are hospitals, dispensaries and public health centres in Majuli at present with 1 Community Health Centre and a PHC at Kamalabari, 4 numbers of mini PHCs—one each at Jengraimukh, Ratanpur Miri, Ratanpur Lahan and Karatipar, 4 numbers of State Dispensaries one each at Bangaon, Dakhinpat, Rangachahi and Ahataguri, a hundred bed sub-divisional hospital at Garamur (established in 2003), and 34 numbers of sub-centres.[137] The growth of the number of hospitals, however, does not speak about actual status of health. There are regular news media reports to that effect. Even a stray visitor has noted in 2002: "To add to the misery, there is only one hospital which has just thirty beds, an inadequate stock of medicines, that is not replenished during monsoon, when they are needed most. Half of the staff of six doctors and eight nurses, that is supposed to be there, are almost always absent. There are eight other dispensaries dispersed throughout the island, and their condition is even worse, if that is possible in the bottomless pit of miseries that Majuli is."[138] The same allegation against heath facility and service systems has also been raised from inside the Department by Dr. Manjurani Devi, a Doctor at the Kamalabari PHC in Majuli.[139] Amidst volumes of allegations it appears that health in Majuli still depends upon its nature to a great extent—climate, food and environment, and more sarcastically, on men's fate, rather than on modern facilities supplied to the island. For, on the basis of those allegations it becomes clear that not only the service rendered by those establishments are unsatisfactory, the entire infrastructure is insufficient to form an independent unit which a geographically isolated place like Majuli really needs. Even today women's mortality rate during child-birth is significantly higher than in any other place of the state. When contacted, Punaram Nath, Head Master of Jakaibowa Kalia M. E. School, has stated that significant number of young women had died in the past in his village during child-birth. Similar was the answer given by Manik Bora, a noted writer from Majuli. Insufficient health facilities in the island, and lack of communication facilities to take patients to the hospital or for emergency treatment outside the island are some reasons for that, he said.

Family planning in rural society in Majuli was not known till recent years. Even at present it is not much known in the villages. There are examples of families of having more than six-seven children each. The growth of mere literacy has not worked in popularizing the family planning system in the island. A kind of fear and suspicion are there that a man undergoing vasectomy operation, or a woman undergoing such treatment, will not remain fit for doing hard labour as ploughing and carrying loads. When asked, almost every aged member expressed his suspicion on family planning measures. It is also true that most of them are not well aware of other systems of family planning due mainly to lack of awareness. Economically too, they are not sound enough to adopt such methods. On the other hand, poor village cultivators have no other pastime for enjoyment than to have sex after the days hard labour in the field or in the river in catching fish.[140] It requires education and understanding of the medieval value system in a modern setting.

Here we shall present an example from a very backward Mising village to show how illiteracy and system of economy have kept the people of that village unaware of the benefits of the family planning system. It is called Kalitapar village within the Namani Jakaibowa Gaon Panchayat. There are altogether 85 families of which we considered 29 on random sampling basis, a 1/3rd of the total. Mainly based on agriculture of a riverine belt, its economy is one of the worst in the island. Prone to the havoc of annual floods, the amount of the *a̱hu* and the *ba̱o* crop collection is not sufficient enough to meet the need of the village for the whole year. On the other hand, number of the service holders is too insignificant. There is only one person who is a graduate; and no woman has studied beyond the 10th standard; and its literacy is mostly confined to the school-going children. The growing poverty and struggle for survival has compelled many of its youths to move to Jorhat and other towns outside Majuli. As reported, 15 young boys have already left the village to be rickshaw pullers in Jorhat. The villagers have to do excessive labour to meet the minimum needs for the year. With such poverty and economic and literacy standards, inhabitants of the Kalitapar village have little understanding to give importance to the family planning system. The average family size of the sample houses is found to be 8.1 which is much higher than the state rate.

FLOOD AND MAJULI—PAST AND PRESENT

The first impression of an outsider on the name 'Majuli' is that it is a land of flood, and, of course, erosion. As we have stated earlier'[141] it was flood that had created the island. Being created and surrounded by the mighty Brahmaputra and the Luhit, it is subjected to annual inundation; and, in fact, inundation has formed part of its culture. It not only brings havoc, and sometimes, untold misery upon the inhabitants, but also gives fertility to its soil, respite to its toiling people,[142] fish, meat and many new items of diet, and above all, a season of games, enjoyments and aspirations. Nirupama Bargohain, a noted writer of Assam, who had the experience of spending some years in Majuli in the fifties of the last century, has noted with emotion about its flood as follows:

> The house which we took on rent was a thatched house. Its floor was not only earthen, it was also very damp. I am not at all a weak lady; I have sufficient mental strength, and a stout body, as stout as a piece of rod. But (during the season) my health broke down due to poor diet and for staying on the damp house. There was incessant rain, and flood everywhere led to collapse of all communication links. In the market vegetables, fish and meat, egg and milk became too dear. Scarcity of dietary items also tolled heavily on my health. Moreover, staying and moving in the damp house from the morning till night created in me a sort of cold and cough which I failed to cure even by using medicine. Finally, under compulsion I had to invite my father from Guwahati, and left Majuli in order to recover my declining health.[143]

This is the picture of a flood season in Majuli when everywhere there is water, water and only water. Neither there is road and communication, nor supply of enough food, nor drinking water. Men often remains hungry due to lack of husked rice (*chaul*), and a place to make the hearth to cook. For even the houses get submerged and water level comes up to knee deep or more, or at times touches the lower portion of the roof of the house. All men irrespective of rich or poor, cut down the plantain trunks and make floating and movable platforms called *bhur* where not only they move but also they make their hearth. The ferocious Brahmaputra criss-crosses the island creating terror not only in the heart of the outsiders, but also among the local inhabitants. There is no man in Majuli who does not pay homage and salutation to the great river when overflowing flood submerges its banks, villages and high *chaporis* creating the scenery of a foggy sea where water touches the extreme end of the horizon. It is in such situations that cattle and tigers live together taking shelter on high patches of land. An eerie sound, not known where it comes from, reigns over the island. It is, of course, enjoyable to the natives, but always horrifying for an outsider.

Every native possesses a boat in Majuli during flood like small traders in the towns having a bicycle. Men, women and children know how to swim and run a boat. Young men now steer their boats to the *chapori* far away from home in search of reeds to make grass for the hungry cattle at home kept almost in confinement on a small mound of the locality, or on the high embankment. They collect the leaves of high reeds in the *chapori* and when the boat is full, they take a morsel of breakfast called *komal chaul* (soft rice) or *pithaguri* and *bhimkal* (dry rice powder with a kind of robust banana) and sail back home. Full of grass and heavy with load, his boat, now an inch above the water level, has every possibility of being sunk into the 'ocean of water'; but he enjoys and spends his return journey by singing a folk song popularly known as the *nawariya* or *bhatiyaliya geet*. John M'Cosh has given a very interesting note about the relationship between the flood and the villagers in Assam as follows:

> The rainy season may be called the carnival of Assam; all the labours of the field are suspended; every one seems happy and contended; and lives luxuriously upon haunches of venison, or steaks of the hog or the buffaloe. The flood of Deucalion is in a great measure realized every year. The timid deer exhausted by long swimming and exertion, is glad to take shelter in a cow house or a cottage. The tiger and the buffaloe swim together in amity, and the elephant and her young with the wild hog and her sucklings. The native anchors his boat to his own roof tree, performs his ablutions on his flooded hearth, and drags his net in his tobacco garden; where the oxen lately ploughed, they swim across to higher pasture; where a field of grain a short time before waved in the rising sun, naught now waves but the muddy water; the sites of large villages are known only by their roofs above the stream; and the situation of others are pointed out only by a few palm trees weeping over the drowned and deserted foundations.[144]

In course of time flood subsides everywhere leaving its imprints—grass fields covered with muddy stains, river water smelling with rotten bodies

FIG. 2.5: POTTERS TRAVEL FROM VILLAGE TO VILLAGE SELLING THEIR POTS

of dead animals, and life in the villages more acute and difficult. Stores of grain (*bharal*) now evaporate, they were under water for some days turning the grain into seeds in germination and thus creating scarcity of food. In the fields *bao* crop languishes after emerging from muddy flood, while *sali* plantation, if there is any, dies instantly. Everywhere there is rotten smell of dead plants, insects and animals. But, this does not continue for long; soon shower comes washing off the fields and the *bao* crops in water. Now everywhere it is green and hopeful. Men now prepare for a second time to grow seedlings for the *sali* crop. But it is already late although fertile fields of Majuli still supply enough energy to them to grow. By November agriculture fields are brown with ripe paddy, and mustard fields are ready to sow seeds. In December, mustard crop blooms making Majuli a globe of yellow flowers. Fields having no end till it reaches the extreme horizon are now bringing new energy and hope for living, merry making, and creating dreams of new conjugal life. So, the months that follow are the months of collecting cash and celebrating marriage.

Potters now travel from village to village selling pots of different sizes (*tekeli* and *kalah*) which could be used for keeping milk/curd that becomes too sticky (*atha doi*) to be used in the *Bihus* and marriages. People of Majuli now forget about the havoc of the last year's flood, and those who have planned to leave Majuli for the Tengani reserve on the Nagaland border,[145] now compromise happily with the fortunes of the winter.

The above picture of flood and consequent life in the Majuli island reflects an occasional situation today, because of extensive measures adopted to prevent it, but has been a regular phenomenon some decades or a century ago. Flood in Majuli now comes in the Brahmaputra and goes along the Brahmaputra; it has little to do with the internal ecology of the island unless it breaks the dykes and embankments. Building of high embankments almost all around preventing water to flow inside as it did earlier in its natural course, and building of a still larger embankment across the Kherkatiya Suti (the northern part of the Brahmaputra) at its junction with the Brahmaputra on the extreme eastern part[146] have totally changed its topography. In fact, Majuli in reality, is not an island today. Prevention of flood at the source has made it a kind of 'Netherlands' during the flood season. Thus, one has either to experience horror and havoc when overflowing flood breaks an embankment, or to experience draught if and when they work well for which they are built. Thus there is a tug of war between the Brahmaputra which wants to flow in its own course and make Majuli a garden of nature, and man who makes utmost attempt to compel it to go aside leaving Majuli, its own child, untouched. Thus flood has now turned into *no-flood* or *over-flood.* The consequence has become horrifyingly pronounced—erosion.

EROSION IN MAJULI: SOME IMPLICATIONS

Erosion has been a natural phenomenon on every river bank, especially in a land where soil is sandy, and geological conditions are evolutionary.[147] It is not known to what extent Majuli was subject to erosion in the past; but as the island which was once extending in the east up to Baiganmang above the mouth of the Dikhow river, and in the west up to Kaliabar in Nagaon,[148] stretching over a length of about 160 miles,[149] has now shrunk to about 75-80 kilometers in length and 7-10 kilomiters in breadth at the maximum, within a period of last two hundred years (1800-2000), there is no need of any other record to persume its intensity. Popular memory supported by records maintain that erosion on the southern bank line of the island has been more serious since the great earthquake of the 1950.[150] Available statistics show that during the last fifty-five years the area of the island has been reduced from 1325.51 sq. kms. to 422.00 sq. kms.[150(a)] It is said that as a result of the earthquake the bottom of the rivers has come up pushing the water level further up consequently raising the flood level and subsequent erosion.[151] Be that as it may, erosion on the southern side from the extreme east to the extreme west has been constantly reducing the area of the island since then eroding hundreds of villages and many a Satras. On the eastern side, many known and affluent villages like Salmara, Lahkar, Ratanpur, Chinatoli have been washed away, while in the west, almost the entire Ahataguri Mauja has been lost. According to a report presented by an eye witness from Ahataguri, about ten Satras and ninety villages have thus been swept away by erosion.[152]

Erosion has great implications for the social history of the island. On one hand, it reduces agricultural and homestead lands, damages Satras, houses, schools and other institutions; on the other, it enhances internal and external migration of the people, and creates a class of landless poor. During our field investigation in and outside Majuli, we came to know how erosion-affected people from Majuli have settled on the other sides of the river and have acculturated the areas to the systems of Majuli. Similar villages are to be found in Narayanpur, Gahpur, Kalabari, Bihpuria and Biswanath on the north bank, and Titabar, Nagaon, Dergaon, Jorhat, Teok, Jhanji, Khowang and Dibrugarh on the south. Thus Kamalabari Satra shifted to Titabar in January, 1975, when its original site had fallen to erosion;[153] and Auniati Satra and many others have shifted further inside the island more than once.[154] The establishment of a big branch of the Auniati Satra at Teok has been a consequence of the Satra's recurring experience of erosion. Even the Dakhinpat Satra which has been able to stay more or less in the original site, has built a branch at Guwahati as a security measure. Thus, erosion has greatly affected its demographic pattern, its ecology and environment, and above all, its social structure and economic growth. It is to be noted that in most parts of the Dhodang *Chapori* area which is but a resultant of the erosion in the Ahataguri Mauja, people who were earlier accustomed to the settled agriculture system, have now adopted to the shifting system due to changing topographic conditions; and winter crops like sugarcane that grows well in the sandy soil of the *chapori*, have begun to dominate its agriculture. Finally, by drastically reducing its geographical territory it has posed a great threat to its very survival. By now most of the southern belt formed by the extended part of the southern mainland has been washed away leaving mainly the northern belt formed by the old and dead bed of the Brahamaputa. It appears that Majuli may once more be converted to a cluster of islands by the renewal of the abandoned courses of the dead channels had not modern technology and science been applied to control and direct the great river.

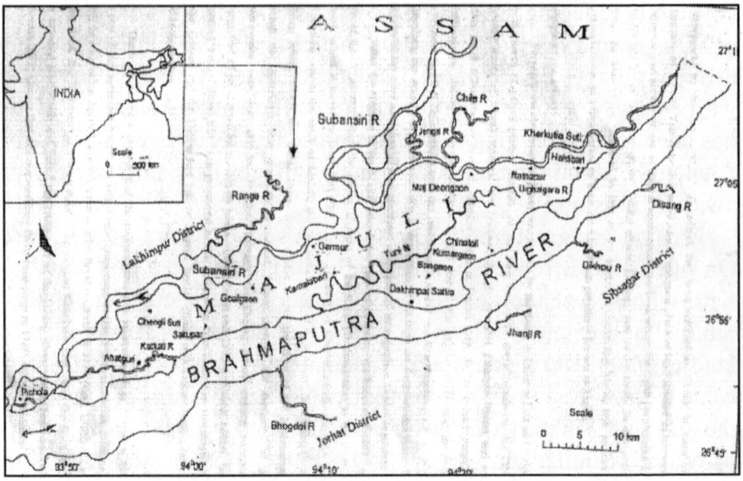

Fig. 2.6 Location Map of the Majuli Island as in 1917
(Survey of India)

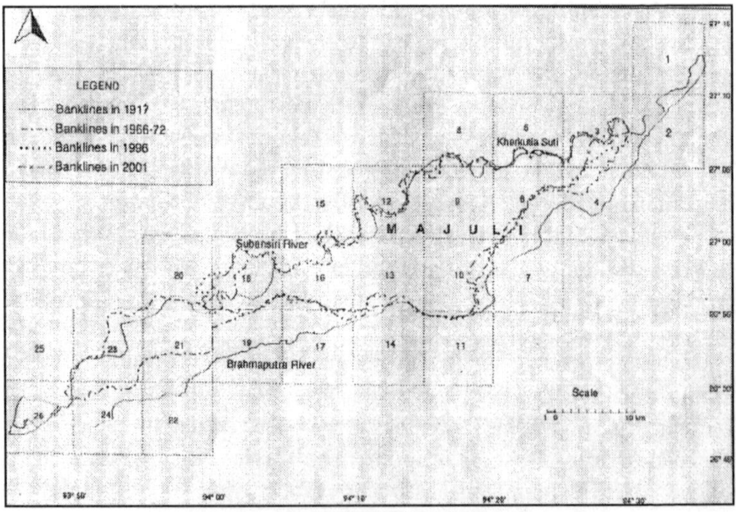

Fig. 2.7: Affect of Erosion on Majuli Island
[From J. N. Sharma loc. cit. (Ms.)]

FIG. 2.8: SPECIMEN OF A SANDY-EMBANKMENT BUILT IN MAJULI

FIG. 2.9: EROSION IN SALMARA KUMAR GAON

FIG. 2.10: EROSION PREVENTION PROCESS IN PURANI KAMALABARI SATRA SITE

FIG. 2.11: A SUMMER SUN-SET ON THE BRAHAMAPUTRA IN MAJULI

DECADES BACK—A WINTER IN MAJULI

Reflection from a Poor Cultivator

It is yet to be morning. The sound of the *urals* (wooden mortar and pestle) from the distant Mising villages of husking rice and the crowing of the cocks inviting the dawn have just touched the ear of Boparam Nath, a poor cultivator, in Puranibari village on the Kamalabari-Jengarai Road. And he is listening to the thin sound of the old Hercules bicycle of Dinsa Ghosh, a Sylhetty milk trader who had his *gakhirar mahal* (milk shop) at Kharjanpar in Madhupur—Puranibari junction on a dead river channel of the old Brahmaputra. Boparam Nath used to hear this sound every morning at 4 coming from over the gravel Garamur-Jengraimukh-Haladhibari road when he was still under the *phatakatha* (a kind of home-made warm cloth/blanket) on his bamboo-bed. Dinsa goes to Jengraimukh about sixteen kms. from his shop to collect milk from the buffalo rearers (*moh-guwal*) with his old bicycle carrying two large steel drums that make sound when the bicycle proceeds over the gravel road. It is rhythimic to Boparam's ears, but unwelcome, as it gives him warning to rise and go to the *ahutoli* field to plough. Going to the field in a winter morning when it was still too dark was something that was not of his preference. It was so cold outside, he even could not sleep well that night as there were leakage holes in the reed-made walls (*ikarar ber*) of his sleeping room by which cold air entered and disturbed him all the night. He would have tried to compensate in the morning. But he has no time, for he must go to the plough. If he does not, he would lose the season's crop, and it will be difficult to maintain his wife and three children for the year. Boparam left his bed hesitatingly with no warm cloth to cover his body. He feels exceedingly cold amidst heavy fogs that had embraced the surrounding. He went to the *gohali* (cow-shed) to take out his pair of the bullock who too are reluctant to follow. But they too would have to go. Boparam took his *nangal* (wooden plough) on his shoulder and the pair of the bullock in his front. His field is at *Pakajara Pathar*; about 3 kilometers away from his house; and he will have to reach there before the sun peeps. He walks and goes as fast as he could. But soon he loses his sense of the foot fingers as it was too cold and he had no footwear whatsoever to prevent the *thetuwai* (cold). So, when he arrives at his field, both his hands and feet lost sense of feeling. In the field he could see nothing beyond a little distance as thickly clouded fogs had covered the field. But he started ploughing. It was only after two hours of labour that he feels some sense when the sun gave him some energy. He ploughed till around ten when he saw the *Bharat Saikia Tata Bus* reaching there starting at Haladhibari at 4 in the morning carrying passengers to the Kamalabari Ferry *Ghat*. Boparam now loosened his bullocks and turned to his house. This time he feels hungry, but not senseless.[155] And Dinsa who left for Jengrai at 4 in the morning, has yet to come back with loads of milk so heavy in his drums for a thin bicycle puller to run on an uneven gravel road.

This was the life style of a Sylhetty milk trader and a poor cultivator in the winter of the early sixties in Majuli. This is however, not the situation now when most cultivators go to the field at 7 in the morning after having 'breakfast'. And few others engage either share-croppers or daily workers working for wage. Agricultural works are now slowly becoming contractual in Majuli.

But, if summer is a season of crisis and a seed-time for the future, winter in Majuli is a time of enjoyment and dream. Winter is the season of harvesting and collection of crops to meet the needs of the family, as far as possible, for the whole year. This nature of the people of upper Assam has been noted with care by Shihabuddin Talish when he came to Assam in the year 1662.[156] Inhabitants of the island now reap the winter paddy—*bao* and *sali*, collect mustard crop and varieties of pulses, and produce various classes of pumpkins and vegetables that grow well in the *chapori* lands, and gather volumes of potatoes (*aluguti*) and preserve them for use in the rainy and flood seasons.

In the villages there is abundant supply of milk and *gur* (jaggery), and the *chaporis* provide the buffalo milk and curd. Food supply now becomes sufficient with collection of various kinds of *sali* crop, such as *bora*, *chakowa*, *lahi* etc. It is a season of enjoyment in Majuli; and *Magh Bihu* or *Bhogali Bihu* falls on mid-January in the form of a gift from God.

Dusk falls at the villages early in the evening inviting the jackals to cry, and leopards to smell and proceed towards the *gohali ghar* (cow-shades). Often young boys, coming back late from the field, are challenged on the way by a group of these jackals (*bonda siyal*) compelling the boys to shout and run home closing the eyes. There are reports from the old generation how leopards often pulled out the young calves from inside the thick bamboo fencing pitched all around the cattle house. And the *hudu* bird (a screech owl) makes the atmosphere grave and awful. In the mean time, sound of the *daba* (big drum) comes from the village *namghar* giving warning to the people to worship God—the Almighty with folded hands for a moment, for it is the time for worshipping Him.

FIG. 2.12: EXTENSIVE FIELDS COVRED WITH MUSTARD FLOWER

FIG. 2.13: A SATRA *NAMGHAR*

FIG. 2.14: WOMEN OF GRAMUR SATRA CHANTING NAM (*NAM LOWA*) IN *NAMGHAR*

FIG. 2.15: A VILLAGE *NAMGHAR*

At six the *randhanee (women cook)* go to the kitchen with the *jal* (a bundle of burning fuel wood) and prepares the evening meal, for it is too cold to wait long for the meal. In the family fire place (*juhal/jui sal*) all children and grand children get together requesting the grand old man or the grand old woman to tell the stories from his/her stock and every one will listen attentively. Such stories are often dominated by the stories of *bhuts* or spirits; and young kids being afraid of the spirits get into a closed and compact unit for more security. In the meantime, drops of dew (*niyarar topal*) begins to fall on the leaves of the plantain trees making a regular but touching sound—*top, top, top*. It appears that night is not as young as it may be. And migratory swans begin to fly over the sky singing songs at regular intervals as if to add music to the sound of the dew drops. In the *chapori*, the birds called *haikali* begin to sing their chorus in rhythm—*haikali haikali haikali, ata dhan chaul kot tholi kot tholi kot tholi, Jiye khale powe khale thak thak thak thak thak*. (O haikali, O haikali, where did you keep your so much of paddy? O my friend, my daughter has eaten, my son has eaten, so, do not make any enquiry.) It is the time for husking rice in the family pedal called *dhenki* where all girls and sister-in-laws are busy to husk rice for the next day. It is a peculiar sound uniformly coming from all around giving a unique experience to any outsider. Soon the dinner is ready, and every one except the ladies have their meal with satisfaction and go to the bed to listen again to the chorus of the *haikali* and the cry of the jackal called *pheura* that follow a leopard who is in search of a hunt. This is the picture of a winter night in Majuli a century or a few decades back. Remembering his experience Tarun Chandra Pamegam, a responsible and an imaginative mind of Majuli, has narrated his sweet memoir of the early thirties of the last century as follows:[157]

> The *naharphutuki*, the *dhekiapotiya*, the *latamakori*, the *kukurnechiya* and *ghong* caused terror in the villages immediately after evening. They searched for the domestic animals and killed cows, goats and pigs and pulled them out from their houses to the nearby forests. There were some hunters to kill tigers to save the villagers and the animals of the households. Pitambardeva Goswami of Garamur Satra himself shot forty four large tigers with his own guns. It is stated that a person is sure to meet a tiger if he moves from one village to another, day or night. As a result, a man traveling from one village to another took with him a long and strong bamboo stick for his protection. In the situation men learnt to behave with these animals and developed their own ways of behaving with the wild animals. It is said that if you see a tiger, you stand still, but if you see an elephant, you run as fast as you can.

The musical chorus of the *haikali* birds in winter nights, solitary cry of the *pheura* (fearful jackal) at the approach of the tiger in the mid-night, and the occasional roar of the *banaraja* (tiger) used to make the winter atmosphere so unique that it is something to be felt rather than described. All these are now tale of the past, said Manik Bora, an eminent writer of modern Assamese literature who hails from Majuli. It is to be noted that, Majuli once sheltered among others, rare species of birds like the peacock and *maina*. T. C. Pamegam has stated that he has heard from the older people that men sometimes killed peacocks at the time of their dance (*chali dhara*).[158] He further writes that during the rule of the British, civil officers from Jorhat used to visit the island during the winter seasons to hunt birds and animals in the jungles, ponds and the rivers. They were helped in their hunting by the head-men of the villages (*gaonburhas*) and the *maujadars* who supplied labour and made temporary residence (*bahar*) for them on the bank of the rivers, or, in the midst of the jungles. The white men had a peculiar technique of killing birds; they flew the birds first from the rivers, and then when the birds are the sky flying en-masse, they shot at them and killed them. The dead or the half dead birds then began to fall on the river or in the pond and the trained dogs which accompanied the hunters jumped into the river and brought them to the banks.[159] Villagers too hunted the birds in various ways, such as by using the *chitika*, (a kind of bamboo instrument driven by a silken thread) and the *dalaghanta*.[160] A rare sight of a flock of migratory birds[161] over areas where there are still some river channels or swamps do not speak about its total past and rich ecological heritage; on the other hand, it indicates how a natural heritage site may die out due to human activity.

That winter is a dead past now. There is no jungle as thick and extensive as to allow the *haikali* to make her nest, nor enough scope to allow a leopard to roam in the narrow village path in the evening. Nor is there any young and energetic boy to sing alone a melody on his flute in the dark winter evening expressing his emotion to meet his darling. There are now only open fields and thickly populated houses at the river banks which were once the shelter of the wild animals and migratory birds. Even the few river channels with fast and strong current (*sapar negur chiga sont*) are now dead and dry allowing internal migrants to 'grow more food' and survive.

Thus, history of ecology in Majuli is the history of social change and decay; inversely, history of social change is but the history of change of ecology and environment. It is sweet to remember the past, but soar to visualize it at present.

RELIGION

Almost all people of the island are Vaishnava by religion; and even those out side it are governed by Vaishnava culture indirectly. Satras and the village *namghars* are the agencies through which religion is administered to the villagers. Even the Barhola Muslim village is governed to a certain degree by its Vaishnavite atmosphere. Similarly, even though the Nepalis of the Sriram Nepali village in upper Majuli follow their own Hinduism, they maintain regular contact with the Dakhinpat Satra.[162] Every village or every family in the caste-society belongs to one or the other of the Satras. The only difference is in their sectarian beliefs as Vaishnavism itself has four internal divisions. In Majuli we find Satras belonging to all the divisions called in the Vaishnavite terminology as *Sanghati*.[163] Thus, Auniati Satra, the largest and the oldest of all, belongs to the *Brahma Sanghati* order. Similarly, Garamur and Dakhinpat of the larger class belong to the same division. The two Kamalabari Satras belong to the *Nika or Nistha Sanghati* order, while Bengena Ati and Chamaguri belong to the *Purusha Sanghati* order. Although there is no Satra of the fourth order, i.e. *Kala Sanghati* order, at present there are a few villages of the Mayamara sect that belonging to that order.[164]

Of the other religious sects practised in some part, mention may be made of (a) Anukul Thakur's sect, (b) Krishnaguru's sect, and (c) the Sankar Sangha and *Ek-Saraniya Bhagavati Samaj*. Their strength is, however, insignificant; some of them are followed by only a few individuals or families.

As mentioned elsewhere,[165] there is only one Muslim settlement—although it is not correct enough to call it a village—with a population of less than one hundred. It has no mosque, but its inhabitants offer their prayer at home without using any loud speaker. When asked, Diju Ahmed, a resident of the village, replied that being in the atmosphere of the Satras, it is not proper to build a mosque. At the same time, almost all inhabitants of the village replied that they use to go to the Satras, Kamalabari and Auniati, when festivals and functions are held there. Thus, despite being Muslim and non-believer, they are under the overall stamp of the Vaishnavite atmosphere.

The tribes have their own ethnic religious beliefs and customs. The Misings, for example, worship their primordial gods *Donyee* and *Polo*, together called *Donyee-Polo*. Ancestor worship in their own tribal way with the offering of wine and meat is one of their major religious practices. It is to be noted that despite being a land of the Satras, few Misings are the disciples of any Satra of the island. As stated by

Indreswar Pegu, retired Principal of Jengraimukh College and a noted writer, it was because till recent years the *Satradhikaras* did not pay much attention to Vaishnavise, and thus sanskritise the tribes through religion because of the caste systems in which the tribes, as a whole, are considered *Kirata* and untouchables.[166] But, the religious atmosphere of the island and men's belief in Vaishnavism together with the hold of the Satras on the minds of the people had slow impact on the tribes too. Thus, an interesting aspect of their belief is the diversity of practices in which Vaishnavite culture plays a significant role. They, like the Vaishnavas, chant *namkirtan* (congregation prayer) in their religious functions despite it is being observed as per tribal ways. Like the Vaishnavas, they close the function by offering blessings (*asirvad*) to the host in complete Vaishnav form and style. They perform *bhaona* and *Ras Lila*, and some of their members also participate in the *Ras Lila* function of the Garamur Satra. Thus, in all their behaviour and social relationship the Mishings maintain a double standard; on one side, they act like Vaishnavas, on the other, they maintain their tribal culture and belief. The present author had a unique experience of being present in a *Saraswati Puja* held in a Mising village school at Jakaibowa-Kalia in northeastern Majuli on the Kherkatia belt where the *pathak* officiated the congregation prayer in a manner which carried both the scent of tribal and Vaishnava musical tune. It is this nature of its culture that has bound the society of the island into one culture-whole. Thus, as stated by R. Bhattacharji, the orderliness of the Vaishnava Satras has moulded the mind of Majuli since the 16th century.[167] The Deoris are all Sakta by religion, believer and worshipper of the *Kechaikhati* (eater of the raw flesh), the primordial goddess of this tribal priestly class.[168] It is interesting that despite being in the Majuli Island, the cradle of the Satras and Assam Vaishnavism, no Deori family is initiated to Vaishnavism till date by any *Satradhikara* of the island. This is due to the orthodox character of the Deori priesthood on one hand, and the same character of the Brahmin priesthood on the other.

The Sonowal Kacharis of Majuli are Vaishnavas enmasse. Among the tribes of Assam they are the only ones to have converted to Vaishnavism en block. It is recorded that during the invasion of Mir Jumla, the Governor of Bengal under Aurangzeb, in 1662, Keshavdeva (1658-1726), the then *Satradhikara* of the Auniati Satra, had to leave the Satra and take shelter in the forest of Sadiya, the place of the Sonowal Kacharis. It was during this time that the Sonowal Kacharis of the place looked after the *Satradhikara* and supplied him with food and shelter. It has been further stated that being impressed by his personality, they took initiation from him and became Vaishnavas.[169] In Majuli as we have stated above[170] there are two Sonowal Kachari villages on the extreme southeastern part of the island, and each has its own prayer hall called *namghar*. They have their own organization for doing *namkirtan* and performing other Vaishnav functions. They also regularly visit the Auniati Satra and pay religious taxes to the *adhikara*.[171] However, the Sonowal Kacharis too, like the Misings, maintain their own tribal beliefs, and worship their own tribal gods and goddess. Thus they are still adhearing to their early animistic beliefs. In a typical Kachari village, as Endle has pointed out, "as a rule neither idol nor place of worship is to be found", but they believe in a vast number of invisible spiritual beings commonly called *modai hamdang*.[172] They believe that any calamity that occurs in the families or in the village is by this *modai hamdang*.[173] These spirits fall into two categories—household gods (*na-ni madai*) and village gods (*gami-ni madai*). *Bathau brai* or *Baithau* worshiped in the form of a *Siju* tree (*Euphorbia Splendens*) is the most important traditional household god of the Kacharis in Majuli. According to Endle, "Of these household gods by far the most important is the ...*Bathau*, who is pre-eminently the guardian of the family interests and family honour. He is never represented in idol form, but is well in evidence through his living symbol, the *siju* (*hiju*) tree (*Euphorbia splendens*), which is often to be seen in the Kachari homestead surrounded by a circular fence of split bamboo."[174] Our field investigation in the Sonowal Kachari village in Majuli justified that statement of Endle who made it almost a hundred years before. Among the village gods there are *Mero Raja*, *Bura Mahadeo, Bura Gosain, Jal Kuber, Thal Kuber, Ih Kuber, Bih Kuber, Kuber brai* (male), and Kuber *brui* (female) and so forth.[175]

From the above it appears that tribal population in the Majuli island despite their being in the Vaishnavite atmosphere, are still nurturing their traditional ethnic religious beliefs and customs. While the Misings and the Deoris are keeping their old beliefs in tact, the Kacharis too, despite their proslytization to Vaishnavism by the *Auniatiya Satradhikaras*, are maintaining their traditional beliefs and customs. Interest on traditional culture and attempt to preserve them have gained new momentum among them in recent years as a matter of their movement for preservation of ethnic identity. It is because of this factor that even Christianity which has developed a foothold in the island, is bound to confine itself to a few families of the Misings alone. It is interesting to note that even the Christian Misings celebrate the *Ali-Aiye-Lrigang*, their ethnic religious festival, with all festivities.

Christianity in Majuli

Attempt to spread Christianity in Majuli had been made by the American Baptist Missionaries since the mid 19th century. But they were not successful in their attempts. But, of late, Christianity has made its hold in the Jengraimukh area of the island with its cradle at the Kumarbari Lakhimi Gaon. As early as the late seventies of the last century a few families of Jangraimukh area were converted into Christianity.[176] It was during the interview with Indreswar Pegu, the then Principal of Jengraimukh College, that the latter had suspected that within a decade almost all Misings of the area will accept Christianity as their religion.[177] Although he did not like to explain the reasons for that, it appeared to the author that he indicated the despising outlook of the *Satradhikaras* towards the tribes. It is true that no *Satradhikara* of the island ever tried to Vaishnavise the tribes and sanskritise their culture. Even Pitambardeva Goswami, the reformer *Satradhikara* of Garamur Satra, cannot claim his authority over these people as their *guru*.[178]

According to an estimation made in the year 1996, there were about five hundred Misings in Jengraimukh who embraced Christianity.[179] The number might have increased during the last one decade. By now the *Bible* has been translated to Mising language, and most missionaries have cultivated the Mising language. It is interesting to note that while visiting the village of Kumarbari Lakhimi Gaon in December, 2005, we have discussions with one Deep Kumbang who was aged 40 years and a Matriculate. He had seven members in his family with his wife and children. He was a businessman. He was converted to Christianity in the year 1994 when his father was still a non-convert. When asked why he had become a Christian, Kumbang replied as follows:

(a) Christianity is a religion where sacrifice of animals is prohibited. But in their traditional tribal religious belief much sacrifice of animals and birds is done. Kumbang, however, did not point to Vaishnavism of Sankaradeva where too there is no place for sacrifice and violence. This indicates that Kumbang was not aware of Vaishnavism and the non-violence taught by it. He also embraced Christianity directly from his traditional tribal belief, and he had no relation whatsoever with Vaishnavism till that time.

(b) Mising traditional religious practices are costly due to the necessity of a large number of animals and birds for offering, and money. And this is compulsory. If a poor family cannot perform the post mortuary rites immediately because of poverty, it will have to perform it even after many years, ten years, twenty years and so forth. But in Christianity there is no hard and fast rule for that.

(c) All irrespective of sex and age can take part in prayer in the Christianity which is not allowed in the Mising systems. So, every one—both young and old, are feeling at home in Christianity.

(d) Rich in Christianity always help the poor. In the time of distress they give money to the poor, or collect public fund for that purpose.

(e) The missionaries love and respect us; they have learnt our language, and translated the Bible into our language.

From what have been stated by Kumbang it appears that there were two major reasons for their conversion to Christianity: (a) Mising traditional religious beliefs are not as comprehensive and comfortable as those of Christianity. This fact exposes another important aspect. It is like this: the Misings in the village were in their traditional tribal beliefs at the time of their conversion, and (b) conversion to Christianity was economically beneficial; the poor get help from the rich, or from public fund at the time of distress.

The method applied by the missionaries to spread Christianity among the Misings of Majuli is thus criticism of their indigenous religious beliefs against the qualities of Christianity, and offer of economic help to the poor at the time of their distress. The missionaries also have shown their sympathy and respect towards tribal culture. Since Misings were till recent years neither formally within the Vaishnava religious society governed by the Satras, nor were themselves well organized on the basis of religion, it was comparatively easy for the missionaries to succeed in their attempt. To this may be added the missionary activities of spreading education in the Mising villages by establishing schools and charitable institutions. In Jengraimukh Kumarbari Lakhimi village the missionaries have established the first missionary school—the St. Paul's High School in Majuli. It was established in the year 1987. This is the first English medium school in Majuli, and the only one till a few years ago in the island.[180] Thus the missionaries took advantage of the Brahmanical and caste policy of the *Satradhikaras*, and built their edifice at the vital centre of Vaishnava faith. As a matter of fact, Christianity has posed a challenge to the name of the island as a land of Vaishnavism and Vaishnava cultural heritage.

FIG. 2.16: AUTHOR (LEFT) SPEAKS TO INDRESWAR PEGU (RIGHT), EDUCATIONIST AND SOCIAL SCIENTIST

FIG. 2.17: MUSLIM HEMLET AT KAMALABARI

FIG. 2.18: THRESHING *MA̱TI MA̱H* IN A *CHA̱PORI*

(b. 1890-D. 1971)
(KESHABRAM BORA)
THE FIRST GRADUATE AND THE PIONEER OF MODERN EDUCATION IN MAJULI

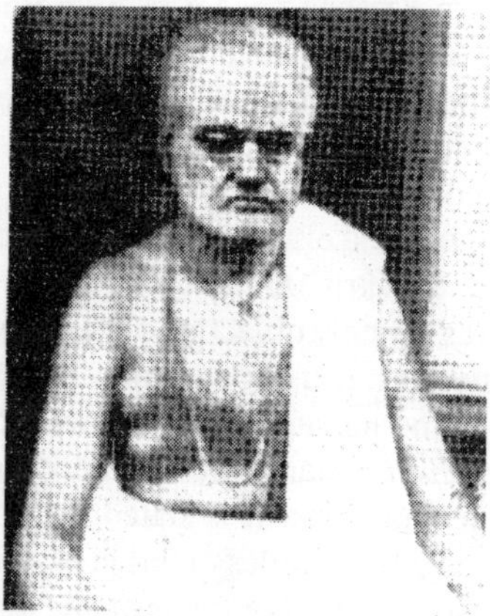

(ADHIKARSHIP 1938-D. 1904)
DATTADEVA GOSWAMI, FIRST ASSAMESE TO PUBLISH AN ASSAMESE PERIODICAL, AND THE FIRST ASSAMESE TO ESTABLISH PRESS IN ASSAM, MAJULI

EDUCATION AND LITERATURE

Despite being cut off from the mainland of Assam, Majuli has a good literacy record—about 74 per cent against the state average of 63.3 per cent. It is interesting that women's literacy rate too in the surveyed villages is a little more than 63 per cent against the state rate of 54.6.[180(a)] This is mainly due to the rapid growth of schools in almost every village and the Government policy of free school education. According to an estimation there are at present 496 Lower Primary Schools in Majuli, 18 Middle Vernacular Schools, 90 Middle English Schools, and 87 High Schools besides 4 higher Secondary and 7 Colleges including 2 junior ones.[181] But, till the colonial period, education in Majuli was purely traditional of the early Indian type imparted at the Satras mainly to the aspirant for either the *adhikarship* or the office of the *Bgagavati*. In the Satras of Majuli it was a custom to appoint tutors to teach the young *adhikara*. The custom was that a Brahman pandit was invited from outside, particularly from lower Assam, who stayed in the Satra for sometime and tutored the young heir to the headship. In the Auniati Satra it was the custom almost since inception. Even in the days of Hem Chandradeva Goswami (1926-1983) one Tirthnath Sarma Vyakaran Tirtha was brought from Kamrup as his tutor.[182] After Tirthanath Sarma was brought one

Pran Krishnadev Misra from Barpeta to tutor him.[183] The same person was appointed to tutor his successor Bishnu Chandradeva Goswami also.[184] The same custom was followed in the other Satras. For example, Pitambardeva Goswami of Garamur Satra has stated that he too was put under such a teacher who took care of his education; and as we have mentioned elsewhere, he was made to study the most difficult grammar—the Sanskrit *Mugdhabodh Vyakaran* at the age of five.[185] Sanskrit learning was the only objective of those tutorial systems. Besides, knowledge was given on texts of ancient scriptures, *Puran* and the epics.

The inmates of the Satras and the village boys were admitted to the *pathsalas* maintained by individual pandits normally hailing from among the Brahmins. It is stated that there were at least one such *pathsala* at every 10-12 miles radius in Majuli, Dergaon and Sivasagar.[186] These were also called *tol* or *chatuspathi* where boys from upper caste Hindus were only allowed to get education. In Majuli *tols* were perhaps maintained in all the large Satras; but specific evidence to that effect is lacking as far as early period is concerned. It is recorded that the Dakhinpat Satra had a *tol* named after its *Satradhikara* Naradeva Goswami called *Sri Sri Naradeva Sanskrit Tol*. It was established in the year 1826.[187] Similarly, the *Auniati Kamaldev Chatuspathi* was established two years after that in 1828.[188] Following them the Purnananda Chatuspathy was established at Bengenaati Satra in 1895.[189] In the Garamur Satra, the *tol* called *Gopaldev Asram* was started almost a hundred years after in the year 1918. Gradually, a few other *pathsalas* or *tols* were established during that century which included those in the Kamalabari Satra, Elcngi Satra, Bhogpur Satra, Natun Kamalabari Satra, and so forth.[190]

Satras also have the tradition of training the inmates in a number of branches of practical sciences such as making of writing paper from the bark of trees called *sancipat* (*agollaca*), calligraphy and painting, mask and boat making. Thus, every Satra has volumes of manuscripts written or copied, and illustrated by the inmates.[191] Similarly, mask making formed a special craft in some of the Satras of Majuli, while boat making, perhaps, was known to all. Training in those crafts are given by the senior inmates of the Satra.

The *pathsalas* were private schools maintained on charity and contributions given by the pupils. Most *tols* were residential, and pupils from distant villages used to stay within the campus with the teacher called *gurudev* or *mahashay* by the pupils and as *pandit* by others. The village *pathsalas* had no specific syllabus, nor even established permanent building. Often they were run in the *namghars*, private houses or even under some big trees. Neither there was formal administration. Its administration and continuance depended on the convenience of the teacher. Declaration of vacation, change or introduction of new syllabus was done by his own will. Usually, the syllabus taught included morals, stories, and reading and writing of the *sastras*.[192]

In the villages technical and professional education came down to the offspring from generation to generation. And professional education, such as rearing of silk worm and spinning thread, making pottery, mat, working on ivory, black-smithy and other such crafts were learnt at home, and were both secret and exclusive.

There was no formal education system that served the common people before the colonial period. The entire system was developed by and meant for the higher echelon of the society consisting of the *Satradhikaras*, the inmates and a few members of the caste Hindus. The only education they got was through the *namghars* and through the systems of the *charit-path* (reading and recitation of the biographical works of the medieval saints of Assam), congregation prayer and *bhaona*. Thus, education of the common people was bound to be informal.

The formal education in Majuli began by the colonial Government who used the tradition and infrastructure of the *pathsalas* to start the primary schools. It should be noted that the American Baptist Christian missionaries visited the island as early as the first half of the 19th century for purposes of proselytization; but they failed to do anything of the kind of conversion or establishment of school in the island due to the influence of the Satras as they could do elsewhere.[193] But, the rest of the years of that century witnessed emergence of a few other L. P. Schools there. As per available record, the first L. P.School in Majuli started by the British was the Karhal Gaon L. P. School which was established in the year 1878.[194] The Kamargaon L.P. School was established in the year 1885. It is said that this school received students from distant villages, as far as from Kamalabari, about ten miles away from the school. Thereafter, the Kamalabari (Opar Katani Gaon) L.P.School was established in 1888. Thus, number of L.P.Schools increased to 44 by the forties of the last century. Bhuban Chandra Thakur, one of the pioneering educationist of Majuli, a student leader of his time, and a social worker, has noted that the names of Betharam Bora, Karka Chandra Doley, Charu Chandra Doley (first Graduate among the Misings of Assam), Devi Gam, Thagiram Bhuyan, Chandradhar Bharali, Dasiram Pegu, Khageswar Hazarika, Maguram Neog, Rajani Bora, Sonaram Saikia, Keshabram Bora (founder Head Master Majuli Auniati Hemchandra High School), Roseswar Hazarika, Sasidhar Barua, Bipin Barkataki, Bholanath Sarma, Rajani Barua and a few others who were to be associated with the growth of early education in the island.[195] It is significant to note that Betharam Bora had devoted his life and labour for the growth of early education in the island in more than one way. He not only was the inspiration behind foundation of so many schools, he himself was a teacher and a colleague of Keshabram Bora in the field of development of modern education in Majuli, and was the Head Pandit of the Bangaon M. V. School (est.1914), the first of its kind in the island. It was after this school had been established that a few other M. V. Schools came up like Auniati M.V. School (1919), the Ahataguri M. V. School (1928), Dakhinpat M. V. School (1940), Ratanpur M. V. School (1942), Sonariati M.V. School (1946), and others in the post-Independence period.[196] One interesting aspect of the system was that education was primarily confined to the members of high caste Hindus and a few emerging members of the Mising community only. The names of the persons associated with the foundation of the schools point to this fact.

Introduction of English education was quite late in the island. The first generation of Middle English Schools came up in Majuli only during the nationalist upsurge in Assam in the early twenties of the last century. Thus, the first ever High School in the island-the Majuli Auniati Hemchandra High School (it was then an M. E. School) was established in 1924 with Keshabram Bora, the first ever graduate from Majuli, (passed B. Sc. from Cotton College in 1920) taking over the charge of its Head Mastership. Thus, a pioneer in introducing modern education in Majuli, his establishment of the Majuli Auniati Hemchandra High School is a turning point in the history of growth of modern education in the island. It was due to his endeavour that people of Majuli experienced a new age of education and knowledge who were so long under the cover of an old world air distinguished by religious orthodoxy and superstitions. Keshabram Bora had opened Majuli to the outside world. For, the Majuli Auniati Hemchandra High School was soon followed by Meragarh Narayandev High School established in the year 1946, the Karatipar High School in 1948, and the Jengrai High School in the same year and so forth. The rest of the high Schools were established in the post-Independence period. Thus the picture of the school education in Majuli has been drastically changed in the late colonial and post-colonial period.

Thus, colonial administration closed the chapter of medieval education in the island as it did in other places. Students from all castes could attend school. But one problem still remained—the problem of caste prejudice in the schools. Even some of the well-known *Satradhikaras* refused to loosen it in the name of tradition and custom based on ancient scriptures.[197] Tarun Chandra Pamegam, who became the Vice President of the *Asam Sahitya Sabha*, has spoken of his experience of caste prejudice when he was the Head Master of Garamur M.E. School.[198] But, the post-Independence time opened a new vista in the growth of education and literacy in Majuli along with the growth of education among the so-called low caste people. Thus, in Rangachai, which is predominantly populated by the people of the Nath caste, we find growth of Rangachahi Tanuram Nath High School in the year 1957 with the financial support from the family of Tanuram Nath, a well-to-do person of that community at that time. Its founder Head Master was Bagaram Nath, who was an M.A. in Assamese, and a brilliant student of his time and one of the pioneering luminaries of modern education in Majuli. Bagaram Nath sacrificed his brilliant career for the good of the backward communities of Majuli. It was mainly for his sacrifice that Rangachahi area is now known for higher rate of literacy and education, and economic and social development. The present author was briefed how his paternal uncle faced such prejudice in the Bangaon M. V. School when he was a student there in 1923-1924. The caste prejudice in the school education was noticed till recent decades. Thus, despised and ignored, people of the so called low castes were not encouraged to send their sons (not to speak of their daughters) to the school far away from home. Naturally, education was bound to be confined mainly to the limited section of the society. This was how, education had an imbalanced expansion among the people of the island. It is due to this historical development that literacy rate in Majuli always remained high among the high castes. Under the conditions, higher was the rate of employment also among them. Inversely, lower was the caste lower was this rate. One has to understand this fact to understand the educational and economic development of Majuli in the 20th century.

Growth of school education contributed to the growth of collegiate education in the island. It is to be noted that the same persons who were at the root of the school education were the pioneering force behind growth of college education also. Thus, with Keshabram Bora as the President of the Governing Body, the Majuli College was established in 1962. Similarly with Indreswar Pegu as the Secretary and the Principal, was founded the Jengraimukh Colege about a decade later in the year 1972. Gradually the Rangachahi College was established in 1983 with Bagaram Nath as its President. In course of the last few decades a few other Higher Secondary Schools, Junior Colleges, and even Degree Colleges, a few music colleges in some of the Satras, and a vocational school sprang up. The rapid and random growth of educational institutions shows that while in earlier times it was a policy to create them for meeting the need of the people, now it has become a necessity to manage the over unemployment problem there.

Growth of literacy and education led to the growth of literary activity in the island. It is known to all that the first Assamese news paper published and edited by an Assamese person, was published from Auniati Satra in Majuli in the year 1871-72. It was *Asam Bilasinee* published by Dattadeva

Goswami (1838-1904), the then *Satradhikara* of Auniati Satra.[199] In the post—*Asam Bilasinee* period too he published a journal called *Asam Tara* (1889-1890). It was edited by Sridhar Barua.[200] In the Satras it was a tradition to compose biographical works (*charit puthis*/*Vamsavalis*) and write drama (*nataka*). This tradition is still continuing at least in the Auniati Satra where every *Satradhikara* on the occasion of his accession to the religious throne is to write and perform some drama[201] Thus, we find volumes of drama composed and performed in the Satra which became popular to the village audience. It was from the Satras that *bhaonas* consequently entered the village *namghars*. At one time learning to read and memorise the dialogues (*bachan*) of the role player (*bhawariya*) was compulsory for all young boys in a village. And this is possibly the cause of a comparatively higher literacy rate among the men there.

Majuli has commendable contribution towards art, culture and literature of modern Assam. Pitambardeva Goswami of Garamur Satra was a well-known writer on religious matters, and an intellectual of his time. He published the journal *Sanatan Dharmar Mukhapatra*, the *Dharmar Bani*, and the *Dharma Sikshya Samaj Rakshya*. Besides, a large number of articles, essays and speeches were written by him which are not only good literature, but also good history. He also translated a few scriptures from Sanskrit to Assamese which were lost before publication during his absence from the Satra. Literary persons and social science researcher like Tarun Chandra Pamegam and Indreswar Pegu are hailing from Majuli. Along with them we find Sridhar Barua, who not only wrote the *Dattadeva Charit*, but also edited the *Asam Tara*, and the later edition of the *Assam Bilasinee*. In the field of social sciences their names are known today. Much contributions in poetry, short stories, research writings, drama, dance and music, painting, mask making and other branches of art and craft are also to be attributed to Majuli. Narayan Chandra Goswami, *Satradhikara* of Natun Kamalabari Satra, and a renowned scholar in Vaishnava literature and culture, was a recipient of the *Sankaradeva Award* for literary excellence. Similarly, Dr. Pitambardeva Goswami of Auniati Satra earned his name in cultural history research and religious literature. In the field of modern Assamese literature the name of Manik Bora, a short story writer, stands among the known writers of Assam. Similarly, Gunamani Nath obtained the literary award from the *Asam Sahitya Sabha* as a novelist and a social science writer. Thus come the names of Beni Madhab Das and Bagaram Nath, both of whom are known for their contributions in journalism and literature respectively. In the field of research in science and humanities too Majuli has its own contribution in the personalities of late Kumud Bora, Babul

Bora, a scientist now working in the USA, Dilip Phukan, a native scholar and Kumud Bora, an economist.

From the above it has become clear that although the society in Majuli is not different from the society of other parts of Assam, it has its own distinction. It remained stagnant mostly due to its geographical isolation and orthodox religious air almost till the late colonial period. It was only towards the close of the colonial rule, particularly since the nationalist period, that it felt a force of change in almost all its aspects, that consequently opened the island to the outside world in the 20th century. Changing political and economic systems and topographic conditions together with growth of education and literacy, have slowly transformed the society in Majuli towards a modern setting. But still, society in Majuli is to be viewed in terms of caste; even the economic classes here is to be understood in the light of the caste system. For, caste and class are very closely related here. Caste rules were always and everywhere maintained; and the Satras act as their preserver. It is significant that a few professional castes such as Katani, Tanti, Patiya, Kumar, Kamar etc. are slowly moving towards or included into the Kalita zone[201(a)] as a result of the decline or death of their traditional professions. Similarly, the Misings among the tribes are attaining a higher scale of mobility towards obtaining a caste status. On other side, men's idea of health and sanitation has developed leaving aside the old ones. This is particularly to be noted among the educated section. All these changes and transition are to be attributed to the late 19th and throughout the 20th century, not to speak of the 18th century as elsewhere in the country.[202]

END NOTES

1. See W.W. Hunter, *A Statistical Account of Assam,* Vol. I, Reprint, Delhi, 1991, pp. 31,117, 237 etc.; Gunabhiram Baruah, *Asam Buranji*, Reprint, Guwahati, 1972, p. 177, B. Kakati, Kalita Jatir itivritta, Guwahati, 1943, for details.
2. Ibid, pp. 17, 114, 237.
3. Interview with a few families of Salmara Kumar Gaon, such as those of Nandeswar Hazarika, Sarupai Hazarika, Gangaram Saikia, Sisuram Kalita and others, led to this conclusion. Also see Gunabhiram Baruah, *op cit.*, p. 178.
4. Prabina Bora, '*Mor Kakadeota Swargiya Keshabram Bora*', in *Majuli Auniati Hem Chandra High School Diamond Jubilee Volume*, Kamalabari, 1998, pp. 12ff.
5. An idea about the caste mobility in rural Assam may be gathered from Audrey Cantlie's *The Assamese,* op. cit.; and B. Lahiri and D. Dev's *Cosmogony of Caste and Social Mobility in Assam,* Delhi, 1984.
6. D. Nath, *History of the Koch Kingdom c. 1515-1615 A.D., Delhi, 1989, pp. 7ff.*

7. See ABSM, pp. 33; DAB, p. 47.
8. See D. Nath, *History of the Koch Kingdom 1515-1615 A.D.*, *op cit.*, p. 58.
9. See *Darrang Raj Vamsavali* (ed.) N.C. Sarma, Guwahati, 1973, vv. 325-328. (Henceforth abbreviated as DRV); D. Nath, *op cit.*, p. 55.
10. The symptom of rifts soon subsided due to the fact that a member of the Koch caste was then elected as MLA from Majuli under the reserved category to which the island is put. With his election the Koch came to occupy an extended political power and domination in the society. This fact minimised, and even negated the social tension.
11. D. Phukan, '*Majulir Jana-Gathani aru Samajik Paribes*', a paper presented in a state-level seminar organized jointly by the Archaeological Survey of India and the Ministry of Culture, Department of Culture, Government of Assam, on 15-16 June, 2005, at the Srimanta Sankaradeva Kala Kshetra Society, Guwahati. (Ms.). This number, however, is not based on actual survey; also see Gunabhiram Baruah, *Asam Buranji*, *op cit.*, p. 179.
12. K. Suresh Singh, (ed.) *People of India, Assam*, Vol. XV, Part-II, Calcutta, 2003, pp. 628ff.
13. Mm. H. P. Shastry, *Haraprasad Shastry Rachana Samgraga*, Vol.II, Calcutta, 1981, pp. 855f.
14. B. Bhattacharyya, '*Tantrika Culture among the Buddhists*', in the *Cultural Heritage of India*, Vol. II, p. 218; SHTN, p. 89.
15. It is generally contended that Nathism spread only among the subaltern class (See N. N. Bhattacharyya, *History of the Tantric Religion*, Delhi, 1999, pp. 23f). But, there are evidences to the effect that even the kings and the queens were its followers. The popularity of the song of the king Gopi Chandra and queen Maynamati (See *Gupichander Gan* by Kavi Sukur Muhammad, (ed.) Abul Kalam Muhammad Jhakaria, Dhaka, 1974 for details) in Assam, and the discovery of the *Ambari Inscription* (see fn.17 below) recording the patronage of king Samudra Pala amply speaks about this. Francis Hamilton in the *Kamarupar Buranji* (ed. S. K. Bhuyan, 2nd edition, Guwahati, 1958, Appendix-C) has also recorded about this fact. For the patronage of the Pala kings of Bengal, see R. C. Majumdar, History of Bengal, Vol. I, Patna, 1973, pp. 418ff.
16. Mm. H.P. Shastry, *Hazar Bacharer Purana Bangala Bhashay Bauddha Gan O Doha*, Calcutta, 1323 B.S. for details. Also see R. C. Majumdar, *History of Bengal*, *op cit.*, pp. 383ff; M. Neog, *Maheswar Neog Rachanawali*, Vol. I, Dibrugarh, 1986, pp. 475ff. Bap Chandra Mahanta has shown that the *bargeets* of Sankaradeva and Madhavadeva were modeled in many aspects on those *charyya* songs of the *Siddhacharyya*. See Bap Chandra Mahanta, *Mahapurushiya Paramparat Satra aru Sangit*, Jorhat, 2003, pp. 249ff.

16(a). See ADB, pp. 475ff; Maniram Dewan, *Buranji Vivek ratna* (Ms.).

17. SHTN, p. 89; ADB, pp. 81, 475; Assamese chronicles mention them as an artisan caste of medieval Assam and called them Katani or Jugi, or combining them together as *Jugi-Katani*. See ABSM, 37; Wade, *An*

account of Assam, op cit., p. 200; ADB, p. 81; DAB, p. 47; *Ahom Buranji*, p. 87. This indicates that the Yogis formed a caste from being a religious community as early as the middle ages; and some of them in Upper Assam (i.e. Ahom kingdom) were brought under the *paik* system and appointed to work on the rearing the *pat* silk worm and spin yarn from its cocoon. Epigraphic records of this period too refer to them as *Jugi* or *Katani*. For example, we may refer to the Land and Servitors -Grant Inscription of *Dakhinpatiya Gosain* of Majuli of the *Saka* year 1707 (1785 A.D.). See M. Neog (comp. & ed.), *Prasya Sasanawali, op cit.*, Ins. No. 86.

18. The *Ambari Rock Inscription* of the year 1154 *Saka* (1232 A.D.) has referred to a *sabasika satra* at Yogi Hati (Guwahati) where the Yogi residing there (*Hati*) conducted the religious affairs of the king Samudra Pala. (See *Prasya Sasanawali, op cit.*, pp. Intro. 9f) It is not unlikely that Sankaradeva took the idea of a *Satra* as a centre of religious activities and proselytisation from the relics of such early Bauddha-Tantrika-Saiva monastic systems. P. C. Chaudhury has opined that even the name Guwahati might have been derived from the word *Yogi Hati*. See 'Significance of the Stone Inscriptions at the Assam State Museum', in *Journal of Indian History*, Vol.XLVIII, Part I, April, 1970 for details). Also see D. Nath, 'Few Significant Derivations from the Ambari Stone Inscription', in the *Proceedings of the North East India History Association*, XX Session, Dibrugarh, 1999, pp. 99ff.
19. GCK, p. 38.
20. Ibid.
21. Ibid.
22. Ibid. M. Neog has rightly opined that "Nathism today is scarcely traceable in Assam, but some influences of Natha legends are still to be felt in Assamese folk songs," (See SHTN, p. 89) although he did not mentioned presence of Natha elements in ths systems of Sankaradeva.
23. K. Suresh Singh, (ed.) *People of India, op cit.*, p. 628.
24. Sureshchandra Nath Majumdar, *Rajguru Yogi Vamsa*, revised and enlarged edition, Calcutta, 1991, p. 388.
25. Reported by Bagaram Nath, a well-known educationist of the community in Majuli. Sri Nath is now 75 years of age (2007).
26. As a result of the schism developed among them, Pitambaradeva Goswami of Garamur Satra had to participate for an amicable solution and give his written comment supporting their claim for assumption of the sacred thread and to be uplifted to a higher social status. See *Letter to Dehiram Nath*, dated 13 *Kartik*, 1883 *Sak*. See Appendix XVI.
27. GCK, p. 38.
28. Ratanpur was known as an ancient village/town. Ensign Wood has mentioned this village as the only one with some notable habitation of people at the close of the 18th century. See H.H.Wilson, *Documents Illustrative of the Burmese Wars* (containing Wood's Map and Survey Report). Cf. Appendix-p.iii (From *Government Gazette*, May 9, 1825).
29. These include tanks, embankments, and shrines. The Basudev Than *alias*

Narowa Satra is contiguous to the place. See M. Neog, *Pabitra Asam*, Guwahati, 1969, p. 14.
30. S. Endle, *The Kacharis*, Reprint, Delhi, 1975, pp. 1ff.
31. W. B. Brown, *An Outline Grammar of the Deori-Chutiya Language Spoken in Upper Assam*, Shillong, 1895, p.Intro.i; HAG, pp. 42f; Neog, *Pabitra Asam, op cit.*, pp. 23f.
32. S. L. Baruah, *A Comprehensive History of Assam*, Delhi, (1985). p. 182.
33. (ed.) S. L. Baruah and D. Nath, *Chutiya Jatir Buranji*, Guwahati, 2007.
34. Ibid, pp. 397ff.
35. H. H. Risley, *The Tribes and Castes of Bengal* (1891). Vol .I, Reprint, Delhi, 1998,376 Also see Gunabhiram Baruah, *Asam Buranji, op cit.*, p. 177.
36. Risley has stated, "Concerning the etymology of the name *Kaibartta* there has been considerable difference of opinion. Some derive it from *ka*, water, and *vartta*, livelihood; but Lessen says that the use of *ka* in this sense is extremely unusual in early Sanskrit, and that thetrue derivation is *Kaivarta*, a corruption of *Kimvarta*, meaning a person following a low or degrading occupation." See, Ibid, p. 376; also see for their movements *Leaflet of the Kaivarta Jatiya Hitakari Sabha*, cf. editorial, *Banhi*, 1838 *Sak*, 7th year 12th issue; Dev and Lahiri, *op cit.*, pp. 28ff. Hem Chandra Barua, *Hemkosh*, 6th edn., 1985, p. 236; R.C.Majumdar, *History of Bengal*, Vol.I, Patna, 1971, p. 591.
37. MDPH, pp. 99ff; Debabrat Sarma, *Non-State Literary and Cultural Organization in the Construction of Assamese National Identiry and Ethos (1873-1960),* a Ph.D. thesis in Social Sciences of Gauhati University, 2000 (Ms.).
38. Ibid; MDPH, p. 99.
39. MDPH, p. 99.
40. Jagatananda had his Satra at Ba-bhaga, Hridayananda at Sarjan, and Bhabananda at Gunakata and so forth. See *Sri Sri Aniruddhadevar Charitra aru Mayamara Gosain sakalar Vamsavali* sby Hridayananda chandra Goswami, Chabua, 1931, vv. 263, 267, 270.
41. See S. Dutta, *The Mataks and Their Kingdom*, Allahabad, 1985, p. 5; D. Nath, in *Dainik Janambhumi*, 'Matak Sakalar Janagosthiya Pariciti', 11-12 February issue, 2007.
42. See Chapter-III, *infra*, pp. 142ff.
42(a). Gunabhiram Baruah, *Asam Buranji, op cit.*, p. 180.
43. Risley, *The Tribes and Castes of Bengal, op cit.*, p. 376; Gunabhiram Baruah, *op cit.*, p. 177.
44. Ibid; R. C. Majumdar, *op cit.*, p. 591; H.K.Barpujari (ed.), *The Comprehensive History of Assam*, Vol.III, *op cit.*, p. 173.
45. Ibid; Cantlie, *op cit.*, p. 8.
46. See Chapter-IV, *infra*, pp. 204f.
47. ADB, p. 508.
48. *Sarsari Asam Buranji*, p. 11; HAG, p. 82; *Asam Buranji* by Harakanta Barua Sadaramin, *op cit.*, pp. 17f.

49. Ibid.
50. *Mahapurush Sri Sankardeva aru Sri Madhavadeve Charit* by Daityari by Daityari Thakur, (ed) H. N. Datta Barua, 2nd edn., Guwahati, 1989, vv.428-438, 311-312.
51. ABSM, p. 32.
52. Ibid. It is stated that later on king Pratap Singha (1603-1641) appointed one Lekai Chetia to make a census of those neo-Brahmans, and bring them back to their original caste or professional status. Lekai, however, took bribe, and whomever he liked, he left untouched. Thus the phrase *lagunar guri Lekai Chetia* i.e. 'Lekai knows the secret of the sacred thread', came into practice. See *Asam Buranji* by Harakanta Barua Sadaramin, cit, p. 32; also ADB, p. 509.
53. See the Chapter IV.
54. Dr. P. D. Goswami, *Satriya Utsavar Parichay aru Tatparyya*, Dibrugarh, 2001, pp. 51f; H.N. Sarma, *Contribution of the Auniati Satra to the Society and Culture of Assam*, Dibrugarh University Ph. D. Thesis in History, 2003, (Ms.).
55. It is interesting to note that while selecting the villages for our investigation out of more than two hundred cadastral villages, no village exclusively dwelt by the Brahmins could be found.
56. It is recorded that king Jayadhvaj Singha died listening to the *sastras* from Vanamalideva, the *Dakhinpatiya Gosain*, whom, according to the record, he gave the charge of his state before he died. *See Banamalideva Charit,* cf.B. Sharma, *Dakhinpat Satra, op cit.*, pp. 42f. It is further to be noted that the *Gosain* of Dakhinpat *Satra* participated in the process of making and unmaking the kings at the court in Gargaon//Rangpur. See, ABSM, p. 86; B. Sarma, *Dakhinpat Satra, op cit.*, p. 42. The role of Pitambardeva Goswami of Garamur Satra has been narrated in the chapter-VI. See *infra*, pp. 291ff.
57. Information obtained from the *diary of Dr. Pitambardeva Goswami, Satradhikara* of Auniati Satra. (Ms.); also interview with a few other *Satradhikaras*.
58. GCK, p. 52; *Hemkosh, op cit.*, pp. 683, 973.
59. Dev and Lahiri, *op cit.*, p. 159.
60. MDPH, pp. 99; Dr. Devabrat Sarma, *Asamiya Jati Gathan Prakriya aru Jatiya Janagosthiya Anusthan Samuh*, Jorhat, 2006, p. 65.
61. ADB, pp. 20f.
62. It is possible that like any other conquered place Sukapha kept a contingent of his *men* in the Majuli island too as a matter of his policy for consolidation of his hold. The two villages might be a remnant of that Ahom colony. See for Sukapha's state formation policy J.N. Phukan, 'The Tai Ahom Power in Assam', in H. K. Barpujari (ed) *The Comprehensive History of Assam*, Guwahati, 1992, Vol. II, pp. 52f; also D. Nath, 'The State—Its Concept to Sukapha—the Founder of the Ahom State in the Brahmaputra Valley', *The Indian Journal of Tai Studies*, Vol. I, 2001, pp. 34ff.
63. *Chaklang* is a Tai-Ahom word standing for the name of the Ahom marriage

systems. In this system the officiating priest called *Deodhai/Bailung/Mohan* lights 101 earthen lamps, and recites *mantra* in Tai language, and then tells the history—*buranji*—of their families before the bride and the groom, the latter holding a long sword in his hand called *hengdang*. The *mantra* and the telling of history of the two families—how they have in the past contributed towards the growth of their state, is indeed significant. The groom promises with the sword at his hand to protect his weded wife and his state. See B.J.Terwiel, *The Tai of Assam and Ancient Tai Ritual*, Vol. I, Gaya, 1980, p. 98; P. Gogoi, *Tai-Ahom religion and Customs*, Guwahati, 1976, p. 7.

64. *Me-dam-Me-phi* is a Tai Ahom word which means worship of the main god of the household and that of the ancestors. It has been the custom of the Ahom kings to perform *Me-dam-Me-Phi* after or before achieving any victory. Of late it has become the symbol of the Ahom unity and a source of strength of their ethnic movement.
65. Cf. HAG, p. 143.
66. Cf. *Asiatic Researches*, Vol. II, *op cit.* p. 131.
67. *Op cit.*, p. 142.
68. p. 356.
69. Ibid
70. Ibid
71. Ibid
72. Ibid
73. Ibid, p. 358.
74. Hunter, *op cit.*, p. 236
75. W. Robinson, *Op cit.*, p. 142/356.
76. Hunter, *op cit.*, p. 239
77. Ibid
78. D. Nath, '*Mising Society in Transition*', in the *Proceedings of the Annual Conference of the North East India History Association*, Vol. IX, 1988, pp. 257f; Indeswar Pegu, 'Parivartanar Ali-Domojat Mising Samaj', in the *Dainik Batari*, 30 March, 2005, p. 4.
79. Ibid.
80. W. Robinson *op cit.*, p. 142/356f.
81. Ibid, p. 357.

81(a) T. C. Pamegam, *Tarun Chandra Pamegam Rachanawali*, Vol. II, *op cit.*, pp. 65f; Nahendra Padun, 'Mising Janajatir Parichay', in Kagyung, *op cit.*, p. 50f.

82. T. C. Pamegam, *Tarun Chandra Pamegam Rachanawali*, Vo II, *op cit.*, pp. 65f.

82(a) See Endle, *op cit.*, for details.

83. HAG, pp. 247ff.
84. Cf. Hunter, *op cit.*, p. 236.
85. W. B. Brown, *An Outline Grammar of the Deori-Chutiya Language Spoken in Upper Assam, op cit.*, p. intro.i.
86. They celebrate it in the most minimum extent; and perform only the rituals.

87. S. N. Das, 'Smritir ManiKothat Kamalabari', in *Majuli Auniati Hem Chandra High School Diamond Jubilee Volume, Kamalabari*, 1998, p. 47.
88. Ibid.
89. D. Nath, 'Satra and Social Change in Majuli', *loc cit.*, pp. 148f.
90. Tradition prevalent in the society of Majuli. Also see *Fathiya-I-Ibriya,* cf. HAG, p. 150.
91. See *Gurucharit Katha*, (ed.) M. Neog, Guwahati, 1986, pp. 62f. (henceforth GCK).
91(a) Ibid, pp. 64f.
92. Ibid, p. 64.
93. Chapter-III.
94. This village is mentioned by Sanjoy Ghose in his diary. See Sumita Ghose, *op cit.*, p. 109.
95. This aspect has been discussed in the chapter III.
96. Robinson, *op cit.*, p. 271, H. K.B arpujari,(ed) *The Comprehensive History of Assam*, Vol.III, Guwahati, 1994, p. 200; also see *Fathiya-I-Ibriya*, cf. HAG, p. 145
97. Cf. *op. cit.*, pp. 192f..
98. *hanh para chagal yi pohe sio pagal* (tr. Those who use to rear duck, pigeon and goat, are simply mad). *Assamese Vaishnava proverb*.
99. *kam charai ranga thot, tate dile sendur phot, deota ai, durakoi nidibi mok* (tr. The Kam charai has red beak, over it is its vermilion stik, o' my father, please do not send me to a distant groom), *Assamese marriage folk songs*
100. For Dak *see* M. Neog, *Maheswar Neog Rachanawali*, *op cit.*, pp. 499f; Barpujari (ed), *op cit.*, Vol. III, pp. 192f.
101. Report supplied by Gunamani Nath, Vice-Principal, Garamur Pitambardeva Goswami College, Garamur, Majuli.
102. Hunter, *op cit.*, pp. 252f.
103. See Chapter-III, *infra*; also see Sumita Ghose, *op cit.*, p. 100
103(a) Jahnabi Gogoi Nath, *op cit.*, p. 172; ADB, p. 472.
103(b) K. C. Bora. *loc cit.*, (Ms).
104. See T. C. Pamegam, "Mising Samajar Sanskritik Jibandhara," in Bhrigumumi Kagyung, *Mising Sanskritir Alekhya*, Revised edition, Guwahati, 1989, p. 78.
105. Pitambardeva Goswami (of Garamur Satra), *Iswar Upasana aru Guru Sewa*, (undated), pp. 13ff; also information collected from the field investigation. Also see Padmadhar Chaliha, 'Asamiya Ganwalia Jivan' in *Banhi,* (Comp.) J. N. Goswami, Jorhat, 2001, p. 384.
106. Ibid.
107. Dr. P. D. Goswami, *op cit.*, pp. 112ff.
108. GCK, p. 65.
109. *See* Dr. P. D. Goswami, *op cit.*, pp. 67f.
110. *See* ADB, p. 493.
111. *See* p. 29 in E. Dalton's, *Tribal History of Eastern India* (1872), Reprint, New Delhi, 1978.

112. *Tarun Chandra Pamegam Rachanawali*, Vol. II, *op cit.*, p. 122.
113. Ibid
114. Ibid, p. 123
115. Ibid.
116. Interview with Phanidhar Tahu, Principal, UMK College, Majuli, on 15th March, 2007; also D. Nath, 'Mising Society in Transition', *loc cit.*
117. For details see Neera Desai and Usha Thakkar, *Women in Indian Society*, Reprint, New Delhi, 2005; and Geraldene Forbes, *Women in Modern India*, OUP, 3rd Reprint, pp. 32ff.
118. Incomplete autobiography of late Keshabram Bora, the founder Head master of Majuli Auniati Hem Chandra High School, and the first Graduate from Majuli.
119. Information supplied by Punaram Nath, son of late Dehiram Nath, and the Head Master of the Jakaibowa Kalia M. E. School, Majuli.
120. Barring a very few, such as Kanaklata Ai and Bhubaneswari, there was no woman to head a Satra. Women are also not encouraged to participate in the religious affairs of a Satra. There is also no system of nunnery in Assam Vaishnavism. *See* S. N. Barman, *Sankaradeva—Kriti aru Krititta*, Guwahati, 1986, pp. 100ff.
121. Bronson Family papers, Box No. 1, Reel I, cf. H. K. Barpujari, *The American Missionaries and North East India*, Guwahati, 1985, p. 176
122. Cf. H. K. Barpujari, (ed), *The Comprehensive History of Assam*, Vol. III, Guwahati, 1994, pp. 194ff; *Sadaraminar Atmajivani*, (ed), K. C. Bardoloi, Guwahati, 1991, pp. 54, 170; Krishna Sarma, *Krishna Sarmar Diary*, Guwahati, 1972, pp. 16, 23.
123. *See* M. Neog, *Sankaradeva*, NBT, New Delhi, 1967, reprint, 1980, p. 40; S. N. Barman, *op cit.*, pp. 100ff.
124. *Op cit.*, pp. 176f. The statement that the husband buys his wife is not correct in the sense the missionary has understood. In fact, there was a custom in the village society of Assam in which the side of the groom was to give some money and other materials to the side of the bride towards making some compensation on account of taking the girl away who was treated as valuable member of the family. It is called *ga-dhan lowa*. The custom is still prevalent among the Assamese people in some modified forms. These forms are known as *telar bhar diya*, *joran diya* etc. This does not mean that the girl was sold to the boy. See, Barpujari (ed), *op cit.*, *The Comprehensive History of Assam*, Vol. III, pp. 184f.
125. Information supplied by Prof. A. C. Goswami, Retired Principal, Majuli College, Kamalabari, and by Mrs. Minati Saikia, Assistant Head Mistress, Garamur Pitambardeva High School, Majuli.
126. *See* chapter III, *infra*.
127. This estimation is derived from our own field investigation. See Appendix.
128. Ibid.
129. D. Nath, *Satras in Colonial Assam: Their Responses to the Emerging Socio-Political Issues,* ICHR, Guwahati; 2007, p. 26.
130. Ibid.

130(a) Called 'Majuli Jila Mahila Samity', the Majuli Women's organization was formally established in 1982, after a long and precarious existance of a women association since 1952.

131. For details see Neera Desai and Usha Thakkar, *op cit.* For understanding the present status of the Kaivarta women in their families, an extract from Sanjay Ghose's *Diary* will be sufficient: "At Maghiram's house, we were served tea by his sister-in-law, who squatted on her haunches and offered up the tea. This is the second time that it had happened, and when I enquired, I was given the usual 'cultural' explanation—qualified by the rider that it happened mostly in Scheduled Caste, rural homes, mostly with visitors, and those with 'in-law' status. Having left Rajasthan behind us, I was getting used to the freedom of women, out of *purdah*, but every now and then there were reminders like this that the underlying base of patriarchy was still active." Cf. Sumita Ghose, *op cit.*, pp. 98f

132. Cf. HAG, p. 142.

133. *See* W. Robinson, *A Descripptive Account of Assam*, *op cit.*, pp 25f.

134. Ibid, p. 21.

135. GCK, pp. 65, also see p 103.

136. The exact date of establishment of a hospital could not be traced. But, as stated by some people, if it was established immediately after the Jubilee celebration of Queen Victoria's declaration as the Empress of Indian Empire in 1877, then it might have been established in the early part of the eighties or in the last years of the seventies of that cenury. For celebration of Queen Victoria's accession to the throne. See ASBS, pp. 252f; also, Chapter III, fn. 93

137. Report collected from the field.

138. R. Bhattacharji, *Lands of Early Dawn*, New Delhi, 2002, pp. 124f.

139. Her allegations were published in the *Dainik Janambhumi*. See July 28th issue, 2005.

140. See also Sumita Ghose, *op cit.*, pp. 103ff.

141. See Chapter-I, *supra*.

142. M'Cosh, *op cit.*, p. 72; *Gazetteer* of Allen et. al., *op cit.*, p. 578; *Sibsagar District Gazetteer*, 1967, p. 1 0; R. Bhattacharyi, *op cit.*, p125; J. N. Sarma, *loc cit.*

143. Cf. Nirupama Bargohain, 'Seuji Surabhi, Uttal Brahmaputra' in *Diamond Jubilee Volume*, Majuli Auniati Hemchandra High School, Kamalabari, 1998, p. 58.

144. M'Cosh, *op cit.*, pp. 72f

145. Tengani is a reserved forest area of Assam on Nagaland border under Golahgat subdivision. Most erosion affected families of Majuli shift to the area and take shelter there. Sanjay Ghose remarks: "After the floods last year, it has taken many months for life to come back to normal. Now you can just about get around everywhere, but often having to by-pass bridges and roads that have been washed away. It is just three months till the next monsoon, and there are no signs of repair starting, but life goes on. In the early mornings there is inevitably a silver of mist hanging

over the island, and as the sun emerges, and the golden yellow mustard fields come into view, it seems like a picture of paradise." Cf. Sumita Ghose, *op cit.*, pp. 135f

146. See Chapter-I of this work.
147. See J. N. Sarma, *loc cit.*
148. Wade, *A Geographical Sketch of Assam*, *op cit.*, p. 32.
149. Ibid
150. Also J. N. Sarma, *loc cit.*
150(a) K. C. Borah, *loc cit.* (Ms.)
151. Ibid
152. Amal Goswami, '*Itihas Hol Ahataguri Mauja*', in the *Dainik Janambhumi*, 19th November, 2006, Sunday issue, pp. 27f.
153. Sonaram Sarma Burabhakat, 'Sri Sri Kamalabari Satrar Satradhikar Prabhujanar Chamu Parichay', in *Souvenir* published on the occasion of *Sisya Samaroh* of Kamalabari *Satra*, 2000, pp. 7f.
154. Prannath Das in his *Padmapanideva Charit*, has given a vivid description of erosion of the Satra. See ASBS, p. 474.
155. Information supplied by Boparam Nath of Puranibari village.
156. Cf. HAG, p. 150; Tarun Chandra Pamegam, *Rachanawali*, II, p. 61.
157. T. C. Pamegam, *Tarun Chandra Pamegam Rachanawali*, II, *op cit.*, pp. 46f.
158. Ibid, p. 46.
159. Ibid, p. 43.
160. It is a process of killing the birds at night by a bamboo pole when the bird, or for that matter, an animal like the deer was silently moving straight towards a light kindled and placed on a bamboo appliance called *dala* carried by a man over his head. This man also uses to beat a bell producing a uniform and incessant sound (*ghanta*) that spread over the entire area. When the bird or the animal was thus looking and slowly moving forward towards the light and the source of the sound, another man following the first instantly killed the prey with a pole that he was taking with him.
161. See Illustration.
162. This was known during our field Investigation
163. See S. N. Sarma, *The Neovaishnavite Movement and the Satra Institution of Assam*, *op cit.*, pp. 92ff
164. See Chapter-IV, *infra.*
165. *Supra.*
166. D. Nath, NEIHA *Souvenir*, 1993, pp. 85fn.
167. *Op cit.*, p. 123
168. See HAG, p. 42
169. ASBS, p. 158; Gahin Sonowal, "Dharmantarkaran aru Sonowal Samaj", in Mohan Sonowal (ed) *Sonowal Saurabh*, Dibrugarh, 2007, pp. 184ff
170. See *Supra*, p. 59
171. See ASBS, p. 158; also as reported during the field investigation
172. *The Kacharis*, p. 33
173. Ibid, pp. 33f

174. Ibid, p. 36
175. Also see Ibid, p. 38
176. *See* D. Nath, NEIHA, *Souvenir*, 1993, pp. 81
177. Ibid.
178. Much has been said about this *Satradhikara's* role in sanskritising the untouchables and eradication of the caste prejudices in the society. But no specific record has been made by researchers from among the Misings themselves about his role in sanskritisation of this tribe as a community who predominate the island's population. Also see D. Nath, 'Satra and Social Change in Majuli', loc. cit, pp. 177ff
179. Cf. Sumita Ghose, *op cit.*, p. 113.
180. One interesting aspect of Christianity in India was its humanitarian activity. M. N. Srinivas has remarked, "Christian missionaries played a notable part in the humanitarian activity, especially in providing education and medical aid to sections of Indian society most in need of them—Harijans, women, orphans, lepers and tribal folk. Equally important were their criticisms of such Hindu institutions as caste, untouchability, the low position of women, child marriage and polygamy. The British-Western attack resulted in a reinterpretation of Hinduism at both the ideological and institutional levels, and the conversion of the lower castes (especially Harijans) to Islam and Christianity was an important factor in producing a changed attitude among the Hindu elite towards caste and untouchability." Cf. *Social Change in Modern India*, Indian edition Reprint, 1972, p. 52.

180(a) According to the Census of 2001, the male literacy rate in Majuli is 85.4 per cent, while that of female is 64.58 per cent.

181. Cf. *Report on Majuli* published on the occasion of the Seminar on *Flood and Erosion Problem of Assam and Protection of Majuli*, organized at Kamalabari, Majuli, by AASU on 8-9 April, 1999.
182. ABSB, pp. 280, 311.
183. Ibid
184. ASBS, p. 353
185. Pitambardeva Goswami, *Confession*, *op cit.*, p. 1.
186. ASBS, p. 280; for *pathsala* or *tol* system see Gunabhiram Baruah, *op cit.*, pp. 185f.
187. B. C. Thakur, 'Sikshyar Bibhinna Disat Alokpat', in *Majuli* (ed) P. K. Mahanta, Jorhat,2001, p. 189
188. Ibid
189. Ibid
190. Ibid
191. *See* Chapter-IV for details. Some list has been given in the Appendix.
192. Ibid, p. 189.
193. See H.K.Barpujari, *Christian Missionaries in North East India*, *op cit.*, pp. 176ff.
194. Bhuban Chandra Thakur has stated that he has collected the information from the first generation teachers of the school like Bagaram Bora, Padma Saikia and Nirmal Bora, Bhuban Ch. Thakur, *op cit.*, p. 190.

195. Ibid, pp. 190f.
196. Bhuban Ch. Thakur, *loc cit*, p. 191.
197. See ASBS, p. 322.
198. *Cf. Rachanawali*, Vol I, *cit*, pp. 272f
199. ASBS, pp. 278f.
200. Ibid.
201. H. N. Sarma, *op cit.* (Ms.).
201 (a) "It is obvious that the Kalita, its core represented by the peasant Barkalitas, absorbed many other groups such as the fisherfolk (Saru Kalita), potter (Kumar), Kamar Kalita (blacksmith), Duliya (palki bearer), Katani (silk weaver), Sonari (goldsm96ith), Bar (Napit), Mali and Nat." Cf. K. Suresh Singh (ed), *op cit.*, p. Intro, XVII.
202. P. J. Marshall, *The Eighteenth Century in Indian History*, OUP, Paperback, 2005, for details. *See* pp. 53-100.

3

Economy

Agriculture, Occupation and Crafts

Economy of the Majuli island, till a few decades ago, was a continuum of the medieval systems, self-sufficient and subsistence in nature, and it has been still continued to a certain degree. The system had its root in the *paik* system of the Ahom days and was dependent on the local geography and environment.

Traces of the *paik* system in the island's socio-economic fabric can be seen in the structure of the villages. In the days of the Ahom monarchy peasants of the state were called *paik*, which meant peasant-cum-warriors who fought in the times of war, and engaged in the civil activities at the times of peace.[1] Every adult male above the age of sixteen, but below fifty, was registered as *paik* and was allotted certain work, such as cultivation on behalf of the king or his officers, making boats, spinning thread and weaving cloth, making mat, building roads and bridges, and so forth, for which he received two *puras* (2.66 acres) of best cultivable revenue-free land from the king.[2] The extent of production was to meet primarily the personal needs of the *paik* family and to contribute some amount towards the maintenance of the state. There was no surplus of significance that could be released to the market. The entire system was concerned with production for subsistence and labour to work. Introduction of the *paik* system in Majuli was duly recorded in the chronicles.[3] It is stated that king Pratap Singha himself was present in Majuli when he appointed his officers to take a census of the people in the island at the beginning of the 17th century.[4] There was a network of administration made up of officers of various ranks who had very smoothly conducted the affairs. In every village of the island are to be found titles like *Bora*, *Saikia*, *Hazarika*, and even *Barua*, *Phukan* or *Rajkhowa*, as evidence of this medieval system.

Villages were organized in terms of either profession or caste. Since one caste followed or was made to follow a certain profession, there was combination of caste and profession, and a village could be marked from the name itself which either spoke of the caste or of the profession of its people. In either case, one could easily distinguish one village from the other simply from the names of the villages. Thus, even now we find in the island, villages like Katani Gaon, Kanhar Gaon, Patiya Gaon, Kamar Gaon, Kumar Gaon, Kanrhal Gaon, Tanti Gaon, Pohardiya Gaon, Mekheli Gaon, and Yogi Gaon, Sonowal Kachari Gaon, Kalita Gaon, Sut Gaon etc. It is true that there are many other villages which do not conform to this explanation. This is because, most of such names are recently coined either due to internal migration and formation of new villages, which derive their names from their geographical location, or from certain historical incidents that have relations with that village. Some of the old names are also substituted by new and modern names.

Besides villages, elements of the *paik* system are to be seen in the Satra administration also. The entire net-work and gradation of the officers which governed the society in the monarchical days, could be seen in the administration of the large Satras today with the *Satradhikara* at the top resembling a medieval feudal lord, and the *bhakats* at the bottom with numerous office bearers of different grades in between.[5]

Agriculture has always been the mainstay of economy in Majuli, and is based on its geography. It has been stated earlier how the climate and its soil system has been conducive to an agrarian economy since known past. Its climate being moist and the soil being alluvial throughout, Majuli has always been suitable for cultivation of various crops, notably rice of summer variety—*ahu* and *bao*, mustard, different types of pulses, vegetables, sugarcane and so forth. The relationship of the climate, and the topographical conditions with its agriculture pattern is noted by different authorities since at least the medieval ages. It has been earlier stated that even Sukapha also noted its flood-prone character for which he found the place around Habung unsuitable for transplanted wet rice culture.[6] But its soil was fertile being annually inundated by flood saturated with high alluvium. Muhammad Cazim, the biographer of emperor Aurangzeb, as early as the mid-17th century, has noted about its cultivated fields which were surrounded by the thick forests where herds of elephants and other wild animals used to roam.[7] A. J. Muffatt Mills in his *Report on the Province of Assam*, has noted in the middle of the 19th century that the island was "formerly well inhabited and cultivated, but is almost entirely over-run with deep grass and forest jungles.... The soil is rich alluvial, calculated for the growth of every kind of crop."[8] Noting down this aspect of its soil and agriculture pattern, the *Gazetteer of Eastern Bengal and Assam*, 1905, has recorded that the island was open to flood and diluvium, and the staple crops are summer rice and mustard.[9] Tarun Chandra Pamegam has recorded about the fertility of the soil in the mid-

20th century and about its alluvial fields lying extensively open, or covered with high reed-jungles inviting the Mising, Deori and other tribal communities to cut down the jungles, burn them and then open them and make settlement there.[10]

LAND SYSTEM

Unlike other parts of Assam where more or less all types of crops can be grown, lands in Majuli were suitable only for growing certain specific types of crops because of its peculiar geographical situation and soil type. It had and still has two types of land—low-lying or *da*, and high or *chapori* lands called *tika*. The low lying lands are classified into several classes, such as *maghuwa toli*, *bao toli*, *sariyah toli*, etc., while *tika* or *chapori* lands are either *kathiya toli* (suitable for growing seedlings), *mah toli* (suitable for growing pulses), *til toli* (land for), *kherani* (land for growing a kind of fern called *Kher*), *bari* (homestead) and so forth. Being a riverine belt, most of its *chapori* lands are temporary in nature, and hence do not come under regular revenue assessment. Again, a good amount of the high and valuable lands here are either gifted lands to the Satras as *devottar bhumi* or treated as grazing lands (*charaniya pathar*). In all the cases, lands here would yield very nominal amount of revenue to the state. As a result, Muffatt Mills stated in the year 1853 that its revenue-yield was small; of the total 282165 acres of land, only 7446 acres paid rent.[11] Lands are also classified on the basis of the nature of their ownership. Accordingly, we find lands with permanent ownership called *myadi* land, and temporary ownership called *ekchana* land. *Myadi* system is of recent origin, especially after Majuli witnessed urban growth centering round its headquarters at Garamur, and around Kamalabari.

The Misings who were, till the early part of 20th century, dwellers of the river banks, particularly, the Suvansiri and the Kherkatiya Suti, had no permanently settled areas. As evidenced by the contemporary British records, till then they used to inhabit the areas bordering the forests and jungles having opportunity to open new lands after every two-three years in search of fertile agricultural fields.[12] A. J. Muffatt Mills has stated that "They are an industrious people; they reclaim lands, cultivate them for two or at the most three years, and then go to another place, where they employ themselves in a similar manner. Captain Dalton tells me that he is endeavouring to induce them to congregate at one or two selected spots on the banks of the Brahmapootra where forest lands abound, and form a colony. This plan is an admirable one, and would tend more than any other parts of Assam."[13] As we have stated earlier, Tarun Chandra Pamegam had noted this shifting nature of the Misings and the Deoris till his own time in the 20th century. This nature of frequent shifting of their settlement and cultivation has had two major impacts on their land and agriculture systems: first, they failed to develop a permanent type of land ownership till recent decades, and second, they could not develop a settled system of agriculture till at least the early 20th century. As pointed out by one of their own scholars, it is a conclusive fact that the Misings had no system of settled agriculture; it was only through their gradual contact with the plains people of the Brahmaputra valley that they slowly became acquainted with the agriculture system of the plains. The presence of the names of most of the agriculture implements in Assamese language and their conspicuous absence in the Mising language point to this conclusion.[14]

Normally lands under the tribal communities, such as those of the Misings, and lands donated to the Satras by the Ahom kings of the middle ages, are not liable to payment of revenue. Records show that while some parts of the island were covered with jungle upto as late as the early 20th century, most of the rest was revenue-free grants made to the Satras by the kings. It is on record[15] that Auniati Satra alone possesses more than one lakh *bigha̱* of revenue-free land till today in and outside Majuli. Similarly, Garamur, Dakhinpat, Kamalabari and Bengenaati also have their own revenue-free lands received as gift from the kings. In the *cha̱poris* the tribes like the Mising and the Deori have most of their lands for which they do not pay revenue. In a sense every family of those communities possesses lands in the *cha̱poris*. Even families of non-tribal communities have portions of their agricultural lands in the *cha̱poris* and on the river banks. As a result, lands occupied by the Misings remained outside the area of revenue settlement. It was therefore one of the reasons why Mills had to mention that Majuli yielded small amount of revenue in comparison to its land area.[16] Even at present, Majuli offers considerably less amount of revenue. As explained by Sri Debendranath Goswami, the *Maujadar* of the Kamalabari *Mauja,*[17] although the demand of the Government has been the same since last 7-8 years, the fact that a good amount of cultivable and other productive lands (about 40-45 per cent of the total) has been either washed away by erosion of the river or has become unusable due to siltation or creation of depressions (*dubi* or *doba̱*) during floods as a result of the breaking of dykes and embankments, has drastically reduced the sources of the land revenue. This has not only reduced the amount of revenue-paying land, but also the peasant's ability to pay revenue. As a result, the only amount of revenue that is possible to collect, can be collected at the time when college and school students receive some money as scholarships from the State Government. It is during that time that peasants can pay some amount of revenue with this money. They would also pay some amount when they (the peasant families) receive any financial assistance from the Government. He has further stated that the Government does not supply revenue papers and standard proforma to the peasants in time. The old custom of *koroki diya,*[18] whereby peasants were compelled to pay revenue, has also become obsolete. Many peasants have no *patta.* All these have led to decrease in the amount of collection of revenue. Since the price of land in Majuli is considerably lower than that of any other place, peasants here do not give importance to the payment of revenue in time. The auction system of land as it was there in earlier times, has also been defunct. This has also lessened the emphasis on payment of revenue.

Table 3.1: Land Revenue Record of Majuli During 2000-2003

Year	Revenue Due	Total Receipt	Remark
2000-2001	Rs.8,00,759.00	Rs.1,52,307.00	
2001-2002	Rs.8,27,280.97	Rs.1,79,864.64	
2002-2003	Rs.8,36,387.91	Rs.1,28,758.26	

Source: Office of the Maujadar, Kamalabari Mauja, Majuli

Extent of land possessed by an individual peasant in Majuli at present varies from 1 *bigha* to 10 *bigha* per family.[19] This could be explained on historical background. During the Ahom age possession of state-registered lands by an individual *paik* was limited to two *puras* only although there was permission that he could occupy more land against payment of a nominal amount of revenue by clearing jungles in the riverine or waste land areas.[20] There is still a belief, therefore, in Majuli, that lands lying in front and at the rear of the homestead always belong to the house owner. It is therefore presumable that families in Majuli during this period who could afford to clear jungles, owned large plots of land of their own. This condition of having more lands is now not in vogue due to reduction of jungle and waste lands.

Recurring flood causing erosion and consequent reduction of cultivable land, growth of population leading to scarcity of lands, and emergence of market and administrative centres at the cost of high and valuable lands, have led to reduction of a part of the valuable lands possessed by the families. This has resulted in attempts by the peasants to convert even the slopes of the high embankments into paddy fields in recent decades, particularly after 1962, when a great flood caused irreparable damage to men's homestead and cultivable field. It is to be noted that while in early times, extent of lands was increased by clearing jungle lands, the attempt has been made in the present times by occupying the swamps, drains, and slopes of the embankments where people either build houses or shops or carry on cultivation. When asked, Makhana Nath of Puranibari Gaon, has replied that he has occupied the slopes of the embankment for mustard and *ahu* cultivation as a portion of his cultivable land was recruited for building roads and embankments. Similar was the answer of Boparam Nath of the same village who also cultivates on the slopes of the embankments due to use of his cultivable fields for excavating drains and building embankments. Examples may be multiplied taking instances from all over Majuli. This shows that frequent building of roads and embankments and breaking of these roads and embankments by flood creating much damage to the agricultural fields has been a great problem to the cultivators of Majuli, who therefore have to resort to using the slopes or sides of the high embankments as supplement to their fields; or have to build their houses on the embankments themselves.

AGRICULTURE

As stated earlier, Majuli was suitable for certain types of crops of which the most important is the summer variety of rice called *ahu* and *bao*. In earlier times both the types were of shifting variety, and were cultivated in the method of slash and burn. Butler, the British officer, travelling in Assam in the mid-19th century, has described the method as follows:

> In January, February, March and April, ... the natives set fire to the jungle to clear the land for cultivation and to open the thoroughfares between the different villages, and the aweful roar and rapidity with which the flames spread cannot be conceived. A space of many miles of grass jungle, twenty feet high is cleared in a few hours.... The jungle is burnt down, and for three successive years two crops are annually realised from it. In February mustard seed is gathered in... and in June the spring rice, sown broadcast, is reaped. After the land has been thus impoverished, it is allowed to remain fallow for three years and fresh jungle land is burnt and prepared in the same primitive way and with most simple implements of husbandry."[21]

This method of slash and burn applied to the *ahu* cultivation was in use till at least the early sixties of the last century when large tracts were still covered by jungle and remained waste. But, slowly, the expansion of the Mising population into the *chaporis* of the northern belt on the bank of the Suvansiri, Luhit and Kherkatiya, led the waste lands contract; and at one time, there were no such lands. In other parts also population growth and internal migration greatly affected the jungle lands. Thus, the Majuli island of which about 2/3rd part was still undiscovered due to forests, jungles and swamps till the close of the 18th century[22] became an open space; and nowhere in it was to be found any strip of a forest, or a piece of waste land by the mid 20th century. This has notably changed the agriculture scenario in the island in recent decades as peasants with small plots of land have no opportunity to use alternate plots for such cultivation. This is why we find the gradual popularity of the multi-crop system in the island.

The *ahu* rice is generally sown broadcast in low and dry lands during December-February, and reaped during May-June. It has two varieties—*ranga* (red) and *baga* (white), the later variety is also called *bar*. But the *baga* or *bar* variety is produced in small amount as it takes comparatively long duration to mature, and production is also smaller in proportion to investment. Sometimes, *ahu* is also cultivated in wet land using water to help germinate the seeds. It is therefore sown during the rainy months, May-June, and is reaped during September-October. It is then called *pharma*. Of the different varieties of *ahu* the most known are the *guni* and *bangah.*

A summer variety, *bao* is sown broadcast in low-lying lands during February-April, and is reaped during November-December. *Bao* requires water, but it is sown when the land is dry. It grows proportionately to the rising water, and settles down as it recedes. With plenty of water it gives a good crop, but without water, it dies. It is therefore a common phenomenon in Majuli to-day to see *bao* crop frequently dying during the receding months of October-November when fields become dry. This is due to building of the road and embankments all around the island which prevent flood water to enter. This system affects the *bao* crop in still another way—when broken embankments allow a major volume of water to enter and clog inside in the low-lying areas. In such condition, cultivators who mainly depend on this variety, have to lose their crop. Of the different varieties of *bao*, *kakuwa*, *amana*, *rangali* and *maguri* are most popular.

Sali or transplanted variety of rice for which land capable of retaining water for long is suitable, is bound to be limited in Majuli. For, lands in the island do not permit the system of cultivation as it is sandy almost all over. Inside the embankments, however, some amount of *sali* is grown where water supply remains constant for a long period. Although outside the embankments lands are regularly submerged by flood, recurring flood, beginning with May till the end of September, does not allow cultivation of this paddy there. Therefore, the *District Gazetteer of 1905* has recorded that "flood rather than draught is the principal obstacle to agriculture. A considerable area of the land is rendered unfit for permanent cultivation by the spill-water of the Brahmaputra and its tributaries."[23]

FIG. 3.1: A CULTIVATOR PLOUGING IN THE FIELD IN WINTER

FIG. 3.2: WEEDING *AHU* CROP

FIG. 3.3: REAPING *SALI* PADDY

Thus, there are certain areas only where transplanted rice is cultivated with profit; but its extent is limited in both local and regional levels. Areas like Jengraimukh, Ratanpur, Phulani, Rangachahi, Tataya Gaon, Mekheli Gaon, Chamaguri and Pahumara in upper Majuli are comparatively better *sali* producing regions than other places. Generally, tribal villages are more accustomed to the shifting variety than permanent *sali* variety. Thus *sali* is comparatively more popular among the non-tribal communities than among the tribal communities, although *ahu* and *bao* too are equally cultivated by them. As a result, we find that *ahu* and *bao* are cultivated by all classes, but *sali* is mainly confined to a few non-tribal areas only.

Sali has two major varieties—*sali* or *bar,* i.e. coarse, and *lahi* or fine variety. In Majuli, like in any other parts of Assam, *sali* or the coarse variety predominates. Among the most popular of the *salis* are the *bara, jaha, bar*, *chakowa*, etc. Of them the *bar* is the most popular again as its yield is generous than that of any other variety, such as *jaha* or *bara*. *Chakowa* including one called *niyar kadam* are used for purposes of preparing breakfast called *komal chaul.*[24] *Bara* is largely used for making varieties of cakes although it is also used for making *komal chaul*. Presently, transplanted rice cultivated during winter called *boro dhan* is also cultivated in some corners of the low-lying areas of the island by supplying water from the nearby swampy areas or through the use of pumps and tube-wells provided by the Government. But here too since the peasants have to supply the fuel on their own to run the power pumps, most poor peasants are unable to grow *boro dhan*. As a result, even *boro* which is meant mainly for the poor cultivators, is bound to be confined to the well-to-do sections of the society only.

Rice (*ahu* and *bao*) grew well and production was plenty till there were sufficient lands to pursue shifting method, buttressed by less number of embankments preventing, like today, the free flow of the river flood all over the island to create alluvium. As a matter of fact, although at one time, the island witnessed healthy growth of crops as noted by the outsiders visiting or writing about the island, but the situation is quite reverse at present. Even in the past, rice was produced mainly to meet the need of the family for the year. Men tried to make some surplus only to meet the emergency when crops failed due to early flood, draught or any other natural calamities. Rice was then treated as goddess Lakshmi (*Lakhimi*), and not even a grain was knowingly left to lie outside. It was therefore not their custom to buy and sell rice in the market. The Mughal chronicler Shihabuddin Talish was astonished to mark this habit of the people here. As pointed out by a historian of agriculture in Assam, "the absence of rice in the list of export of agricultural products to Bengal even as late as the 19th century could be explained from this point of view."[25] Rice is still regarded as the most sacred of the products, and seldom goes for sale. Naturally, rice sale is a rare phenomenon in Majuli. It is also true that volume of rice produced at present is not sufficient to meet the demand of the inhabitants and their visitors. Naturally, Majuli has to import rice from outside to feed its swelling number of inhabitants and visitors. In this process of import of rice, some families having man-power and money, purchase or take in mortgage certain amount of lands outside, normally in Lakhimpur, where they cultivate and produce rice either by themselves, or on *adhiar* or share-cropping basis. *Adhiyar* or share-cropping system is also practised in Majuli by the able families. Thus, most school teachers get their lands cultivated by others on the share-cropping basis.

With most agricultural lands lying fallow after one crop till the next season, the scenario of cropping pattern in Majuli indicates in general that peasants here are less concerned about optimum use of cultivable lands by doing double or triple cropping. Thus, a land where *ahu* is sown in winter to be harvested in summer, is used for mustard in the next autumn to be reaped in the winter before *ahu* is sown again. Similarly, lands used for jute are sometimes used for *sali*, and/or *robi* crop. With the same picture remaining constant, the concept of double cropping system has become slowly popular with certain sections due mainly to the growing scarcity of cultivable lands, and a few cultivators today are becoming conversant with the system of double cropping. Information obtained from the agriculture department in Majuli for the year 2003-2004 has pointed this out. It is stated that during that year out of a gross crop area of about 56389 hectors, 28452 hectares were net sown area, and about 20943 hectares were under double cropping system, while 4294 hectares under triple cropping.[26] The same department supplies information also about the major pests and diseases that attack crops in the island. These pests and diseases include *stem borer*, *hispa*, *rice bag* in paddy, *army worms* in pulses and mustard, *cut worms* in vegetables, *late brigand* in potato, *aphids* in mustard, UFRA in *boro* paddy and so forth.[27]

It is significant that lands once lying fallow have now been brought under regular and incessant cultivation.[28] The records presented above show that double cropping system has been gradually becoming popular in the island. During our investigation it was found that the popularity of this system is not only because of the growing knowledge of the cultivators about optimum use of the land, but it is also due to the necessitey to feed the growing number of population.[29]

Besides rice, various kinds of pulses are produced in the Majuli island.

These include *matimah* (*phaseolus max*), *mug mah* (*phaseclus minimus of rumph*), *kalamah* or *khechari mah* (*lathyrus sativus*), *arahar* (*eajanus caijan*) and few others. But the most popular is the *matimah* followed by *mug*. *Mug* is largely used in the religious functions as offering (*mah-prasad*) to the deities. Cultivation of peas is also becoming popular for it needs little labour to grow and less vulnerable to calamities. Seeds are sown broadcast on the *bao* or *sali* paddy fields when the land is still soft and moist, and allowed to grow after the rice is harvested. It is a kind of winter crop, and at the same time, it supplies a good part of the food for the peasant families in the villages. As a result, its popularity is growing. Of the other winter crops that supply part of their food is wheat that has become popular since the days of the *Green Revolution* of the 1970s. It is interesting that most peasant families having no tradition of the cultivation of wheat, and not conversant with the system of its harvest, thrashing and preparing the *chapatti* from its flour, now have started cultivating wheat and have adapted to the habit of taking *chapattis*. *Chapattis* made of this wheat are very sweet and tastful. One significant aspect of outlook of the peasantry towards wheat is that, being accustomed to the production and use of rice as the only item of subsistence since unknown past, families here do not like to welcome *chapatti* as a kind of supplement to rice-food; and therefore, it is considered a kind of upstart over their culture. As a result, eating *chapatti* as a substitute to rice is often considered a symbol of poverty in Majuli.[30]

Of other major crops mention may be made of sugarcane. As the soil of the island is suitable for growing sugarcane, the crop grows well here. Referrineg to the sugarcane, Shihabudddin Talish has noted that three varieties of sugarcane were grown in Assam—red, white and black; but they were full of worms.[31] Similarly, more than a hundred years later, Captain Welsh also noted the same when he wrote that sugarcane was cultivated in almost every part of Assam.[32] *Gur* (rough sugar/jaggery) as it is called, the product of sugarcane, once dominated the items of breakfast and all sorts of offerings in the religious and social functions of the villagers. In fact, it was a kind of industry that encouraged a few subsidiary crafts in Majuli like pottery, and provided men with other amenities of economy. Hot juice of sugarcane called *pakarahi* was so popular, says Mohan Barua, a cultivator of Rowmara village under Majuli Development Block, that many old generation people still enjoy remembering it. Another popular item of good taste made of sugarcane was *micha* which was but a small bundle of the fibers made from the trunk of the squeezed sugarcane and then made wet and boiled with the hot juice. Production of *gur* is done through a machine involving a simple technology. It is called *kunhiyar sal* (squeezer) pulled by a pair of bullocks, or a buffalo, or by half a dozen men. The *sal* consists of a machine for squeezing the sugarcane, a big flat iron tray called *thali* or *phelahi*, a fire place called *jaleegant*, a bamboo appliance called *ghotani/larani* and a chieve called *chalani* or *chakani*. Most cultivators in Majuli had a squeezing machine in the past.

Cultivation of sugarcane is now not popular in the mainland Majuli as it did till around the seventies of the last century. Lack of sufficient land, growing unitary families leading to reduction of manpower[33] and more particularly, its unprofitability in terms of labour and time investment, has made its cultivation unpopular. When asked, Mr. Mitharam Nath of Puranibari village, who was once known for sugarcane cultivation, replied, "We have now not much land suitable for sugarcane cultivation. All such lands where we once had sugarcane crops, have now been converted to homestead lands for building houses to accommodate members of the proliferated families. We have also no sufficient manpower to go for sugarcane." Such is the situation almost all over the mainland Majuli.

Table 3.2: Land Area under different Crops, 2004

Name of the Crop	Target		Achievement		Remarks
	Area in Hctr.	*Amount Produced in MT*	*Area in Hctr.*	*Amount Produced in MT*	
Early *Ahu*	840	1340.00	8485.00	11454.00	
Boro	180	284.00	206.00	278.00	
R/*Ahu*	4350	4000.00	3263.00	4405.00	
Sali	3500	11201.00	5181.00	10109.00	
Bao	7500	18668.00	8720.00	9360.00	
Sugarcane	50	2508.00	130.00	6500.00	
Maize	15	10.00	15.00	9.50	
Jute	65	706.00	80.00	1010.00	
S/vegetable	210	2449.00	590.00	7730.00	
B/gram	1090	764.00	2100.00	—	Harvesting not then complete
G/gram	260	167.00	780.00	—	-do-
Pea	2300	1786.00	3150.00	—	-do-
Lentil	220	130.00	800.00	—	-do-
Other pulses	220	146.00	32.00	—	-do-
Sesamum	20	12.00	51.00	—	-do-
Rap & Mustard	12000	7200.00	6998.00	—	-do-
Wheat	1070	1391.00	870.00	—	-do-
Potato	1550	12400.00	730.00	—	-do-
Robi Vegetable	719	11688.00	418.00	—	-do-
Garlic	—	—	635.00	—	-do-

(*As furnished by the Office of the SDO, Agriculture, Majuli*)

Today, therefore, one rarely witnesses sugarcane fields in the island which once made the land distinguished with high and green sugarcane bushes. The crop today is mainly cultivated in the peripheral areas, such as those lying outside the mainland island near Dergaon on the south of the Brahmaputra. During our field survey in the Dakhin Ahataguri and the Dhodang *Chapori* areas, it was found that sugarcane was cultivated by almost all the families of the *chapori* and it formed their major crop. When asked, Suresh Bora and his neighbour Sonaram Bhuyan of the Ghuriya Gaon (Charai *Chapori*) under Dakhin Ahataguri Gaon Panchayat replied that sugarcane was the only hopeful crop that could be produced in their area in the context of its geographical situation.

Of the most known agricultural cash crops popular all over the island mention may be made of jute and mustard. Traditions and literature speak much about the production of mustard all through the island. During the Ahom rule people opened new lands by clearing jungles and brought them under cultivation of ahu and mustard crop. After the *ahu* was harvested, those lands became suitable for cultivation of mustard. It was then an established fact that every family must produce oil of its own to meet the need for the whole year. Besides, there was a *khel* or guild of the *paiks* called Teli who were exclusively engaged to produce oil.[34] Kings used to donate suitable lands to the Satras and the temples. It was from the produce of those lands that oil lamps and other aspects of expenditure were met.[35] There were different classes of traders called *mudoi* and *saud* who used to collect mustard in Upper Assam and buy them for sale in Kamrup, i.e. lower Assam.[36] During the British, Marwaris used to collect mustard in their *golas* from the peasants and exported them to other parts of the country.[37] The story of Assamese peasants and Marwari traders is a long history of *Mahajan* and cultivators relationship, and that of the exploiters and the exploited[38] In the 20th century, mustard was a major crop that fetched some cash to the cultivators besides jute, which was, of course, not as cash rewarding as mustard was. Jute was largely used for domestic purposes—in the making of rope of different sizes, rope for binding buffalo and cow, making thread and masks and so forth. With ample amount of low-lying areas, Majuli provides suitable lands for growing jute. Even today, viilagers produce some amount of jute at least to meet the needs of the family.

Majuli is also known for production of tobacco since the middle ages. Although it is stated that tobacco was imported to India by the Portuguese in the middle of the 16th century, during the reign of Akbar (1556-1605),[39] there is ground to suspect that some kind of tobacco plant was not unknown to the people of Assam even before that. On the contrary, it is possible that tobacco was largely produced and there was a tobacco market called *dhuwa hat* (*dhuwa* = smoke, *hat* = market) in Majuli during the time of Sankaradeva (1449-1568) where the saint established his monastery.[40] It is to be noted that Madhavdeva (1498-1596) discarded tobacco and *ganja* smoking as irreligious and unethical.[41] Jahnabi Gogoi Nath has noted in this connection that "if this is believed, then there is a possibility of existence of a local variety of tobacco in Assam even before its introduction by the Portuguese."[42] It is relevant here to note that a trader from Kamrup, then under the Mughal rule, came to buy tobacco in Upper Assam (Ahom kingdom) to sell it in Bengal.[43] Tobacco plant of a special variety with thick and round shaped dark green leaf was grown in Majuli, and the same was used to make a special kind of consumable variety called *maladhapat* prepared through a process of mixing the grinded tobacco leaves with granulated *gur* called *lali,* and then putting them into the bamboo tubes called *chunga*. It is still prepared and used by the villagers with betel-nut in Majuli where the crop is grown.

It is not known to what extent poppy called *kani* was cultivated in Majuli. But that it was known to the people even before the coming of the British to this state is evidenced by local records.[44] S.K. Bhuyan has stated that the drug might have been imported by some of the border tribes to Assam from China and in sufficiently earlier times.[45] This is not improbable when W. Robinson has said about the Miris (Misings) that they used to produce opium in large amounts. He says that the Misings in the plains "employ themselves chiefly in growing opium, and as they always cultivate new lands, their fields in general yield them large returns. They seldom use the drug themselves but they make a very large profit by bartering it to the Assamese for grain and other necessaries. They also cultivate cotton to a large extent and engage in manufacture of cotton rugs,[46] peculiar to themselves."[47] The *Auniati Satrar Buranji* has recorded that Dattadeva Goswami, the *adhikara* of the Satra (1838-1904), had to pay a fine of Rs.500.00 for poppy being cultivated in his land by some of his disciples.[48] Similarly, Benudhar Sharma has noted that Basudeva Goswami of Dakhinpat Satra (1828-1870) also had to pay the same amount of fine for the same kind of offence.[49] It is even stated that Bishnudeva Goswami (1780-1820), *Satradhikara* of this Satra, could gallop more than 300 grams of opium at a time.[50] Pitambardeva Goswami (1885-1962), the *Satradhikara* of Garamur Satra in Majuli, had to launch a campaign against opium addiction in Majuli in the early part of the 20th century.[51] Poppy however, ceased to be produced in the island in the post-independence period.

Majuli was and still is famous for production of varieties of fruits. Mango, banana and coconut were once plentiful. Among the citrus fruits mention may be made of varieties of lemons, such as *kagji* and *gol*, *amara* (*spondias amara*), tamarind, olive, shaddock, *amlakhi* (*embica officinalia*), *kardoi* (*overrhoa caranbola*), *thekera* (*thaikol*) and others. One of the interesting citrus fruit is *outenga*, a wild fruit, but very popular among the people of Majuli island. *Outenga* and fish curry is a favourite dish for the people of Majuli which tease the taste buds in the mouth of the people here. Majuli is also famous for production of varieties of chilies, garlic and vegetables.

Table 3.3: Cropping Pattern of Majuli Sub-Division during 1997-98, 1998-99, 1999-2000

Sl. No.	Name of the Crop	1997-98		1998-99		1999-2000	
		Area in hectares	% total crop area	Area in hectares	% total crop area	Area in hectares	% total crop area
1.	Paddy	24418	45.48	22521	45.77	26406	54.92
	(a) Summer paddy	9612	17.90	9661	19.63	8646	17.98
	(b) Winter paddy	14453	26.92	12503	25.41	17100	35.57
	(c) Autumn paddy	353	0.66	357	0.73	660	1.37
2.	Rape and Mustard	9223	17.18	10962	22.28	11125	23.14
3.	Wheat	1250	2.33	3120	6.34	915	1.90
4.	Black gram	1968	3.67	1650	3.35	1292	2.69
5.	Peas	1580	2.94	808	1.64	1077	2.24
6.	Potato	1574	2.93	1508	3.06	1518	3.16
7.	Mung	196	0.37	144	0.29	232	0.48
8.	Lentil	320	0.60	580	1.18	355	0.74
9.	Others	13160	24.51	7912	16.08	5160	10.73
	Total	53689	100.00	49205	100.00	48080	100.00

Source: SDO, Agriculture, Majuli, Garamur.

Production of Certain Crops Decreasing

The above table gives a picture of decreasing volume of production of certain indigenous crops in Majuli. Among them one important crop is mustard which is also the major cash crop there. As we have stated, in the pre-colonial days peasants produced this crop in large amounts to meet their needs of edible oil for the whole year. A part of the collection was also exchanged for other essential items for meeting the need of the family.

Production of mustard crop has now decreased to a significant extent. This is evidenced by the official records also as shown in the table IV below. This is due mainly to the scarcity of land suitable for this crop on one hand, and the loss of fertility of the soil on the other. To this may be added the age-old method of cultivation without much improvement in the technological aspects. The same age-old appliances and techniques are still in use barring a few cases where only the rich use fertilizer and tractors. Thus, when asked, Sri Boparam Nath, a poor cultivator from the Puranibari village, told the present investigator that he could not collect enough money to purchase fertilizer, nor he had enough capital tools to use in cultivation. Similarly, Jabar Deori, of the Majar Deori village under Cherepai Gaon Panchayat, who cultivates mustard in 4 *bigha* of land, has neither modern machinery nor he can afford to use chemical fertilizer. But, Kalkiran Deori of the same village uses both tractor and fertilizer. On an average, however, more than 95 per cent of the surveyed households of the village still use traditional technology and do not use chemical fertilizer. One important aspect in this regard is that extensive embankments preventing river flood from submerging the lands as we have mentioned above, have significantly reduced the fertility of the soil in recent decades. Naturally, the yellow-globe-picture of the island during November-December in the past has now become a nostalgic memory.

Table 3.4: Decrease of Production of Certain Crops during 1991-2004

	1991-1992 in Matric ton	2003-2004 in Matric ton	Decrease in the Volume of production	Rate of decrease %
Sugarcane	15,22,000	9,81,0005	41,000	35.54
Jute	8,66,000	6,65,000	20,1000	23.21
Wheat	1,05,000	73,000	32,000	30.47
Oil seed	1,69,000	1,52,000	17,000	10.05
Mustard	1,58,000	1,30,000	28,000	17.72

Source: Staff Reporter, *Dainik Janambhumi*, July 10, Sunday, 2005.

According to an estimation made by the Agriculture Department in Majuli, there were 23666 peasants of different categories in 1991 classified on the basis of possession of landed property. Accordingly, there were 962 marginal farmers, while the rest were above that category. The average land-holding per farmer was 9.95 *bigha**. The Department has also traced out the problems and constraints faced by agriculture in Majuli. Thus it has pointed out the following problems:

Problems

1. Frequent occurrence of flood.
2. Erosion.
3. Silt/sand deposition in the field.
4. Water stagnation after flood.
5. Heavy pest/diseases infestation after flood.
6. UFRA diseases in *bao* paddy field.
7. Inadequate supply of seed and fertilizers in time.

8. Lack of irrigation facilities.
9. Adoption of new technology of production by the farmers.
10. Poverty of the farmers.
11. Lack of proper credit facilities to the willing farmers.
12. Lack of planting materials for horticulture development.

Constraints

1. Inadequate market facility.
2. Poor transport and communication facilities.
3. Inadequate agricultural service facilities.
4. Lack of basic infrastructure facilities.

Source: SDO, Agriculture, Majuli, Garamur.

Fertiliser

There is no record of use of any sort of fertilizer in agriculture in early times, except perhaps cow-dung.[52] This was more so in case of Majuli where natural fertility of the soil was abundant due to alluvium deposited during flood which was once a regular phenomenon in the island. Even in other parts of Assam also, additional fertilizer was almost unnecessary. Hiuen Tsang, the Chinese pilgrim who, visiting early Assam (Kamarupa) during the reign of king Bhaskaravarvaman (c.594-650 A.D.), stated that the climate of the land was moist and lands were fertile and crops grew abundantly.[53] In the mid-16th century, Shihabuddin Talish, the Mughal official historian, has recorded that its soil is fertile and whatever they sow, or plant grew well. The chief crop of the country was rice.[54] Similarly, all early British records testify to its fertile character. John M'Cosh, for example, has observed in 1837 that though "the country is at all generally swampy, and intersected with half-filled channels and stagnant lakes, yet in the dry season it is very susceptible of cultivation, and amply repays any labour and expence bestowed upon it by producing abundant crops."[55] Similarly, William Robinson has recorded: "The alluvial deposits of the Brahmaputra and of its tributary streams may be considered as another, and the third, great general division of lands in Assam. These lands are very extensive, especially so along the channel of the great river, and are of great variety of fertility and elevation, from the vast churs of pure sand subject to annual inundations, to the great islands….."[56] The same kind of fertility of the mainland Majuli was there till a few decades ago when not much encompassing of the island by man-made embankment was done to prevent the natural washing by flood. Even now, said Padmeswar Pegu, Professor of Jengraimukh College, fields lying outside the embankments on the northern part of Majuli but to the south of the Suvansiri river are as fertile as it were centuries back. Similar is the answer of Shri Aputi Rajkhowa of the Madhuur Gaon who has all of his cultivable lands outside the Kamalabari-Garamur-Jengraimukh-Haladhibari road-cum-embankment towards Suvansiri. Sri Rajkhowa, who is a marginal cultivator, said that he is completely dependent on this part of his land alone as the other parts of his cultivable lands lying inside the embankment and devoid of natural inundation, are not yielding much to him.

Decrease in fertility of the soil and, against it, the need to produce more to meet the growing demands of the increasing population accompanied by publicity about the use of chemical fertilizers have, of late, made some peasants support the utility of fertilizer use to gather more crop. This is not only known from our investigations in the model villages, but is also reflected in the State Government records. An illustration from the Mohkhuti village corroborated by another from the village Tataya in upper Majuli can be placed here for illustration. When asked about the use of fertilizer, Khageswar Nath from the Mohkhuti village under Garamur Gaon Panchayat, replied that he managed to use a tractor to plough his field and used fertilizer in order to produce enough from his small plot of land to meet the need of his large family. Similarly, Bhogram Saikia of Tataya village under Rawanapar Gaon Panchayat, uses chemical fertilizer in his six *bigha* plot to produce enough to meet the demand of his family. Below, we have placed the record about the use of chemical fertilizer in Majuli during the decade 1994-2003 as supplied by the Office of the SDO, Agriculture, Majuli Sub-Division.

Table 3.5: Record of Fertiliser Consumption in Majuli—1994-2003

Year	Fertilizers Used			
	Urea (in qntl.)	SSP (in qntl.)	MOP (in qntl.)	DAP (in qntl.)
1994-95	36.7	52.5	10.00	17.00
1995-96	38.6	54.3	10.8	18.9
1996-97	40.75	59.5	12.8	22.4
1997-98	44.25	66.3	15.7	25.15
1998-99	60.30	89.6	19.65	36.8
1999-00	94.70	101.6	23.85	44.3
2000-01	98.00	116.8	29.35	52.1
2001-02	106.5	120.00	31.00	55.5
2002-03	120.2	130.00	46.35	72.6
2003-04	140.00	150.00	65.00	80.00

The above table shows that consumption of fertilizers in Majuli is a late development, but its popularity has been slowly increasing since at least the last two decades. Field survey shows this trend, but not to the extent as indicated in the table supplied by the Agriculture Department. It has been found during our field investigation that villagers under our survey are still not much accustomed to the use of chemical fertilizers, and more than 95 per cent of the cultivators still go without fertilizers and modern technology. Chemical fertilizer and machine technologies are available to those only who could afford to purchase and/or maintain them.

CRAFT AND INDUSTRIES

Besides agriculture there are certain other aspects of the economic life of the people of the island. Among these may be included certain crafts, such as sericulture, weaving, gold washing in medieval times, pottery, wood and bamboo work, poultry farming, etc. Sericulture includes production of Assam *pat* (mulberry silk), *eri* and *muga*. While production of mulberry silk has been a known craft ever since in Majuli among the people of the Katani/ Yogi or the Nath caste inhabiting the island, *eri* has been extensively produced almost by all people irrespective of caste affiliations although it is more popular among the Misings at present. Villages like Puranibari, Balichapori, Baruabari, Meruwabari, Chengelibari, Baraguri, Barbam, Rangachahi, Nagaon, Pahumara, Sonariati, Phulani Gatiyala are some of the thickly populated villages of those people who engage in production of mulberry silk. However, production of mulberry has been swiftly declining during the post-independence period due mainly to the fact that rearing of mulberry worm was treated in the society as one of the lowest of the professions; and educated generations accustomed with the process of status-mobility do not prefer to go for it now. When asked, Ms. Labanya Nath of the Sonariati village replied that she and her villagers do not now prefer that job as it is regarded as the profession of the low castes. It should, however, be noted that in the middle ages *eri* cloth was produced by almost all families, and it was used by the common Assamese people to meet their requirements of warm cloths for the winter. Nowadays *eri* is a popular culture among the Misings of Jengraimukh and its neighbouring villages; and very beautiful *eri* cloths are produced in their family looms. *Eri* cloths produced in Jengraimukh and in Dhakuakhana on the Lakhimpur side, are known for their quality and design all through the state. *Eri* cloths from Majuli are also exported. Weaving of the cotton cloth was once popular among all sections of the people. It was the system during the Ahom rule that every family should produce its requirements of cloth at its own loom, which every family used to have one set at least. It is stated that every woman was expert in weaving, and it was very difficult for a girl to be married if she did not know the art of weaving.[57] This is, however, not the case today. Most girls today have no family loom, and therefore, do not know how to weave. Growth of markets and availability of varieties of cloths at cheaper rates, and supply of money at the hands of the affluent class are some of the reasons for the decline of the *pa̱t* and the *eri* industry. Basavi Pegu of Kumarbari Lakhimi village in Jengraimukh and Kadami Nath of Puranibari village replied to our quaries that both *eri* and *pa̱t* are not economically profitable in face of growing market supply of machine-made items. This explains how in the face of the emergence of modern technology and market economy any medieval craft is bound to give way to all that is modern and scientific.

FIG. 3.4: EXCAVATING POTTER'S SOIL ON REVER-BANK

Of the traditional crafts still practised in Majuli, pottery is the most significant. People expert in the vocation of making pottery called *Kumar* is a class of the old residents of the Majuli island. They inhabit the southeastern part of the island on the bank of the Brahmaputra where soil suitable for making pottery is available about 20ft. below the surface of the river bank. Both men and women, even the children, are engaged in the craft. During our field investigation it was found that children instead of going to the school were engaged in the process of making pottery. It was stated during investigation that the craft had fallen to disrepute and very small margin of profit was derived nowadays as there were certain factors which had decreased its importance in the society. Discovery and use of various systems of preservation of milk for which pots of different shapes and sizes were once used, use of electricity replacing oil-lamps of medieval types in both religious establishments and houses, and above all, its unprofitable nature[58] have lessened the importance of the pottery as a craft in the rural Majuli. Besides, the continuous erosion of the banks of the Brahmaputra on the southeastern side of the island, and making of the potters responsible for that,[59] is one of the major causes for its decline. During our field investigation it was also found that most of the potter villages located on the bank of the Brahmaputra had, by that time, shifted to other places of the state.[60]

Wood, bamboo and cane works are popular in the island. During the monarchical days, Majuli was full of forests with valuable timbers, cane and bamboo. Even today, Majuli can be called a land of the bamboos with lines of grooves surrounding the villages. British records say that the entire island was made beautiful by the thickly grown cane bushes all around.[61] There were timbers *like karai, gomari, ajar, simalu, uriam, autenga, maj* and so forth. Each of these woods was used for some of the very specific purposes, such as building of houses, making of boats, and furniture and so on. The wood called *ajar*, still found in Majuli, although not in abundance, was used for making boats. There were several factories for making boats called *naosal* in the island of which those of Salmara, Saraibari and Auniati were very famous.[62] Making of boats from the *ajar* wood is still practised, and is a popular craft in Majuli, and a section of the people in Salmara and Auniati still earn their bread by making boat and selling them. There are records to the effect that all *Satradhikaras* of Majuli had their special boats made for the purpose of travel built by the expert craftsmen of the Satras. We have reference to the fact that Hemchandradeva Goswami of Auniati Satra built a *pinish* (*panchoi*) boat with unique design and craftsmanship for his personal tour.[63] The American Christian Baptist missionaries have recorded that such a boat could be as large as 100 feet in length.[64] It is a culture of the people in the island to have one boat in each family, for a family without a boat is sure to be in trouble during the flood seasons. Bamboo is largely used in building houses, and for making furniture and other domestic appliances. They have different types, such as *jati*, *makal* and *bhaluka*. *Makal* and *bhaluka* of the short variety well-known for their thorny and thick bushes (*jatiya*) are extensively grown in Majuli used normally to form defense walls against the strong currents of flood, and often, wind. Bambo is also used for making masks which is a known craft in the Chamaguri Satra[65]. Some people in every village are expert in making bamboo appliances.

FIG. 3.5: SILVER TRAY DONATED BY KING JAYADHVAJ SINGHA TO GARAMUR SATRA

They also sell them in the villages or in the markets and earn some money. It is interesting that some castes are incapable of or inefficient in making bamboo appliances and wood works. Like pottery or mulberry silk other crafts also have some caste-relations. For example, the Brahmins are habitually unaccustomed to physical work, while the Kaivartas put more emphasis on fishing than on other crafts.

Mask-making is a well-known craft in the Satras of Majuli, more particularly at the Chamaguri Satra. Locally available materials like bamboo and varieties of colours prepared by the craftsmen are used to make various masks for the purposes of using in the *bhaonas*, *Ras* festival, and other religious occasions. There were some huge masks which needed more than one person to handle in the stage or in the *namghar*. Painting is a part of the mask making craft. Animal and human figures of different forms and colours are skillfully depicted on the masks to make them attractive. Mask making is a hereditary craft in the family of the *Satradhikara* of the Chamaguri Satra. The present *Satradhikara* Koshakanta Goswami is a recipient of the *Sangeet Natak Academy Award* for his proficiency in the art.[66] In the same way, his cousin Hem Chandra Goswami is a well-known mask artist of high calibre. The design and art of the main entrance gate of the Garamur Satra (see illustration) is an example of his work. Mask making is also an economically profitable craft. Hem Chandra Goswami has stated that he earns a good amount of money through his craft.

Satras are often the centres of cane work also. The Auniati and the Kamalabari Satra are famous for making cane-fan beautifully embroidered with floral design made in what they call as *makhmal* cloth. An Auniati-made embroidered cane fan is not only able to fetch as much as Rs.300.00-500.00 per piece in the local markets, but they also form items of export and gifts. When asked about this craft, Khagendra Nath Lekharu, the *Majindar* or the record keeper of Auniati Satra, has told us that an inmate can make as many as 20-30 such fans in a season, and by selling them he can earn, on an average, Rs.10,000.00 per annum.

Besides fan, various other items of cane were made in the past. Important ones were *japa, pera, sarai, saja, pola, khaloi* and others. These are now gone crafts, of course. Opening of lands for settlement and cultivation by cutting down the jungles and cane-bushes leading to the scarcity of the raw material, and use of substitutes available in the markets at lesser price, have made them crafts of the past. Similarly, there are villages of the *Patiyas*, a caste that once was engaged in making mat of a kind of reed called *patidoi/gogol* that grow in the swamps. The craft of making mat from the *gogol* is now dead.

Fishing and selling fish is an important economic activity in the island since early times. Being endowed with vast varieties of ponds and *bils,* it is a natural breeding ground of fishes. Its rivers, swamps and ponds were once full of varieties of fish. In early times, Majuli was a cluster of island's and numerous dead river channels, ponds and marshes. But, as has been stated already, most of these ponds, marshes and river channels are now dead and have been either converted to cultivating fields or have become shallow due to various reasons.[67] But still, there are a number of these to encourage a section of the people to take fishing as a vocation. Naturally, all people except the *Satradhikara*s, who, as a matter of custom, are necessarily vegetarian,[68] are fond of eating fish. The Kaivartas were, and still are, the only major community of people who catch and sell fish. There were several methods of catching fish, the most popular being by using nets and various kinds of bamboo implements like *pala, jakoi, gui, pauri, elengi, khuki, chepa, pacha,* and so forth. Various kinds of nets have been in use since at least the late 19th and early 20th century when the Bengali fishermen, particularly those from erstwhile East Bengal, used to pour into the island and engage in fishing.

Selling of fish was once entirely at the hands of the Kaivartas although in recent years it has spread among some of the other communities also, particularly, to the Misings. In earlier times, there were two classes of fish traders—small trader called *pohari*, and *bepari* and big trader called *vishaya* (lessee). *Poharis* were women traders who brought fishes to the villages inhabited by high caste people, and exchanged them in retail for

FIG. 3.6: *MUKHA* (MASK) OF RAVAN CHAMAGURI SATRA

FIG. 3.7: *MUKHA* (MASK)

FIG. 3.8: *DABA* (DRUM)

rice or vegetables or fuel woods. Their profession was treated as inferior in the villages, and such women were addressed as *bai,* i.e. a sister. As we have mentioned elsewhere,[69] *poharis* played significant role in the inter-village relationship and in the system of communication in the village societies by carrying information from one village to another. The *pohari* system has now sharply declined in the society. *Beparis* are of two classes—small *bepari* and big *bepari* who sell fish in the villages or in the market places for money. In the true sense of the term, the *beparis* have replaced the *poharis* from the market, a fact, which indicates that money market has replaced the barter, men have replaced women, and a sense of dignity has slowly replaced ridicule. Small traders (*beparis*) either catch fish by themselves or buy from big traders and then sell in the local markets for retail.

When going to fishing in the river, the life of a fisherman is always at risk, particularly in the summer season. Sometimes the whole day and the night is spent without any catch. In such cases the fisherman's family has to remain without the day's meal as their food depends on the sale of the catch. Sanjoy Ghose has given a vivid description about small fishermen's trade and fortune in Majuli as follows:

> The fish in the morning provides for the evening meal after it is sold in the market. If the catch is good, people will cycle down to Kamalabari, where the prices are the best. If not, they will sometimes go to Garamur, and sometimes to the Rangashahi market, both about five kilometres away. The family I was staying with was not involved in '*pohari*', or barter, which even among the Scheduled Caste is considered an inferior vocation. *Pohari* families exchange the fish for vegetables, rice and other commodities. I tried to understand why this was considered so inferior—after all, did not the money from the sale of fish serve exactly the same purpose ? The answer was surprising and complex. There was nothing inferior in act of exchange—this was an accepted pattern amongst themselves. What was galling was having to go to houses of higher caste people (referred to here as the 'general caste', to differentiate them from the tribals and the post-Mandal other backward castes), and there not be allowed access, not be treated with respect, and to have to do all sorts of other odd jobs in the household—like cleaning the house, etc.[70]

Catching and selling of fish, i.e. fishing as a profession has taken a new turn in the last few decades. Many of the *bils* earlier used for fishing are now dead and have got converted into either shallow water pond, or agricultural fields; and almost all the rest have been brought under the revenue system. Consequently, poor fishermen have to depend on the *vishayas* who have taken it from the Government against payment of revenue, and pay for catching fish. This necessitates him to directly go to the market in stead of going to the villages as they earlier did, and sell his share with some amount of profit; and there are customers who have both money and the habit of purchasing them. Thus a confirmed selling class and a confirmed buying class consisting of the job-holders from both inside and outside the island have been slowly emerging. Haren Hazarika of the Kharjanpar Gaon near Garamur has said that he has about 5 *bighas* of land; but he lends it to others on share-cropping basis. As against this he sells fish both at the market and at the village to certain specified families who are his permanent customers. With the profit he thus earns, Hazarika manages his four children's education and maintains his family. One interesting aspect in this connection is that all Government officers going from outside and having the habit of buying fish at comparatively higher rates of prices, have largely contributed to the growth of fish markets in Majuli. The result is that the man who would have earlier exchanged a fish for rice, or would have consumed it at home otherwise, now readily avails himself of the market opportunity to sell it and get some money. Kanpai Das of Natun Kamalabari village about eight kilometers away from Garamur, the headquarters of the Majuli sub-division, is a small fish trader; and he sells even a small quantity of fish in the market or at somebody's house in order to earn his daily expenses. When asked, he said "I can normally collect one or two kilograms of fish from the neighbouring *bils* controlled by certain *vishayas*, and sell them either at Garamur or at Sonariati market. Even a small fish weighing ½ or 1/4th of a kilogram I would be taking to the market for I need money to run the family. We have scarcely any opportunity to eat a good fish at home." Similar is the answer of other *beparis* like Bheluwa, Mahendra and Nilamani of the same village. Thus, the two facts, scarcity of fish and availability of market facility, have led to commercialization of the entire social relationship which, at least half a century ago, was understood in terms of intimate contact between two social groups. And therefore, Majuli is now neither known for abundance of fish nor for providing enough fish to the peasant community who do not have sufficient money power to buy them, or who have now no right to fish in the revenue-paying rivers or *bils*. Gradual ecological change, development of a money economy, and growth of a class of confirmed fish buyers have been responsible for all this change.

It is since a long time past that Jorhat has been an attractive market for the big traders from Majuli. Kan Das, one of such a big traders from Natun Kamalabari village, said, "We collect fish from small traders at Majuli and export them to Jorhat where our agents receive and sell them in the markets. Normally we send the baskets of fishes in the morning ferry from Majuli to Jorhat so that the whole day is at our hand to handle the business of the fishes. Only those fishes which we cannot export to Jorhat due to certain unexpected developments, such as lack of ferry due to a *bandh* call, we sell at Majuli. In that case we lose certain amount of profit as the market prices here are lower than those in Jorhat." Jorhat market is a significant factor in controlling the fish markets at Majuli. It is interesting that Majuli markets are often full of imported (*chalani*) fishes from outside to meet the requirements of the people. In the daily markets at Garamur and Kamalabari one is sure to see baskets of such fishes displayed for local buyers who inherit a tradition of abundance of 'local' fishes!

Fishing as a vocation has now taken a new significance as it has also spread to the hands of communities other than the Kaivartas, although the latter still hold the major share. Change of men's outlook towards traditional communal crafts and professions, educational growth and economic need, and revenue and leasing system of the *bils* and the rivers to the competitive bidders have slowly opened the border of fish trade from the hands of the Kaivartas to the members of other communities.

It is possible that the declaration of Kamaldeva Goswami (1904 1922), *Satradhikara* of Auniati Satra, that the Kaivartas could be uplifted to higher social status only if they sell fish at water,[71] must have some impact on the overall psychology of the society who perhaps bagan to think that selling of fish at water to be dignified. As a result, many people now bid for taking lease of *bils* and ponds or rivers, and trade in fish indirectly. The process possibly began immediately after his declaration, for it is stated that the Congress volunteers during the Non-Cooperation and subsequent phases of the freedom struggle used to sing a slogan in Majuli that was directed to prevent the *Vishayas* to bid for fishing in the *bils* and the rivers.[72] Trade in fish through indirect procedure is now popular among some members of the new generation. Thus, Ranjit Nath of Puranibari Gaon, an M.A. in Sociology from Dibrugarh University, is such a bidder who takes the *Yogi Ghuli* in lease and trades with fishermen on 50 : 50 basis. Ranjit is not the only such fish trader, there are many others who belong to different castes of higher social status. Poultry and pig farming, however, is still confined to the Mising community alone as it is considered an untouchable business in the orthodox circle. But, it is not improbable that poultry farming too would be soon spreading to the educated generation breaking the age-old tradition of its confinement to the tribes alone.

FIG. 3.9: TOWNSHIP AT GARAMUR

FIG. 3.10: YOUNG GRADUATES PURSUING TRADE IN FISH

FIG. 3.11: MAKING POTTERY IN A KUMAR FAMILY

LABOUR

There is no such class as could be called as 'labour class' in Majuli. Here every one is a labourer of one's own family. According to a recent estimation, about 40 per cent population of the island is reportedly of workers of which about 80 per cent engage in cultivation.[72(a)] In the middle ages people of rank used to have some slaves (*da̲s*/*da̲si*), servants (*cha̲kar*), or bondsmen (*bandha̲* or *bandhayowa*).[73] In the Satras are found a class of inmates called *a̲ldhara̲* who is a kind of personal labour attached to the *adhika̲ra* for life.[74] *Pa̲chanis* are also attached to the establishment of the *Satra̲dhika̲ra* whom the latter engage to get some of his personal works done.[75] In the villages, life was based on community codes in early times; every one helping the other in building houses, making roads, building *pandals*, and in reaping, harvesting and so forth. They all worked for the village in common (*haj kara̲*) and served the need of their common prayer halls (*na̲mghars*). There was no system of hired labour, nor any body offered to work for a wage. W.W. Hunter has stated that in 1871-1872 here in upper Assam waiting for the whole day for a person offering for doing labour against wage would go fruitless. No body here offers to work for daily wage.[76] Abundance of lands and better economic conditions prevent them from doing works for wage. This habit of the people is still there; and till a few decades ago, physical labour was done in Majuli for wage by the labourers from Bihar or immigrants from East Bengal.[76(a)] They were the people who excavated tanks, built roads, caught fishes through net and so forth. But, this has been slowly changed; and due to shortage of land and growth of population and consequent economic pressure, men now would not hesitate to labour for wage although it is too low. In this connection a new trend has arisen recently in Majuli. In our investigation it was found that almost the entire labour force in the island—truck and taxi drivers, wage earners, and the like, is now supplied by the Misings. A good number of the rickshaw pullers in nearby Jorhat town also belong to this community, and are from Majuli. Sampol Nara of Kalitapar Mising village, has stated that about fifteen boys from his village are now engaged in different wage-earning works at Jorhat. It is due to their joining such jobs that the number of Bihari labourers called *nuniya* is now sharply declining in Majuli. Even the technical labourers engaged in building houses are mostly from among the Misings. It is not improbable that they will soon govern and control the labour market of the island. The comparatively less pressure of the foreign nationals (Bangladeshis) on Majuli is to be explained in the light of this development, said Gunamani Nath, Vice Principal, Garamur Pitambardeva Goswami College, Majuli. Even for building the embankments and roads which was done by the Biharis before, Mising labour force has now become indispensable. "Without them no embankment building is possible at Majuli now", said Dilip Bhuyan, a first class contractor from Garamur. Even agriculture, which was once the business of all the members of a family, has now been done in the employed circles, by the share-croppers or by labourers on wage.

There are, of course, domestic labourers in the rich or affluent families; and wage earners who work for daily wage. Young boys and girls are sometimes mortgaged for money on monthly payment basis. It was a regular feature in the society of Majuli till a few decades ago. One may feel a distant echo of the old slavery system that was practised in the society of Assam in the middle ages. The abolition of *dola* system by Pitambardeva Goswami, the *Satradhikara* of Garamur Satra, in 1921, considering it as a remnant of the feudal system of the middle ages, must have an impact on the gradual eradication of the domestic servant system in the society. The universalisation of education of children of both sexes and all classes too must have struck a strong blow to the system.

EMPLOYMENT AS OCCUPATION

Majuli has no industry as such, nor any employment generating source. The only significant sector other than agriculture where the maximum number of the educated youths are engaged, is teaching in schools and colleges. According to the office of the Deputy Inspector of Schools (DI) of Majuli there were in 2005, 496 Lower Primary Schools, 108 ME Schools and MV Schools, 87 High English Schools, 5 Higher Secondary Schools, and 2 Junior Colleges and 4 Degree Colleges besides 1 Basic Training Centre for teacher training. While a small part of the schools are financed by the State Government on 'deficit system,' the rest run on their own or on non-recurring ad-hoc grants. In the context of severe unemployment problems, establishing a school and engaging oneself therein as teacher is a kind of lease to the life of an ordinary graduate in Majuli now. This has therefore become a normal phenomenon in the island. Noting this aspect of education and employment in Majuli, Sanjay Ghose has given a very interesting account as follows:

> The other mystery about schooling in Majuli (and I suppose all over the state) is the profusion of 'venture' schools. Started by a couple of enterprising graduates from the village, the way the programme works in theory is very different from the way that it finally plays itself out in

the field. A concerned village group gets together and donates land for setting up of a school. The entire community contributes the labour to build the school, and the teachers are employed for free, as volunteers. As and when the school gets recognized (provincialised) by the government, the teachers are entitled to salaries, and the students to some basic facilities.... The motivation of the boys who teach is not merely social service, but the clear idea of getting a 'government' job once the school gets recognized."[77]

In the present economic system in Majuli school teachers occupy a respectable place—a section of them serving under deficit system of schools being comparatively affluent. They have a better living condition and are able to give higher and professional or technical education to their children.

There are three categories of people in the society of the island who possess monetary strength—school and college teachers, service holders and contractors. It is often said that Majuli is the 'heaven of the contractors.' Thus with money and social dignity teachers are the leaders of the society; and almost all politicians in the island are teachers in schools or colleges, at present or in the past. With money and power, contractors are the most powerful segment in the socio-political network. It has already been noted that caste is a significant factor in understanding the economy of the people in the island. Most of the service holders are from among the Kalitas, Brahmins and the Koches. A good part of them are also from among the educated Misings. But this is not the case with the Scheduled Castes or other such backward communities. For example, data collected from the village Kharjanpar Kalvarta Gaon, one of the advanced villages belonging to the Kaivarta community in Majuli, revels that out of about 100 families inhabiting the village, almost 100 per cent are engaged in small trade in fish; and only a few are engaged in employment belonging to the lower earning group. It was reported that in that year (2005), out of 11 employed in the Kharjanpar village, 9 were 4th grade employees, while 2 belonged to the 3rd grade.[78] This scenario also applies to many other villages peopled by Scheduled Caste and/or Scheduled Tribe and other backward communities. Similarly, very few contractors are from among the lower echelons in the society except possibly one or two from among the affluent families of the Kaivartas.

At the absence of different avenues of vocation, unemployment is a rising problem in Majuli for both educated and uneducated youths. The following data supplied by the Employment Exchange Office at Majuli as recorded in June, 2005, reveals the unemployment scenario of the island:

Total Unemployed Registered Candidates:

Scheduled Caste	:	**1261**
Male	:	985
Female	:	276
Scheduled Tribe	:	**5822**
Male	:	3749
Female	:	2073
OBC	:	**2978**
Male	:	2038
Female	:	940

Table 3.7: List of Educated Unemployed in Majuli (*Excluding the Post Graduate Degree Holders*), 2005-2006

Sl No.	Education Standard	Male	Female	Total
1.	HSLC	1056	742	1798
2.	HSSLC	3615	1357	4972
3.	B. A.	1422	363	1785
4.	B. Sc.	204	66	270
5.	B. Com.	28	nil	28
6.	Diploma Holder (ITI)	23	7	30
7.	Others (Steno)	25	11	36

In our household surveys it was noted how employment rate was horribly low in the villages, particularly among women. The following table shows women's employment percentage in Majuli. This table also shows that even the overall percentage of employment is not satisfactory at all.

Table 3.8: Employment Rate in Majuli, 2005

Sl No.	Name of the Village	Number of Surveyed Population	Employment			Agriculture & traditional age	Business	Wage earner	% of employment per village
			M	F	Total				
1.	Na-Mati	36	1	nil	1	—	1	1	2.7
2.	Purani Mati	44	—	—	nil	—	3	2	0
3.	Barpamua	299	9	4	13	—	2	nil	4.34
4.	Chamaguri (Karatipar)	143	—	1	1	—	12	7	0.69
5.	Chaorekia	130	4	2	6	—	—	—	4.61
6.	Roumara	47	—	—	nil	—	—	—	0
7.	Salmara Kumargaon	162	5	3	8	—	29	—	4.93
8.	Sriram Deori	163	3	4	7	—	—	1	4.29

(*Contd.*)

(*Contd.*)

Sl No.	Name of the Village	Number of Surveyed Population	Employment M	Employment F	Employment Total	Agriculture & traditional age	Business	Wage earner	% of employment per village
9.	Sonowal Kachari	166	3	—	3	—	2	1	1.80
10.	Ujir Ati	55	2	5	7	—	—	—	12.72
11.	Ghuriya Gaon	46	2	0	2	—	4	—	4.34
12.	Major Deori	178	9	2	11	—	—	—	6.17
13.	Milanpur Bengali	88	5	1	6	—	9	2	6.81
14.	Puranibari	46	4	1	5	—	2	1	10.86
15.	Natun Deodiaati	77	6	0	5	—	2	—	7.79
16.	Sankopara	74	2	0	2	—	5	—	2.70
17.	Ahataguri Seraati	56	2	0	2	—	3	5	3.57
18.	Sriram Devottar Nepali	68	2	1	3	—	1	4	4.41
19.	Kumarbari Lakhimi	145	3	3	6	—	3	3	4.13
20.	Kaniajan	137	8	1	9	—	3	8	6.56
21.	Kamalpur Kamalabari	110	9	7	16	—	5	1	14.54
22.	Khallhamari	82	3	0	3	—	5	1	3.65
23.	Mohkhuti Bania	70	—	—	nil	—	3	2	0
24.	Natun Pohardiya	92	10	1	11	—	1	—	11.95
25.	Phutchang	89	3	0	3	—	2		3.37
26.	Gopalpur	82	4	1	5	—	5	—	6.09
27.	Tataya gaon	114	9	1	10	—	5	—	6.77
28.	Dakhinpat Kaivarta	163	1	0	1	—	5	—	0.61
29.	Dhapak Gaon	140	12	2	14	—	1	1	10.00
30.	Dolkhowa	59	3	1	4	—	2	—	6.77
31.	Namani Jakaibowa	99	3	0	3	—	—	3	3.03
32.	Thakurbari Sensowa	85	5	0	5	—	3	3	5.88
33.	Barhola Muslim	90	—	—	nil		12	7	0
	Total villages	**3435**	**132**	**41**	**172**	—	**130**	**53**	**5.00**

The above table shows that only 5 per cent educated people are employed in different jobs, while 3.78 per cent are engaged in business, and 1.54 per cent in wage earning works, and the rest in agriculture and community profession. Among women only 1.19 per cent are employed. Thus about 89 per cent people in Majuli solely depends on agriculture and traditional caste-professions whereas the state rate of dependents on agriculture is only 65 per cent.[78(a)]

DEVELOPMENT OF COMMUNICATION SYSTEM

Majuli is connected with Jorhat, the District Head Quarters, by ferry service through (1) Kamalabari-Neamati, (2) Sumoimari-Neamati, (3) Dakhinpat-Neamati, (4) Salmara-Neamati, and (5) Phulani-Neamati Ferry *Ghat* on the south. On the north, it is connected with Bihpuriya through Majuli-Bihpuriya Ferry *Ghat,* and with Lakhimpur town through Luhit *Ghat* near Garamur. The 27 mile long *Lakhimpur-Kamalabari Road* that connects Kamalabari with North Lakhimpur town across the Luhit and the Khabuli (a local name of the Suvansiri river) rivers, was built in the year 1885. It is recorded that the labour force derived from the prisoners (*kaidis*) kept at the Kamalabari jail was used to build the Majuli part of this road.[79] The island is connected with Dhakuakhana on the northeast by an embankment built by the E & D Department of Assam Government across the Kherkatiya Suti in 1979, leading to a man-made reconfiguration of its topographic peculiarity.

In the 19th century there was only one road worth the name connecting the ferry *ghat* across Kamalabari and Garamur.[80] The *District Gazeetteer* has recorded that in 1903-04, there were 237 miles of unmetalled road throughout Sibsagar district maintained by the Public Works Department, and 705 miles maintained by the Local Boards.[81] Road and communication system, however, improved along with the growth of administrative networks and urban growth in the early 20th century. At present, inside the island there are PWD Roads running from east to west—one along the northern and the other along the southern parts. The first is called *Kamalabari-Jengraimukh-Haladhibari Road*, built in the year 1957, and the second is called *Majuli Road.* It was built in the year 1954 from Salmara in the east to Badatighat in the northwest.[82] This was the first ever PWD Road built in Majuli. Prior to this all communication roads were under the Local Boards. The *Haladhibari-Bechamara Embankment* (*mathauri*) of about 17 miles in length had been built two years before, in 1952. According to the records supplied by the Public Works Department in 2005, inside the island there are about 1236 kilometers of PWD road connecting different places of which about 20 kilometers are only made *pakka*.[83] Most *bils*, dead river channels and swamps consequent upon breaking of dyke or roads during floods, are spanned by bamboo and wooden bridges. Thus the Tuni river, the only river inside Majuli, was spanned by a bamboo bridge till at least 1954 near the present (Kamalabari) *Thana*, and a boat-man used to ferry a part of the passengers in small boat across the river. The boat station on the river was called *Thana Ghat*. This was the means of communication across the river on the major road connecting Lakhimpur, Garamur, *Badati Ghat* and Kamalabari with the ferry *ghat* at the Brahmaputra. The bamboo bridge over the Tuni river was replaced by a wooden bridge built in the year 1954.[84] Similar provisions were there over all the river channels and ponds falling on the communication ways. As an alternative to this system seasonal boat services, in some of the cases during rainy seasons, were also provided, a system which is still there at *Dariya Ghat* (at *Dariya Dubi*) on the *Kamalabari-Garamur Road*, and at Chamaguri over the dead channel of the Tuni river near Rawnapara in the absence of bridges.[85]

In earlier times boats were the major means of transport in Majuli during the season of flood, and every family had its own boat made by itself from particular classes of tree-trunks locally available. John M'Cosh has stated that Assamese families used to have boats like utensils of everyday use.[86] This was more appropriate in case of Majuli. For the *Satradhikara*s who form the highest class in the island, there were *panchoi* boat for long travel, and palanquin called *dola* borne by human beings for short distance travel. This system of travel was in vogue till the twenties of the last century. But, as a result of the nationalist movement, Pitambardeva Goswami of Garamur Satra, and following him, all others of his class, abandoned it.[87]

Common people used to travel on foot during winter and by boat during summer seasons to visit neighbouring villages and relatives whose villages lay at a day's distance.[88] It is not known whether the embankments built during the Ahom rule, such as the *Meragarh*, or the *Dhuwachela Garh*, were ever used as communication road. The *Gazetteer* of Allen *et. al.* has, however, very clearly maintained that old embankments built by the *paik* labourers during the Ahom rule were used as travel road; and the one lying on the north of the Brahmaputra at Majuli was used for that purpose.[89] During the colonial rule, there were very few roads built by the Local Boards; all other places outside the periphery of these roads were full of jungles, and men used to travel through small jungle-covered foot-ways resembling the natural corridors which, during summer, became submerged with water. Tarun Chandra Pamegam, while narrating his experience in the thirties of the last century, has stated that "during that time there was no proper road and communication systems in Majuli. One was to go from one place to another through some narrow foot-ways lying amidst the jungles. We had to travel on foot a distance of four miles

FIG. 3.12: THE WAY MAN TRAVELS TO JORHAT FROM MAJULI ACROSS THE BRAHAMAPUTRA

FIG. 3.13: A VILLAGE BAMBOO BRIDGE IN JAJULI

FIG. 3.14: THE WOODEN BRIDGE ON THE RIVER TUNI

to the school from our village through such a wild road. Not to speak of the other wild animals, even tigers sometimes appeared on the roads."[90] But on the roads, bullock carts, elephants, horses and bicycles were in use since the British times. Possessing an elephant or a bicycle was, however, very rare, for common people did not have the ability to buy these. Most of the old generation people now remember with pleasure their excitements when they first saw motor-bikes (they called *dhapdhapi*) running on a Majuli road in the early fifties of the last century.

Building of roads and embankments in the post-Independence period led to introduction of buses, lorries and jeeps, and finally, cars and motor bikes. The first ever bus service was introduced by one Bharat Saikia of Kamalabari. His Tata make small bus introduced in the sixties ran between Haladhibari and Kamalabari Ferry Ghat.[91] The ASTC bus service was introduced as late as 1986 when Lalit Rajkhowa, the then PWD Minister of Assam, provided with two red coloured ASTC trade marked buses to run on the same route. One of those buses is still in service. Today there are even taxies, besides personal vehicles, used for travel within the island.

Postal service was introduced in Majuli in the year 1897 along with the establishment of a Post Office at Dakhinpat and another at Auniati. In 1906 the second Post Office was established at Kamalabari. After a long time, in the year 1953 wireless communication system was introduced in Majuli through the Police Station which was established at Kamalabari in 1929.[92] Telephone service was started in 1994-95. There were five telephone exchanges in Majuli during that year. They were Kamalabari, Garamur, Phulani, Jengraimukh and Nayabazar Exchanges. Today Majuli is under the *Cell-One* and reliance mobile networks. Similarly, electricity was introduced in Majuli in mid seventies. At present (2006), almost all villages are covered by electricity connection, although the power supply is very insufficient.

Majuli had medieval system of communication net-work till at least the time of Independence. But the post-Independence period saw the gradual development of the road and communication systems. The establishment of the Post Offices and the Department of Public Works, Government of Assam, had brought about a significant change in the communication system of the island. This, however, did not exceedingly increase the speed of its development. It had to wait till the eighties of the last century to see more other developments in the communication systems, at least in the field of its communication with the other parts of the state.

Growth of communication network has broken the age-old tradition of its aloofness from the rest of the world, and this contact, while contributing towards the island's economic growth, exerts significant impact on its cultural heritage as well.

URBAN GROWTH AND EMERGENCE OF NEW TRENDS IN ECONOMY

Majuli was an isolated place with much more isolated villages. Even till the beginning of the 20th century, most parts of the island were covered by jungles, dead river channels and ponds which had separated the villages one from the other. The system of economy was self-sufficient. After the occupation of Assam by the British in 1826, Majuli came under the British rule, and slowly modern economic system touched the fringes of the island. It was during this period of the beginning of the growth that the present Kamalabari town, the first of its kind in Majuli, was developed.[93]

"Extending to the eastward six miles in length and four in breadth, and bounded by the Tuni nullah", Kamalabari, at the close of the 19th century,[94] was the only place of importance as a centre of trade and communication. The existence of the Tuni river (the local name for the part of the Dikhow flowing inside Majuli) facilitated this development. It is recorded that a trader (*Mudoi*) named Kamala Mudoi had his house on the bank of this river in the early 17th century.[95] It was here that Badala or Badula Padma Ata had established his Satra in later times which came to be known as Kamalabari Satra.[96] Thus, existence of a Satra and a trade house is no less significant in understanding the historical background of Kamalabari regarding its growth into a township. Connection with Jorhat, the last capital of the Ahom state,[97] was one of the major factors for the growth of Kamalabari as a market centre during the colonial period. During the initial period of the British rule the road known as the *Commissioner Ali* was built connecting Jorhat with Neamati *Ghat*, a distance of about 13 miles, and maintained at an average cost of 50 pounds per annum.[98] After the introduction of the Railways in Assam in the late 19th century, particularly for trade purposes in Upper Assam, the *Jorhat (Kakilamukh) State Railway* was built, and extended to Kakilamukh near Neamati *Ghat*[99] through which all shipments to Majuli were brought. It is interesting to note that the *Jorhat State Railway* is older than the *Assam Bengal Railways* which was established in 1910.[100] Tirthanath Sarma has recorded how this traffic was used for carrying pilgrims and devotees to the ferry *gha̱t* to visit the Auniati Satra across the great river during its various religious functions.[101] The British established a shipyard at Kakilamukh and a station at Kamalabari. Since then *Kamalabari Ghat* became a centre of trade. Small traders had their shops in the *ghat,* and even big traders too had their centres of business there. Thus, Hiralal Thakur (1902-1968), one of the pioneers of the freedom struggle and the growth of primary education in Majuli, had his centre of business in the ferry *gha̱t*. He ran the ferry service between *Kamalabari Ghat* and

Kakilamukh for about 12 years on lease and had business links with Calcutta, Dhaka and Bihar.[102]

In their own interest, the British Government took some measures to connect Kamalabari with other parts of Majuli by some roadways and other means of travel. Thus by the close of the 19th century, in 1885, as we have stated elsewhere,[103] was built the *Kamalabari-Lakhimpur Road.* The building of this road connecting Kamalabari with the ferry service station (*Kamalabari Ghat*) in the south, and with the North Lakhimpur town in the north across the Luhit and the Subansiri rivers, had largely contributed towards growth of the modern Kamalabari township. The river Tuni was then spanned by a bamboo bridge to be converted to a wooden one in 1954. Thus a regular road service developed connecting Kamalabari with all important places of Majuli besides Lakhimpur and Jorhat outside it.

In 1906 the Post Office was established at Bhalukar Chuk village at the periphery of the present Kamalabari township.[104] But, after the 1950 earthquake, when much dislocation and erosion altered the entire situation, it was shifted to the present place near the SDC office. Similarly, all shops located at the *Kamalabari (Ferry) Ghat* had also to be shifted to the present township site for the same reason. In 1935, a Police Station and the office of the Sub-Deputy Collector (SDC), in 1945 the office of the Department of Supplies, a few years later, in 1953, the Block Development Office were established. Kamalabari thus emerged as an administrative centre by the close of the 19th and the first half of the 20th century where people with different traits and from various corners of the state participated. Slowly, shops and markets emerged to feed the growing population. Thus developed shop-keeping in Kamalabari with the Marwaris taking the lead. The most known businessman of this township of the early 20th century, as we have mentioned above, was Hiralal Thakur. There were shops beginning from betelnut sale to the wholesale of cloths, and from the tailors to the cobblers, started by both local and immigrated shop-keepers.

Growth of business and administration had brought many other changes to Kamalabari, particularly, in the field of educational progress. Thus, in 1888 was established a Primary School at Kamalabari. This school then had a large catchments area, but due to lack of easy communication systems, number of pupils was small. As a result, Kamalabari had to wait for about half a century to have an English School in 1935 when the M.E. School, established in 1924 and shifted from place to place till 1935, was finally shifted from Rawanapar, a place in upper Majuli, to Kamalabari. The school building was then rebuilt permanently with the financial assistance of Hemchandradeva Goswami (*Adhikara*: 1926-1983), the *Satradhikara* of the Auniati Satra in the same year. The school was therefore renamed as *Majuli Auniati Hemchandra Institute* after the *Satradhikara*'s name. Thus, Kamalabari, which emerged as an administrative-cum-trade centre, now became also a centre of education and learning.

The new trend of development inspired the local elites to start many other cultural activities. In 1938, at the initiative of the elites of Kamalabari like Keshabram Bora, Sasi Barua, Roseswar Hazarika, Bhola Sarma, Thagi Bhuyan, and others, the *Majuli Milan Sangha* (club) was established with a public hall for organizing meetings, holding cultural shows and theatrical performances. The building was made purely on public contributions. It is recorded that one Tirthnath Medhi of Dhekiajuli village, offered Rs.100.00 (one hundred rupees) towards that end when the *Bihu* (Bihu dance and *huchari kirtan*) was organized for collection of fund for that end.[105] The beginning of the *Majuli Milan Sangha* opened a new chapter in the cultural history of the island. It was here that the first modern stage theatre was performed. The drama was *Chandrakanta Singha*.[106] In 1962 was established the first Degree College at Kamalabari. This is the Majuli College today, the pioneer of higher education in the island. Early in the century was established the Veterinary Hospital and the Kamalabari Health Centre. The latter was promoted to a full fledged 30 bed-hospital in 1986. A year before, was established the *Majuli Sanskritik Kendra* (the Majuli Cultural Centre).

Coupled with the process of the development of transport and communication system, growth of trade, administrative net-work, education and culture, Kamalabari experienced growth of population. Besides local Assamese from the neighbouring villages, Kamalabari now became the shelter of various peoples coming from different parts of the country—Bengali, Marwari, Bihari, and East Bengalis (Sylhetty) in the main. By the close of the 20th century, Kamalabari emerged as the largest semi-urban centre of Majuli.

Following Kamalabari, a few other places also emerged as semi-urban market and administrative centres. It is to be noted that most of such centres grew round either some educational institutions or some Satras. Among such emerging small townships Garamur, which became the headquarters of the Majuli sub-division in 1978, deserves to be mentioned. Garamur as a Satra of the Ahom days, had been a well-known pilgrim's place since at least the mid-17th century. The embankment called *Choatalar Garh* built during the rule of king Pratap Singha (1603-1641) ended here. J.P.Wade has mentioned that there was a high causeway directly to the north of Garamur across the Luhit (old Brahmaputra) that connects Garamur with the northern parts of the state.[107] This high causeway was no other than the northern part of the *Chotalar Garh* and the kernel of the present *Kamalabari-Lakhimpur Road.*

During the colonial rule Garamur Satra attracted the attention of the Government due to the supposedly reactionary policy of its three *Satradhikaras*.[107(a)] Early British records are full of appreciation about the attractive environment of the Satra.[108] It was during this period that Garamur became a centre of trade and commerce with a market. Although no record is available as to its beginning, it started with a weekly market (*hat*), held every Tuesday. Traders used to go there from Jorhat for selling clothes to the locals. During the month of March till mid-April, i.e. till *Bohag Bihu*, Garamur was once a very flourishing market, and people from all parts of Majuli, used to buy cloths there on the occasion of the *Bihu.* One important aspect of the market was that Mising people from distant villages, as far as from Daphalakata, Jengraimukh and Jakaibowa visited the market in large numbers and bought clothes of their choice at the highest of the prices.[109] Both men and women, particularly of the younger generations, used to go to the market in groups, singing *Bihu* song (*ainunitam*) and beating drum (*dhol*) all the way from their home to the market and back. It was an amazing sight. There was, however, some limitations in the nature of the goods bought and sold in the market.[110]

With the emergence of Garamur as the headquarters of the Majuli sub-division (in 1978) with usual growth of markets and shops, Majuli has now witnessed the growth of a few market centres with increasing features of urbanization. They include Rangachahi, Jengraimukh, Nayabazar (Ratanpur), Bangaon and Rawanapar in the main—all providing facilities for daily shopping.

Rangachahi is a large area covering a number of villages. The name was derived from a village called Rangachahi which was formed by people migrating from the neighbourhood of Garamur. As a result, this particular village is still known to some people as *Garamuriya Gaon.* Located at a swampy area, Rangachahi was once surrounded by Gatanga, Pahumara, Balichari and Batamari *bils* making it completely an uninhabitable area. But, the 1950 earthquake and consequent human activity slowly converted the area to a cultivable land in course of which Gatanga, or for that matter, all other *bils* became agricultural fields. Thus, Rangachahi slowly emerged as an agriculturally developed area. Affluent economy accelerated the growth of education too. Thus early in the 20th century was established an M.V. School here at Sonariati village. In the pre-Independence period, a few notable men of education and culture organized a movement for growth of education in the area following Kamalabari. Among them the names of Dinaram Nath Bayan in the early decades, and his younger brother Bagaram

Nath later, come to the forefront. It was at their initiative that a High School was established in the village in 1957. This High School (Rangachahi Tanuram Nath High School) has made a large contribution towards the growth of education in the area. In the same year in 1957 the *Rangachahi Pragati Ranga Mancha* was established which served as the public hall for all kinds of meetings and cultural functions. It is to be noted that among the public halls where the *Ras Lila* festival is held and stage performances are presented with participation of both sexes, the *Rangachahi Pragati Ranga Mancha* is one of the pioneers.[111] In 1982 was established the *Rangachahi College*. Thus with the growth of schools and colleges and with better economic condition, Rangachahi emerged as a centre of importance. One important characteristic of the *Rangachahi-Sonariati* market centre is that here all shopkeepers and business men are from among the local Assamese communities.

Jengrai is the name of a small river. It has fallen into the Kherkatiya river near the present Jengraimukh town. The origin of the name is not known. It is possible that the name is derived from some tribal words. However, it appears that the name is an old one, for an Assamese chronicle, while narrating the games of king Gaurinath Singha (1780-1795), has mentioned the name of Jengraimukh as a game sanctuary.[112] It appears that Jengrai is included in J.P. Wade's account prepared at the close of the 18th century within *Pohmara* (Pahumara) 'district' of Majuli. If this is accepted as true, then Kumargaon (Wade's Khoomargown) was its 'chief town' indicating that the present Kumarbari, the heartland of Jengraimukh, was then a settled area , possibly by people of the potters community.[113] This shows that the Jengraimukh or the mouth of the Jengrai river with the Kumarbari village area within it, formed a village as early as the middle ages.

Jengraimukh has some advantages—(i) it is located on a high land normally not much affected by flood water, (ii) it is located on the bank of the two rivers—Kherkatiya and Jengrai, and (iii) it has an ecological advantage for agriculture and commerce. With these aspects of advantages, Jengrai was an affluent village at least in the 20th century. It is known that the present Mising villages in and around Jengraimukh are immigrants from the north of the Kherkatiya Suti who migrated to this place in the early decades of the last century due mainly to the attack of the epidemics like Cholera affecting the villages at large.[114] Thus Jengrai did not develop as a centre of business and trade till at least the second half of the 20th century. It was after the building of the *Haladhibari-Bechamara Embankment* in 1952 about 17 miles in length, and the *Kamalabari-Jengraimukh-Haladhibari* PWD Road in 1957 that

Jengraimukh slowly emerged as a market place. A few persons of eminence like Dasiram Pegu, Santu Pegu, Dambar Pegu, Gopong Doley, Pakkali Doley were the early businessmen of Jengrai.[115] However, initiative in this regard was taken by a Marwari (called *Keyan*) trader who had his shop there to collect cash crops and supply consumption goods to the people.

When Majuli became a reserved constituency for the tribal communities in the Parliamentary political systems since the general election of 1957, Jengrai took advantage of it, as most people of Jengraimukh with strong economic position had large share in Majuli's politics. Gradually, Jengrai became a place of the MLAs and other high executive officers of the island. It also became a centre of education and learning with the *Jengrai High School* and *Jengrai College*. The name of Indreswar Pegu, a renowned thinker and writer of the Mising community, has been associated with the educational and cultural march forward of the place. Today Jengrai with its first ever English medium school—the *St. Paul's High School*, a public storage, and many other educational and cultural organizations, is a major market place in Majuli.

Items of purchase and sale and the nature of the buyers and sellers in the market places are fast changing in recent years.[116] Things like chicken and animal meat which were once prohibited at all market places, are now common items of sale everywhere. In the daily market held by the side of the *Majuli Milan Sangha* at Kamalabari, one finds all sorts of fishes and certain kinds of meat. In the neighbourhood of the Garamur township, it was noted during our field survey, that all the Mising villages have one or more slots for selling pork. Such centres were at Phutukichapori, Sonapara and Chitadarchuk. Similarly, in the suburb of Kamalabari, in the villages of Dhapak Gaon, and Sumoimari pork selling was noted to be a regular feature as in the township of Jengraimukh in Ujani Majuli. In the weekly markets at Phulani (Friday), Kaliagaon (Wednesday), Kalitapar (Sunday), Jakaibowa (Saturday), and at Barunchuk (Wednesday) at lower Majuli, pork is sold. It was found that along with pork, these markets supply Mising rice beer called *apang*, vegetables, clothes, and many other items of domestic use.

In the past there was no custom of selling and buying goods of everyday consumption in the villages. However, field investigations reveal that almost every village in Majuli has now at least some vegetable shops in a corner. All items which were once either exchanged or given free of cost to the neighbours, are now sold in these village shops. This is an impact of commercialization of the life-styles of the people. Thus money-economy has changed the traditional systems in the island leading to the change in its value system. This is reflected not only in the caste-craft relations, but also in the overall psycho-social structures. Once, when everything was produced at home, or could be procured by exchange, families were happy to have a visitor (*alahi*) for a night or a week; but the picture is reverse now; poverty and scarcity has made village life deplorable; and they will be rather happy not to have a guest for the night, not to speak of for a week, said Jagat Bora, Head Assistant of Majuli Auniati Hemchandra High School, Kamalabari, and Secretary to the *Satradhikara* of the Auniati Satra. The same answer is derived from Kanpai Das of Natun Kamalabari Gaon. This does not, however, indicate that they have lost their habit of being a class with good hospitality. To an outsider, they still have a kind heart, and are helpful, and happy to find one as their guest. But some amount of commercialization of men's outlook towards visitors can now be noted in the face of growing demand for tourism development and commercialization of men's life styles.

One new trend in the economic growth in Majuli today is the emergence of a few business-women. During our field investigation it was found that women who were never a partner in the trade and business, are now not as hesitant as they were earlier to participate in the affair. In the Garamur sub-divisional township market we found Arati Deka, a graduate in Arts, Archana Dutta, Sikhamoni Bhuyan, Jyotshna Bhuyan, Ranju Goswami, Ranjana Das, and Mrinali Saikia—who have stores of clothes or various other consumers' articles and stationeries.

RATANPUR-NAYABAZAR

A Field Investigation Report

Emergence of small townships at places like Garamur, Kamalabari, Jengraimukh, Ratanpur-Nayabazar, Phulani, Rangachahi, Bangaon, and growth of market places at different corners have indicated a new trend in the economic life of the island. In our own investigation it was found that amongst 120 shops at the Ratanpur Nayabazar township in upper Majuli bordering Dhakuakhana on the other bank, 75 belonged to Marwari, Bihari and Bengali businessmen including 2 Muslims. While in this native dominated township there are only 18 shops belonging to the Mising and 27 to the non-Mising Assamese businessmen. 38 shops out of a total of 45, owned by Assamese shopkeepers (Mising and non-Mising combined), were started in the 90s only. Their major items of business are fish, betelnut and leaf (*tamol-pan)*, vegetables, teaching and typing in computers, and keeping PCOs, while the outsiders are found to have been dealing with medicine, grocery, cloth, hardware, rice and so forth. Interestingly, all the Assamese shopkeepers are educated and most of them are above 12th standard pass.[117] This shows that a sense of going for business is slowly growing among the educated Assamese youths at this remote township. But lack of capital deposits have bound them to undertake small business only. The local MLA, Sri Rajib Lochan Pegu, however has stated that when any bank-loan is granted to a youth, he uses to expend it for his comfort rather than in doing business. "It is interesting", he said, that "on the day of the withdrawal of the loan amount from the bank, and for a few days immediately after, fish and meat markets swell with local and young customers. And this is where we find the nature of utilization of capital granted to the unemployed young businessmen in Majuli."

Thus, despite the emergence of a local, petty business class, peripheral markets are dominated by the outsiders. The Kamalabari township, the largest and the oldest of the kind in Majuli, better be called the cultural centre of the island, however, local businessmen dominate. Similar is the situation in Bangaon, Rangachahi and other non-tribal areas. It appears that in the market centres of the tribal areas traders from outside predominate. Thus Hunter's observation that the inhabitants of this District are described as a contented and happy people, having but few wants, that paddy is almost the only article grown for food, and that they still live the same primitive way as their forefathers,[118] now needs scrutiny and reorientation one hundred and fifty years after his comment. Economy of the island is no longer confined to agriculture alone as it was a century or fifty years ago. Nor are there ample forest products to make the people here much dependent on this resource. Although medieval agrarian economy predominantly characterized the Majuli island till the mid-twentieth century, it has undergone fast and significant changes during the last century. This is reflected on all fronts—agriculture, land and labour systems, employment, art and craft, and in the living standards of the people.

END NOTES

1. HAG, p. 239; S.K. Bhuyan, *Anglo-Assamese Relations*, *op cit.*, pp. 10ff; Jahnabi Gogoi Nath, *op cit.*, pp. 94ff.
2. Ibid.
3. *Purani Asam Buranji*, (ed) H.C. Goswami, Reprint, Guwahati, 1977, p. 60; ADB, p. 119; SAB; p. 21; HAG, p. 86.
4. Ibid.
5. B.Sharma, *Dakhinpat Satra*, *op cit.*, pp. 13ff; Dr. P. D. Goswami, *op cit.*, pp. 48ff.
6. See Chapter-I for details.

7. Cf. *Asiatic Researches*, Vol. II, p. 131.
8. p. 503.
9. p. 159.
10. See *Tarun Chandra Pamegam Rachanawali*, II, pp. 54, 57.
11. *Op. cit.*, p. 504.
12. Robinson, *op cit.*, p. 356; *Orunodoi*, (ed.) M. Neog, 3rd year, 11th issue, p. 280.
13. cf. *op cit.*, p. 651.
14. Dr. Basanta Kumar Doley, 'Mising Sakalar Krishi Paddhati aru Bhumi Vyavastha' in B.K. Barua (ed). *Pu-Lan-Chi*, December, 2006, 6th issue, p. 72.
15. D. Nath, *Adhunikatar Unmeshat Shri Shri Auniati Satra, op cit.*, (Appendix) pp. 131-136.
16. *op cit.*, p. 503.
17. In territorial sense there are only two *maujas* in Majuli now—Salmara and Kamalabari. The third—Ahataguri, has been almost completely swept away by erosion. At the time of this investigation (2005), there remained only two villages in that *mauja* Kerkeri and Misamara.
18. *Koroki diya* was a process by which the *maujadars* used force (*tekela*) to get the land revenue paid by a peasant who fails to pay the same. By this method everything of value that a family possesses may be taken away and may be auctioned. This system was introduced during the British when money as medium of payment was introduced. The process has been well-explained by P. N. Gohain Barua in his drama called '*Gaoburha*' (1897). Cf. *Gohain Barua Rachanawali*, 2nd Print, Guwahati, 1987, pp. 275f
19. *See* Appendix IV.
20. Jahnabi Gogoi Nath, *Op cit.*, p. 37.
21. Butler, *Sketch of Assam with some Accounts of the Hill Tribes by an Officer*, London, 1847, cf. A. Guha, *Medieval and Early Colonial Assam*, Calcutta, 1991, pp. 63f.
22. Wade, *A Geographical Sketch of Assam*, *op cit.*, p. 33.
23. *Gazeetteer* of Allen *et. al.*, p. 578.
24. *Komal chaul* means soft rice, a kind of dried boiled rice which is taken as a kind of breakfast by immersing it into the water for a short while making it instantly soft. *Komal chaul* is also used as items of offerings in rituals and functions.
25. Jahnabi Gogoi Nath, *op cit.*, p. 70.
26. The record says about the cropping pattern as follows: (a) *ahu* followed by *sali* (b) *ahu* mixed with *bao* followed by pea/oil seeds/wheat (flood prone low lying areas), (c) *ahu* followed by *robi* crop (d) jute followed by *robi* (e) *sali* followed by *robi*, (f) *boro* replaced by pea in all areas (g) mixed inter-cropping in case of horticultural crops, and (h) *robi* crops folloed by *bao* and *ahu*. (Information obtained from the SDO Office, Agriculture, Majuli.)
27. Ibid.

28. John M'Cosh wrote—"As I have already observed, agriculture is not in a forward state; and though famine or even scarcity of provision is seldom known, yet the produce is little more than the consumption. Immense tracts of country are lying waste that might be under profitable crops, and little cultivation exists but in the vicinity of the principal towns." See *Topography of Assam*, *op cit.*, p. 29.
29. During our visit to the family of Sri Piyada Hazarika of the Sonowal Kachari Gaon under Ujani Majuli Development Block, we were informed by Hazarika that he uses his 3 *bigha* land again and again for growing various crops—putting them under double, and even triple cropping systems to feed the 13 members of his family.
30. It is the custom of the people in the island to ask a person at the time of dinner or lunch if he had taken his meal. If the person in question had had only *cha̲pa̲tti* in stead of rice, he would be hesitatingly answer that he just took *cha̲pa̲tti*. (*bha̲t to na̲yei, ruti pitha̲ke dukhanma̲n kha̲lo a̲ru* ! tr. No rice. Therefore took two or three pieces of *cha̲pa̲tti* only).
31. Cf. HAG, p. 142.
32. Alexander Mackenzie, The *North East Frontier of India* (1884), Reprint, Delhi, 1999, p. 387.
33. Aphorism of Dak says—*chay po chay na̲ti tehe kariba̲ kuhiya̲r kheti* i.e. grow sugarcane only when you have six sons and six grandsons. For Dak see M. Neog, *Maheswar Neog Rachanawali*, *op cit.*, pp. 499ff
34. Amalendu Guha, *Medieval and Early Colonial Assam*, *op cit.*, p. 110; H.K Barpujari (ed.) *The Comprehensive History of Assam*, Vol.III, *op cit.*, pp. 175ff.
35. For example, see the *Copper Plate Inscription of Konwarbhag and Pubpar Pargana*, cf. *Prachya Sasanawali*, Ins. No. 64.
36. D. Nath, *History of the Koch Kingdom*, *op cit.*, p. 155.
37. Mills, *Report on the Province of Assam*, pp. 503f; H.K.Barpujari, *Assam in the Days of the Company*, Guwahati, 1963, pp. 262f.
38. Ibid.; Amalendu Guha, *Medieval and Early Colonial Assam*, *op cit.*, p. 251; Omiya Kumar Das and Liladhar Barua, *Asamat Mahatma*, Guwahati, 1969, p. 56.
39. Irfan Habib, 'Technology and Economy of Mughal India', *Indian Economic and Social History Review*, Vol.XVII, Pt. I, p. 4; Jahnabi Gogoi Nath, *op cit.*, p. 72.
40. GCK, p. 65.
41. Ibid., p. 55.
42. Cf. *op cit.*, p. 88, fn.131.
43. DAB, p. 110; *Purani Asam Buranji*, *op cit.*, p. 63.
44. Jahnabi Gogoi Nath, *op cit.*, p. 73.
45. S. K. Bhuyan, *Asam Buranjir Katha*, Gauhati, 1989, p. 92.
46. This piece of rug measures in average 2.5 metres in length and .75-1.00 metre in breath. See Tarun Chandra Pamegam, 'Bayan Silpat Mising Jiyari', in B.Kagyung, *op cit.*, p. 323.
47. Robinson, *op cit.*, p. 357.

48. ASBS, p. 250; *Orunodoi,* (Comp.) A. Saikia, Nagaon, 2002, pp. 83f.
49. *Dakhinpat Satra, op cit.*, p. 70; Ibid.
50. Ibid., p. 60.
51. MDPH, pp. 44ff.
* This statement, however, deserves scrutiny as revealed from our field work.
52. See Jahnabi Gogoi Nath, *op cit.*, p. 67.
53. Cf. K. L. Barua, *op cit.*, pp. 54f.
54. Cf. HAG, p. 142.
55. M'Cosh, *op cit.*, p. 5.
56. *A Descriptive Account of Assam, op cit.*, p. 7.
57. Barpujari (ed.), *The Comprehensive History of Assam, III, op cit.*, p. 114.
58. It was reported that a family could produce a minimum number of utensils working for the whole year. Sri Sisuram Kalita of the Salmara Kumar Gaon told the present investigator that his family income in a year hardly amounts to Rs.10,000.00. Similar was the answer of Temaram Hazarika of the same village.
59. J. N. Sarma, *loc cit.* (Ms.).
60. *See* Chapter II.
61. *Gazzetteer* of Allen, *et al.*, p. 159
62. Wade, *An Account of Assam, op cit.*, Intro. p. XXXV.
63. ASBS, p. 327; D.Nath, *Adhunikatar Unmeshat Shri Shri Auniati Satra, op cit.*, p. 28.
64. *The Whole World View*, cf.H.K. Barpujari, *The American Missionaries and Noth East India*, Guwahati, 1986, p. 191.
65. *See* Chapter IV.
66. *See* Illustration (mask of Ravana) as an example of his art.
67. *See* Chapter 1, pp. 29f.
68. Dr. P. D. Goswami, *op cit.*, p. 218.
69. See Sumita Ghose, *op cit.*, pp. 140f.
70. *Ibid.*, pp. 103f.
71. *Kaivarta Jatiya Hitakari Sabha Leaflet*, cf. *Banhi*, 1838 *Sak*; Devabrat Sarma, *Asamiya Jati Gathan Prakriya etc.*, *op cit.*, Jorhat, 2006, p. 63.
72. T. C. Pamegam, *Tarun Chandra Pamegam Rachanawali*, II, *op cit.*, p. 274. "*era bhang kani, bilati pani, swaraj hobor eyehe upai,.....nadakiba bil ghat nepelaba paicha tat, taka loye pathaba bilat*"—(tr. Avoid opium and *ganja*, avoid drinking intoxicating liquor, this is the way to obtain *swaraj;* do not bid for *bils* or *ghats,* do not throw money on that, they (the British) will send them immediately to London".

72(a). K. C. Borah, *loc cit.*, (Ms.).
73. Jahnabi Gogoi Nath, *op cit.*, pp. 127ff; D. Nath, *History of the Koch Kingdom*, *op cit.*, pp. 135ff.
74. S. N. Sarma, *op cit.*, pp. 139ff; H. N. Sarma, *op cit.* (Ms.).
75. Ibid.
76. Hunter, *op cit.*, p. 249.

76(a). These labourers came to Majuli only during the late 19th and early 20th century, during the British when Assam was included in the British Indian empire.

77. Sumita Ghose, *op cit.*, p. 108.

78. Data collected from Haren Hazarika, a resident of the Kharjanpar village near Garamur Satra.

78(a). K. C. Bora, *loc cit.* (Ms.), p. 146.

79. Prior to the establishment of the Kamalabari Thana, there was a jail at the place, and prisoners from Lakhimpur were brought and kept here. cf. S. N. Das, *Majuli Auniati Hem Chandra High School Diamond Jubilee Volume*, loc. cit., p. 44.

80. *Gazetteer* of Allen *et al.*, p. 580.

81. Ibid.

82. S. N. Das, *loc cit.*, p. 45.

83. Records obtained from the office of the SDO, PWD, Garamur, Majuli

84. Ibid.

85. A detail list of Road and Bridges in Majuli is given in the Appendix.

86. M'Cosh, *op cit.*, p. 28.

87. MDPH, p. 37; D.Nath, *Adhunikatar Unmeshat Shri Shri Auniati Satra, op cit.*, p. 28; ASBS, p. 275.

88. There is a folk saying that a girl for marriage should be selected from a village of a day's distance, while a cow be bought from a call's distance. (*Chowali aniba dintor batat, garuto kiniba ringtor batat*).

89. p. 580.

90. *Tarun Chandra Pamegam Rachanawali,* Vol. *I, op cit.*, p. 272.

91. S. N. Das, *loc cit.*, p. 45.

92. Ibid.; Information supplied by Jagat Bora, Head Assistant, Majuli Auniati Hem Chandra High School, Kamalabari.

93. In the growth of the Kamalabari township, the role of the Kamalabari Satra was significant. It is known from the records of the Sastra that on the occasion of the celebration of queen Victoria's declaration as Empress of British Indian Empire (1877), organised at Sibsagar in 1878, the inmates of the Satra performed the *Rajasuya Yajna Bhaona*. The performance was so perfect and satisfying that being highly pleased at their performance, the Company Government rewarded the Satra with the grant of a *mauja*, a *thana*, a post-office, a hospital and a ferry *ghat*. (Information obtained from Narayan Chandra Goswami, *Satradhikara* of Natun Kamalabari Satra. See, also H.C.Bhattacharyya, *Asamiya Natya Sahityar Jilingani*, 2nd edition, Guwahati, 1970, pp. 104f; Kamalakanta Bhuyan, 'Kamalabari Satrar Sanskritik Avadan ', in S.Hazarika (ed). *Asamar Satriya Parampara aru Shri Shri Badala Padma Ata*, Dibrugarh, 2006, p. 225.)

94. Wade, *A Geographical Sketch of Assam*, *op cit.*, p. 33.

95. *Bar Charit* by Dina Nath Bezbarua, Guwahati, 1987, vv. 3608-3651.

96. Ibid.

97. Purnanda Buragohain had shifted the capital from Rangpur to Dichoi nagar—Jorhat, during the Moamariya Rebellion in the year 1794. Since

then Jorhat remained the capital till Assam was annexed to the British Indian Empire in 1826, See S. K. Bhuyan, *Anglo-Assamese Relations*, *op cit.*, p. 231.

98. Hunter, *op cit.*, p. 259.
99. Ibid.; Benudhar Sharma, *Benudhar Sharma Rachanawali* (*Majiyar para Mejaloi*), Guwahati, Guwahati, 1986, p. 58.
100. Ibid.
101. ASBS, pp. 268ff.
102. See Premananda Thakur, 'Hiralal Thakurdevar Sangkhipta Jiban Charit' in the *Majuli Auniati Hem Chandra High School Diamond Jubilee Volume*, *op cit.*, pp. 18.
103. *Supra*; above fn.79.
104. Ibid., p. 155
105. *See* S. N. Das, *loc cit.*, pp. 44ff.
106. Ibid.
107. Wade, *A Geographical Sketch of Assam*, *op cit.*, p. 33

107(a). For details, *See* Chapter 6 of this work.

108. *See* Chapter 1.
109. D. Nath, 'Mising Society in Transition', loc.cit, pp. 255ff.
110. For example, no trader was allowed to sell meat, or wine or any intoxicating liquor in the market. Most items of sale constituted clothes brought by traders from Jorhat, and local agricultural products sold by the villagers. Also *see* fn. 116 below.
111. Today there are about 30 such public halls all over Majuli. But at the time of its establishment, there were only three—one at Kamalabari, one at Garamur, and the other at Bangaon. See Appendix-XVIII. Also information supplied from the office of the Cultural Officer, Kamalabari Majuli.
112. *See Tungkhungiya Buranji*, (ed) S.K.Bhuyan, 2nd edition, Guwahati, 1964, p. 93 (henceforth TB)
113. The name *Kumar* (i.e. potter) bari is interesting as there is no potters village at present in or nearby Jengraimukh. It is possible that once the area was inhabited by the potters community, and that might have been either before the (old) Brahmaputra had shifted to the south, or till the river bank could be exploited for making pottery.
114. Information supplied by Prof. D. Doley, Retired Professor, Department of Sociology, Dibrugarh University in July, 2007. Prof. Doley hails from Jengraimukh, Majuli.
115. Ibid.
116. I remember, on a Tuesday afternoon, the day of the Garamur weekly market (called *Mangalbariya hat*), an unknown man (a Bengali immigrant from erstwhile East Pakistan who used to settle in the *chapori* on the north) killed a goat by strangulation in a corner of the market for sale. Killing of a goat for sale in the open market till then was not known in Majuli, particularly within the sphere of a Satra. The news of this event therefore spread all around like a wild fire, and hundreds of men gathered there to *gherao* the man who killed it. We were minor students

attending our class in a room which was adjacent to the place of the event. So, when there was much hue and cry outside, there was an unruly situation in our class room too. The incident was so interesting for our childhood mind that without caring for the attending teacher, we just jumped out over the windows and rushed to the spot. Peeping inside through the gaps of the gathering I remember how a helpless butcher was trembling with the dead animal lying in his front. Suddenly we heard, Pitambardeva Goswami coming with his usual posture with the cane stick at his hand. And all people kept aside allowing the *Satradhikara* to punish the 'culprit.' The rest of the event was as usual. He gave him 14 beats with his cane stick and let go with the kill and throw it on to the Luhit river flowing nearby. And I believe no body would dare to repeat such an act after that event. That was about half a century ago in early 1962.

117. A detail chart has been given in Appendix IX.

118. *Op cit.*, p. 249.

4

Satras of Majuli

The Neo Vaishnavite Institutions and Practices

EARLY HISTORY

The Satra institution of Assam is associated with the Neo-Vaishnavism of Sankaradeva (1449-1568), the great Vaishnava saint and social reformer of 15th-16th century Assam. But the idea of the Satra institution, as we find it today, was perhaps not there in his vision although he had started some congregational gathering for the purpose of cultivation of religion and pursuit of cultural activities when he was at Belaguri Dhuwahat itself in Upper Assam (1520-1546).[1] "It may be recalled" writes M. Neog, "that in Sankaradeva's days the daily sittings of the monks and such lay disciples, as used to attend them, were held in the open or under the shade of trees. Such meetings, independent of any construction whatsoever, probably formed the nucleus of a Sankarite satra with the *kirtan-ghar*, and the residences of the Superior and the monks only came later to be associated inseparably with the notion of a satra."[2] For the full fledged development of the Satra as an institution we have to wait till after his death when his follower Damodardeva in Patbausi and Madhavdeva in Barpeta organized it with all infrastructure and attributes.[3] In order to understand this development, we have to look into the historical background.

Sankaradeva's Vaishnava movement aimed at teaching the common people simple ways of living, equality of all men in the field of religion, and practicing non-violence and doing away with the belief in sacrifice of birds and animals which was largely prevalent in the society of that time in the name of religion. At the same time, complicated and elaborate systems of rituals and practices associated with propitiation of various gods and goddesses under the canopy of Brahminism exploited the commoners in all possible ways.[4] Sankaradeva through the simple way of congregational prayer, *nama-kirtana,* to one Supreme God in the form of Lord Vishnu or Krishna, attempted to simplify this ritualism. The two aspects of his teachings—belief in and submission to one Supreme God, and rejection of caste distinctions in the religious plane as an attempt to create an unified society of universal brotherhood thereby uniting men in a single platform through congregational prayer, was not liked by the Ahom feudal state system. This, therefore, became an intriguing factor to the Ahom royalty as they demanded undivided submission of the subject population and did not allow them to gather together in any kind of common assembly. Thus the state looked at the movement, almost from the beginning, with much suspicion and planned to curb it especially when Sankaradeva proselytized Madhavdeva at Belaguri Dhuwahat (about the year 1522) in Majuli which was then within the Ahom kingdom, and preached non-violence openly.[5] As a result, both Sankaradeva and Madhavdeva had to leave the kingdom for Kamrup in lower Assam, then under the Koch king Naranarayan (1540-1587). It was here in the Koch kingdom that Sankaradeva died in 1568 leaving two important apostles to succeed him—Madhavdeva (1498-1596) and Damodardeva (1488-1598) in the helm of his religious affairs. The presence of two great personalities in the field, however, led finally to the division of the faith with Damodardeva deviating from the stream and creating his own branch. Schism gradually proliferated. For, later two other leaders—Gopal Ata *alias* Gopaldeva and Purushottam Thakur, a grandson of Sankaradeva, also formed their own divisions. Consequently, after the death of Madhavdeva, his disciple Mathuradas Burha Ata, founded the last and his own order to retain the original features of the sect in tact. These divisions were popularly called *Samhati* or *Sanghati.*[6] Despite differences in minor aspects due to differences of personalities and contexts of developments, they share in common the basic elements of Vaishnavism initiated by Sankaradeva. The historic divisions took place in lower Assam by the close of the 16th century.

While the movement grew in Kamrup, Upper Assam, the heartland of the Ahom kingdom, remained almost out of its impact since the great saint had left in the mid-16th century. In the mean time, Aniruddhadeva (1553-1626), disciple of Gopaldeva, founder of the *Kal Sanghati* order, had returned from Kaljhar, where he had been with his *guru* Gopal Ata, and began to preach in his native place at Narayanpur on the north bank of the Brahmaputra in the year 1601.[7] Gradually Aniruddhadeva's activities spread all around. He then went to the Majuli island and established a Satra there, it is said, on the bank of a pond called *Moamari bil* and began to preach among the Kaivarta people inhabiting there.[8] It is said that the name *Moa̲mariya̲* or *Ma̲ya̲mariya̲* meaning the people who were converted to his sect, was coined from this fact of his proselytizing the Kaivarta people who lived on fishing the *Moa* fish in the *bil* (pond) called *Moamari*.[9] This Mayamara or Moamara Satra was consequently washed away by the Brahmaputra leaving no trace behind; but the name and the creed thrived; and it is still a very significant branch of the Vaishnavism of Sankaradeva. The biographical work of Aniruddhadeva records that after his death his eldest son Jagatananda had further advanced upwards and proselytized the Kaivartas of other places in the island with his Satra*s* at Sarjanpar and other places.[10] The Moamariya disciples of Majuli played significant role in the Moamariya Revolt of 1769, and ruled the island for a time being by making one of them called Hauha, chief of their clan. This has been discussed elsewhere.[11] Their role in the Revolt, however, created a large schism between them and the disciples of the other Satra*s* whose strength was so large that the Moamariyas known in Majuli as 'Matak' soon became insignificant, and then isolated. There are at present nine villages of the Matak Kaivartas in Majuli, their parent body being located at Sensowa village near Rawanapar; but they have no Satra there.

Following Aniruddhadeva, and realizing the void in the process of spreading the tenet in upper Assam (Ahom kingdom), Madhavdeva (1496-1598) and Damodaradeva (1488-1598) deputed their respective disciples of rank and personality to go to the Ahom kingdom and preach their faith there, among whom Vamsigopaldeva was the foremost.[12] Vamsigopaldeva, who had the advantage of being a disciple of Damodardeva, and trained by Madhavdeva, and who got the warm association of Sankaradeva too for sometime,[13] left for the Ahom kingdom early in the 17th century. By now the Ahom state could realize the growing popularity of Neo-Vaishnavism, and the challenge it may pose to the state, if at all, its popularity was not channalized for the good of the kingdom by allowing it to flourish under the royal patronage itself which might work as some kind of safety valve. As a matter of fact, despite oppositions and challenges at the initial stage, Vamsigopaldeva was able to establish, among others, the Kuruwabahi Satra on the junction of the Brahmaputra and the Dhansiri river.[14] He, however, died soon after leaving his Satra at the hands of his disciple-cum-adopted son Misradev. The latter too incurred royal displeasure, and died in the royal custody soon after leaving Jayharidev, cousin of Vamsigopaldeva, in charge of the Satra.[15] Jayharidev also died early leaving Niranjandev, a reader of the *Bhagavata* (*Bhagavat Pathak*) in charge of the Satra as the son of Misradev was then too young to shoulder the responsibility.[16] All this happened before king Jayadhvaj Singha came to the throne in 1648.

Auniati Satra

King Jayadhvaj Singha (1648-1663) had much bent towards Brahmanical religion. It is said that once when the state was attacked by natural calamities, the astrologers of the state reported to the king that this misfortune was because of some past misdeeds on part of his predecessors, indicating thereby, the death of Misradev Gosain of Kuruwabahi Satra in the custody of the state before his time.[17] He, therefore, in order to make some amends for the past misdeeds of his forefather, decided to establish a grand monastery for the son of the Kuruwabahi *Gosain* with all sorts of royal grants including lands and servitors and himself becoming its disciple.[18] When this intention of the king was forwarded to Gosain's widowed wife, it is stated, she refused to send her minor son to the king on suspicion that her son too may be killed like his father.[19] On persistent request on part of the king's men, however, she finally gave way and sent Niranjandev, the *Bhagavati* of the Satra, in stead of her son, to the king.[20] Presuming him to be the son of the *Gosain*, the king became his disciple and made him a *Satradhikara* by establishing for him a grand new Satra at Auniati in the Majuli island.[21] According to the official records preserved in the Ahom chronicles, this was in the year A.D. 1653-54. (*Sak* 1575-1576).[22] This record further says that king Jayadhvaj Singha himself (formally) laid the foundation pillar of the *manikut* (i.e. the sanctum-sanctorum where the *Bhagavata* is placed) after a year or two in the *Saka* year 1578, in the month of *Chaitra,* it being a Wednesday.[23] King Jayadhvaj Singha thereafter established two other Satra*s* of the same school in the island—they were Dakhinpat and Garamur Satra.

Dakhinpat Satra

From the sequence of events narrated in the Assamese chronicles and the *charit puthis* it appears that king Jayadhvaj Singha brought Banamalideva from Koch Behar sometime after his foundation of the Auniati Satra.[24] It is known from the *Sri Sri Vamsigopal Devar Charitra* that Banamalideva was a disciple of Vamsigopaldeva and spent his early years at Kuruwabahi. But after Vamsigopal's death[25] he left for Koch Behar and joined Damodardeva there at his Vaikunthapur Satra.[26] Here he found the company of two other disciples of Damodardeva—Paramananda and Baloram. It is stated that while he was at Koch Behar, king Jayadhvaj Singha performed a great *yajna* at Dauka Chapori on the north of the Brahmaputra to where the *Auniatiya*, *Garamuriya*, *Kuruwabahiya* and a few other *adhikaras* (*bapu*) were invited; but Banamalideva, being then at Koch Behar, could not attend due to prevention by king Prannarayan (1632-1665 A.D.). It is stated that after this event the king excavated a tank at Bhatiyapar near the capital city of Rangpur. But, there was no water till almost its complete excavation. In the mean time, Baloram and Paramanda died, and Vanamalideva too left for Jagannath in Orissa and thencefrom to *Asama,* the Ahom kingdom, following the earlier invitation from its king.[27] It was now that on hearing his supernatural power, king Jayadhvaj Singha accorded his second invitation to Vanamalideva to offer *puja* when there was no water in the tank excavated at Bhatiyapar.[28] It is further recorded that the tank became flooded with water immediately after Banamalideva's presence at the site.[29] As a mark of gratitude king Jayadhvaj Singha established him first at Jatkara and then at Rangalubahar at Dakhinpat making a grant of 300 *puras* of land and sufficient number of servitors, and himself becoming his disciple.[30] From the sequence of events as narrated in the chronicles, it appears that this event took place some time after the establishment of the Auniati Satra in 1578 *Sak* (1653-54 A.D.) and Garamur Satra in 1657-08.[31] This fact makes it clear that of the three royal Satra*s* of Majuli Dakhinpat was established in the last.

Garamur Satra

Garamur Satra was established by the Ahom king Jayaddhvaj Singha about the year 1657-1658 after the foundation of the Auniati Satra in the year 1553-54. It is recorded that when Misradev Gosain, the *adhikara* of Kuruwabahi Satra, and the successor of Vamsigopaldeva (1548-1634), the founder of the Satra, died a prisoner in the Ahom court, his son Ramkrishna was too young to shoulder the religious throne. As a result, according to the *Vamsigopaldevar Charitra,*[32] Jayharideva, a cousin of Vamsigopaldeva, and a grandson of his paternal uncle, came to occupy the headship of the Satra.[33] But he too died soon after giving the headship to Niranjandeva, the *bhagavati* of the Satra, and a Brahmin by caste.[34] As stated above, by the turn of events, king Jayaddhvaj Singha took initiation from him taking him to be the son and successor of Misradeva, the *adhikara* of the Satra who died in the royal custody.[35] But the truth soon came to light, and king Jayadhvaj Singha, finding that he took initiation from the *bhagavati* but not from the actual *adhikara*, now took to the alternative measure of establishing him to the status of the highest of the *adhikaras* by establishing him in a new Satra at Auniati in the Majuli island and giving him all sorts of material wealth and social status including the image of lord *Govinda* (*Govinda Mahaprabhu*), the tutelary deity of Kuruwabahi Satra.[36] This status of Niranjandeva of being the preceptor of the king, had made both Ramakrishna and Lakshminarayan, the latter a nephew of Jayharideva, jealous of him (Niranjandeva) who then appealed to the king for the return of the *Govinda* image and grant of some other facilities to them also.[37] Thus a part of what Niranjandeva had taken away from Kuruwabahi was given back to the Satra; and for Lakshminarayandeva, the king established a separate Satra at Garamur, and by giving the image of *Vamsigopala* (*Vamsibadan*) brought from the temple of Jagannath for that purpose, had made him its *Adhikara.*[38] Maniram Dewan too in his *Buranji Vivek Ratna* has stated that a relation (*bhai-bhatri*) of Vamsigopaldeva, attached to the Kuruwabahi Satra, had established the Garamur Satra at Majuli at the instance of the king Jayadhvaj Singha.[39] While Maniram Dewan's statement is not much clear as to the identity of the person, according to a record submitted by the Satra to the Government in 1904, the founder *Satradhikara* of the Satra was shown as Jayharideva, the nephew of Vamsigopaldeva, but not as Lakshminarayandeva.[40] But there is no historical record to support such a statement. On the other hand, it simply contradicts with the information derived from the original records. It is also chronologically not possible to make Jayharideva to have founded the Garamur Satra in the year 1658, or in 1660, as shown in one of the popular genealogies preserved in the Satra as he died at Kuruwabahi long before Niranjandeva was established at Auniati by king Jayadhvaj Singha[41] unless we consider that Jayaharideva had been at Garamur on the bank of the Luhit river (old Brahmaputra) where he was hiding himself for some time during the days of the crisis in the Kuruwabahi Satra when Misradev Gosain was in captivity of the Ahom king.[42] This, however, does not speak of foundation of a Satra, that too with the royal patronage. It appears that showing Jayharideva as the founder *Adhikara* of Garamur Satra[43] is either a wrong historical recording of the origin of the Satra on part of its scribes, or it may be the result of a deliberate attempt to trace the genealogy of the Garamuriya *Satradhikaras* from a close descendent of Vamsigopaldeva, which fact has made it unavoidable to show Jayharideva as the founder of the Satra (as no Satra among the big three in Majuli can exclusively claim Vamsigopaldeva as its founder *Adhikara*). It is interesting to note that the genealogy of the Garamuriya *Satradhikaras*, shown as official, is not only wrongly dated, but also wrongly recorded, and even among the internal historians there is no one opinion about the genealogy.[44] Be that as it may, at the absence of more other genuine records, it may be stated that Lakshminarayandeva of the family of Vamsigopaldeva was the founder of the Garamur Satra in Majuli in the year 1657(or 1658), a few years after the foundation of the Auniati Satra by Niranjandeva in the year 1653.

Garamur Satra has a branch Satra existing almost as its parallel and within the same religious and territorial jurisdiction, although in both its physical establishment and administrative structure it is an independent Satra. It is the Saru (small/junior) Garamur Satra. It has now no *adhikara* of its own after the death of Chitra Chandradeva Goswami in 1895, the father of the reformer *Satradhikara* Pitambardeva Goswami. The *adhikara* of the (Bar) Garamur Satra acts as its pontiff.

Kamalabari Satra

The Kamalabari Satra, belonging to the *Nika Sanghati* order, is another important Satra in Majuli. It was established by Badala/Badula Padma Ata, a disciple of Madhavdeva, in the year 1673.[45] The *Katha Guru Charit* has mentioned that Madhavdeva in his last year invited Badula *alias* Padma Ata, his beloved disciple, to his residence at Barpeta and directed him to go to the Ahom state in upper Assam to preach his tenes which was not yet done after he and his *guru* Sankaradeva had left the state for Kamrup.[46] It is narrated in the biography of the saint that Badula Ata then travelled far and wide encamping at different centres and preaching among the common people before he finally settled at Kamalabari, a garden of orange fruit belonging to the ancestors of *Sahityarathi* Lakshminath Bezbaroa.[47]

There are three Kamalabari Satra*s* at present. The original Kamalabari Satra is at Titabar (Jorhat) now. It shifted to this place in 1975 as a result of erosion of the Satra by the Brahmaputra. In the mean time, the Satra had proliferated creating two of its branches, now both at Majuli, one called Natun Kamalabari Satra nearby the site of the old establishment, and the other, a little to the north of it, called Uttar Kamalabari Satra. The Kamalabari Satra is known for its cleanliness[48] and for the performing arts of music, dance and drama called *ankiya natak* originally composed by Sankaradeva and his disciple Madhavdeva.[49] *Satradhikara* Narayan Chandra Goswami of Natun Kamalabari Satra is known for his scholarship for which he obtained the *Sankaradeva Award* from the Government of Assam for the year 2005.

Chamaguri Satra

The Chamaguri Satra was in Bangaon within the Salmara Mauja. Chakrapanidev, son of Keshavpriya, daughter of Purushottam Thakur, and Niranjan Gabharugiri *alias* Petphala Ata (her husband), established this Satra in the year 1585 *Saka* (1663 A.D.)[50] There is also one Chamaguri Satra at Kaliabar in Nagaon. The Purani Chamaguri Satra claims that it possesses the footwear (*paduka*) of Sankaradeva, a *ghati* (pot), a part of the *padasila* (foot-print stone) originally preserved at the Belaguri Satra and Bardowa, and a leaf from the *Dasam* (10th Book of the *Bhagavata*) written by the saint. himself.[51] It is stated that when the couple was at Jania in Kamrup, Niranjan had introduction with the Ahom prince Chakraddhvaj Singha. Their intimacy increased, and the prince, it is said, promised to establish for him a Satra if he would someday become the king.[52] So, after his accession to the throne, Chakraddhvaj Singha brought Niranjan (then an '*Ata*') to his capital; but Niranjan Ata died before the king took initiation from him. So, the king established his son Chakrapani at Chamaguri in Majuli and granted 7000 *puras* of revenue-free land at Bahgara.[53] The Satra has a new branch called Natun Chamaguri Satra situated near the market centre of Rawanapar established in the year 1824 *Saka* (1902 A.D.). The Chamaguri Satra is famous for mask making.

Bengenaati Satra

Belonging to the *Purusha Sanghati* order, the Bengenaati Satra was established by one Muraridev. It is recorded that Purusottam Thakur, son of Ramananda, eldest son of the great reformer Sankaradeva, selected six disciples from among the Brahmans, and six others from among the Sudras, and asked them to move to different places of Kamrup and *Asam* for establishment of Satra*s* to propagate his creed. The Satra*s* founded by those pontiffs were known as *Bar Barajaniya* Satra*s*.[54] At his instruction, his younger brother Chaturbhuj Thakur too on his part, deputed twelve disciples to such places, who also established twelve other Satra*s* which came to be known as *Saru Barajaniya* Satra*s*.[55] Among the twelve disciples sent by Purusottam Thakur was one called Murari who established the Bengenaati Satra in Majuli about the year 1773.

Other Satras

These are the major Satra*s* in Majuli established either at the royal patronage or by the *Satradhikaras*' own endeavour. There are many other Satra*s* to be counted in this regard. For example, Satras like Bhogpur, Owa, Belesidhiya, Sankopara, Gajala. Pahumara, Phutukichapori, Garamur Saru Satra, Elengi and others were established during the 17th century. Thus by the reign of king Rudra Singha (1696-1714), Majuli became known as the place of the Satra*s* popularly called '*Etaka Mahantar than*' meaning thereby that Majuli was the place of the *Satradhikaras*, who are also called *Mahanta*. In recent times number of the Satra*s* proliferated either due to internal feuds between the aspirants to the headship of a Satra, or due to clashes between Sudra *adhikara* and Brahman inmates.[56] Whatever be the cause of proliferation, it is believed that at one time there were more than a hundred Satra*s*. In this connection the term *etaka mahantar than* is also interpreted as indicative of the number of the Satra*s* in the island. It is stated that at one time there were sixty four Satra*s* in the island so that giving one *paisa* to each of them amounts to a total of one rupee from which fact the term *etaka mahantar than* is said to have been derived.[57] This however, does not test scrutiny if we trace the origin of the term to the reign of king Rudra Singha when one *paisa* coin was yet to be introduced.[58] It is sometimes believed that the term *etaka mahantar than* implied the place of those *adhikaras* who had complete knowledge of the four sacred things of Assam Vaishnavism (called *bastu*)—*guru* (preceptor), *deo* (God), *nam* (name of God, congregation prayer) and *bhakat* (devotee).[59] In another way, the same is interpreted as the place of the big four Satra*s* which form a complete unit—*etaka*, like four quarter rupee coins—*siki* form a complete rupee—*taka*.[60]

CLASSIFICATION OF SATRAS—MONASTICISM AS A WAY OF LIFE

Satra*s* in Majuli are found in two distinct types—(a) monastic, with its celibate inmates (*kewalia/udasin bhakat*) and the celibate pontiff (*udasin adhikara*), or celibate pontiff with house-holding inmates (*grihi/grihasthi/vishayee bhakat*), and (b) house-holding (*grihi* or *grihasthi* Satra), with house-holding inmates (*vishayee bhakat*) and house-holding pontiff (*grihasthi/vishayee adhikara*). Of the monastic Satra*s*, the big ones, Auniati, Dakhinpat, Garamur and Kamalabari (two), and Bhogpur are situated in the Majuli island. These monastic Satra*s*, being the ideal representative of the kind, are most well-known and influential in the society. Being favoured with lavish gifts by the medieval rulers of Assam almost all of them are possessed of extensive amount of landed property which they once received as revenue-free grant from the Ahom kings of Assam,[61] and which the British rulers later retained with the Satra*s*,[62] and the national Government too, on its part, endorsed them to a certain extent. These (monastic) Satra*s* have their own physical identities, with a secluded territorial jurisdiction, a structural establishment with the common prayer hall (*kirtanghar / namghar*) at the centre and the cluster (*hati*) of houses of the inmates (*baha*) and the pontiff all around, lay disciples (*sisya*) scattered all over the state, and a kind of administration with the hereditary pontiff at the head and a layer of office holders under him with mass of the celibate inmates at the bottom resembling the medieval state structure.[63] The entire structure forms a distinct society with its own identity. This was what made the Satras a feudal organization with a distinguished and a well-defined society. These monastic religious institutions bear resemblance to the early Buddhist monasteries, and also to the medieval *mathas* of India.[64]

A Monastic Satra: How Does it Look Like

A monastic Satra can be distinguished by any onlooker from a distance. It is an independent establishment away from the hub-hub of the township, like the Buddhist nunneries, possibly looking like an ancient day hermitage (*asrama*). Scholars say that the concept of a Satra has been borrowed from the concept of the hermitage of the *Risi* Saunak in the Naimisha forest where the hermits used to assemble to listen to the recitation of the *Bhagavata* for a thousand years at a stretch performed by the monk Suta[65] It is, however, not unnatural that the Satra institution of Assam had derived its inspiration from the 'sect' or '*sangha*' systems of early India. For we know that Vaishnavism did not encourage monasticism till at least the 11th-12th centuries A.D. when the *Bairagi Movement* initiated it.[66] It is interesting to note that about the same time, the Yogis who derived their source from early *Siddha-Yagi cult* and indebted to a certain degree also to sectarian Buddhism and Hindu Tantrikism, emerged in the peripheral regions including Assam.[67] This is also testified by local epigraphic evidences.[68] Be that as it may, the Satra*s* grew as a secluded and solitary place suitable for conduct of all religious, philosophical and devotional discussions. It is interesting to note that the Ahom kings took into account this aspect of territorial exclusiveness of the Majuli island within the large river streams in order to establish the great Satra*s* in the mid 17th century.[69] Being situated in a solitary area, the Satra has to be approached through a long road till one reaches its gateway called *karapat* or *batchora* that resembles the *toranagriha* of a Hindu temple.[70] Beyond the *batchora* is seen the establishment enclosure of the Satra situated in a quadrangle having the residential quarters (*baha*) of the celibate devotees all around in four lines, and that of the pontiff in the midst by the side of the great prayer hall called *namghar/kirtan ghar*. The *namghar* of the Auniati Satra in Majuli is a huge building that could accommodate more than five thousand devotees at a time during the congregational prayer, or during the performance of a drama, or a dance. Attached to the *namghar* is the sanctum-sanctorum called *manikut* that contains the *Bhagavata* in manuscript form and the image of Lord Krishna called by the name *Govinda Mahaprabhu.*[71] The wooden pillars of the *namghar* of the Dakhinpat Satra, cut out from solid block of woods at the time of the establishment of the Satra in the mid 17th century, are still to be seen holding the old building of the *namghar*.[72] When visited one is struck by the beauty and artistic designs of the pillars with which these were made, and by the atmosphere that prevails inside. The atmosphere of the Garamur Satra is still more impressive. The *District Gazetteer* of Sibsagar, 1905, records the following about the apparent look of the Garamur Satra in Majuli:

The building of the Satra are approached by a good road which is constructed at some expense. The *namghar* is a huge structure, the roof of which is supported on huge wooden pillars and the great floor space is entirely bare save for one or two lecturns on which the sacred writings are reposing. The actual shrine is a separate building closely adjoining the eastern end of the *namghar*. The shrine is very different from the penetralia of the Sakta temple. There is no trace of blood or grease; there is nothing distinguishing or grotesque and the whole place is dominated by the note of decency and propriety which is so marked a characteristic of Vaishnavism of Majuli.[73]

This picture of the monastic Satras in the Majuli island has, however, been significantly changed at present due mainly to the changing geographical and environmental conditions, swift modernization of life-styles, and more importantly, due to the growing economic relations and politicization of the Satra systems. This has been reflected in both material and spiritual life of the inmates. Similarly, extensive erosion caused by the river Brahmaputra and loss of forest, marshy and grazing lands has compelled the Satra*s* to seek shelter elsewhere. Thus, of both natural and man-made causes monastic Satra*s* now look almost desolate in their original seat of settlement.

The Pontiff—His Changing Life Styles

A monastic Satra has a pontiff called *adhikara* or *Satradhikara* who heads the Satra. He, like all residential devotees, is invariably a celibate person, and always belongs to either Brahman or the Kayastha community.[74] It was a custom with the Barpeta Satra in Kamrup alone, which is now a semi-monastic Satra, that the headship is theoretically supposed to be open for members from all castes, and filled up through a process of selection/election.[75] But the custom has now become essentially meaningless as the office has been for last few centuries occupied by Brahman pontiffs alone although a kind of election to the post is held at the time of succession.[76] In the Majuli island there is no Satra at present where the *Satradhikara* is ever elected; he is invariably a Brahman or a Kayastha, and is normally chosen from among the relatives of the existing *Satradhikara*, and he can never be dethroned in his life time.[77] The only exception was Kamalabari where the *adhikara* was selected by the inmates at the initial stage.[78] The concept of superiority of the Brahmans and the idea of the Brahmans being the authority of religious life, which was rejected by Sankaradeva, are so strong here that even the Kayasthas pretend to be Brahmans by assuming the surname of the former, who in order to distinguish themselves in the manner of Bengali Brahmans, used to assume the title *Goswami* since at least the middle of the 19th century.[79] It was in the process that the Auniatiya Satradhikara Deva Dattadeva assumed the title *Goswami* for himself, and seeing him, his counterparts in the other Satras too followed his footsteps.[80] One of the best examples of this historical development was Krishnakanta Goswami (c.1834-1857) of Kamalabari Satra who also was the first *Goswami* of his Satra.[81] There were examples of clashes between the Brahmin devotees and the Kayastha pontiff in at least one Satra, i.e. Kamalabari Satra, where two Brahman disciples left the Satra refusing to acknowledge the authority of the Kayastha *Goswami*.[82] This fact even led to division of the Satra about the middle of the 19th century.[83] Even the *Satradhikaras* of the *Kala Sanghati* order which emphasized much on the upliftment of the backward communities,[84] particularly the Kaivartas, Moran-Mataks and other such tribes, subsequently confined itself to the Kayasthas alone.[85] It is interesting that the *Satradhikara* of the Mayamara Tiphuk Satra in the district of Dibrugarh, who was originally a member of the Moran tribe,[86] treats himself as a Kayastha by assuming all sorts of caste paraphernalia in course of time, and has ceased to maintain intimate relationships with his ethnic kinsmen.[87] Thus, the Satras which played instrumental in the spread of Neo-Vaishnavism whose creator Sankaradeva despised caste disabilities and preached equality of men in the field of religious practices,[88] had soon after his death, becomc an inheritable institution to bc always headed by a member of the Brahman or the Kayastha community; and this is one of the reasons why despite all contributions they have made towards creation of a fabric of Assamese nationality, Satras have failed to embrace the subaltern communities whose numerical strength still distinguishes the population pattern of the Brahmaputra valley. It is interesting that caste factor is so strong among the inmates of a Satra that a single house (*baha*) may have more than one hearth on ground of castes of its members.

Normally, every monastic Satra has two *adhikaras*, one junior and heir to the religious *gaddy* called *deka adhikara*, and the other senior—the *adhikara* or *Satradhikara* who is the actual head of the Satra. It is not known from when the system of having two heads came into being. Early records do not testify to this system. Even Sankaradeva, the initiator of this system, did not have a junior formally nominated although he did so at the time of his death when he nominated Madhavdeva as his successor.[89] This fact, however, led consequently to the division of his sect under different claimants.[90] Even the Auniati Satra which has now three in line of succession including the junior-most called *Govindapuria*, had no custom of having two pontiffs initially.[91] It appears that when the qualification of caste became compulsory for being a *Satradhikara* the superior used to select one of his relatives whom he brought to the Satra and trained him up to finally succeed him to the *adhikara*'s position. Pitambardeva Goswami, the late *Satradhikara* of Garamur Satra (1908-1962), has stated that when the line of Vamsogopaldeva, the founder of the Brahmanical line of the Satra*s* in Upper Assam, came to an end at his Satra, his uncle Chitra Chandradeva Goswami was brought to Garamur Satra from the Kuruwabahi Satra, which is a collateral branch of the earlier family of the line of Vamsigopaldeva. And he was brought to the Satra at the age of a little more than four by his uncle to be the prospective *adhikara* of the Satra.[92] It is interesting to note that not only caste, but even the lineal status also became a subject of consideration in later times. There are examples where a slight deviation from the lineal status in selecting a boy for being a *Satradhikara*, had been criticised. The *Charit Puthis* maintain that after the death of Badula Padma Ata, the founder of the Kamalabari Satra, who died without nominating his successor, inmates had to exercise much labour to find one for the job.[93] As a matter of fact, caste qualification for a *Satradhikara* became a custom in subsequent times for all Satra*s*. The *deka* or the junior *adhikara* is trained for the headship mentally and culturally during his apprenticeship; and when the *Satradhikara* dies, he is installed ceremoniously to the religious throne by performing the coronation ceremony as per vedic rites.[94] As per record, the coronation ceremonies of the *adhikaras* of the big four Satras of the Majuli island (Auniati, Dakhinpat, Garamur and Kamalabari) resembled that of the coronation of the king in the middle ages.[95] It is their custom that the installation of the new *adhikara* be solemnized by one of their class.[96] One aspect of such a coronation was that after the ritual was over, the king was to approve the succession by duly making announcement to the public declaring the succession.[97] The same kind of announcement and approval was done during the colonial Government when the enthronement was duly recorded and published in the state *Gazette*.[98] The system is still continued, of course, in a modified form, and the Government has to approve their succession. It is considered necessary because it carries economic prospects for the Satra and is a matter of prestige.[99]

Both the senior and the junior *adhikaras* have their independent establishments. In the Auniati Satra they have three separate and independent establishments with a number of attendants attached to their respective establishments to work for them.[100] The *adhikara* is the religious head and spiritual guide of the flock under his care, and is normally well-versed in all the scriptures. Most of the *adhikaras* of the big Satra*s* of Majuli were the *gurus* of the Ahom kings in the pre-colonial period, king Jayaddhvaj Singha (1648-1663) being the first of their class to be the disciple of Niranjandeva, the first pontiff of the Auniati Satra and also of Banamalideva of Dakhinpat Satra.[101] Even in the post-Ahom period also they have disciples of the rank of ministers and high executives of the state. Naturally being the proselytizer of the king and his ministers throughout the centuries, the *adhikaras* were much powerful in medieval period and no less revered at present so far as the most known ones are concerned.

An *adhikara* is distinguished by his own dress including the head-dress called *pag,* a style which his class imitated either from the Ahom kings who had established them with all sorts of paraphernalia resembling the monarchs themselves, or the Buddhist monks who used to put them on.[102] He thus felt himself a god, and would never put his feet on the ground, and used to travel by artistically designed boats[103] or on elephant[104] or by human carrier called *dola.*[105] It is recorded that disciples vied with each other to carry the *dola* used by an *adhikara* of the great Satras.[106] The custom of using human-transport (*dola*) and avoiding putting of foot on the ground in public continued till the first quarter of the last century when Pitambardeva Goswami, the reformer *Satradhikara* of Garamur Satra, had initiated the process of its abolition beginning with his own Satra.[107]

FIG. 4.2: A *KHEL NAO* (A TOUR/GAME BOAT)

The *Satradhikara* is the initiator of disciples in almost all cases unless necessary when the *deka adhikara*, and at his absence, the *raj-medhi*[108] (a representative of the *adhikara*), uses to do this duty on his behalf, particularly in distant places. He is addressed (by all) as *jagannath* (Lord Almighty, Lord of the Earth), *prabhu iswar* (Lord God), *tera* (He, the

God), *iswar purush* (in the Person of Lord God), etc.[109] His authority on the inmates and lay disciples was thus immense in the past; he was the Lord Almighty; and everybody was at his disposal from the man on the street to the king on the throne. This status he still enjoys in the rural society, and in part, in the urban society also.

INMATES OF THE SATRA: FROM TRADITIONALISM TO MODERNISM

The devotees called *bhakat* or more specifically *kewalia̲* or *uda̲sin bhakat* live in small houses consisting of one or two rooms called *baha̲* cloistered in a row of such houses called *ha̲ti*. They are, as a matter of rule, celibate persons with supposedly perfect celibate character; but at liberty to leave the life of a celibacy if at any time they find the restraint of celibacy irksome.[110] This has a resemblance with what has happened to many sectors of modern Buddhism in East and South Asia.[111] Celibacy was once a great attracting aspect of the Satra system. It was considered a superior way of life respected by all, and even aspired for by anybody in the society.[112] When on tour to the villages for few days they received very warm welcome from the villagers who used to supply everything that was necessary for their living. It is interesting to note that village folk, men, women and children—all hopefully waited to have a share of the food cooked by such a visiting monk. Having a life of the monk in medieval Assam was also considered to be fortunate when vocations of life were too limited and feudal administration governed men's movements. Sir Edward Gait, the historian of Assam, has noted that at one time in the last part of the 17th century, there were some more than three thousand celibate inmates enrolled in various Satra*s* alarmingly creating a deficit in the man power revenues of the state.[113] Opening up of new vocations in the colonial period, particularly, in the post-colonial times, when men came out of medieval feudal bondage, and had the opportunity of education and employment, celibacy as a system gradually became less popular. The Auniati Satra in Majuli which had once more than a thousand inmates, has at present only three hundred and forty four inmates, the Dakhinpat sixty three, and Kamalabari and Bhogpur each having similar numbers.[114]

The *bhakats*, as the inmates are called, are brought to the Satra in their childhood in order to bring them up in the celibate life style and create a mental makeup in them throughout their youth.[115] Not only mentally, but also physically they were to create a certain class of people quite distinguished from others in their dress and behaviour with long hair which they used to keep twisting on the back of their head, a simple dress consisting of a long white *churiya*, a cotton wrapper called *chadar*, and a towel (*gamocha*) and with moderate and soft speech distinguished by limited, devotional, and passive words. Their food habit was also modified from what they had developed at home, meat and drink being totally prohibited in the Satra. Even the process of one's eating was also changeded in that they now cook their food with a spiritual mind, by one who has a certain standard of spiritual attainment, and before they took it, they used offer it at the name of in the God Almighty and so forth. This again has great similarity with the style of the Buddhist monks in some of the Southeast Asian countries. Peter Harvey has stated that in "South-east Asia monks do not 'eat food', but 'glorify alms-food."[116] Above all, they had to distinguish themselves by cultivating a sense of sacrifice and detachment from all this worldly affairs. The *Sibsagar District Gazetteer* of 1905 referred to the above records about their life style as follows:

> In a square round the garden stand the lines of huts in which the resident monks live. They consist of well-built rows of rooms which are much more specious than those ordinarily occupied by village folk and are kept scrupulously clean. There is singularly gracious and pleasing feeling in the whole atmosphere. Everything is fresh, neat and well to-do. The well-groomed smiling monks are evidently at peace with themselves and with the world at large and even little boys that flock around them are unusually clean and well behaved. The children are recruited from the villages and trained to be devotees.[117]

As stated above, celibacy as a way of life has lost its early popularity. No economically able parents would like to send their sons to a life of celibacy today. In our investigation in the Dakhinpat Satra in 2005 it was found that of the 43 residing inmates of the Satra enrolled at that time there was none whose parents could provide for education of their children. As a matter of fact, most celibate inmates are bound to be confined to the poorer section of the society who had little scope for adopting vocations based on economic affluence of their parents. In the case of Auniati Satra, which had about 350 inmates during our investigation in the same year, almost 99 per cent of them were found to have come from poor families.[118] In the Satra also they lead a poor life reflected well in their small houses (*baha*) with a deserted and melancholy look resembling lines of small huts in a poor urban sub-urb. The income of the *Satradhikara* that includes the contributions from the individuals, religious taxes paid by the disciples, and also the recurring and non-recurring grants obtained from the State Government belongs to him alone, although a small portion he parts with the *Deka Adhikara* and a few of the office holders of the Satra. Interestingly, while the inmates lead a depressed life, a few of the *Satradhikaras* own even tea-gardens. Thus, there remain economic differences between the inmates and the pontiffs. This is however not the case with Garamur Satra, where some of the inmates maintain affluent life than the *Satradhikara* himself. The poverty of the inmates could be seen not only in their economic life, this is also noted in their daily life-styles. It is possibly because of this reason that almost all inmates who had education and a source of earning, like employment, were found to have left the Satra and the life of celibacy in favour of having a married life. It is interesting to note that to our queries as to why they have left celibacy a handsome number of those who have left the Auniati Satra in the past, had replied that they had left the Satra to look after the helpless family at home.[119] In fact, their leaving the Satra is a kind of escapism from poverty and wretchedness. Naturally, the smiling faces of the inmates which once attracted Allen and others, now hardly dazzles the atmosphere of a Satra, nor the inmates have enough scope amidst the hub-hub of the growing urban life all around to make it a place of delight. A visit to the site of the Dakhinpat Satra which is governed by a melancholy atmosphere all around, would explain all about this aspect.

There is no record to show that Sankaradeva, the founder of the system, had ever introduced celibacy as a matter of discipline for the inmates of the Satras. Rather, he was in favour of avoiding it when his most intimate disciple Madhavdeva took it as a way of life. Even Madhavdeva had openly expressed that celibacy was too difficult for an ordinary person, and it was rather advisable not to imitate him in this regard. It is however, not compulsory for any inmate to remain a celibate if he desires to marry finding celibacy difficult to maintain, or if any urgency compels him to do so.[120] In that case, however, he is to leave the Satra and go back home, or live elsewhere.[121]

It is interesting that despite sacrificing a life of house-holder the inmates possess a kind of imaginary family, where the head of the house (*burha bhakat*) considers his juniors as his children, and nominates one of them to succeed him to the headship and perform obsequial rites at his death.[122] Devotion (*bhakti*) to the *guru*, the most distinguished of his aspirations, is his wife, which he cannot leave at any cost.[123] Thus, the idea of being a house-holder, has still been a part of his mental make-up. A question often raised is: whether like the Roman Catholic Church in the pre-Reformation age when the life of the church monks was characterized by many sorts of immoral activities,[124] the inmates of the Satra also have such experience. The answer is not always negative as reported by some of the inmates of a grand Satra of the island. Early biographical works have recorded that even as early as the time of Madhavdeva, some inmates had to break celibacy when circumstances so allowed.[125] Rumours about such relationships of some young inmates with women of the neighbouring locality could be heard. On investigation it was found that most of the inmates who have left the Satra for leading a married life, have married girls of the neighbouring villages with whom they have ample opportunities for introduction, or to mix up during their stay in the Satra.[126] It was possibly realizing this aspect of danger that Pitambardeva Goswami, *Satradhikara* of the Garamur Satra, had abolished celibacy from his Satra in 1915. He also requested the other Satra*s* to follow suit for a better future of the institution.[127] He has stated in his own records that he himself was prepared to marry; but opposition from the other Satra*s* and orthodox section of his disciples finally debarred him from changing the age-old system.[128] It is from his time onwards, therefore, that this Satra became a semi-monastic Satra with the married inmates and celibate pontiff.

Life-styles of the inmates were once governed by certain code of conducts, such as living on bare income earned from begging, not earning more than what was necessary to maintain one's life, wearing simple dress consisting of a *dhuti* and a *chadar*, and keeping long hair.[129] They were to be busy in the pursuit of culture and learning traditional literature and language. On investigation, however, it was found that all inmates today irrespective of their status, ordinary inmates or the pontiffs, go for modern education in the schools and colleges including learning of English as against the tradition of learning early Assamese vernacular and Sanskrit. This has changed the entire life-style of the community. This has been discussed in a subsequent context.

SATRA AND SOCIETY—CASTE AND SOCIAL CHANGE

Understanding Satra as an institution in continuum from the middle ages carrying the heritage of Sankaradeva's tenets, brings the question of caste and inequality, and responses of the Satras to this question. The Neo-Vaishnavite movement led by Sankaradeva of which the Satra institution is a legacy, preached the ideal of caste equality at least in the religious plane and opposed untouchability.[130] Naturally, society of Majuli was a fertile field for the Vaishnava reformers to work and materialise their ideals. Records, however, point to the otherwise. Field surveys have revealed that caste was, and still is, an aspect of consideration for the Satras, of course, in varied degrees according to their affiliations. According to Cantlie, who visited Majuli for several times for the purpose of studying the Satra systems, the "degree of Brahmanization is greatest among the Satras of *Brahma-samhati* which contain the largest proportion of Brahman disciples. The *adhikaras* are also, with a few exceptions,

Brahman. Caste distinctions among the disciples in respect of seating and commensality are carefully maintained in the Satra Name House."[131] She has further noted that the *Purusha Samhati* maintains an intermediate position as regards the observance of caste distinctions. The *Satradhikaras* are both Goswami (Brahman) and Mahanta (Kayastha). The Satras of *Nika-Samhati* have little interest in these matters, being mostly concerned with maintenance of ritual purity. Even in the Satras of the *Kala-Samhati*, according to her, caste distinctions have a comfortable place.

> "In 1971 I visited Puranimati Satra near Jorhat, the main branch of the famous Mayamara Satra. The principal Name House had been blown down in a storm and a new one was in course of construction. In the meantime all the disciples were using the other Name House which was ordinarily reserved for the Kaibarttas (fishermen) who are a scheduled caste. At Name they sat together and ate the raw offering (*prasad*), but at feasts of cooked rice (*bhoj*) the Kaibarttas did not sit with the others. The new Name House was to be for the use of the clean castes only and some of the Kaibarttas were objecting to this arrangement. Caste distinctions in varying degrees have entered into the organization of all Satras."[132]

It is to be noted here that the Kaivartas form a significant group among the inhabitants of the island, but were treated with contempt in the Satra circles. It was possibly due to such outlook of the Satras and of the people attached to them that the Kaivartas rose in revolt against the Ahom monarchy as early as the 18th century during the Mayamara civil war (1769-1805)[133] and led a movement against oppression in the early 20th century.[134] This has been discussed in the chapters II and VI respectively of this work. Similar movements were also to be launched by the Ahoms in the post-monarchical days[135] whose rulers had once made Vaishnavism a royal religion and established the Satras with all kinds of grants including land and labour. The book called *Ripunjoy Smriti* published from Jorhat in the early 20th century bears evidence about the role of the Satras on the question of eradication of caste prejudices.[136] While going to note about the role of the caste in the society of the island, Sanjay Ghose, a social worker and who spent a few years in the island doing social work and mixing up with its people, has recorded his experience as follows:

> The issue of caste is interesting. Seeing from the outside this society seems egalitarian, classless, casteless. But from within, the perception is quite different... ....True, not the kind of vicious caste discrimination one is used to seeing at close quarters in Rajasthan, people sitting at different levels, drinking water in different glasses, practicing

untouchability—but there is a difference here, subtle, yet deep rooted. This was apparent at every step on my journey.[137]

Another caste which had to fight strenuous battle against the orthodox caste attitude and the role of the Satras, were the Suts, as has been mentioned in Chapter-II. It is recorded that they prayed for a lift in their social status in response to which the Auniati *Satradhikara* set on them certain conditions of penance to accede to their demand, thereby indicating his refusal.[138] During the movement led by Mahatma Gandhi for abolition of untouchability, there was a public demand from all over Assam requesting the Auniati *Satradhikara* Hemchandradeva Goswami (1926-1983) for comment on the issue of maintenance of untouchability. In response to this demand, as Tirthanath Sarma, the revered historian of the Satra, had remarked, Hemchandradeva published and circulated a leaflet titled *Hindu Samajaloi Gohari* (an appeal to the Hindu society) wherein he emphatically stated that "he cannot reject the conventional rituals and customs sanctioned by the *Srutis* and *Smritis*. *Satradhikara*s like him come to conduct the affairs of a Satra for some time as a matter of rule. They have no right whatsoever to break the rules and regulations maintained by the Satras since inception."[139] It seems that the *Satradhikara* thereby rejected the essence of the movement for eradication of untouchability led by Gandhiji by saying that 'it was not proper that rules laid down by *sastras* be violated by enacting law. If the door of the heart of men in the high society does not open itself to embrace the untouchables they cannot be embraced into the temple by application of law.'[140]

This, however, does not speak the whole truth. Even Hemchandradeva's comment could be interpreted otherwise, because there is no doubt that unless high society embraces the subalterns, no law could change the system. But, to what extent the high society can be open ? There is a case in this regard. A few years ago the *gosain* of a Satra in Majuli and his accompanying inmates were not received well by his counterpart in another Satra as is usually done simply because the team was accompanied by a young boy who was not a *bhakat* of the Satra and who belonged to a caste that is considered low in the Satra circle. As reported by the boy, the visiting team had to cut short its programme in order to avoid further interactions. This was exactly the view of most of the Satras on the matter of caste equality and fraternity till at least very recent decades. There is no doubt that the nature of caste prejudices was more stringent a few decades before, and more than that before a century. As a matter of fact, going against such social outlook was very difficult, particularly on part of those who have enjoyed higher social and economic status since feudal days. As a result, although the farsighted and intelligent Pitambardeva

Goswami of Garamur Satra who was trained in the ideals of the father of the nation, acceded to their demand and certified and approved their lift,[141] his approval did not bring higher status to the Suts. He himself said, "Even after the penance, the caste Hindus never looked up to the Suts.... Some of the Gosains and Mahantas of Ahataguri mauja came forward to harm me because I performed that penance for the Suts."[142] He, however, opened his *namghar* to the Suts and paved the way for their assimilation in his Satra with members of the caste Hindus. He also threw open the door of his Satra to the Kaivartas, the Misings and similar other communities of his neighbourhood. For Pitambardeva Goswami too it was not easy a task to go against prevailing caste prejudices. Once he was to seek permission from the disciples of his Satra to allow him to proselytize different tribal and backward communities of Assam like the Kacharis, Lalungs and Mikirs.[143] But the Satra community did not approve of his plea on the ground that for doing such an arduous job, the *Satradhikara* would have to lose his dignity while moving from place to place like an ordinary man. Pitambardeva Goswami also lamented that he found no time to work among the tea-garden people and the Nagas in the hills.[144] The root of untouchability as a social crime thus remained although it became gradually loose and looser. It is clear that barring a very few, most Satras did not undertake any serious and systematic attempt at sanskritising the tribes and other depressed people in the island which fact left best opportunities to the Christian missionaries to make good of their footholds in the island in recent decades. It is interesting that majority of the Misings in Majuli do not belong to any Satra located in the island.

Caste consideration marks also the internal atmosphere of the Satras in matters of dining and social relationship. As known from the Satra sources, a Brahman inmate does not take food cooked and served by a Sudra inmate; and a Sudra of a higher caste will not take cooked food from the hand of a fellow *bhakat* if he belongs to a caste lower than his.[145] It is a normal rule in the Satras that a man especially belonging to the lower castes who visits the Satra, shall have to wash or throw away the plates, normally earthen pots or plantain leaves, himself/herself if he/she is to take food at the premises of the residences of the inmates. Such convention is, no doubt dictated by procedure of maintaining cleanliness, but it is equally true that there is a strong element of caste prejudices in the convention. But that is not always the case with visitors of higher castes, or of higher echelons. The only exception but interesting aspect is that when an educated and a man of status visits the Satra, even though he belongs to a lower caste, the *bhakats* themselves arrange for doing such works. This is what may be considered as a prelude to the victory of knowledge and modernity over all that is old and traditional.[146] In this matter an attempt was made by Pitambardeva Goswami of Garamur Satra against untouchability and caste discrepancies and allowed all including tribal members to have entrance to all agenda of his Satra. Tarun Chandra Pamegam, who belonged to the Mising tribe of the village Bargaya, a few kilometers to the west from the Garamur Satra, was appointed his personal Secretary. This fact explains how this *Satradhikara* by liberalising his treatment towards the depressed classes living around his Satra, gave them significant uplift in the ladder of their culture. It was due to his endeavor that members of all depressed communities within the sphere of influence of Garamur Satra got an opportunity to be a part of the culture system of the Satra. And this makes the society of the Garamur Satra and its neighbourhood apparantly distinguished from those of any other parts of the island.

Caste in the Organization of the Satras

Inmates of the Satra are recruited from the families of certain castes only which enjoy higher positions in the caste hierarchy. At present (i.e. at the time of collection of materials for preparing this work) there were 344 residential *bhakats* at the Auniati Satra in Majuli out of which 43 were Brahmans, 1 Kayastha, 188 Kalitas, 71 Koch and 42 Keot. The *Satradhikara*, the *Deka Satradhikara* (heir to the headship), the *Barpujari* (chief worshipper) and the *Bhagawati* (reader of the *Bhagavat*) were invariably Bramans.[147] In the Natun Kamalabari Satra which is headed by a Kayastha *Satradhikara* there were 163 inmates among whom we found during our investigation 1 Brahman, 1 Gosain (Kayastha), 66 Kalita, 38 Koch and 31 Keot members. Similarly, in the Dakhinpat Satra which is headed by a Brahmin pontiff, there were 63 inmates among whom we found 18 Kalita, 19 Brahmin, 18 Koch and 8 Keot members. This shows that inmates were recruited from among the Brahmans, Kayasthas, Kalitas, Keots, and to a lesser degree, from among the Kochs only; and rest of the inhabitants of the island, such as the Chutiyas, Naths, Suts, Kaivartas, Misings, Kacharis, Deoris, or members from any other community for that matter, were not recruited, to the residential *bhakatship* of a monastic Satra. Dr. Pitambardeva Goswami, the present *Satradhikara* of Auniati Satra, writes that since the head of a *baha* normally selects a boy of his choice to bring him to his *baha* and bestows on him the responsibility of performing his mortuary rights after his death, he normally selects a relation of his; and this fact leads to concentration of *bhakats* in the Satra of certain castes only.[148] While his statement is not untrue, it is, at the same time, seen that even in those *bahas* where *bhakats* of different castes reside, and therefore its head has the option open to recruit a boy from any caste, he always selects one only from among the castes mentioned above; invariably not from among the Chutiya, Kachari, Kaivarta, Nath or Katani, Sut, or Mising. This shows that although the head of a *baha* normally brings a boy of his own caste, and if possible, of his own relation, no head brings any boy to his *baha* from other than the Brahman, Kayastha, Kalita, Keot or Koch caste even when he can apply more flexibility in this case. This is certainly due to the norms maintained by the Satra since inception. This is exactly what is going on in other Satras of Majuli as well and most other Satras of Assam. And this is why, Satras are sometimes alleged to have been able to unify only certain fraction of the society, and not the whole, to justify its credit of being considered as a symbol of Assamese nationality.[149] This shows that caste factor which was earlier rejected largely during the days of Sankaradeva and immediately after in the organization of the centres of practices, it became an important element in the later periods in the organization of the Satras and in the social relationship within the Satra itself. It is perhaps because of such aspects that opinions differ as to the nature of role played by the Satras in the formation of an Assamese nationality. According to a recent research, therefore, the assertion that the Satras helped in the emergence of an Assamese middle class, which acted as the agent of nationality formation, 'flies in the face of simple truth'.[150]

Satras and Material Wealth

Early Vaishnava preachers emphasized on attainment of knowledge and morality; and less importance was laid on material wealth and prosperity. There were such *Satradhikaras* who even despised wealth in the form of the king's gifts as detrimental to the purpose of teaching morality and devotion. But slowly Satras became attached to them, and material prosperity began to govern a major aspect of Satriya life. The major Satras of Majuli, particularly Auniati and Dakhinpat, being the owner of enormous landed properties gifted by the Ahom kings, and their *adhikaras* being the religious preceptors of lakhs of disciples scattered all over the state, these Satras pause to be royal, and their *adhikaras* assumed in the past the life style of a class of lords in imitation of the Ahom kings. It is the normal procedure on part of a *Satradhikara* of those Satras to anoint themselves through the *abhisheka* ceremony that often resembles the coronation ceremony of the early kings of the state. It is recorded by the writer of the *Auniati* Satra*r* *Buranji* that the 50th and the 60th year jubilee of Dattadeva Goswami's (1838-1904) coronation was observed in the Satra with such pomp and grandeur that it resembled the coronation ceremony of queen Victoria;[151] and his *adyasraddha* ceremony was attended by more than one lakh devotee.[152] The total expenditure incurred in this function cannot be estimated without going through the entire proceedings of the ceremony.[153] Similarly, the *adyasraddha* ceremoney of Naradeva Goswami (1895-1925) of Dakhinpat Satra was attended by 7000-8000 Brahmans and more than 20,000 people.[154] Their mode of travel was also similar to that of a lord; palanquins borne by human beings were a part of their means of surface travel till at least the middle of the last century. Cantlie has remarked that "the *adhikars* of famous Satras, who are in theory almost totally withdrawn from worldly affairs, cannot be touched and do not set foot on the ground outside the Satra precincts. When they go out on tour with their retinue to visit their disciples in the cold weather, they travel by boat or are carried in litters to camps specially built for them by the villagers, and cloths are spread on the ground before them as they walk."[155] She has further noted as follows: " When I was a child of four, the *adhikara* of Auniati Satra paid visit to my father who was at that time Deputy Commissioner of Sibsagar District. I remember that a carpet was ordered from Calcutta for the occasion and laid on the stairs of the house just before his arrival so that no foot had trodden on it before his."[156] According to a scholar "with lust for money, power and prestige.. they ceased to be agents of social and spiritual progress and became sad symbols of cultural inertia."[157]

At present, however, much liberalization in their life styles has set in, and the present *adhikara* of Auniati Satra, Dr. Pitambardeva Goswami, has been an example in this regard. It is stated by the inmates of the Satra that Hemchandradeva Goswami was so strict in maintaining the schedule of his work that he did not allow any body, disciple or otherwise, to see or meet him if they fail to do that in time already fixed, and as per programme scheduled sufficiently earlier like very very important political leaders of the country. Thus, the *Satradhikaras* of the large Satras despite being pleased to have millions of disciples (*sishyas*), had led a secluded life far above the mass society in order to maintain his class distinctions. Considering this attempt to maintain a class character detrimental to the growth of the nationalist upsurge in the country, Pitambardeva Goswami, the late *Satradhikara* of Garamur Satra, relinquished the palanquin in 1921 as means of travel, when the question of equality, liberty and fraternity came to the fore during the freedom struggle of the country.

The above description, however, does not apply equally in case of all Satras and *Satradhikaras*. Satras with weak economy and comparatively less number of disciples, are unable to lead a life of pomp and afflorescence. On the other hand, there were certain *Satradhikaras* who were happy to relinquish extensive landed property during the time of the British. Thus, Garamur and Kamalabari *Satradhikaras*, of their own accord, gave away much of their landed properties under the colonial pressure. Even after independence, most Satras, including Auniati, had to relinquish their ownership over certain portion of their lands as a matter of Government policy of ceiling. Be that as it may, lands possessed by the Satras form a part of the agricultural fields of the peasants, and Auniati Satra has the credit of lending out large extent of its lands to the cultivators of the state although at the cost of payment of a part of the produce as revenue.[158] In other aspects of the economic life the Satras have little to do, except possibly in the field of certain crafts, such as boat making, which has been an indispensably required qualification of the islanders. A few other crafts, such as making of embroidered cane-fans by the inmates of the Auniati and Kamalabari Satra, and the mask making by the family of the *adhikaras* of the Chamaguri are known to people even from outside. This has been discussed in the Chapter on Economy. It may, however, be presumed that in the context of commercialization of arts and crafts, and growth of cultural tourism as an industry, Satras in Majuli have ample scope to become significant sources of its economic growth.

PERFORMING ART IN SATRA

Music and Dance

Satras are centres for cultivation of various performing arts, notably music and dance.The Neo-Vaishnavite Movement brought in its trail a new horizon to the traditional cultural activities of the people of Assam. Sankaradeva himself composed a number of devotional songs. M. Neog has stated that although there was culture of Hindu music in Assam, there was no specimen of *raga* music composed at a date anterior to Sankaradeva.[159] "Music and poetry", he says, "promoted the propagation of *bhakti* by making it attractive and drawing people to its side."[160]

FIG. 4.3: CHANTING *NAM-KIRTAN* IN A *BAR-SABAH*

Songs composed by Sankaradeva, and his disciple Madhavdeva are still sung in the Satras. Among them the most well-known are the *bargeets* sung in particular melody (*raga*) which is mentioned at the top of the *geet*. The *bargeets* are composed in a language called *Brajawali/Brajabuli*, although a good number of them composed by his disciple Madhavdeva deviate from that.[161] *Bargeets* occupy the most sacred place among the devotional songs of the Satra. In the Auniati Satra they are included in the list of the *nitya* (daily) songs. They are also practiced and taught to the novices at the Satra, and sung in three different agenda of the *naimittika* (occasional) schedule of work, in the morning agenda called *prabhati*, in the orchestral songs called *gayan-bayan*, and in the evening prayer called *arati*. They form a special agenda in the functions of the birth and death anniversaries of the saints.

The next class of *geets* popular in the Satras are the *ankar geet*. They are the songs of the dramas. According to M. Neog, they "do not differ from *bargeetas* in musical execution except in that the former is always accompanied with rhythmic beats and is rarely or never executed without it. The *tala* of each *ankar geet* is, therefore, always indicated along with its *raga*."[162] *Ankar geets* are always performed during the presentation of a drama which 'mark occasional monastic or village festivities.'[163] *Ankar geets* are also composed in *Brajawali* language. *Ankar geets* form a part of the *naimittikar geets* that include *ankar geet, janmastamir geet, rasha lilar geet, tithir geet, gopal vairagyar geet* (Auniati Satra), *geet-govindar geet, panchali geet, bihur geet* and *guru bandana geet*.[164] M.Neog includes in the list also the congregation prayer *kirtana* or *nama-kirtana* or *kirtana-ghosha*.[165] *Nama-kirtana* is easy for all classes of singers as it is sung in chorus with a leader called *nama-lagowa* setting the singing. Being easy this form of music is popular both in the Satra and in the villages. Indeed, in a village *namghar*, or in a family religious function performing *nama-kirtana* is a normal feature. *Nama-kirtana* is accompanied by use of musical instruments like *khol*, *mridanga*, *nagara*, and cymbal called *bar-tal*.[166] A different set of music known as *oja-pali* is popular in all the Satras of Majuli. A band of singers consisting of four or five members use to perform the song. There is a leader called *oja*, and his supporters called *pali*. It is a distinct form of dance-music performed in form of a chorus and similar to the *nama-kirtana*. The *charit puthis* of Auniati Satra record that this class of music has a long history in the Satra.[167] Be that as it may, *oja-pali* is both a song and a dance. The song consists of recitation of the stories from the *Ramayana* or the *Mahabharata*. It is stated that Mathuradas Burha Ata (later *adhikara* of the Barpeta Satra in Kamrup) was earlier an expert in this form of singing before he became a disciple of Madhavdeva. And the style of his singing was called by the inmates as *vangadesi-m*a̲*ta*.[168] The tradition was later brought to the Satra system of dances, and was reoriented.[169]

FIG. 4.4: PERFORMING *KHOL* IN CLASSICAL ASSAMESE FORM

Ga̲yan-ba̲yan forms another class of dance-cum-choral music performed by a group of artists called *ga̲yan* and *ba̲yan*. It is a part of the regular activities of any Satra, and is an indispensable part of the performance during the presentation of a *bha̲ona̲*. The *ga̲yans* who preserve the manuscripts on songs with them, use to sing the solos, while the *ba̲yans* perform the instrument called *khol* and the *ta̲l* (cymbal). It is a choral song accompanied by dance.

Of the various other forms of dances important ones include the *sutradha̲ra na̲ch* or *sutra bhangi*, *gosa̲i prabesar na̲ch* or *krishna bhangi*, *gopi prabesar na̲ch* or *gopi bhangi*, *ca̲li na̲ch*, *jhumura̲*, *nritya bhangi*, *ra̲sa nritya*, varieties of dance forms associated with *bha̲ona̲s*, such as the *yuddhar na̲ch* (fighting dance), and so forth.[170] The dance of *sutrabhangi* is associated with performance of a drama; and in a sense, it is the inaugural of the *bha̲ona̲*. By the *gosa̲i prabesar na̲ch* Krishna enters the audience in the *na̲mghar* in dancing movement. Similarly, *gopi bhangi* is the rhythmic movement of the milk-maids of Vraja along with Yasoda, Krishna's mother. Of the dances *ca̲li na̲ch* deserves some elaboration. According to M.Neog, "Some *bargeet*s and songs from the dramas representing actions and sentiments of women are presented in a dance form, *ca̲li na̲c* (dance resembling *ca̲li* or 'the spreading out of tail of a peacock or similar bird'), or, simply *natuwa̲ na̲c*." He further notes that "*natuwa̲ na̲c* or *cali nac* is a dance performed by young monks, dressed as women as in *gopi—bhangi*, but which can sometimes be separated from the body of a dramatic representation and danced independently on special occasions. In the rich Satras of Majuli as many as twelve different types of *natuwa nac* are made out (the difference, however, being only in the difference in rhythms of the *ramdani*), and these are sometimes divided into *hajowalia* and *pakhuaji* styles, which name indicates the later day imbibed features of dances of the temple women of Hajo and of some style of northern India. The Auniati Satra particularly speaks of an *apsara bhangi* or the style of nymph dance.... In some features, particularly in the costume *natuwa nac* seems to have some sort of relation with the Manipuri school of dance."[171]

Among the distinct dance forms of the Satras of Majuli mention may be made of *jhumura* in the performance of which the dancers put on a kind of dress when he is appearing half male and half female. The term *jhumura* has been taken from the dramas of Madhavdeva like *Chordhara Jhumura, Ras Jhumura*, and the dance is believed to have been developed by Madhavdeva.[172] It is specific to the Kamalabari Satra. During this dance songs from the dramas of Sankaradeva and Madhavdeva, and *bargeets* expressing women sensuality are sung. During this dance both *khol* and *tal* (cymbal) are used. It is further believed that this dance is expressive of the mental and physical condition of the *gopis* in Vrindavan when Krishna departed from the midst of the *gopis*.[173] In this dance form 2-4 young inmates (*bhakatar lora*) participate.

Other dance forms include *nadu-bhangi* which is a dance presenting the sweeming posture of Krishna in the Kaliya lake where he tamed the demon Kalinaga. It is performed by the young inmates of the Satra.[174] Other forms of Krishna-centred dances include the *ras-nritya*, the 'circling dance of the *gopis* of Vrindavana. Introduced by Sankaradeva and Madhavdeva through their plays, *ras nritya* is popular in all the Satras of Majuli. There are various other forms of dances performed in the Satras and village *namghars*, such as *yuddhar nach, bhawariya pravesar nach, dhemali* or preliminary dance which is performed before the *bhaona* begins, and so forth.

Dance and music involves the use of various kinds of musical instruments of which the drums called *khol*, and cymbals called *tal* predominate. Both the types are found used in the devotional songs in the Satras and in the villages. The *khol* is a hollow wooden instrument covered with animal skin finished by a layer of special iron-mix soil-paste called *loachu* at both ends. *Mridanga* is another type of instrument made of dry clay and skin. "Both *mridanga* and the *khol* are barrel-shaped; but the former looks more tapering at the ends and has smaller drum heads than the latter."[175] *Tals* are of three varieties—big or *bar tal, bhot/ bhor tal* (cymbal originally imported from Bhutan by Sankaradeva), middle sized (*patital*) and small sized (*khuti tal/saru tal/mandira*). *Khol, mridanga*, and *tals* are used in the performance of various kinds of dances, drama and devotional songs. Two other types of bamboo instruments called *kara tal* and *ram tal* respectively are also used in the singing of devotional songs. A very large wooden and skinned drum called *daba* (kettle drum) is kept in every Satra and village *namghars*. It is used in congregation prayer, and in the evening as a symbol of announcing the time for prayer. In that sense it works as the church bell.[176] *Nagara* is another type of wood and skin instrument used in pair during congregation prayer. It is more popular in the Auniati Satra than any other Satras of the island. Among other instruments we find *banhi* (flute), a small bamboo instrument used in performance of devotional songs, and *khanjari* (tambourines) used for the same purpose. Two other varieties of instruments the *kali* and the *bheri* are also in use, particularly in the big Satras like Auniati and Dakhinpat or Garamur. They are used to indicate the arrival of the *Satradhikaras* after completing tour, or on arrival of important persons at the Satra. They are specially used during the *Palnam* festival.[177]

During the British rule some changes in the style of presentation and in the forms of music and musical instruments were brought to the system practiced in some of the Satras of Majuli. It was during this period that most of the enlightened *Satradhikaras* had their contact with Bengal through the British colonial rulers who always tried to impress upon the *Satradhikaras* the superiority of their (British) culture. Records preserved by the Auniati Satra mention that it was during the period of Dattadeva Goswami (1838-1904) that a few Western musical instruments entered the Satra culture.[178] Tirthanath Sarma has noted that Dattadeva was greatly impressed by Jenkins towards Western music.[179] He has further informed us that during his long stay at Guwahati, after his assumption of the headship, he was deeply influenced by Bengali musical systems and there he cultivated many of the Bengali songs and rhythms which, later on, he introduced into his Satra systems.[180] He was also a regular reader of the Bengali news papers and journals.[173] It was perhaps because of this habit that he was deeply impressed by the Bengali language and some of the other developments in the 19th century Bengal. Reflection of the impact of the Bengali language in his composition can be noted in his songs.[182] As a result, men used to allege that Dattadeva allowed entry of *bare-bangaluwa* culture to the society of Assam.[183]

H. N. Sarma, who has done surveys of the Auniati Satra, has stated that there are three varieties of music and dance in the Auniati Satra, *hajowalia*, *bangalua* and *ankiya*.[184] He states that the *natuwa nach* and the *apsara nach* are performed in the Satra in the *hajowalia* style, while the *Krishna nritya* is presented in the *bangaluwa* style.[185] All this shows that two factors have influenced the music and dance style of the royal Satras—one is the patronage of the Ahom kings and the other is the 19th century contact of Assam with Bengal and the colonial British. As a result of this, modern Satra art forms are sometimes seen to reflect some extra-Vaishnavite influence in their performance.

Satras of Majuli are the workshop of Assamese drama called *nata* or *nataka*. Sankaradeva introduced drama (*nataka*) in the form of *bhaona* in Assam to be followed by his disciple Madhavdeva, and then by Gopaladeva, the founder of the *Kala Sanghati* order. As an instrument of spreading the Neo-Vaishnavite ideals among the mass of people, dramas were, and still are, the best agency that transmit Neo-Vaishnava teachings and the story of Lord Krishna into the villages with which the saints were primarily concerned. And performance of a drama in the Assamese Vaishnava style involves presentation of almost all aspects of devotional songs and music. Thus an Assamese drama as performed in the Satras as well as in the villages in Majuli is both a drama and an art of dance and music. Kamalabari Satra (all the three) is well-known for performance of such drama of which the *Ram Vijaya, Rukmini Harana, Parijat Harana* of Sankaradeva are most famous.

Dramas composed by Sankaradeva and Madhavdeva are called *ankiya*, a term applied to them by the writers of their biographical works.[186] According to M.Neog, "It is very likely that the Assamese drama as an one-Act piece came to be called *anka*, in imitation of the Sanskrit terminology (*anka, utsristikanka*) in spite of the fact that Sankara's or Madhava's dramas do not conform to all the requirements of the above definition of *anka* or *utsristikanka*. On the other hand, it also cannot be dismissed as improbable that Assamese variety of drama was called *anka* just because it continued a single act."[187]

Dramas are normally performed at the common prayer hall both in the Satras and in the villages of Majuli. There are however, examples when dramas are also performed in open *pandal* called *rabha*. Madhavdeva himself staged dramas in such open houses called *rang ghar* or *rangiyal ghar*.[188] Being religious in character, there is always the role of Krishna or Ram in the Assamese Vaishnava dramas. Among the other players called *bhawariya*, meaning one who represents other's character,[189] the *Sutradhara* or *Sutradhari* is the most important in the *ankiya* drama who carries forward the story of the drama till it closes. There is no woman player in *bhaona*; women roles are played by young inmates of the Satra, and in a village *namghar* by the young boys. The language of the dramas composed by Sankaradeva and Madhavdeva (*Kaliya Daman, Patniprasad, Keli Gopal, Rukmini Haran, Parijat Haran, Ram Vijaya* are written by Sankaradeva, while *Arjun Bhanjan, Chor Dhara Nat, Pimpara Guchuwa, Bhumi Letowa, Bhojan Behar Bhushan Herowa Kotora Khela, Ras Jhumura* are dramas of Madhavdeva) is called *Brajabuli* or *Brajawali bhasa* except in certain recitative *payaras* within the drama where old Assamese used by Sankaradeva himself in some of his other works are used.[190] In course of time, *Brajawali* was gradually replaced by the Assamese vernacular language. It is possible that later day composers, notably the *Satradhikaras*, could not achieve such excellence in the use of the *Brajawali* like the preceding preachers, or may be that Assamese as the common man's language became more effective in carrying the lessons of the dramas to the village. Thus, use of common man's vocabulary became a usual practice in the dramas composed in the Satras. As we have mentioned elsewhere (Chapter-II) in the Auniati Satra there was and still is a custom that every *Satradhikara* after his accession to the headship, has to compose a drama and perform it in the Satra under his direction. It seems that composing drama and directing it effectively was considered a qualification for a *Satradhikara* which is still in practice. Thus composing drama and performing them is a culture in the Satra in Majuli; and it was from the Satras that it spread to the villages. In earlier times Auniati Satra used to perform *bhaona* also at the court of the kings.[191] It was on such an occasion that the inmates of the Satra received Jai Singha, the fugitive king of Manipur, with *gayan-bayan* and dramatic performance at the Ahom court at Rangpur.[192] It is not therefore unlikely that many aspects of Vaishnava culture of Manipur including *gayan-bayan* and *ras lila*, were imported from Auniati Satra. This is further corroborated by the fact that the worshipful deity of Manipur Vaishnavism is the same as that of the Auniati Satra—the *Govinda Mahaprabhu* who is called there as *Govindaji.*

Besides *ankiya* drama, in the Kamalabari Satra we find a different kind of drama called *dhura* or *faujiya natak*. Its *Satradhikara* Krishnakanta Goswami is said to have introduced this class of *bhaona* about the middle of the 19th century possibly in imitation of the Bengali *yatras*. It is stated that Krishnakanta Goswami learnt a special class of melody called *bandha rag* from one Lokai Gayan Barua of Jorhat and introduced it in the Satra by composing a class of drama to play on this *raga*.[193] There are, therefore, differences between an *ankiya bhaona* and a *faujiya bhaona* [194] in so far its *rags* are concerned. This class of drama includes *Rajasuya, Rukmini Harana, Duti Sangvad, Kangsabadh, Aghasur Badh, Bhojan Vyavahar*, and *Mukta Harana*. They are composed respectively by Krishnakanta Goswami and his successors.[195] These dramas are very popular in the villages. It appears that *dhura bhaona* is an impact of Bengali culture which became so widely practiced in the Satras in the 19th century that it is not improbable when it is known that even the title *Goswami,* the surname of the *Satradhikaras,* was an imitation from Bengal. It is to be mentioned here that impact of the 19th century Bengali culture was not only traced in the life and culture of the *Satradhikaras*, of Kamalabari Satra, but also in those of other Satras of the island. In this regard Vishnu Chandradeva Goswami (1983-1998), successor of Hemchandradeva Goswami (1926-1983) of Auniati Satra, has remarked that, in course of time, the Bengali *yatras* entered the towns and cities of Assam and exercised much influence on the Assamese society before the First World War.[196] It was since then that many writers began to compose drama in Assamese using sources from the *Puranas* or histories. And thus, a new chapter began in the history of Assamese drama which soon spread into the cultural life of the Satras.[197] This is how a separate class of drama known as *matri bhashar natak* (drama in mother /vernacular language) came into being. In present times, these dramas in vernacular language are more popular among the common people.

It is not astonishing to find that dramas composed and performed in the Satras of Majuli are invariably religious in contents with subject matters taken from the epics and the *Puranas*. The only exception in this regard is to be found in the Auniati Satra where its *Satradhikara* Kamaldeva Goswami (1904-1922) had composed a secular social drama called *Yugal Milan* in modern Assamese language. The drama was published by Durgeswar Sarma of Jorhat in the year 1910.[198] The drama reflects on the contemporary Assamese rural society, its beliefs and customs, vocabulary, social evils like opium consumption and so forth. According to T.N.Sarma, "use of modern Assamese prose in the Satras, like Auniati and Dakhinpat, began much earlier; and it was also the demand of the time. Chief objective of a drama is its aspect of popularity, but old vocabulary fails to serve this purpose to the extent desireable. The *Satradhikaras* realised this drawback. Thus Dattadeva, Kamaldeva and the present *Satradhikara* Hemchandradeva—all of them used modern vernacular in their dramas."[199] Thus, 19th century opened a new horizon in the drama culture in the Satras; and the trend of the old order of the time of the *Mahapurushas* was reoriented to suit the need of the society; and Majuli played a vital role in this regard.

FINE ARTS IN THE SATRAS—MANUSCRIPTS PREPARATION

Preparation of manuscript was an old art of the people of Assam. After the growth of the Neo-Vaishnavite movement in the 16th century the art became more popular and widespread. Now onwards, every Satra had some inmates expert in preparing a kind of paper called *sanci pat* from the bark of a class of tree called *sanci.*

As a center of cultivation of *Bhakti* religion the Satras in Majuli has been also a centre of cultivation of Sanskrit and vernacular literature since inception. Thus it was a kind of library of multitudes of manuscript works prepared or collected since inception many of which are still preserved. According to S.N.Sarma, "Big Satras like Auniati and Dakhinpat once contained more than a thousand manuscripts, some of which are being preserved in the different antiquarian institutions."[200] Considering the volume of manuscripts which still remains enormous by voluminous even after centuries of damage and loss due to flood, natural calamities, ignorance of men and warfare in medieval times, and many other causes, the statement of Dr. Sarma is not an exaggeration.[201]

Objective of Preparing/Collecting Manuscripts

One of the major objectives of the Neo-Vaishnavite movement in Assam was to enlighten the common people with the stories of the epics and to imbibe them with the moral lessons derived from them. The preachers of the period therefore translated the epics, in full or in part, into the vernacular Assamese for the edification of the masses.[202] Both Sankaradeva and his disciple Madhavdeva spoke of the backward castes and tribes—the *Mlecchas* and the *Yavanas* while indicating the good effects of their cult on the tribal and unclean society of the north-east.[203] Thus the Satras, which form the core institution of the Neo-Vaishnavite movement, became the centre of study of scriptures including the epics for proper and quick expansion of the sect. It was for this purpose that the preachers and devotees who were well-versed in Sanskrit as well as Assamese, used to collect and/or translate the Sanskrit works into Assamese (verse), and they also used them to form the kernel of many of their dramas.

In this context it should be mentioned that all manuscripts preserved and/or produced in the Satras are not always Assamese manuscripts; there were scholars like Sankaradeva, Madhavdeva, Ram Saraswati and Ananta Kandali whose works included Sanskrit compositions also. Most of the *Satradhikaras* too were Sanskrit scholars who never relegated the traditional view on the language. As a matter of fact, many a manuscripts thus preserved were Sanskrit manuscripts. The Auniati Satra, for example, still possesses in its collection the Sanskrit manuscripts of the *Bhagavata-Cantos IX, VII-IX, Kumar Sambhav, Sri Chandogra Sulapani bajra Binirgata Rajapratyengika Strota, Mahapuja Bidhi, Jyotish-Muktawali, Gopal Sahasra Nam, Bhatti Kavya and the Sri Hastamuktavali* (with Assamese prose translation).

Nature of Subjects

The boundary of the subjects selected for translation, collection or preservation of manuscripts became expanded enough beyond what was during the time of Sankaradeva and immediately after. While most of the early works were religious scriptures or parts of the epics, works produced in the Satras of post-Sankaradeva period were combination of both—secular and religious subjects. The *Hasti Vidyarnava* or the *Gajendra Chintamani* preserved in the Auniati Satra has been an unique example of secular works. Similarly, the oft-noted *Chitra Bhagavata* may be an illustration of the religious works. So far as Assamese manuscripts are concerned, the most numerously preserved are those of the *Bhagavata*, the *Mahabharata*, the *Ramayana*, works of Sankaradeva and Madhavdeva, and other works including astrology and astronomy. The later group includes among others the *Puran, Kavya, Vyakarana*, historical work, and a few manuscripts of devotional songs. But the most voluminous of this group consists of the biographical works of the Vaishnava saints called *Charit Puthis.* The Auniati Satra is probably the richest in this class of manuscript preserve where biographies of all the *Satradhikaras* till the time of Hem Chandradeva Goswami have been preserved. Thus, manuscripts collected and preserved in the Auniati Satra, and as such, in all other Satras of the state are on varieties of subjects although religious works, notably the *Bhagavata,* the epics and the works of Sankaradeva and Madhavdeva predominate. Gait, in this regard has pointed out that " the subject dealt with are various. Many are of a historical character; others described the methods of divination in use amongst the Ahom Deodhais and Bailungs; others again are of a religious nature while a few contain interesting specimens of proper folklore."[204] Similarly, S.N.Sarma has also pointed out the same nature of collection when he states, " It is not that only religious scriptures were preserved, but books on music, dance, medicine, literature, philosophy, and even painting were preserved."[205]

The causes for the variety of subjects selected for preparation of the manuscripts may be varied; but the most plausible cause for advent of secular subjects into the store may be found in the royal patronage of the Satras as well as of the Assamese literature. For, both religion and literature in post-Sankaradeva Assam grew under the alliance between the Satras and the state.[206]

Method of Preservation

In view of the amount of labour involved in preparing a manuscript, number of copies was always few. As a result, the translator of the

Mahabharata has requested the readers to preserve the manuscript properly and take extreme care while handling it in the process of reading and reciting it. He further says that only the copiers and the writers know how much labour and pain do they have to take in their work.[207] Despite such warning or request from the writers or the copiers there was apparently no properly developed method as such for proper preservation of the manuscripts. As stated by Gait, manuscripts were made into bundles being wrapped up with pieces of cloths and put either inside the sanctum sanctorum of the prayer hall called *namghar*, or else on the platform above the family loom. Hundreds of years passed during which the manuscript was either recited in the *namghar*, or worshipped like a sacred item, or kept for years unseen or unnoticed during which it might be eaten by mouse, or white ants or may be damaged due to moisture, rain or water. The present author saw boxes of manuscripts in the Auniati Satra being carelessly put inside an iron trunk for decades. It is however to be noted that the Auniati Satra has since inception maintained a Department under an officer called *Lekhaṟu* who is invariably a *Majindar* or Secretary of the *Satraḏhikaṟa* to maintain and preserve the manuscripts as the custodian of them all with the power to replace, revise or make new copies of any manuscript which are worn out, lost or damaged.[208] He is assigned for that duty with an extensive estate called *khaṯ* from where he collects through his agents a share of the produce of the soil, mostly in kind.[209] This officer is responsible for registration, preservation, exhibition, and lending out of the manuscripts for recitation in the *namghar* or elsewhere.

There is no trained person to take care of the manuscripts. Neither there is enough precaution to protect them from natural calamities from which most Satras, particularly those in the Majuli island suffer. The only positive aspect in this regard is that the preserver considers them to be sacred, and therefore, considers any act that affects the manuscript to be immoral. But the most important of all causes for relegation of the manuscripts is that nowadays inmates of the Satra, almost all of whom are educated in modern systems, lack the knowledge of reading the manuscripts written in old Assamese characters. While this is one aspect, the other aspects include the impacts caused by printed books and their easy availability in the markets. Neither the *Satraḏhikaṟa* nor the inmates are now interested in preparing the *sanci* bark, or that peculiar ink for writing them prepared through a very complicated process,[210] or, would like to use wooden or feather pen (*pakhi kap*) and spend months together, doing that tedious job. As a result, there is a lack of both a writers and readers class of manuscripts in the greater society.

FIG. 4.5: THE BELIEF THAT PURANI CHAMAGURI SATRA POSSESSES A PAGE FROM THE *KIRTAN-GOSHA* WITH HAND-WRITTING OF SANKARADEVA HAS NOW BECOME A MYTH

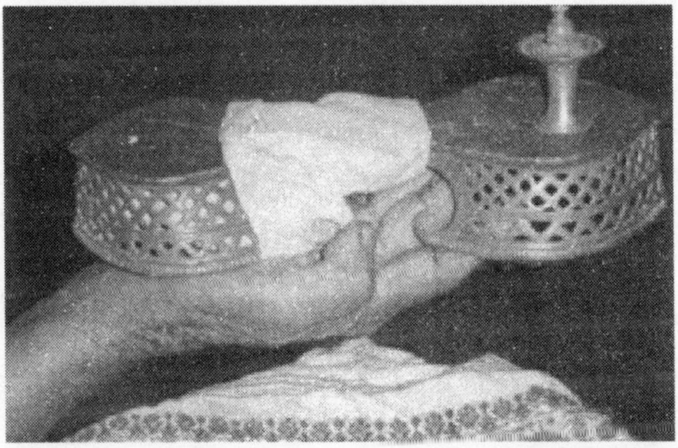

FIG. 4.6: SHOWN AS THAT OF SANKARADEVA THE PURANI CHAMAGURI SATRA POSSESSES THE ABOVE *PADUKA* (FOOTWEAR) MADE OF BRASS

FIG. 4.7: SPECIMEN PAINTING FROM THE MANUSCRIPTS PRESERVED AT THE SATRAS

FIG. 4.8: THE *NAMGOSHA* OF MADHAVDEVA WRITTEN ON MUGA-CLOTH AND PRESERVED AT PURANI CHAMAGURI SATRA

FIG. 4.9: BUNDLES OF MANUSCRIPTS THUS PRESERVED IN THE SATRAS OF MAJULI

FIG. 4.10: RESIDENCE OF PITAMBARDEVA GOSWAMI OF GARAMUR SATRA

Most of the manuscripts are full of paintings, sometimes lavishly. The art of painting became popular along with the expansion of the Neo-Vaishnavite movement and consequent multiplication of manuscript writing. Paintings of great historical value and artistic skill like the 'seven vaikunthas' of Sankaradeva himself, and an elephant on the cover page of his work *Gunamala* are well-known to the world.[211] Sankaradeva's other famous painting was that of Lord Krishna's childhood woven in the sheet of a cloth which was 120 cubits long.[212]

It was in this process that the *Bhagavata Purana*, the main scripture of the school of Neo-Vaishnavism, came in for illustration.[213] The paintings of the Xth Book of the *Bhagavata* better known as *Chitra Bhagavata* in printing[214] is an illustrious example of the paintings in Assamese of the medieval age. According to M.Neog, "the paintings of the *Chitra Bhagavata* seem to be the work of some sattra artist and a representative work too of the Assam school."[215] Among the other most well-known manuscript paintings those of the *Hastividyarnava* are outstanding. The Auniati Satra still possess a copy of this book titled *Hati Puthi* which is probably a collection of the Satra or a gift received by it from one of the nobles of the Ahom administration. We find the name of the owner of the manuscript inscribed therein in Tai-Ahom script to be one Choladhara Phukan of the family of Chiring Phukan.[216] It is to be noted that almost all manuscripts still in the custody of the Satras of Majuli are illuminated with miniature paintings of both religious and secular nature. We have found a wonderful set of astrological works illustrated with lavish paintings preserved in the Purani Chamaguri Satra. Similarly painted manuscripts are also preserved in Garamur Satra and other Satras of the island.

The art of preparation and preservation of manuscripts was once a respectable job in the Satras as well as in the villages. It was due to the popularity of this craft that despite mounting expenses in terms of labour and time, thousands of manuscripts on various subjects, religious and secular, had been produced which served the purpose now served by printed books. It were these manuscripts that contributed chiefly towards the growth of Assamese literature and cultivation of Sanskrit in pre-modern period, and provided a vocation for some people in the Vaishnava monasteries as well as in the villages. But preparing and preserving them in Majuli like any other place of Assam has been no longer in practice at present. Predominance of modern technology including printing press, availability of finished paper, ink and fountain pen has now made the craft of preparation of manuscript obsolete thus making the once thriving and respectable job die at the face of a competitive culture. This shows that any culture however much paying it might have been in the past, would give away to one that holds superior technology and status. The story of manuscript preparation and preservation in the Satras and the reasons behind its discontinuance point to this fact.

Satras in the Life of the People

The mainstream society of the island consisting of the higher echelons is directly associated with the Satras—in both their formation and functioning. As stated before, Satras are headed by the Brahman or Kayastha *adhikaras*, and peopled invariably by members of the caste-Hindus who also include the highly Brahmanised ethnic communities like the Kochs and the Keots. Satras being centres of cultural activities including music and dance, it is no wonder to note that till a few decades ago when performing art was not much commercialized, it was purely confined to the high caste people alone. It has been only a few decades since that the Satra culture in almost entirety in Majuli has begun to spread into the peripheral villages, particularly since the days of Krishnakantadeva Goswami of Kamalabari Satra, Kamaldeva Goswami of Auniati Satra, and Pitambardeva Goswami of Garamur Satra. It is to be noted that following Garamur Satra, all its neighbouring villages, now participate directly or indirectly in the performance of the *Ras* festival in the island. At present several Mising villages also perform *Ras Lila* in Majuli. However, the case was a bit different for the Mayamara Kaivartas who have a few villages in the island at present. There is no Satra at present belonging to the Mayamara affiliation in Majuli; these people have to be initiated by Satras like Dinjay Mayamara of Chabua, Modarkhat Satra of Dibrugarh, or for that matter, any other Satra of that school. They have their own system of performing art which they themselves teach and learn. Thus, a few members from the Sensowa village in upper Majuli are best known for their skill in performing *mridanga*. It is, however, interesting to note that their style of music and dance is again confined to themselves alone as they have formed almost an isolated segment within the greater society of the island since the days of Aniruddhadeva, the first preacher of the sect, and his successors, more so after the Moamariya Revolt of 1769.

Thus, so far as art and culture is concerned, higher the caste, higher is the extent of learning and association with the Satras. But as far as the social outlook and behavioural pattern is concerned, impact of the Satras is clearly discernible on almost every one irrespective of caste, economy or religion. For example, a few Muslim families forming a small settlement area in the heart of the Kamalabari township, reported to the present investigator that they use to visit the Satras on every great occasion, and offer prayer along with others. They have no mosque, not because they are not allowed to have it, but because they themselves do not like to have one in the midst of the Satras. In the Jengraimukh area, *Ras Lila* is performed by the Mising people who include the converted Christian families of the place as well.

Impact of the Satras are noted in the life-styles of the inhabitants of the island, in their food and dress habits, in their speech and behaviour, and above all, in their moral and spiritual life. A man from the island is easily distinguishable from others due to their own and distinct style of living. In the village society, poverty is habitually attributed to the fate, and people are taught to consider it a gift of God in the line of the *kaivalyavadi* ideals of the Satras.[217] No morsel of food goes to the stomach unless it is first offered to the unseen, nor a living creature is habitually molested for purpose of food except, of course, fish. Neither anybody dares to take intoxicating liquor in the public barring the tribal society for whom production and consumption of liquor is a part of their culture. Even those whose culture it is, hesitate to visit a Satra when drunk. The *namghar* and the *manikut* which every village use to have a pair, once served the society as the court of judgment, and till a few decades ago, no one dared to tell a lie looking at the sacred *sastra* (the *Bhagavata*) placed in the *manikut*. No person rides a bicycle or drives a car in high speed when he/she passes a *namghar*, or an assembly sitting in the *namghar*. An outsider when passing by a village *namghar* in the evening would have to stop for a while to listen to the recitation of the *Bhagavata*, or the *Kirtan Ghosha* along with the beating sound of the evening drum called *sandhyar daba*. Listening to the sound of the *khol* in the evening of the Spring coming from a distant village in the midst of a quiet atmosphere is a unique experience in Majuli. The whole year is an agenda of cultural activities for the villagers, and their *namghar* is the centre of all the programmes. Performing *bhaona* every year is a part of their cultural agenda, and attendance of a *Satradhikara* /*Gosain* in the *bar-sabah* (big congregation) preceding it is a must. Every family has its own prayer house or prayer room (*gosain ghar*) where the head of the family recites the *Bhagavata* or the *Kirtan Ghosha* of Sankaradeva placed in the *thapana* (sacred space made of wood earmarked for putting the *sastra*), and perform prayer (*nama-prasanga*). It is their habit to pray in their family prayer-house to offer something for the propitiation of God when some new projects are undertaken, or some calamities occur. Holding an annual prayer in each of the families inviting the elderly members of the village is a part and parcel of their culture. Even the *Bihu* festival here is accompanied by *nama* called *huchari-kirtan*. It is interesting that life-styles of a celibate inmate was once considered an ideal aspect of imitation for any gentleman of the society; and in Majuli one would still come across persons in the attire of a celibate inmate with *dhuti*, *chadar* (scarf), *gamocha* (Assamese traditional towel), *chandan* (vermilion) and long and twisted hair. A gentleman born and brought up in Majuli is therefore naturally distinguished, and psycho-socially different from another person.

It is not, however, true to say that Satras have revolutionized men's life-styles, beliefs and customs. For, despite their lasting impacts as discussed above, people of the island are still under some of their early tribal beliefs and customs. They believe in *tantra-mantra* (incantation), *jara-phuka* (trying to recover a diseased person through the application of *mantra*), *bhut-pret* (spirits), *buradangariya* (village god), *jal devatar dosh* (displeasure of the water god) and so forth. In the tribal societies Satra systems seem to have insignificant impact—in their beliefs, customs and rituals. It is interesting that while Neo-Vaishnavism of Sankaradeva did not approve worship of and belief in various gods and goddesses other than Lord Vishnu or Krishna, people in Majuli believe in numerous gods and goddesses and worship them in various ways. For example, in most schools in Majuli goddess Saraswati is worshipped with or without image, and Dakhinpat Satra perform the *Ras Lila* as a kind of *puja* (ritual worship of), while Auniati perform in the same way the *Kati Bihu,* and Bengenaati the *Dol Yatra*. The only significant legacy of Sankaradeva's tenet is that nowhere in the island *Durga Puja* with its indispensable accomplishments is celebrated.

SATRAS—INTERNAL CHANGES

Satras, however, have undergone significant changes within themselves during the last few decades, more especially in the post-eighties of the last century.

It is, of course understandable, that the Satras in Assam today are competitive among themselves, to obtain more power and publicity, and more precisely, to exercise more political influence than exercising the strength of their institution on sanskritisation and social development process for which early Vaishnava preachers devoted themselves. The problem is that while in the medieval and colonial society Satras with learned pontiffs had a need to look into the matter of social reforms, at present villagers know better hygiene and have greater scientific temper than a *guru* with a medieval outlook could give them. This is because while the entire Satra system remained stagnant and confined to their old and orthodox horizon, public in general are going far ahead in education and learning, and in attaining sophistication and modernity. In fact, inmates of the Satras are lagging far behind than their counterparts in the villages. The present investigator noted how once parents offered their sons to the

FIG. 4.11: A *GURU-ĀSAN* (SANCTUM-SANCTORUM) WHERE SACRED BOOK IS KEPT

FIG. 4.12: THE NEW *NĀMGHAR* OF AUNIATI SATRA AT TEOK, JORHAT

Satras to accept monkhood thinking it as a pious gift, but the same parents are now unwilling to send their kids to the Satra to become celibate inmates.[218] Pitambardeva Goswami of Garamur Satra, in one of his confession papers, has noted his experience as apprentice to the Satradhikara of the Bar Garamur Satra who was his own uncle, to where he was brought at the age of five. Remembering his experience of those days, he has simply commented that he had lost his talent and all that was good of him during this period of apprenticeship, and that had he not been brought to the Satra, he would have been certainly a gifted man of much higher ability than what he had now become.[219] Now modern literate parents have learnt to have one or two offspring only so that they can take sufficient care of their children for their upbringing. They give more importance to having modern education than to send their sons to learn traditional arts at the Satras which parents can manage by paying money. Performing arts practiced and taught in a Satra can be purchased as a commercial product now, or can be cultivated in professional schools or teaching centres. All these have diminished the popularity and importance of the Satras among a class of the public; even those who were once its constituent parts, and a class of ardent supporters, are beginning to look elsewhere for the upbringing of their children. Weak economic condition of the parents was one of the most considered causes for sending their sons to the Satras to become celibate inmates where some kind of guarantee of their maintenance was assured. This was evidenced from our own field investigation in the celibate Satras of the island.[220] Men's growing scientific temper too has a significant role to play in this regard; no parents today attribute the reasons for the early death of their children or for their remaining childless to any divine cause or curse. Most parents in earlier times suffered from this superstition, and wanted to rid themselves of this misfortune by dedicating the first born son, or one of the sons, to the Satra. Parents today would go to the doctor, rather than to the *Satradhikara* for amelioration.[221] This has opened the traditional eyes of some of the *Satradhikaras* who now allow the inmates to have modern education, to practice arts outside the Satra, and more importantly, to mix up with the open society. And this has become a turning point in the long history of the Satra system. The preference of the present Auniatiya *Adhikara* Sri Sri Dr. Pitambardeva Goswami for a Ph.D. degree and his attendance and participation in various national and international seminars and conferences mixing up with varieties of people, his having a computerized press and a TV set, and other *Satradhikaras* following him instantly, indicate a significant historic change in the system. Presuming perhaps the possibility of such changes in the Satra system in near future, Pitambardeva Goswami of Garamur Satra, advocated them for the inmates long time before, in the early twenties of the last century, when all other *Satradhikaras* were in slumber. His permission to the *bhakat*s to marry was looked down upon by his contemporaries; but the gradual attachment of the Satras and their inmates to material life soon became apparent; and Pitambardeva Goswami perhaps did the right thing which, Sankaradeva, the *Mahapurusha*, had approved more than five hundred years before.[222] A survey conducted by the present author in the Auniati Satra has shown that as many as hundred inmates of that Satra, having had modern education and service, have left the Satra and become householder. Garamuriya *Satradhikara* Pitambardeva's decision acted as a safety valve to the exploding situation of desire among the inmates of the Satra.[223]

Till recent years Satras did not look at modern education for the *bhakats* liberally. Maintenance of Sanskrit *tols* inside the Satras for education in Sanskrit for the Brahman inmates was the normal way of maintaining a system. Establishment of schools and colleges near some of the Satras in the post independence period, however, brought the *bhakats* nearer to the modern education system. This is how almost all *bhakats* of the younger generation of Auniati and Dakhinpat Satras, not to speak of Garamur Satra with the married *bhakat*s, are now school, college or university goers, and thus educated in modern systems. A survey taken on the Auniti Satra in 2004 (August) shows that out of a total of 343 *bhakat*s including old and adult, more than 50 per cent are educated in the modern systems, and as we have stated above, the *Satra̱dhika̱ra* is an M.A. Ph.D. This fact of growth of modern education among the *bhakat*s and the *Satra̱dhika̱ra* has introduced them to the modern amenities of life. It is his inspiration and liberal outlook that has encouraged the *bhakat*s to pursue modern education and other amenities of life. When asked at his residence, the *Satra̱dhika̱ra* replied in favour of modernization of the Satra including in the field of education and outlook. His comment to our query indicated that old ideals would not be able to stand against open and liberal civilization.[224] Similar was the opinion expressed by Harideva Goswami, the present *adhikara* of the Garamur Satra. We have not been able to contact the *adhikara* of the Dakhinpat Satra. But inmates of this Satra too were found to have spent their leisure times by viewing T.V. in their residences.

SATRA AND WOMEN

The outlook of the monastic Satras towards women was once rigid and derogatory. Till recent years Auniati Satra did not allow women to visit the Satra and stay there.[225] But such rigidity has now been relaxed. Willing women are now not only initiated by the *Satra̱dhika̱ra*, and allowed entrance to the Satra, but they can now also stay there in times defined as need.[226] In the Garamur Satra, women play important role along with men in socio-religious matters. This has happened since its conversion to a semi-monastic or half-*grihi* Satra in the early twenties. Thus, Pitambardeva Goswami's policy was the pivotal factor in uplifting women's position in the Satra when he encouraged them to play roles in the stage performance and *Ra̱s Lila̱* performed in the Satra. The well-known cinema actress Ila Kakoty was a product of this Satra of Pitambardeva's times.[227]

It is a fact that societies everywhere have undergone tremendous changes in the 20th century without being influenced by the Satra*s*. The fact that early in the 19th century when the British first appeared in Assam (1826), Majuli presented 'an old-world air' pervading all its atmosphere despite the fact that there were already innumerable Satra*s* including the aristocrats of the kind for about two hundred years; and for about three hundred years after Sankaradeva and Madhavdeva had opened their 'market of religion' (*dharmar beha*) there.[228] It is therefore understandable that Pitambardeva Goswami's (Garamur Satra) reform programmes that brought about many significant changes to a part of the society in the island which rejected the 'old air', was inspired not by his Satra, but by the air which then pervaded the progressive minds of the country. Pitambardeva Goswami himself said in his *Confession* how contemporary happenings in Bengal consequent to the great *Partition* as published in the contemporary news papers and periodicals, had impacted upon his mind and inspired him to undertake the reform measures advocating equality of men and amelioration of the downtrodden.[229] Thus the force of equality and fraternity sponsored by modern education and science was much more powerful than theocratic ideals advocated by the Satras which have, therefore, to fight for their own survival with all kinds of cooperation with modern thoughts and technologies. And the revered *Satradhikara* Dr. Pitambardeva Goswami of Auniati Satra today claims to stand for that.[230] Thus it is not the Satra*s* alone that have brought about changes to the society, but the societies themselves which have also brought changes to themselves and to the Satra*s*.

The Satra*s*, however, still govern the island-society to a large extent in shaping the various castes and ethnic groups into the form of a compact society which have certain fundamental characteristics. These are reflected in their maintenance of the caste rules, food ethics, religious, mortuary and cultural functions, and above all, in their speech and behaviour. It is to be noted that once the opinion of a *Satradhikara*, particularly those of Garamur, Auniati and Dakhinpat, was considered final in settling a dispute in connection with an unsocial or sinful activity like extra-marital relationship, inter-caste marriage or marriage within nearest genealogical relationship, addiction to intoxicating liquor, killing of cows and so forth. Even today, no Hindu family perform a *sraddha* or celebrate a marriage without offering something which include some money and a *chadar* to the *gurughar* (house of the preacher). In this connection it would be relevant to say that despite differences among various groups of people in their social status, education, economy, culture, etc, the Satra institution has given to the people of the Brahmaputra Valley, particularly the Hindus, a common identity which is often equated with the identity of the Assamese people;[231] and the Satras of the Majuli island have a large share in it. Indeed, it will be rather difficult to see the Satras separately from the society which is intrinsically interwoven with the life of the people. Thus, despite growing detachment of the younger generations with this old heritage institution, people find solace in the Satras, and families in Majuli attach themselves to one or the other of the Satras directly or indirectly.

END NOTES

1. *Mahapurush Sri Sankaradeva aru Sri Madhavdeva Charit* by Daityari Thakur, V. V.; KGC, pp. 171, 248; also *see* SHTN, pp. 208ff; S.N. Sarma, *op cit.*, pp. 145f.
2. SHTN, p. 312.
3. Anil Raichaudhury, *Asamar Samaj Itihasat Nava-Vaishnav Bad*, Guwahati, 2000, p. 112.
4. SHTN, pp. 80ff.
5. Sankaradeva convinced Madhavdeva about the utility of non-violence and about the futility of worshipping various gods and goddesses making much bloodshed and sacrifice. This was at Belaguri Dhuwahat, a place which was then within the kingdom of Suhungmung Dihingiya Raja, who immediately after his accession to the throne (1497-1539), conqured the Bhuyan territories of Panbari and Habung. See HAG, p. 86. The theory of *tarumula* was advocated by the saint here at the island. See GCK, p. 38.
6. SHTN, p. 153; S.N. Sarma, *op cit.*, pp. 92ff.
7. *Shri Shri Aniruddhadeva Charit*, vv.114-121.
8. See S.Dutta; *op cit.*, p. 16; HAG, p. 59.
9. Ibid.
10. *Shri Shri Aniruddhadeva Charit*, vv.274ff.
11. *See* Chapter 6.
12. *Shri Shri Vamsigopaldevar Charitra,* (ed) M. Neog, Guwahati, 1872 *Sak* (1950), vv. 174ff.
13. Ibid.
14. Ibid., vv. 885-890.
15. Ibid., vv. 950-955.
16. A person who uses to read the *Bhagavata* to the gathering assembly of the inmates in the Satra, and explains its meaning is called *Bhagawati* or *Pathak.* Ibid., vv. 1180-1193.
17. ABSM, p. 63; *Shri Shri Vamsigopal Devar Charitra*, vv.1166-1205; also Introduction, pp. 17f.
18. Ibid., vv. 1214; also Introduction, p. 18.
19. Ibid., Introduction, pp. 18f; Maniram Dewan, *op cit.*, p. 26.
20. See Maniram Dewan, *op cit.*, p. 26.
21. Ibid.
22. SAB, p. 160; D. Nath, *Adhunikatar Unmeshat Shri Shri Auniati Satra*, *op cit.*, pp. 196ff.
23. Ibid., p. 198.

24. ABSM, 73f. For details see B.Sharma, *Dakhinpat Satra, op cit.*, pp. 40ff
25. vv. 1214-1215.
26. Ibid., vv. 1248-1249.
27. Ibid.; *Guru Lila* by Ramraya, (ed). S. C. Goswami, Barpeta, 1869 *Saka*, v. 908; *Damodaradeva Charitra* by Nilakantha Dasa, (ed). S. C. Goswami, Jorhat, 1927, vv. 418-419, 603; *Chakaripheti Buranji*, cf. H. Barbarua, *Banhi*, 6th yaer, 7th issue; *Dakhinpat Satra*, p. 38; SHTN, p. 130f.
28. *Bania Kakati Vamsavali Puthi*, cf. B.Sharma, *Dakhinpat Satra, op cit.*, p. 40.
29. *See Dakhinpat Satra (Charit)* by Dvija Bolorama, cf. *Dakhinpat Satra, op cit.*, pp. 40ff.
30. ABSM, p. 74; also see *Banamalidev Charit*, cf. *Dakhinpat Satra, op cit.*, p. 41.
31. Ibid.
32. (ed.) M. Neog, vv. 1193-1201.
33. Ibid.
34. Ibid., vv. 1200-1205
35. Ibid., 1166-1179; D. Nath, *Adhunikatar Unmeshat Shri Shri Auniati Satra, op cit.*, p. 10.
36. ADB, p. 508; HAG, p. 140; D. Nath, *Adhunikatar Unmeshat Shri Shri Auniati Satra, op cit.*, p. 10.
37. *Santa Samprada Katha*, DHAS, Ms.13b; cf. SHTN, pp. 144f;
38. Ibid.
39. Ibid., p. 26f.
40. *Gazetteer of India*, 1905, pp. 95f; MDPH, p. 390.
41. See *Shri Shri Vamsigopaldevar Charitra*, vv.1194-1202; MDPH, p. 397.
42. *ShriShriVamsigopaldevar Charitra*, vv. 1166-1183.
43. MDPH, pp. 422f.
44. Ibid.
45. *Badala Padma Ata Charitra*; cf. Narayan Chandra Goswami, *Satra Sanskritir Swarnarekha*, 2nd edition, Guwahati, 2005, pp. 820ff.
46. It is said that Madhavdeva sent Padma Ata for preaching in upper Assam on his behalf as he himself was then unable to do this because of his old age and breaking health. That Padma Ata was sent as his substitute, was the reason why he was called *Badala* or *Badula*, i.e. a person sent as substitute of one's body. *See* GCK, p. 428.
47. *Bar Charit* by Dinanath Bezbarua, vv. 3619-3636.
48. *See* M. Neog Foreword to Narayan Chandra Goswami, *op cit.*
49. *See* Narayan Chandra Goswami, *op cit.*, for details.
50. *Chamaguri Satra Buranji* (Ms), preserved in the Satra; SHTN, p. 74.
51. Ibid.
52. Ibid.
53. M. Neog, *Pabitra Asam, op cit.*, p. 74.
54. *See* SHTN, p. 148f.
55. Ibid., p. 149
56. *See* Narayan Chandra Goswami, *op cit.*, pp. 832f.
57. Dr. P. D, Goswami, *op cit.*, p. 2.

58. Jahnabi Gogoi Nath, *op cit.*, pp. 149ff; Nicholas Rhodes and S.K. Bose, *Coins of Assam*, Vol.II, Guwahati, 2004, p. 42
59. *Hemkosh*, p. 150.
60. Dr. P. D. Goswami, *op cit.*, p. 2; ASBS, p. 151. Gunabhiram Baruah has given a different meaning. To him, the term *etaka mahanta* stands for 1280 number of Satras. He explains that giving one cowri to each of the Satras would make a rupee (*taka*), thus making it to stand for the land of the Satras and the *Satradhikaras*. See *Asam Bandhu*, Vol. I, 10th issue, *Kartik*, 1885 (cf. ed. N.Saikia, Guwahati, 1884), p. 329.
61. Jahnabi Gogoi Nath, *op cit.*, pp. 38ff, pp. 41ff; Amalendu Guha, *Medieval and Early Colonial Assam: Society, Polity and Economy*, *op cit.*, pp. 39ff
62. Amalendu Guha, *Planter Raj to Swaraj*, Reprint, New Delhi, 1988, p. 49; T.N.Sarma, *Auniati Satrar Buranji*, Auniati, 1975, p. 235; D.Nath, *Adhunikatar Unmeshat Shri Shri Auniati Satra*, Appendix, pp. 131ff.
63. Satras established under direct patronage from the king followed the state system in their net-work of administration with the *adhikara* at the apex of the system enjoying the services of a set of officers appointed by him with the designations, powers and functions similar to those in the king's court. While some of the monarchs helped the system grow, some others resented it. Thus, king Gadadhar Singha (1681-1696) tried to curb the power and wealth of Auniati, Dakhinpat, Kuruwabahi and other Satras as early as the eighties of the 17th century; but his son Rudra Singha encuraged them to grow. See TB, pp. 23ff; also see HAG, p. 171.
64. SHTN, pp. 310fn.
65. Ibid., pp. 309ff; S.N. Sarma, *op cit.*, pp. 143ff.
66. Louis Dumont, 'World Renunciation in Indian Religion' in his *Homo Hierarchicus: The Caste System and Its Implications*, Complete Revised English edition, OUP, 5th impression, 2006, pp. 184ff; and Romila Thapar, 'Renunciation: the making of a Counter Culture' in *Ancient Indian Social History*, New Delhi, 1978, pp. 76f, for details; SHTN, pp. 326ff; Peter Harvey, *An Introduction to Buddhism—Teachings, History and Practice*, Cambridge University Press, 1st South Asian Edition, New Delhi, 2004, pp. 217ff.
67. Romila Thapar, *loc cit.*, pp. 77ff.; also Satish Chandra, *Essays on Medieval Indian History*, OUP, 2005, pp. 292ff.
68. The *Ambari Rock Inscription of king Samudrapala* dated 1154 *Saka* (1232 A.D.) speaks of a *tantrik satra* (*savasika satra*) headed by a Yogi in the heart of the present city of Guwahati. For details, see M. Neog, *Prachya Sasanawali*, *op cit.*, pp. Introduction (*bhumika*), 9f; P.C.Chaudhury, 'Significance of the Stone Inscription at the Museum, Guwahati', *Journal of Indian History*, vol.XLVIII, Part-I, 1970; D. Nath, 'Few Significant Derivations from the Ambari Stone Inscription', in the *Proceedings of the North East India History Association*, XX Session, Dibrugarh, 1999, pp. 99ff.
69. D. Nath, 'Luitar Majuli—Majuli Dvip etc.' NEIHA *Souvenir*, *loc cit*, pp. 81ff.

70. S.N.Sarma, *op cit.*, p. 148; SHTN, pp. 330f.
71. ASBS p. 380. Different royal Brahmanical Satras have different worshipful deities, e.g. for Garamur Satra it is *Vamsigopala*, and for Dakhinpat it is *Jadavrai*. See B.Sharma, *Dakhinpat Satra*, Guwahati, 1963, pp. 3, 22.
72. Benudhar Sharma, the revered historian of the Dakhinpat Satra, remarks, "A Satra is always a Satra. The heritage of a Satra exists only when stamp of old systems and traditions prevail both inside and outside it, and thus it remains a wonder for the changing society." Cf. *Dakhinpat Satra, op cit.*, p. 3.
73. *Sibsagar District Gazetteer*, 1905, p. 95; cf. S.N. Sarma, *op cit.*, p. 141; Cantlie, *op cit.*, p. 175.
74. SHTN., p. 335; Cantlie, *op cit.*, p. 175.
75. The tradition with the Barpeta Satra is that the community of the inmates called *samuh* use to gather together after the death of an *adhikara* to nominate the next *adhikara.* In the process any person having efficiency for the assignment was nominated to the headship. See Anil Raychaudhury, *Asomar Samaj Itihasot Nava Vaishnav Bad, op cit.*, pp. 112f. Also see his article. '*Nava Vaishnav Satrar Artha-Samajik Dis*', in S. N. Barman *et al.* (ed) *Oitihya aru Itihas—Amalendu Guha Abhinandan Grantha*, Guwahati, 2005, p. 28.
76. It is stated that the choice of the *adhikaras* shuttled between the range of the Keots in the bottom and the Brahmans on the top although Mathuradas Burha Ata, its founder, did not belong to any of them. Since disciples of an *adhikara* are his electors, normally the same person having more disciples was elected to the headship time and again. Thus, for the last many years the family of a Brahman has occupied the post in the Barpeta Satra. Interview with Anil Raychaudhury on 15/11/06.
77. Haliram Dhekial Phukan, *Asam Buranji*, incorporated in *Haliram Dhekial Phukan Rachanawali*, (ed.) L.N.Tamuli, Guwahati, 2005, p. 71.
78. S.N.Barman et.al., *op cit.*, p. 28; E.T. Dalton, 'Note on the Mahapurushiyas, a Sect of Vaishnavism in Assam', in JASB, 1851, Vol.VI, for details.
79. There was once a long debate about the use of the title 'Goswami' by the *Satradhikaras* (see See *Banhi*, 1834, *Sak*, 10th issue, pp. 240ff) who earlier used no surname, but were invariably called 'Deva" in imitation of the names like Sankaradeva, Madhavdeva, Damodardeva etc. (See ASBS, p. 245, 248; Narayan Chandra Goswami, *op cit.*, pp. 31ff; D. Nath, *Adhunikatar Unmeshat Shri Shri Auniati Satra, op cit.*, pp. 16f.) The *Dattadev Charit* records how Garamur and Dakhinpat *Satradhikaras* also became '*Goswamis*' at the same time. See *Sri Dattadeva Charitra* (ed) N.Saikia, Guwahati, 2004, pp. 197f; ASBS, pp. 488; also D.Nath, *Adhunikatar Unmeshat Shri Shri Auniati Satra, op cit.*, p. 17f.
80. *See* fn. 79 above.
81. Narayan Chandra Goswami, *op cit.*, pp. 31f; 983f.
82. Ibid.
83. Ibid.
84. Annie Hazarika, *Asamar Itihasat Shri Shri Aniruddhadev aru Mayamara Vaishnav Sampraday*, Guwahati, 2000, p. 73.

85. Cantlie, *op cit.*, p. 25.
86. Annie Hazarika, *op cit.*, p. 148.
87. Cantlie, op. cit, pp. 25f.
88. SHTN, pp. 360ff.
89. S. N. Sarma, *op cit.*, p. 29. Sankaradeva was not an *adhikara*, nor was Madhavdeva or Damodardeva. The system of *adhikaraship* developed later. See Anil Raichaudhury, *op cit.*, p. 112.
90. Ibid., pp. 92ff.
91. *See* Neog, *op cit.*, p. 335. In the Auniati Satra, the largest of the class all over Assam with about three hundred and fifty celibate devotees at present (2005), there are three, the most junior being an apprentice undergoing necessary training under the care of the *adhikara* for the headship in future. The history of having three is interesting. As this Satra is the richest of all the Satras being established by the Ahom kings, with grants of enormous wealths, the pontiff here lives a life of pomp and grandeur of the type of a lord, or else, like an early Ahom king who lived with all classes of retinue and maintained a majestic life style. This fact of distribution and ownership of wealth led to development of conflict between the *adhikara* and his junior—the *Deka-Adhikara*, who has no such authority to utilise the resources, but who is the legal claimant to the headship after the death of the *adhikara*. The *adhikara* having thus found a challenge to his power and dignity in the person of his junior, brought a third one in order to maintain balance of power, and by giving him all sorts of training to the office, made him his possible alternate choice. Since then it has become a practice to keep a second claimant to the 'throne' in this great Satra enhancing the power of the *adhikara* and giving him options to choose his successor. But this is still not the custom in other Satras of the island. See H.N. Sarma, *Auniati Satra—A Study of its Contributions to the Socio-Cultural and Political Life of Assam*, a Ph. D. thesis in History, Dibrugarh University, 2003, (Ms.).
92. Cf. P. D. Goswami, *Confession, op cit.*
93. *Sri Sri Badula Padma Atar Charitra* by Nityananda Atoi, (ed) Bhavakanta Goswami, Jorhat, 1888 *Sak*, vv. 948-954; Narayan Chandra Goswami, *op cit.*, p. 899.
94. D. Nath, *Adhunikatar Unmeshat Shri Shri Auniati Satra, op cit.*, Appendix, pp. 152ff; also see ASBS, pp. 260, 268ff, 315f.
95. Ibid.
96. For details *see* T. N. Sharma, *op cit.*; B.Sharma, *op cit.*
97. Haliram Dhekial Phukan, *Assam Buranji, op cit.*, p. 71; Harinarayan Sarma, *op cit.* (Ms.).
98. *Sadaraminar Atmajivani*, (ed.) K. C. Bordoloi, Guwahati, 1991, p. 28; Harinarayan Sharma, *op cit.* (Ms.).
99. Ibid.
100. Harinarayan Sharma, *op cit.*, (Ms.); ASBS, p. 315
101. ASBS, pp. 116ff
102. Peter Harvey, *op cit.*, p. 220
103. ASBS, pp. 35, 327f. A piece of beautifully designed boat called *khel-nao*

(sporting boat) made in the Kamalabari Satra is preserved in the Assam State Museum at Guwahati. Also see R.M. Nath, *The Background of Assamese Culture*, *op cit.*, Appendix, pp. 146f; also illustration.

104. The Garamur *Satradhikara* possessed a herd of male and female elephants, which the *adhikara* used for various purposes, including hunting of tigers. MDPH, pp. 25, 130.
105. Ibid., p. 37.
106. ASBS, p. 350.
107. MDPH, p. 37.
108. ASBS, pp. 394ff; H.N.Sarma, *op cit.* (Ms).
109. Ibid.
110. SHTN, pp. 326f; S.N.Sarma, *op cit.*, p. 194.
111. See Harvey, pp. 218f
112. Madhavdeva, the most intimate disciple of Sankaradeva, and a great literary genius of Assam of all times, has in his *Namghosha* spoken about the status of an absolutely devout *bhakat* who does not even aspire for salvation (*muktita nispriha yito/sehi bhakataka namo/rashamayee magoho bhakati*) to be superior to all; and it is this *bhakat* whom he would like to adore and salute. Harvey has stated that "most Buddhist schools see monasticism as a superior way of life, one that all should respect and aspire to join in this or some future life. In the *Theravada*, it is said that a lay stream-enterer should even bow to a monk of lesser attainment, as a way of showing respect to his way of life." Ibid., *op cit.*, p. 218.
113. HAG, p. 169, also TB, p. 17.
114. Data obtained from our field investigation. Also see D. Nath, 'Satra and Social Change in Majuli', *loc cit.*
115. Pitambardeva Goswami papers—*Confession*; Dr. P. D. Goswami, *op cit.*, pp. 51f.
116. *Op cit.*, p. 218.
117. *Op cit.*, pp. 95f.
118. D. Nath, *Adhunikatar Unmeshat Shri Shri Auniati Satra*, *op cit.*, Appendices, pp. 137ff.
119. Ibid., pp. 101f.
120. D. Nath, *Adhunikatar Unmeshat Shri Shri Auniati Satra*, pp. 96f; Dr. P. D. Goswami, *op cit.*, p. 53.
121. Dr. P. D. Goswami, *op cit.*, p. 53.
122. D. Nath, *Adhunikatar Unmeshat Shri Shri Auniati Satra*, pp. 102f.
123. Ibid., pp. 96f; Dr. P.D. Goswami, *op cit.*, p. 53. This information was also obtained from Khagendra Nath Lekharu, *Majindar* (accounts officer) of Auniati Satra.
124. J. Nehru, *Glimpses of World History*, 2nd Indian edition, New Delhi, 1962, pp. 290f; MDPH, p. 33.
125. *Sri Sankaradeva aru Sri Madhavdeva Charit* by Daityari Thakur, vv. 1001-1008.
126. D. Nath, *Adhunikatar Unmeshat Shri Shri Auniati Satra*, *op cit.*, pp. 102f.
127. Pitambardeva Goswami's paper *Confession*, p. 4; MDPH, *op cit.*, p. 33.

128. MDPH, p. 33.
129. *ekanta bhakata yara hay, kicho artha tara nabanchay,/ maha adabhuta hari guna namamay;/ parama mangala Krishna yasa, atapare ana nahi rasa,/ parama ananda samudre maji rahay*. (tr. Those who are single minded and intense devotees, do not desire any other objects but remain absorbed in the ocean of great joy consisting of Krishna's fame, than which there is nothing sweeter, which is highly beneficent, full of the attributes and names of Hari and most wonderful.), cf. *Mahapurush Shree Madhava Deva's Nam-Ghosha*, (ed. & tr.) H. M. Das, Guwahati, 1957, v. 684, p. 332. For a critical appreciation of monasticism, Louis Dumont, *Homo Hierarchi cus-The Caste System and Its Implications*, *op cit.*, pp. 184ff.
130. *parama nirmala dharma, harinama kirtanata/ samasta pranira adhikara;/ Etekese harinam samasta dharmara raja,/ ehi sara sastrara bechar* (v.118) (tr. All beings (or creatures) have right to sing *Harinam* which is the most pure form of religion. So is *Harinam* the king of all religions; this is the essential decision of the *Shastras*). (cf. *Namghosha* by Madhavdeva, tr. H.M. Das, *op cit.*)
varnasrama dharma yata yara yena bihi ache,/ tarese kewala adhikara;/ harinama kirtanata nahike niyama eko/ etekese dharma maje sara. (v.119) (tr. In the *varnasrama dharma* rights and attributes are distinctly prescribed for different *varnas*; one can not encross upon others. But in the religion of *harinama-kirtana* there is no such specification; and this had made it distinguished from all such religions.) ibid.
131. Cantlie, *op cit.*, p. 175.
132. *Ibid*, p. 176.
133. See *infra*, Chapter VI.
134. *Leaflet of the Kaivarta Jatiya Hitakari Sabha*, cf. editorial, *Banhi*, 1838 *Sak*, 7th year, 12th issue; Dev and Lahiri, *op cit.*, Delhi, pp. 28ff.
135. The *Ahom Association* under Radhakanta Handiquse had opposed the satriya view on caste and caste-prejudices by holding a meeting at Jorhat. See Keshab Dihingiya, 'Gananeta Surendranath Buragohaindevar Rajnaitik Aru Samajik Matadarsa Samparke Eti Chamu Alochana' in Devabrat Sarma (ed), *Surendranath Buragohain,* Jorhat, 2005, pp. 64ff.
136. *Ibid*; Devabrat Sarma, *Non-Stae Literary and Cultural Organizations in the Construction of the Assamese National Identity and Ethos 1873-1960* (Ms). *op cit.*
137. Cf. Sumita Ghose, *op cit.,* pp. 105, 109.
138. MDPH, p. 98; Dev and Lahiri, *op cit.*, p. 34.
139. cf. ASBS, pp. 321ff.
140. Ibid.
141. Even Pitambaradeva Goswami also enjoined some ritual procedure which the caste was to pass through to obtain a touchable status. See MDPH, pp. 98ff.
142. Ibid., pp. 104f.
143. Ibid., pp. 96ff' 185ff, 212ff.
144. Ibid., p. 214.

145. Information obtained from field investigation. Also D. Nath, 'Satras in Colonial Assam etc.', *op cit.*, pp. 137ff.
146. D. Nath, *Adhunikatar Unmeshat Shri Shri Auniati Satra*, *op cit.*, pp. 14ff.
147. D. Nath, 'Satras and Social Change in the Majuli Island', *loc cit*, pp. 133ff.
148. Ibid., p. 136f; Dr. Pitambardeva Goswami, *op cit.*, pp. 53f.
149. Devbrat Sarma, *op cit.* (Ms.).
150. R. Saikia, *Social and Economic History of Assam 1853-1921*, Delhi, 2000, p. 163.
151. Cf. *op cit.*, p. 257 cf. *op cit.*, p. 257.
152. Ibid.
153. Cf. ASBS, pp. 287f; D.Nath, 'Satras in Colonial Assam etc.', *loc cit.*, pp. 44f.
154. Cf. B.Sharma, *Dakhinpat Satra*, *op cit.*, p. 82.
155. Cantlie, *op cit.*, p. 154; also *see* 180fn.
156. Ibid.
157. R. Saikia, *op cit.*, p. 162.
158. D. Nath, *Adhunikatar Unmeshat Shri Shri Auniati Satra*, *op cit.*, pp. 131f.
159. SHTN, p. 277.
160. Ibid.
161. Ibid., p. 278.
162. Ibid., pp. 278f.
163. Ibid.
164. H. N. Sarma, *op cit.*, (Ms)
165. Ibid., p. 279.
166. Ibid.
167. *Keshavdeva Charit* by Dvija Ambarish, vv. 454-455.
168. KGC, pp. 265f; SHTN, p. 292.
169. *See* SHTN, p. 293; Karuna Bora, *Sattriya Nrittyar Rup Darshan;* Kamalabari, 2007, pp. 156ff.
170. SHTN, pp. 294ff.
171. Ibid., p. 298.
172. Narayan Chandra Goswami, *op cit.*, p. 46f.
173. Ibid., p. 47.
174. Ibid., p. 52f.
175. SHTN, p. 289.
176. Cf. Ibid., p. 290.
177. information gathered from the Satra during investigation; also H.N. Sarma (Ms.), *op cit.*
178. D. Nath, *op cit.*, pp. 16ff; ASBS, pp. 279f.
179. ASB, p. 245.
180. Ibid., p. 248-251.
181. ASBS, p. 279.
182. The following specimen of his songs may be noted:
dinanath din gela edine ebar daya kara/ami ati abhajan: najani bhajan/ bishay bishapane haye tatpar/deha daba dhan bhabiye apan/ mayai mugdha mana karechi bhraman/ bhranta hoyea gyana harayea nakorilam

o pada smaran/ duranta bishay bhoge durasaya/haiyache chanchal mati atisay/ abhaya charane dehi me sarana/datta kohea dasa baliye dhara. Cf. *Sri Deva Dattadeva Charitra*, *op cit.*, p. 146.

183. ASBS, p. 279.
184. *Op cit.*, (Ms).
185. Ibid.
186. *Mahapurush Sri Sankaradeva aru Sri Madhavadeva Charit* by Daityari Thakur, v. 527; *Guru Charit* by Ramcharan Thakur, (ed) H. N. Dattabaruah, Guwahati, 506 *Sankarabda*, vv. 3314-3332; *Gurucharit* by Ramananda, 150-155; SHTN, p. 264.
187. SHTN, p. 265.
188. *Guru Charit* by Ramcharan Thakur, vv.3964-3974; SHTN, p. 267.
189. See SHTN, p. 268.
190. Ibid., p. 257.
191. TB, pp. 51, 92, 177f.
192. *Ibid*; D. Nath, 'The Rangpur Reception of King Jai Singha', in the *Proceedings of the North East India History Association*, Vol. XXI, Imphal, pp. 63ff.
193. Narayan Chandra Goswami, *op cit.*, p. 777.
194. The term *faujia* ordinarily means armed forces. But as used in the *charit puthis* (as in Daityari, v.128), it means a group of artists who perform the *raga*, meaning thereby that a large number of persons are needed for its performance. See Ibid., p. 778.
195. Ibid.
196. Vishnu Chandradeva Goswami, *Abhimanar Parinati Ba Jatrabhinay*, Auniati Satra, 1914 *Sak*, Preface.
197. Ibid.
198. ASBS, p. 433.
199. Cf. Ibid., p. 438.
200. *op cit.*, p. 223.
201. See Appendix XII.
202. Cf. B. Kakati (ed), *Aspects of Early Assamese Literature*, Gauhati University, 1959, pp. 219ff; H.C. Goswami (ed), *Asamiya Sahityar Chaneki*, Vol. I, Reprint, Guwahati, 2002, p. 166; *Darrang Raj Vamsavali*, (ed) N.C. Sarma, Pathsala, 1973, vv. 606-607.
203. Sankardeva's famous translation of the *Bhagavata sloka* (Canto-II, v.474) makes the list as follows:
    kirata-kachari khasi garo miri
    yavana kanka goal
    asama muluka rajaka turuka
    kuvacha mleccha chandal
    Madhavdeva also mentions their names in his *Namghosha* (vv. 473, 501).
204. HAG, Appendix-D.
205. *Op cit.*, p. 223.
206. D. Nath, *Adhunikatar Unmeshat Shri Shri Auniati Satra*, pp. 1ff; D. Nath, 'Satra and Social Change in the Majuli Island', *loc cit.* for details.

207. Ram Saraswati, a 16th century *Mahabharata* scholar of Kamrup-Assam, has noted the pain of the copiers as follows:
Kikohibo mainee likhanata yata klesa
Bidyanese jane dukh yata
Anubhava kare save jane sabisesha
Garbhinise jane yena srama prasavata
Pristha kantha kati desa jana yena bhage
Sarpese dekhaya yena sarpara charan
Adhumukhe sthira chakhyu dekhibaka lage
Lekhakese jane lekhakara dukha gan
Samasta sarira praya achala howaya
Eteke sabako kaho kari shorapani
Hasta bahu niruddhiya likhibe lagaya
Yatane palana kara ito sastrakhani
Nilikho pustaka ami hena parisrame
pathaka bargaka karo mainee nivedan
Itaraka bujaibe napari kona krame
sabadhane ito grantha kariba pathan.
(cf. Manuscript preserved in the Auniati Satra, cf. D. K. Phukan, *Auniati Satrat Sangrakshita Prachin Grantha Samuhar Vivaranatmak Talika*, Auniati, 2004, Introduction-*batchora*).
(tr. How can I describe the pain of copying a manuscript? It can only be felt than described. It breaks one's back, neck and waist, for one is to keep one's eyes fixed downwards (at a stretch for long). Hands and shoulders have to be kept firm. Thus the whole body becomes stiff, and loses its flexibility. I promise never to write/ copy any book in future. Ignorant cannot understand the nature of this pain. Only the wise and learned know the pain of being expert in the art (of writing manuscript) like the pregnant woman who only knows the pain of child birth, and the snake who knows where their legs hide. Similarly, only the writers know the pain of writing out a manuscript. So, with my folded hands I appeal to every body—please preserve and read the manuscript carefully (so that it may not be damaged).

208. Information obtained from the present incumbent Sri Khagendra Nath Lekharu *Majindar* of Auniati Satra, Majuli.

209. *See* H.N. Sarma, *op cit.* (Ms.); This was also coming to light during interaction with Khagen Lekharu of Auniati Satra.

210. SHTN, pp. 301f.

211. *Katha Guru Charit*, (ed) U.C. Lekharu, Nalbari, 1952, pp. 36, (henceforth KGC): 187; SHTN, p. 304.

212. KGC, p. 210; SHTN, 304.

213. Cf. SHTN, p. 306.

214. *Op cit.*

215. SHTN, p. 306.

216. The name of the owner is scribed on the outer side of the cover page of the manuscript in Tai alphabet (but not the language) as follows:

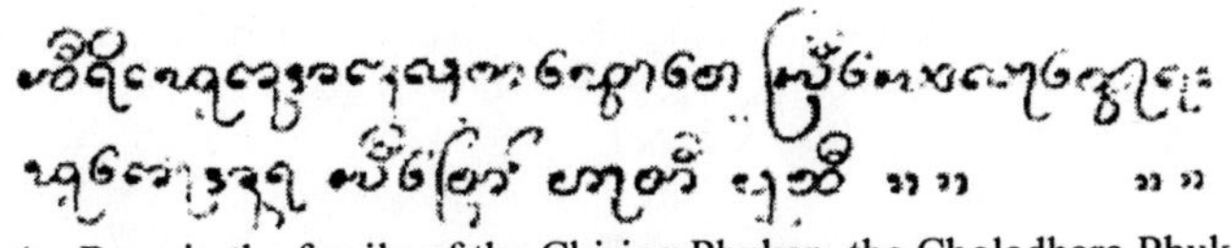

(tr. Born in the family of the Chiring Phukan, the Choladhara Phukan is the owner of this illustrated *Hati Puthi*)

217. S.N. Sarma, *op cit.*, pp. 195ff.
218. *See* D. Nath, 'Satra and Social Change in the Majuli Island', *loc cit.*, p. 150.
219. *See* Pitambardeva Goswami, *Confession, op cit.*
220. It was found that almost all the boys brought to the Satra for being initiated to celibacy hail from the poor families. The reasons shown by the *Auniatiya Satradhikara* in his work *Satriya Utsavar Parichay aru Tatparya* (*op cit.*, pp. 53ff) indicates this aspect of the life of the inmates of a monastic Satra.
221. D. Nath, 'Satra and Social Change in the Majuli Island', *loc.cit.*, pp. 150f.
222. The *Guru Charit Katha* (GCK) mentions that Sankaradeva had advised Madhavdeva to fight by building fort so that life remained secured. By this statement he meant that Madhavdeva should marry so that in the pursuit of his spiritual life he would not have to slip from the right path. See p. 60.
223. *See* his *Confession, op cit.*
224. *See* D. Nath, *Adhunikatar Unmeshat Shri Shri Auniati Satra, op cit.*, p. 82.
225. H.N. Sarma (Ms.), *op cit.*
226. Ibid.
227. Ila Kakati was a known cinema artist of Assam of the late sixties and seventies of the last century. She got her first training in the performing art in the Garamur Satra itself and during the time of Pitambardeva Goswami himself. See D. Nath, 'Obituary to Ila Kakati', *Purbanchal*, Special Sunday Issue, 19 October, 2003.
228. *See* Chapter 2.
229. See Pitambardeva Goswami, *Confession, op cit.*
230. He said, "By 'modern' I understand the demand of the present times and conditions. It is experimented and scientific. But such changes will have to be rested on our tradition and culture." Cf. D. Nath, *Adhunikatar Unmeshat Shri Shri Auniati Satra, op cit.* p. 82.
231. Also see Manorama Sarma, *Social and Economic Change in Assam: Middle Class Hegemony*, Delhi, 1990, p. 129.

5

Cultural Life

Religious Festivals and Secular Celebrations

Cultural life in Majuli is mainly dominated by religion. Being the land of the Satras, most of its beliefs, customs, functions and festivals are governed by the Satras. Even a secular festival like *Bihu* is not out of the influence of a religious tone. Below we have given a detailed list of socio-cultural festivals and functions popular in the island:

PALNAM

It is a religious festival organized by the Satras of Majuli, particularly by the Auniati Satra. *'Palnam'* is a compound word, *pal* and *nam*. *Pal* (Sanskrit-*paryaya*—one after another) means by turn, and *nam* means congregational prayer; chanting the name of God. And so, *palnam* means holding of incessant congregational prayer or chanting of the name of God by the inmates of the Satra in group and in rotation.[1]

In the Auniati Satra *Palnam* is held during the last five days of the *Kati* month (October-November). Initially, it was a monthly festival held during the last five days of every month. But being too expensive it ultimately became an annual affair; the person behind this change was Harideva Goswami (1737-1760), the 5th *adhikara* of the Satra. The objective of holding *Palnam* is defined as seeking welfare for all living and non-living beings of the world.[2] *Palnam* is organized by other Satras too. But they have options to select the dates and duration for holding it. For example, in the Garamur Satra it is celebrated for one day only which starts on the closing day of the *Palnam* at Auniati. In the Bengenaati Satra it is held in the month of *Bhadra.* While in this Satra it is held for the whole month, in Chamaguri it is held for one day only. In the Dakhinpat Satra *Palnam* is not organized. In the Kamalabari Satra (s) it is organized for three days in the month of Jeth. Earlier it was a seven-day festival in imitation of the beginning set by Sankaradeva himself.[2(a)] But, the period has been reduced to three days in course of time due mainly to economic reasons. Often *P<u>a</u>ln<u>a</u>m* is organized by individual persons also on some special occasions.

The origin of *P<u>a</u>ln<u>a</u>m* is to be traced to the mid-16th century. It is recorded that when Madhavdeva was kept in confinement by the men of the Ahom king Suhungmung *alias* Dihingiya Raja (1497-1539) on charges of his failure to capture elephants on his behalf with threates of dire consequences,[3] all devotees then, at the advice of Sankaradeva, started a kind of unending prayer for his life and release.[4] It is further recorded that it was during a session of such congregation that Madhavdeva came back safe and delighted the chanting inmates by offering his salutation and with whatever amount of rice and salt he had with him.[5] It is from this fact that *P<u>a</u>ln<u>a</u>m,* meaning continuous chanting of the *n<u>a</u>ma* of God, or prayer by groups of devotees, came into practice among the Vaishnava circle; and making gift of salt and rice became a custom in the agenda of the *P<u>a</u>ln<u>a</u>m.*[6] In imitation of this prayer the inmates of the Auniati Satra also undertook the same kind of prayer for the security of the life of Keshavdeva, who had to keep himself in hiding in the jungle of Sadiya to escape the wrath of king Gadadhar Singha.[7] Edward Gait has recorded from the evidence of the Assamese chronicles that "Gadadhar Singha bore a personal grudge against some of the leading Gosains for having refused to shelter him in the days when he was in hiding, and for having endeavoured to dissuade the Barphukan from his design to set him up as king in place of Lara Raja. He, therefore, resolved to break their power for good. Under his orders many of them were sent to Namrup and put to death there. The Auniati Gosain, Kesab Deb, escaped this fate by hiding in a Chutiya village."[8] Thus the tradition of *P<u>a</u>ln<u>a</u>m* began at the Auniati Satra.

The ritual beginning of the function of the *P<u>a</u>ln<u>a</u>m* in Auniati Satra starts when certain dignified functionaries of the Satra—the *Bar <u>A</u>sirvadiy<u>a</u>*, the *Bar N<u>a</u>mlagow<u>a</u>*, the *Sravani Dhupiy<u>a</u>*, and the *Maliy<u>a</u>* formally (in fact, ritually) seek permission from the *Satr<u>a</u>dhik<u>a</u>ra*, who has been then sitting inside the sanctum (*manikut*), considered by the devotees as Vaikuntha, the abode of Lord Vishnu/Krishna, to chant *n<u>a</u>ma.*[9] The Vaishnavas believe that the *n<u>a</u>ma* originates at Vaikuntha, symolised by the *manikuta* in the earth.[10] The functionaries then come out of the sanctum (*manikuta*) with the *Bhagavata* and starts *n<u>a</u>ma* by putting the sacred book inside a golden boat in the midst of the prayer house (*n<u>a</u>mghar*).[11] The boat symbolizes the agency for salvation (*bhavat<u>a</u>rana*) of the soul. Then the *Bhagavata*, which is presumed to be the representation of God Hari (Krishna/Vishnu), is put inside the boat, and thereby they establish *nama* as they call it as such. The inmates then take their seat on both sides of the boat and begin to chant *n<u>a</u>ma* in group.

There are three turns (*pal*) in a day—early turn (*ag pal*), middle turn (*maj pal*) and the last turn (*sesh pal*). The chanting of *nama* in *Palnam* does not require clapping of hands (*hatchapori*) as done in case of normal *nam-prasanga*. The *nama* constitutes selected chapters (*ghosha*) from the *Nam Ghosha* of Madhavdeva, and a few other books composed by the Satra's late *Satradhikaras*. The congregation is attended by many thousand devotees from all over the state everyday during its sessions.[12]

At the end of a *pal* (turn) it is the custom that the *Satradhikara* and his juniors, the *Deka Adhikara* and the (third) *Govindapuriya*[13] prostrate before the Vaishnavas and offer salutation (*sewa*). During the pause between the *pals assembled* devotees and other believers offer *naivedya* and obtain blessings. Their offer includes among other items, salt (*lon*) as it is a tradition in the Satra to gift salt since the days of the origin of the *Palnam.*[14] In medieval context, gift of salt is considered as equal to the gift of gold.[15] In this way four days pass during which thousands of people from all over the state come to the Satra and offer prayer. On the fifth day the *Satradhikara* and his juniors accompanied by the senior Vaishnavas of the Satra (*sat-man-bhagiyas*) take out the *Bhagavata* in a procession and move around the *namghar* four times at the end of which the party enters the prayer hall. The whole procession ends amidst beating of drum (*daba*), bell, horn (*singa*) and playing of conch shell (*sankha*). Inside the *namghar* five silver trays called *Rangali Sarai* (painted tray) containing *dakshina* consisting of gold, silver and other valuables, are placed in the *namghar* on behalf of the *Satradhikara* and his juniors, who, after coming into the hall, lay down on the ground and fell prostrate before the Vaishnavas who offer blessings (*asirvad*) wishing welfare of all living and non-living creatures. Then the *Satradhikara* and the others enter the *manikut* and reinstate the *Bhagavata* in its proper place. All this is done before it is dawn. In the morning the *nitya-prasanga* (daily system of prayer) is started to be followed by *hiyanam*, *dihanam* and *gayan-bayan*. The *Satradhikara* now prostrates again before the assembly of *bhakats* and obtain blessings (*asirvad*) from the Vaishnavas. It is followed by distribution of *prasad*. Thus ends the festival of the *Palnam*. All visitors and devotees then return to their home. During this time devotees attending the *palnam* are fed from the store of the Satra.[16]

RAS LILA

Among the superb Indian classical performing arts popular in Majuli, the *Ras Lila* (*Krishna Lila/ Ras Yatra*) is the outstanding, and largely participated by the people both inside and outside the Satra circle.

Like the *Palnam*, the *Phalgutsav,* and the *Janmastami*, about which we shall discuss shortly, the *Ras Lila* is an annual festival being performed on the full moon day (*purnima*) in the months of October-November (*Kati-Aghun*) during the autumn season. It is not known for certain in which Satra *Ras Lila* was first introduced in Majuli as a performing festival. According to Benudhar Sharma, *Ras Lila* organized and performed at the Dakhinpat Satra during Basudeva Goswami (1828-1870) is the earliest.[17] His statement is based on the fact that this *Satradhikara* of Dakhinpat Satra composed a drama on *Ras Lila* and also prepared a code for the performance of the *Ras Puja* (*Ras Puja Bidhi*) in the Satra taking sources from the *Bhagavata Puran*, the *Brihat Gautami*, *Hari Vamsa*, *Krishna Janma Khanda,* etc.[18] Writing a drama and preparing a code, however, do not speak about the antiquity of the *Ras* festival in Majuli. Even for Dakhinpat Satra his statement suffers from self-contradiction when he says that "after having renovated the *manikut* and the *namghar* (destroyed during the Burmese invasions) the *Satradhikara* installed all the images old and new, in their places through proper procedure, and wrote a drama on the *Ras Lila* and performed it in a novel way on the day of the *Ras* festival of the *Sarat Kal* of the year 1772 *Sak*". He further says that since then it became a three-day affair and a regular annual agenda of the cultural activities of the Satra.[19] Sharma's statement neither bears evidence if other Satras had no *Ras* festival till that time (although he swears in the name of history without any evidence, of course, to insist on believing his statement), nor he argues well why Basudeva Goswami had termed the day of his performing the *Ras Lila* as the *Ras* festival day of the autumn season (*Sarat Kal*). The only summary of his

FIG. 5.1: ON FESTIVAL DAYS SUCH AS *RAS-LILA* AND *PAL-NAM*, MANY THOUSAND PEOPLE VISITS MAJULI FROM ALL OVER THE STATE (THIS IS A PICTURE AT NEAMATI GHAT AT JORHAT.)

very ambiguous writing[20] may be that Basudeva Goswami wrote a drama on the *Ras Lila* which he elaborated later on with a revision to include the episodes from the birth of Krishna to the killing of Aristasur and performed it on the *Ras* festival day of the year 1772 *Sak.* He also prepared a code to make the *Ras* a *puja* which he termed as *Ras Puja Bidhi.* And since then *Ras* festival in Dakhinpat Satra begun to be performed according to this code or regulation. This does not necessarily mean that Dakhinpat Satra had introduced *Ras Lila* in Majuli.

On the contrary, there is sufficient ground to believe that all Satras, including also perhaps Dakhinpat, had the culture of performing *Ras Lila* since the beginning as it was introduced by Sankaradeva himself who not only included a detailed chapter on *Ras-Kriḍa* in his *Kirtan-Ghosha,* but also composed the drama of *Keli-Gopala* and got it performed at Patbausi in Barpeta on the request from Rama Raya, his brother.[21] Since that time *Ras Lila* has been performed in Assam in the form of *bhaona.*[22] According to Narayan Chandra Goswami, *Satradhikara* of the Kamalabari (Natun) Satra, it was on the basis of this drama of Sankaradeva, that a number of dramas on the *Ras Lila* have been composed in Assam, and Majuli remained the centre of the festival.[23]

In a subsequent context we shall try to show that even Manipuri *Ras Lila* may be an import from Assam during the time of the king Rajeswar Singha (1751-1769)[24] It is not likely that when Sankaradeva himself started the festival by composing a drama, Satras in Majuli had to wait to perform it till the late 19th century (*Sak* 1772 = 1840 A.D.). The plausible assumption could be that Dakhinpat *Satradhikara* Basudeva Goswami had composed the *bidhi* and converted the *Ras* into a *puja* from a *bhaona.*

As in other Satras, Auniati Satra also observes *Ras Purnima* as a form of worship (*puja*) following the Dakhinpat Satra. The *Ras Lila* is the story of the life of Lord Krishna presented in the performing art form. It begins with the birth of Krishna, his upbringing at the house of king Nanda, his tending the cows at Gokula along with his fellow cowherds, his childhood activities, his killing of the demons like Bakasur, Putana, Kaliya, and of Kamsa, his maternal uncle, at various times of his youth and on various other occasions.[25] Finally his amorous play with the Gopis including Radha form the kernel of the story of the *Ras Lila* as presented in Majuli.[26] The *Ras Lila* in the Dakhinpat Satra, however, maintains some of its own specifications. As pointed out by S.N. Sarma, "The dual worship of Radha and Krishna as is usually done in *Ras-puja* is not prevalent in the satras. It is observed strictly in conformity with the narration of the *Bhagavata-Purana* where Radha is conspicuous by her absence. Devotional services performed on this occasion are usually related to the *Rasakrida* episode. The five chapters of the *Bhagavata* (*Ras panchadhyaya*) are read and explained to the assembled devotees. At night *Ras* dance is performed by boys donning female costume."[27] The *Ras Lila* is the epitome of *bhakti* represented through the relationship between Gopi and Krishna, but symbolized in the merger of the *atma* (soul) with *paramatma*, (the great Soul—God). The presentation indicates that our soul will have to finally take shelter with the great soul, the *param brahma* in the form of Lord Krishna.[28] Thus, the *Ras Lila* was created to successfully spread the contents of *Bhakti* among the commoners. Sankaradeva borrowed the story from the *Bhagavata Purana* and made it a part of his sacred book—the *Kirtan Ghosha*.[29] The drama of the *Ras Lila* was written later by the *Satradhikaras* from the story narrated by Sankaradeva in his *Kirtan-Ghosha* and the drama *Keli-Gopala.*

The *Ras Lila* is performed with music and dance. It has great impact on the life and culture of the people of Majuli in particular, and those of the entire state in general. In Dakhinpat Satra *Ras Lila* is still performed as an offering (*puja*) as it used to be in the beginning in the late 19th century. All its participants are the celibate inmates of the Satra—the *bhakats*. The performance is done in the common prayer hall (*namghar*) of the Satra, and mostly in the day time. From Dakhinpat it spread to many other Satras as a grand religious festival.

Ras Lila was made into a stage performance by Pitambardeva Goswami of Garamur Satra in the year 1934, and a few years after he built the *Vamsigopal Natya Mandir* in the Satra for presentation of such performing arts.[30] It is to be noted that Pitambardeva Goswami was the first person in the island to allow women participation in the *Ras Lila*. In the year 1950 he permitted the girls of the Satra to take roles in the *Ras Lila* and dance.[31] Today, in most of the centres women participation is the normal way to carry on the *Ras Lila* performance.

The *Ras Lila* in the Majuli island is a part of the culture of the Satras, although as a festival, it is performed also by many of the villagers. It is reported that at present there are about twenty such centres, Satras and villages together, where *Ras Lila* is performed. During the festival every man and woman and children remain busy receiving visitors and performing different duties related to the festival. There are reports to the effect that during the festival that lasts for four to five days at a stretch, lakhs of outsiders visit the island, and every family is to receive and keep one or more of them for those days.

FIG. 5.2: *RAS LILA* PERFORMED BY THE INMATES OF A SATRA IN THE *NAMGHAR*

FIG. 5.3: THE *KARAPAT* (ENTRANCE ROAD) OF GARAMUR SATRA

FIG. 5.4: *MATI-AKHARA* PERFORMED IN NATUN KAMALABARI SATRA

Performance of the *Ras Lila* involves various classes of musical instruments, music and dance, and artifacts including mask and painting. These constitute Assamese classical music and dance. Although masks are used in all the Satras in the performance, masks made and used in the Chamaguri Satra are the most distinctive in their fineness and style. These are painted in various colours prepared from indigenous ingredients. The instruments used in the musical performance include *khol* (a kind of hollow wooden instrument made of animal skin in both ends), *tal* (symbal), *banhi* (bamboo flute), and the songs called *bargeets* (celestial songs composed by Sankaradeva and Madhavdeva). Various classes of artists are engaged in the process—actors and actresses, musicians, instrumentalists, painters, and the dressmen of the actors and so forth. In fact, performing *Ras Lila* is a group work involving a whole village or the entire community of a Satra.

Ras Lila was earlier presented for the public in the *namghar*. But now it has become a stage performance and commercialized. Increase of expenses, development of techniques, and above all, professionalizing the art has made it commercial. Now one has to pay money for enjoying the performance in most of the centres in the island where it is presented within closed stage-halls. It is significant to note that many artists now teach the art of performing *Ras Lila* outside Majuli for money. Besides, *Ras Lila* is also exhibited on request and invitation from others. It is recorded that in the last part of the 18th century king Jai Singha of Manipur came to Assam seeking shelter and help from its king Rajeswar Singha (1751-1769). During his stay here at the Ahom capital at Rangpur for more than six months the Assam king arranged for presentation of various kinds of performing arts in his camp in honour of the visiting king's pleasure and entertainment.[32] It is also recorded that when Jai Singha was going back home, he was accompanied by a group of *bhakats* from Assam who carried with them the tradition of performing arts of the Satra.[33] It is possible that these inmates (*bhakats*) from Assam popularised the Satriya culture in Manipur including the *Ras Lila* in later times. In this connection it is to be noted that when the presiding deity of the Auniati Satra is *Govinda Mahaprabhu*, that of the Manipur Vaishnavism is the great *Govindaji*, the temple of which was built consequent to the visit of king Jai Singha to Assam.[34] There is, therefore, ground to suspect that Manipur classical dance and its *Ras Lila* were brought from Assam.

JANMASTAMI

Janmastami or the birth day of Lord Krishna is celebrated with great festivity in all the Satras and in the villages of Majuli. Some of the Satras perform it for two days, while in some others it is performed for one day.

In all the villages, except those of the Misings and the Deoris, and perhaps, all non-Assamese villages, however, it is performed for one day. The *Janmastami* falls on the eighth lunar day of the dark fortnight in the month of *Bhadra*. It is marked by offering of *puja*, holding of the congregational prayer—*nam-prasanga*, fasting—*brat*, and performance of drama depicting the birth of Lord Krishna.[35] It is believed that fasting on the day of *Janmastami* would bring immense religious merit (*punya*) equal to the offering of *pinda* (oblution) at Gaya on the Ganges.[36] On the contrary, those who do not observe fast shall take their birth as demon (*rakshasa*)[37] An interesting belief associated with the *Janmastami* is that coconut which is indispensable as an item of offering in all other religious functions, is prohibited to be offered in the *Janmastami*; on the other hand, *pakamithoi* is a special item of the offerings in this festival.[38]*Janmastami* too is held both as a *puja* in some of the Satras, although *nam-prasanga* predominates over all forms of observances. In the Dakhinpat Satra, however, it is *puja* that predominates the agenda.[39] During the *nam-prasanga* the inmates of a Satra use to recite from the *Krishna Janma Khanda* of the *Kirtan-Ghosha* of Sankaradeva. The day is observed with performance of dances of various forms. But in Garamur Satra, certain forms, such as *natuwa* dance, *gayan-bayan*, *ojapali* and *hiyanam* are not presented. Similarly, in the Auniati Satra *natuwa nach* is conspicuously absent.[40] But one finds here various classes of devotional songs like *hiyanam, uthanam, dihanam,* etc, performed by the inmates.[41] In the Garamur Satra, *Janmastami* is celebrated with much pomp and merry-makings. Here it is celebrated for two days. In the evening of the first day, the 8th day of the lunar month, is organized special congregational prayer called *janmastami geet* in the Satra prayer hall. *Mah-prasad* along with *paka mithoi* is the normal offering served on that occasion. The inmates gather at the *namghar* early in the evening, and continue to sing the *janmastamir geet* till late at night. In earlier days when the inmates were celibate, it was their habit to recite from the Xth Canto of the *Bhagavata* preserved in the Satra itself in manuscript form till the close of the chapter on Krishna's birth.[42] In the Kamalabari Satra *Janmastami* is noted for *nama-kirtana*. *Janmastami* is belived to be a day of thick cloud and heavy shower with much thunderstorm, and if the night passes without rain and thunderstorm, people consider the day to be unenjoyable.

GURU TITHIS

Although *Guru Tithi* initially meant observance of the death anniversaries of the two great saints only—Sankaradeva and Madhavdeva, it subsequently expanded to include the death anniversaries of all the preceptors of the post-Sankaradeva times. Accordingly, the *tithi* of the following Vaishnava saints are celebrated in the Satras: Damodardeva, Vamsigopaldeva, Bhavanipuriya Gopal Ata *alias* Gopaldeva and the *tithi*s of the late *Satradhikaras* of the Satras. *Guru-Tithis* are also called *Atar Tithi* as the preceptors were also addressed as *Ata*, a word which is a *prakrit* form of the Sanskrit *atma* (soul).The normal procedure is that on the day of the anniversary (*tithi*) the inmates organize *annadan (gift of cooked food)*, *nam-kirtan*, varieties of classical dance forms—*natuwa nach*, *ojapali nritya,* etc.

Guru *Tithis* are observed in different Satras with variations in the day's agenda. For example, emphasis is laid on the *tithi* of Damodardeva, the founder of the *Brahma Sanghati* order, in the Satras like Auniati, Dakhinpat and Garamur, while in a *Nika Sanghati* Satra like Kamalabari, the same amount of emphasis is laid on the *tithi* of Sankaradeva, Madhavdeva and Badula Padma Ata. Similarly, in the Satras of the *Kala Sanghati* order Gopal Ata's *tithi* is observed with much celebration. In a *Purush Sanghati* Satra like Bengenaati or Chamaguri much emphasis is laid on Sankaradeva's *tithi* with elaborate agenda. In the same way, in the Mayamara system of the Satras, Aniruddhadeva, the founder of the Mayamara sect, receives highest elaboration (although no such Satra is in Majuli now). An interesting aspect of performing of the *Guru Tithis* is that all Satras, irrespective of their affiliation, use to perform the *tithis* of Sankaradeva and Madhavdeva, although with variations in the nature and extent of the celebration. While Satras of *Nika Sanghati*, *Purush Sanghati* and the *Kal Sanghati* observe their (Sankaradeva and Madhavdeva) *tithis* in the same manner, as they do in case of their respective founder *gurus*, those of the *Brahma Sanghati* order like Auniati, and Garamur, give less emphasis on them, and Dakhinpat not at all.[43]

In the Auniati Satra the *tithi* of Damodardeva, and its founder Niranjandeva are observed with much pomp and grandeur. Dr. Pitambardeva Goswami, the present *Satradhikara* of Auniati Satra, has stated that there are differences in the style and agenda in the celebration of the *tithis* of the *Mahapurushas* (Sankaradeva, Madhavdeva, Damodardeva, Gopaldeva, Aniruddhadeva), and those of the *Satradhikaras*.[44] While in the performance of the *tithis* of the *Mahapurushas* emphasis is laid on *nam-kirtana, natuwa nach, ojapali nach*, reception and feeding of the guests giving it an air of a festival,[45] those of the *Satradhikaras* are marked by offering of *pinda* and performance of other cultural programmes like *bhaona*, distribution of alms called *chaul sidha* among the visitors and invitees, extension of daily cultural agenda and so forth.[46] In the Kamalabari Satra, another Satra of the non-Brahmanical groups, the *tithi*s of the *Mahapurushas* are observed with much celebration continuously for a number of days.[47] In the Bengenaati Satra they are celebrated for three days. Performance of *ankiya bhaona* and *bargeet*, and recitation from the *Bhagavata*, the *Kirtan Ghosha*, and the *Namghosha* are compulsory in the agenda of those days.

The Satras belonging to the *Kala Sanghati* order of Gopal Ata, such as the Ahataguri, Sankopara, Gajala and Chakala, observe the *tithi* of Gopal Ata, the founder of the sect, for three days with an extended agenda of performance. In the first day, among others, the *Basudeo* (Vasudeva) image is worshipped in public with performance of music called *bangla badya bajana*.[48] In the afternoon of the day a drama called *Janma Yatra* composed by Gopaldeva, is performed; and a few dramas composed by Sankaradeva like *Rukmini Harana* and *Parijat Harana* are performed.[49] The major agenda of the next day is the *charit path*, i.e. recitation from the biography of the saint. The third day is often called valedictory.

At present there is no Satra of the Mayamara sect started by Aniruddhadeva in the island. Disciples belonging to this sect celebrate the birth and the death anniversaries of Aniruddhadeva every year collectively at their respective *namghars* by undertaking various cultural agenda and reciting from his *Bhagavata*, the *Bhakti Mangal Ghosha* and other *Sastras*.

An interesting aspect of the functions and festivals organized by the Satras is that almost all non-tribal villages in the neighbourhood irrespective of caste and creed, join the function either as participants or audience or as lay invitees. In either case, *tithi* of a *guru* is considered as a sacred festival where one is to contribute to the extent of one's ability and will. In that sense the Satras act as an integrating force and as a common organization for all.

PHALGUTSAV/PHAKUWA/DUAL YATRA

Phalgutsav, *Daul Yatra*, or more commonly, *Phakuwa* is a festival of colour stated to have played at Lord Krishna's birth place at Gokula between Krishna and the *gopis*.[50] In some of the *bargeets* also Sankaradeva and Madhavdeva have narrated how Lord Krishna played *rang* or *ahira* with his fellow friends[51] As this festival is observed in the month of *Phaguna* (Feb-March), it has been called *phalgutsav*, i.e. festival observed in the *Phagun* or *Phalgun* month, while the term *daul yatra* has been derived from the fact that the image of Lord Krishna is brought out in a temple like house (*daul*) and then taken to move in a procession all around the Satra. It therefore means travel of the image of Lord Krishna sitting inside a temple called *daul*.[52] During the travel of the image of the Lord villagers in the neighbourhood come out to the streets and offer prayer along with some *dakshina* and other articles.[53] It is stated that *phalgutsav* was first introduced by Sankaradeva himself in the Bardowa *than*, Sankaradeva's birth place, within modern Nagaon district, and then at Barpeta Satra.[54]

Phalgutsav is special to Bengenaati Satra where it is observed in a grand scale. There it has certain interesting agenda of which the one called *mesh-dah* or burning of the goat is the most interesting. In a small cottage built of grass and reeds a goat is kept and worshipped. At the end of the worship the cottage is put to fire and the goat is set free after burning some of its furs. Ramcharan Thakur in his *Guru Charit* has given a detailed narration of the act of '*mesh-dah*' during the *Phalgutsav*. He has gone to the extent that Sankaradeva himself got a *sukla chagal* (white goat) bought for him and performed the *yajna*.[55] As pointed out by Narayan Chandra Goswami, *Satradhikara* of the Kamalabari (Natun) Satra, and a noted scholar of the Vaishnava literature and culture, historicity of this information is not beyond doubt as Sankaradeva in his own writings has never referred to his inclination to any kind of sacrifice except devotion to only one Supreme God (*ekamaivadvitiyam*).[56] From the conspicuous absence of such information in the writings of Sankaradeva himself, and in the early series of the biographical works, it appears that Ramcharan's narration might have been a later addition, which he, or some of the copiers of the work, had done to suit certain circumstances, such as accommodating certain Brahmanical and tantric elements. It should be mentioned that burning of a few furs of the animal indicates that once in early times where and when this agenda was discovered, the animal was really sacrificed. Thus burning of the fur of the goat as an agenda of the *Phalgutsav* in Majuli is a symbolic killing of the goat. This is however, not exclusive to Majuli alone; it has been an all-India culture.

BARSIK BHAONA-SABAH/BAR SABAH

Bhaona-sabah, meaning performance of a religious drama and holding of a grand congregation prayer, is the most universal festival of the villages in Majuli. Every non-tribal Assamese Hindu village in Majuli perform an annual congregation, called *bar-sabah*[57] followed by performance of a religious drama (*bhaona*), where not only the organizing village but also many of the neighbouring villages participate. It is the most important festival in a village in Majuli possibly next to the *Bihus*. The time for organizing a *barsik sabah-bhaona* is not the same for all the villages; but the normal time is during the months of May and June, although it may sometimes be held even in the last part of April or first part of July. June-July being the harvesting time of the summer crops—*ahu* rice, and it being the season of rain and flood, the chosen and the most convenient time for organizing a *bhaona-sabah* is immediately after the *Bohag Bihu* which falls in mid-April. Among the agenda of the *barsik sabah-bhaona*, are congregation prayer that includes *uthanam* and *hiyanam*, reading of the *Bhagavata*, distribution of *mah-prasad*, reception of the invited guests in both village and family level, and above all, performance of the *bhaona* in the night.

It is said that in Majuli, March and April are the days when one is accustomed to the hearing of the sound of the *dhol*, while May and June is the time for hearing the sound of the *khol*. This means that men prepare for the *Bohag Bihu* in the months of March and April by beating the *dhol* which is the symbol of the *Bihu*, and prepare for the *Barsik Sabah-Bhaona* by playing on the *khol* which is again the symbol of the *bhaona*. An evening in a village of Majuli in the months of May and June is, therefore, is always unique when one, traveling alone through the village road, or together with one's friend, hears only the musical sound of the *khol* coming out of a family house or from a distant *namghar* breaking the silence of the dark or disturbing the cry of the *jackal* that comes from the jungle.[58]

Villagers prepare for the *bhaona-sabah* since at least a month before the actual function. When asked about how they prepare, Punaram Nath of Puranibari Gaon under Kamalabari Mauja, narrated the story as follows:

> *Bhaona* is very sacred for the villagers. To them it is coming from the heaven. *Mahapurusha* Sankaradeva had brought it from heaven for the welfare of the common people about five hundred years ago. He developed the *bhaona* for edification of the illiterate masses in the knowledge of the scriptures. We therefore consider *bhaona* to be the heart and soul of the people.

The drama for a *bhaona* is composed by learned people of the village, or they collect one such drama from outside, and make a copy of it for the villagers. Normally, dramas are composed by the *Satradhikara*s and then performed in the Satra. When the villagers visiting the Satra attend the *bhaona*, or come to know about the drama, they borrow it for sometime and make a copy of it for their own use. A drama is normally selected at the elderly level for a particular year's performance, and then some one is given the responsibility to collect it from elsewhere if it is not at the village, and then write the dialogues called *bachan* in separate sheets of paper. When writing of the *bachans* are finished, a meeting attended by both young and the old is held at the village *namghar* to distribute the *bachans* among the possible players. Female roles are given to those young boys who resemble girls, or who are supposed to be suitable for the role. Normally, no body desires to do a female role. Some times there are problems arising out of the distribution of roles as more than one persons aspire for the same role consequently leading to conflicts between them. This, however, is always settled at the instance of the seniors. After distribution of the roles, rehearsal is carried out for about a month almost every evening until it is decided that the practice is perfect. Then a day is fixed after making due astrological calculations and in consideration of family problems like, students' examinations, and so forth. When the day comes nearer, information and invitations are given to the neighbouring villages, Satras, relatives and so forth. On the day before the day of the *bhaona-sabah* all sorts of preparations are reviewed, responsibilities are distributed among the male persons, and dresses of the role players (*bhawariya*) are collected. In the evening of that day final review of the rehearsal is made. It is called *bar-akhara* (big-rehearsal). All role players pray for their welfare, good memory, and good health next day. Thus after a long endeavour, aspiration, labour and hope of enjoyment the fixed day comes.

From early in the morning of that day every member of the village engages in his/her duty fixed by custom or by the society, or by the family. By late in the morning guests from the other villages begin to arrive. At noon formal function of the reading, recitation, and congregation prayer starts. The whole *sabah* closes in the afternoon with distribution of the *mah-prasad*. Now there is the time for recreation for about three hours. At about 7 p.m. every role player comes to the dressing/green room where the appointed artists, normally a few experienced men from other villages, are waiting to make them up. Making up takes about one hour to two. And *bhaona* starts when the *namghar* is full of audience, on one side are female members, while on the other side are the males. No person in alcoholic condition is allowed to enter the *namghar*.

The *bhaona* starts by the dance of the *sutradhar* or *sutradhari* who inaugurates it. The first scene normally starts with either by a king or by the appearance of Lord Krishna. In the second case, all in the audience bow down their heads considering the person in guise to be the Lord Krishna Himself. Thus a month's labour and plan finds its reality. And thus the *bhaona* starts. It lasts till the next day morning, and some peasants go to the field directly from the *namghar*.

Bhaona-sabah has great social value. It enhances relationship between different villages and between different social groups. Today a village *namghar* is full of audience coming from all castes and tribes and from various walks of life. In the congregation also members from different communities participate; and inviting *bhakats* from various castes and communities to participate in the *bhaona-sabah* under a single canopy called *chandratap*, has become a fashion in certain villages. An interesting aspect of this function in the past used to be that *bhaona* was a secluded cultural function confined to the Satras alone; and therefore, its participants were also mainly the inmates of the Satra and their family members. It is not known when did *bhaona* culture entered the villages; but it is surely presumable that *sabah* or congregation prayer and the common prayer hall (*namghar*) became part of the village culture along with the spread of Vaishnavism although it certainly did not become part of a family agenda then as it does today.[59]

It appears that spread of *bhaona* culture in the villages was mainly due to the initiative of the Kamalabari Satra. Punaram Nath, referred to the above, remembers how his grand-father Titaram Nath (1830-1910) was a *Bayan* and a *Muktiyar* of the Kamalabari Satra under its *Satradhikara* Krishnakanta Goswami (c. 1834-1857 A.D.) who deputed some of the inmates of his Satra to train the villagers in the culture of *gayan-bayan* (to play on the *khol* and sing religious song in a chorus), *sutradhara nritya*, and organize *bhaona*. His family till today holds that honourable job of *bayan* (head of the village artists' group who play on *khol*) and the title of *Muktiyar*.[60] It is to be noted that Krishnakanta Goswami was the only person from Majuli who had also contact with Maniram Dewan (1806-1858), the martyr of 1857 Revolt.[61] The fact that initially *bhaona* was confined to the Satras alone, and that members of certain castes and all the tribes were not allowed to enroll as resident inmates (*bhakat*) of any Satra, were possibly the reason why *bhaona* culture had a late entry to the villages. It is not that only villages peopled by tribal or peripheral Hindu castes, but villages of the caste Hindus too were out of the *bhaona* culture till perhaps 19th century. The reason for that is clear. The grand royal Satras had a different status: their *adhikaras* never having the custom of putting the foot on the ground,[62] nor the habit of staying in a village *namghar*,[63] nor contact with common villagers, had been aloof from the villagers. Even today, it is easy to reach the *Satradhikara* of the Kamalabari Satra at his residence, and for that matter, those of Bhogpur, Chamaguri or Owa Satra, but it is not that easy for a lay villager to meet the *Satradhikara* of the Auniati, or Dakhinpat or that of Garamur Satra.[64] Popularising *bhaona*, therefore, was the work of the smaller Satras, mainly of Kamalabari. This Satra still has its largest performance record outside Majuli including achievement of national awards by its inmates.[65]

Bhaona is a popular traditional culture in the villages in the island. This is irrespective of caste and tribe or rich and poor affiliation. The role of Pitambardeva Goswami of Garamur Satra[66] who invited the young members from the neighbouring villages and allowed them to participate in some of the cultural functions of the Satra, particularly, in the *Ras* festival, is significant in gradually loosening the watertight barrier between the Satras and the villages. More recently, due to the 'open-door' policy initiated by the Auniati Satra, perhaps under the compulsion of the modernity effect, open economy and globalization, *bhaona* and other branches of Satriya culture have not been now confined to the Satra premises alone; it has slowly embraced a section of the urban people also, although mostly in an exhibitive form. The organization of the *bhaona* as a grand festival in Majuli at the initiative of the Auniatiya *Satradhikara* Dr. Pitambardeva Goswami,[67] followed by his Kamatabari counterpart Narayan Chandra Goswami, is an example of such grand exhibition in the expansion and preservation of this traditional culture of Majuli. This is, however, only one aspect of the *bhaona* culture; for it is noticed that being a medieval tradition in continuum, it has been loosing its earlier attraction among the younger generation and the growing elites in Majuli itself. It is interesting to note that younger generations in Majuli today have developed significant interest in enjoying a cinema or a TV serial or such other programmes more than their traditional cultures.[68] This is where one can see the impact of modern technology on the traditional and intangible cultures.[69] Thus intangible culture in the form of traditional knowledge systems in the island has slowly been challenged by modern cultural trends. It is significant that the organization of the *bhaona* competition on all Assam or all Majuli basis by some of the *Satradhikaras* and other public organizations is but a response to this challenge posed by modern technology and culture towards the traditional local cultures in the island.

BIHU

Bihu is the national festival of Assam. There are three *Bihus* in Assam, held in three different times of the year, perhaps fixed according to the urge of early human habit in a particular topographical context. They are *Bohag Bihu*, *Kati Bihu* and *Magh Bihu*. The first is observed in the middle of April, the second at the close of the Hindu month of *Asvin* or *Ahin* and beginning of *Kartik* or *Kati* (middle of October), while the third is observed at the close of the Hindu month of *Pausha* or *Puh* and beginning of *Magh* (middle of January). Of the three *Bihus*, the *Bohag Bihu,* also called *Rangali Bihu,* is the most popular and widespread over all sections of the people irrespective of caste and religion. In fact, this is the *Bihu* which is the national festival of Assam and has a secular character.[70] The popularity of this festival among the various communities, and its composite character with the folk elements of the society, show that at the beginning there was only one *Bihu,* and it developed among the aboriginal communities of the land.

Scholars have attempted to show that *Bishuva* (Capricorn) is the origin of the term *Bihu*[71] trying thereby to show that *Bihu* is of Brahmanical origin. Dr. Pitambardeva Goswami of Auniati Satra supporting this view has stated that the *Bohag Bihu* is originated from *Maha-Bishuva*, the *Magh Bihu* is originated from *Makar-Bishuva*, and the *Kati Bihu* is originated from the *Jala-Bishuva*. He therefore says that since the three *Bihus* originated from the three *Bishuvas*, the term *Bihu* had its origin in the term *Bishuva*.[72] This is, however, no more than an attempt to argue against ethnic origin of the *Bihu*. In fact, *Bishuva* has been connected with *Bihu* in order to aryanise the non-Aryan term *Bihu* to make it Sanskrit and Communicable as it was so widespread and popular that ignoring or despising it like some of the 19th century members of the Assamese middle class elites[73], would be not only diplorable, but also suicidal to the aryanising authorities themselves. It was in the process of such an attempt that there was addition of two other *Bihus*, the *Magh Bihu* or winter *Bihu* (interpreted as worship of the fire god *agni*), and the *Kati Bihu* (organized as worship of the god *Kartika*).[74]

There is no difference in observing the *Bihus* in Majuli with those in the other parts of Assam. The only significant aspect to be noted is that despite a secular character, Bihu has attained here a religious tone too which could be detected in the celebration of the *Bihus*. For example, the *Bohag Bihu* is marked by bathing and feeding of the cows, recitation of the verses from the religious scriptures reflecting the activities of Lord

FIG. 5.7: *BIHU* DANCE ON STAGE

Krishna and Radha, use of *khol* and organization of the *smaran-kirtan* (popularly called *Charan-Kirtan*).[75] Organization of the congregation prayer at the village *n<u>a</u>mghar* on the *sankr<u>a</u>nti* day (first day of the *Bihu*), are some of the best aspects of religious impact on the *Bihu*.

FIG. 5.8: MISING *BIHU* DANCE DURING *ALI-AYE-LRIGANG*

To be more specific, one will see how on the previous day of the *Bihu* (first day of *Boh<u>a</u>g*), a festival is organized for the cows called *Garu Bihu*. On this day cows are bathed in the rivers or ponds, and then they are fed with pieces of gourd, brinjal, amber and *kerela* (the bitter gourd *momordica charatia*). In the evening they are fed in cakes, given new ropes (called *pagh<u>a</u>*), and the cowshed is besmeared with thick smoke created by burning a heap of husks, grass and a special kind of herb called *m<u>a</u>khiyati*. It is believed that the smoke produced by burning the *m<u>a</u>khiyati* tree would burn the mosquitoes and other insects, and thereby it will contribute towards good health and breeding of the animals and increase their number. The next day (the first day of the month of *Boh<u>a</u>g*) is the actual day of the *Bihu*, often called *M<u>a</u>nuhar Bihu* (*Bihu* of men) as against *Garu Bihu* or cow-*Bihu*.

The *M<u>a</u>nuhar Bihu* continues for a long period, at least for a week. It is marked by what is called *huchari* and *Bihu* dance; the latter meaning singing of *Bihu* songs, beating of drum called *dhol*, playing of bamboo instruments like *gagan<u>a</u>*, *tak<u>a</u>* and buffalo-horn called *pep<u>a</u>*. *Bihu* teams consisting of young and male members of the village go from house to house, singing *huchari kirtan* (a kind of congregation singing/ chorus), and performing *Bihu* dance. They bless the householder and collect whatever amount of *dakshina* (contribution) he could offer to the team. It is customary that the *dakshina* should include a piece of *gamocha* (an Assamese towel), a symbol of gift of a piece of cloth (*bastra dan*) which is considered of great religious merit. This goes on for days, and even weeks.[76] Slowly monsoon sets in, and rains begin to shower leading to the peeping of occasional but minor flood in the rivers called *barhani pani* or *na-pani* (new water). It is the time for weeding the fields (*dhan nirowa*) which get covered with vegetables, herbs and grass attacking the paddy crops, and the sugarcane and the jute fields. *Ahu* crops in the low-lying fields are by now getting matured, and within a short time they will be ready for harvesting. In the mean time, seasons come for germinating the seedlings (*kathiya para*) for the wet rice (*sali kathiya*) crops. Slowly, rains become frequent and that is the season of catching fish which begin to breed (*ujan para*) at the first shower, and the villagers get busy with harvesting their crops and catching fish.

But, this is the time for spread of various diseases, like measles, cholera, malaria and goiter and so forth. Men now turn their attention to the *namghar* where they find solace and solution to all their problems. And this is the season of the *barsik bhaona-sabah*.

FIG. 5.9: KACHARI GIRLS PERFORMING *BIHU* DANCE ON STAGE

It has been stated elsewhere that population of Majuli consists of various communities religious, ethnic and linguistic. The *Bohag Bihu* as narrated above is mainly confined to the Assamese Hindus although non-Assamese inhabitants like Biharis, Marowaris and Bengalis too participate in the festival. The Deoris, Kacharis and the Misings have their own systems of celebrating *Bihu*. While the Misings celebrate the

Bihu in the same way as the Assamese Hindus do, the Deoris celebrate it a few days after the *Manuhar Bihu*, and in their own way. This has been narrated in appropriate contexts.

Magh Bihu is celebrated on the day of the *makar sankranti* (mid-January) in Majuli, like any other place of Assam. The *Magh Bihu* is significant in a few ways: (i) first, it is celebrated at the close of the season of harvesting of the winter crops—*bao* mainly, and *sali*. (ii) second, it is the season of availability of all sorts of food items—milk, curd, cream, rice, fish, pulses, *gur* and other things. Thus, after harvesting, it is time for recreation and feeding. So, this *Bihu* earns its name as *Bhogali*. But, this being the season of cold, the major way of celebrating it is to make heaps of firewood, or dry paddy straw called *nara* and make what is called *meji* in open or in the paddy fields, and to arrange grand feasts on the previous night called *uruka*, i.e. the day before the actual *Bihu* that falls next day, the day of the *Makar Sankranti*. Various kinds of cake (*pitha*) and breakfast items (*jalpan*) are prepared by the villagers The next day, people gather at the village *namghar*, and perform congregational prayer. In some of the villages, people arrange a grand feast on that day. This *Bihu* is not popular among the tribal communities in Majuli.[77]

People of Majuli observe the *Kati Bihu* on the *Ahin-Kati Sankranti* day. It has a bad name being called *Kangali,* i.e. poor. The season of October-November is one of scarcity, particularly in Majuli. The season of rain has just ended, paddy fields are green but not yet brown, domestic animals are yet very thin having passed the flood season in pain due to lack of grazing areas leading to scarcity of milk and milk products. Sugarcanes are not yet mature for making *gur*, and so forth. Thus like two other *Bihus*, *Kati Bihu* too is interpreted by men in terms of economy. Be that as it may, men celebrate it according to their ability. It is the custom of the people to plant the *tulasi* (basil plant) specially for that day which they use to worship on the evening of the *uruka* day, and some amount of cakes and *jalpan* are prepared for the next day. Villagers go to the paddy fields in the evening to light candles (*banti*) praying for God Almighty's grace for good of the harvest and for destruction of the insects that may destroy crops.[78] It is a custom for the cultivators in the Majuli island to go to the fields next day to see the growing crops. At noon that day, they go to the *namghar* and organize congregational prayer, i.e. *nam-kirtan*, distribute *mah-prasad*, and offer salutation to the God Almighty for the welfare of all. This *Bihu* lasts for one day only. The tribal communities have no *Kati Bihu.*

The Satras have their own method of celebrating the *Bihus*. A description of the system of celebrating the *Bihus* at the Satras, as collected from the Satras themselves, is given in Appendix XI. It is interesting that the Satras have given a religious and spiritual colour and interpretation of the *Bihus* in their own way. For example, Narayan Chandra Goswami of (Natun) Kamalabari Satra, has stated that worship of *tulasi* plant destroys sin (*pap*) and earns religious merit (*punya*), for *tulasi* is the beloved of the God.[79] Similarly, interpreting *Magh Bihu* he says, "The *Bhogali Bihu* of the month of *Magh* is a very old festival. It is a life giving festival, and very pure. Bali, the traditional Asura king (demon) was sent to the other world (*Sutal Puri*) one day before completion of his enjoyment on the earth on the *Sankranti* day of *Pausha*. The day left un-enjoyed by Bali was enjoyed by men on earth with all sorts of affluence and happiness."[80] *Kati Bihu* is celebrated in the Auniati Satra with much pomp and grandeur. On that day the inmates organize what is called *akas bati jalowa* (lighting of the lamp in the sky) in nearby the common prayer hall (*namghar*). The preparation takes a long time, at least a month preceding the *Bihu,* and many inmates of the Satra are engaged in the work of preparing for the *akas bati*.[81] Dr. Pitambardeva Goswami, *Satradhikara* of the Satra, has stated that the tradition of *Kati Bihu* as practiced in the folk society has obtained a religious perfume in the Satras.[82] Thus, here the *Satradhikara* has accepted the folk-origin of the *Bihu* although on the earlier occasion he attempted to derive the term (*Bihu*) from the Sanskrit word *Bishuva*.[83] The fact that *Bihu* is celebrated at the Satras, is a kind of an attempt to sanskritise it in the Brahmanical fashion. It is natural that being born and brought up in the same society, inmates of the satra carry the *Bihu* culture from the villages when they come to be enrolled as *bhakat* in the satra. This is how, the preceptors could not exclude *Bihu* from the whole of the Satra festivals and giving it a religious character. As a result, *Bihu* in Majuli has two sides, one secular and ethnic, and the other religious and Brahmanical.

Bihu has now slowly become detached from the village life. Growth of modern technology and multiple amenities of life has made even the *Bohag Bihu* a business of the urban people for preserving it as a piece of intangible culture. Making love and marrying some one dearest, the core essence of the *Bohag Bihu*, does not now need one to meet his/her fiancée in the *Bihu* dance organized under a solitary tree in a corner of the village (called *jeng bihu*); nor cow is the main source of economy today to worship and feed in cake, nor it is necessary to light candle in the evening field during the *Kati Bihu* to kill insects that destroy paddy. In fact, it is the *Magh Bihu* alone that still has some relevance to the society irrespective of its standing—urban or rural. As a matter of fact, *Magh Bihu* is now celebrated more than *Bohag Bihu* in traditional form. *Bihu* is now greatly modernized.

ALI-AYE-LRIGANG—THE MISING FESTIVAL

Like non-tribal peoples, tribal societies in the island also have their own festivals. As we have noted above, there are three ethnic tribal communities in the island—Misings (earlier mentioned as *Miri*), the Deoris and the Kacharis, each having their own socio-religious festivals with the *Bihu* common to all.

Among the most widely popular festivals of the Misings having both religious and secular tone is the one called by them as *Ali-Aye-Lrigang*, the spring festival, observed on the first Wednesday of the month of *Phagun* at the beginning of the spring season. It is the national festival of the Misings to be equated with the *Bohag Bihu* of the others. The term *Ali-Aye-Lrigang* means the festival of sowing seeds; *ali* means paddy or seed, or root called *alu*; *aye* means fruit, and *lrigang* means the day of sowing seeds. The entire term means the day of sowing seeds.[84] Nahendra Padun, one of the researchers of the community, has stated that in earlier times there was no fixed date of the month of *Phagun* for the festival, but it was only since 1956 that the first Wednesday of that month has been fixed as the day of the festival.[85] Although he has not stated the cause of this late fixation of the date of the festival, it can be presumed that gradual Assamisation and formalization of the tribal festivals led to development of such formalities and arrangements in the cultural life of the Misings.

On the very Wednesday, early in the morning, the members of a Mising family go to the field under the leadership of the mother or the head woman of a family who by hoeing certain amount of a plot of land sow the seeds. Tarun Chandra Pamegam has stated that at the field during the time of sowing the seed the sower will say, "I shall give it to the *guru*, I shall give it to the *bhakats*, and I shall feed the transitory physical bodies."[86] It appears that this Vaishnava system of dedication[87] is a new development in the Mising society, after they have come into contact with the socio-cultural systems of the plains, particularly that of Majuli. Thus, it may be a later addition to the celebration of the festival.

The festival is performed by consuming and offering fish, meat and cake made of *bara* rice. For that purpose, a fish and meat collection drive is undertaken collectively by the whole village using knife and other iron and bamboo implements. Nahendra Padun has mentioned that at present hunting is done not by using the old instruments, but by using guns and other modern instruments.[88] It is to be noted that even hunting which was once an indispensable part of the festival, has now become obsolete as few jungles, *bils* or rivers are available for hunting or fishing. Indreswar Pegu, one of the most known scholars of the Mising community, has answered to a query of this writer to that effect. This was supplemented by Ghanakanta Nath, Principal of Pitambardeva Goswami Junior College, and a resident of the Mohkhuti village, a part of which is also inhabited by the Mising people, who has stated that no hunting is now undertaken by the Mising villagers on the eve of the festival which was once its significant feature. On the other hand, Phanidhar Tahu, Principal of the UMK College, Majuli, has emphatically shown that *Ali Aye* today, like the *Bohag Bihu*, is observed in public platforms under decorated stages.[89] Thus a tradition that has been continued since unknown past, has been now undergoing transition.

Performing music and dance like those in the *Bohag Bihu* of the Assamese non-tribal people is a special aspect of the *Ali Aye Lrigang*. On that occasion the young men and women would visit the house of a well-to-do family of the village, preferably the family of the headman or the *Satola*, and organize the *Bihu* where every one of the village irrespective of old and young, shall participate. This merry-making shall continue for days together and the rich men of the village will supply all sorts of rice beer, fish and meat by making lavish expenditure. *Ali Aye Lrigang* is popularly called by the non-Misings as *Mising Bihu.* And *gumrag,* the most distinguished of the dance forms of the Misings, dominate the whole festival.

P'orag or *Nara Chiga Bihu*

Like *Ali Aye Lrigang*, *P'orag* is an agricultural festival of the Misings. It is observed at the post-harvesting seasons—during August-September (Assamese *Ahin* month) after the harvesting of the *ahu* crop, or during November-December after harvesting the *sali* and the *bao* crops.[90] As it is observed at the close of the harvest when the straw has rotten to pieces, it is popularly called by the non-Misings as *Nara Chiga Bihu*.[91] This, like the *Ali Aye*, involves a very elaborate system and needs year long preparation. Young boys use to build a common hall in front of the village large enough to accommodate inhabitants of the whole village and the invited guests. It is called *Murang*. Also called *Deka Chang*, it is mainly the house for the young boys of the village who used the house in earlier times to sleep together at night as a body of protectors of the village when it is in danger of being attacked by enemies.[92] *P'orag* is celebrated in the *Murang* with singing of songs called *oi-nitam* and dance where all people including the invited guests gather and participate. These dances are mimetic 'suggesting sowing, reaping, weaving etc.'[93] *P'orag* is considered by the Misings as a symbol of unity and brotherhood among them.[94] Of the other minor and major socio-religious festivals *Dabur* is to be mentioned. A religious festival, *Dabur* is a kind of *puja* of the

Misings. Here the community worship their primordial gods—the moon and the sun—*danyee-polo*.[95]

Festivals of the Deoris: The *Bisu* Festival

The Deoris have their own festival of which the *Bisu* (*Bihu*) is the foremost. Although it does not synchronize with the *Bohag Bihu* that starts on the day of the *Visuva Sankranti*, the *Bisu* of the Deoris begins in the first Wednesday of the (mid-April) month of *Bohag*. The *Bisu* is both a secular and a religious festival. Preparations for the *Bisu* festival are made for the whole month of *Chot* preceding the festival. The actual festival starts on the first Wednesday of the *Bohag* month along with the worship of their god *Kundi-Mama* (*Hara-Gauri*) with the sacrifice of thirteen fowls at the *sal* (shrine) of the priest. The *Bar Deori*, the *Saru Deori*, the *Bar Bharali* and the *Saru Bharali*—all their priests perform this sacrifice. On the first day, the young and old together go to the house of the chief priest and spend the whole night dancing and singing there. The next morning they go to the river and take common bath and also bathe their cattle. Since that day till the next Wednesday the young girls and boys of the village dance and sing at the open *Marang* house of the *Gosani Sal*. This is still the major feature of the *Bisu* festival. In the past, they used to gather at the house of the priest for the entire month.[96] But, as reported by Ram Prasad Deori, one of the known popular writers of the community, this custom of dancing and singing in the house of the chief priest for the whole month has now become obsolete.

On the second Wednesday, called the day of *Bisu/Bihu Uruwa*, all people irrespective of age and sex gather together at the *Gosani Sul*, the shrine of the goddess *Kechaikhati* (eater of the raw flesh) for merry making with dance and singing. During this day there is also *deodhani* dance, 'the shamanistic dance of a woman who make prophecies.[97] "At night, *Bisu* is cut off in a river or a piece of waste-land. This is symbolically done by throwing away the bamboo clapper or the stick used to beat out rhythm."[98] After the *Bisu* festival, the Deoris organize *Ras Kebang* at the close of the month (*Bohag*) when 60 hen, a couple of duck and 4 pigs are sacrificed.

On the third Wednesday of the month the villagers sacrifice four pigs, two ducks and fifty four hen and propitiate the goddess *Minucchi Midi* (goddess Lakshmi) and god *Acchiya Midi* (*Opar Devata* or gods in heaven) and seek welfare to the village for the year. On the next and last Wednesday they worship *Kundimama* with the sacrifice of three goats and ten hen. Pegions are also offered, but not by the villagers as a whole, but individually. It is called *Metuwa Puja*.

Another religious festival of the Deoris of the island is the *Saoni Puja*. On that occasion thirteen hen are sacrificed for the propitiation of their ancestors. On this occasion even the insects and flies also are offered for propitiation of the ancestors at the village shrine.

Festival of the Sonowal Kacharis

Like other ethnic and culture groups, the Sonowal Kacharis have their own tribal socio-religious festivals. The most known of these festival cum *pujas* are the *Gajai Puja,* the *Monai Puja*, the *Batho* or *Baithau Puja*, the *Deori Puja*, *Guru Maga* and the *Bihu.*[99] *Gajai Puja* is twice celebrated in a year—one in the month of *Bohag* (April), and the other in the month of *Kati* (October). *Gajai*, a god of the tribe, has no image. People worship him in a village temple where there is a shrine inside made of cement concrete. Although a duck is sacrificed, no liquor is offered. *Gajai Puja* involves worship of the goddess earth (*Vasumati*) also. *Manai* is *Gajai*'s brother. His worship is held once a year in the month of *Bohag* (April). This worship is organized in the courtyard of the village prayer house (*namghar*). No sacrifice is made, but he is worshipped with *mah-prasad*, and offering of feast with fish.[100]

Celebrated in the month of *Phagun* (February-March), *Batho or Baithau Puja* is the worship of the god *Batho*, equated with lord Siva, the primordial god of the Kachari tribe.[101] For the *Batho Puja* a *Siju* tree (a kind of euphorbia) is always necessary, for this *puja* is impossible without this plant. As a matter of fact, planting a *Siju* tree in the courtiyards of each of the Kachari families is a custom of the tribe. People make an image of the god with rice powder (*pithaguri*) and put it under the *Siju* tree that is encompassed by a bamboo fencing. Inside the enclosure a pair of fowl is sacrificed, and at the close of the function *mah-prasad* is offered. Outside the fencing there is feast with offerings of rice beer. This function is a kind of agricultural festival.

Of the other festivals, the most gorgeously celebrated is the *Bohag Bihu*. During this *Bihu* the Kacharis sing their traditional tribal song called *haidang geet*, and accompanied by dance they present it from house to house in choral form called *huchari gowa*. During the performance of this *haidang geet* a bamboo pole is posted in the middle of the courtyard of a family, and with regular beating the bamboo pole the performers dance in a uniform circle and sing.

Festivals of the Kacharis are a mix of both tribal and Vaishnava features. While gods and goddesses are of ethnic origin, methods of worship are frequently characterized by Vaishnavite idioms. This is due to their conversion to Vaishnavism retaining, at the same time, their old tribal culture.

Festivals of the Bengali Community

Although among the local Assamese communities *Kali Puja* as such is not celebrated, it is popular among the Bengali community of Majuli. It is celebrated every year on the *amabasya* day (the last day of the black fortnight) of the month of *Kati*. As reported by Anil Sarkar of Milanpur village, there are two methods of holding this *puja*—by Vaishnava method which does not involve sacrifice, and the *Sakta* method where sacrifice is allowed. Surely, we find here an impact of the Vaishnava atmosphere of Majuli. Other festivals of the Bengali community include *Lakshmi Puja, Saraswati Puja, Makar Sankranti, Phakua, Sarak Puja, Bhatri Dvitiya,* etc. Congregation prayer called *Sankirtan* of the Sri Chaitanya order is much popular among them. The function of *Sankirtan* (Assamese *charan-kirtan*) has no fixed date and month. Generally, it is celebrated on the full moon day in the month of *Bohag* (March-April). One interesting aspect of their socio-religious festivals is that they also, like the local Assamese people, celebrate *Bihu* festival.

Like the Bengalis, the Nepalis, the Biharis and the Marwaris celebrate their own festivals which are normally religious in character. Among them various kinds of *puja, Rakhi Bandhan, Dewali* are significant where all, irrespective of Assamese or non-Assamese, participate.

Thus, it is found that festivals of Majuli are of two types: religious and secular, but the former dominate over the latter. Of the religious festivals the Vaishnavite ones dominate where all, irrespective of tribal and non-tribal affinities, loosely or steadfastly participate. Large festivals include the *Bihu, Ras Lila* and the *Pal Nam*. Of the tribal festivals the *Ali-Aye-Lrigang* dominates over all others. Of late marked changes are noted in the observance and functioning of these festivals. Such changes are noted in two aspects again. Festivals are becoming more exhibitive; and while *Ras Lila* has been commercialized, *Bihu* and other festivals have lost their medieval rural fragrance. This exhibitive character has significant impact on the beliefs and customs associated with the functions and the festivals. The growing sense of culture protection, as reflected in the act of the *Auniatiya Satradhikara* when he organizes a state level *bhaona* competition, and in the organization of the Majuli festivals by some NGOs, and the trend of commercializing them have been significant developments in the field of cultural life of the island in the 20th century. One interesting development in this regard is that Satriya cultures have slowly been released to be exhibited in the socio-religious functions like *Durga-Puja* in some of the major metropolies of the country This exhibitive character is noted for both tribal and non-tribal cultures. Thus for those who would like to see them from a heritage point of view, it will be a bit discouraging; but from a historical point of view it is certainly interesting.

END NOTES

1. S.N. Sarma, *op cit.*, p. 189.
2. Dr. P.D. Goswami, *op cit.*, p. 154.

2(a). *Sri Sankaradeva aru Sri Madhavdeva Charit* by Daityari Thakur, vv.

3. Also see Chapter-IV, *Supra*, p. 169; SHTN, pp. 111f.
4. *Bar Charit*—

   Yi dinata madhavaka dute laiya gaila,
   Sankara chintita mane pathe chahi raila;
   Aneka bilamba bhaila mane gurujan,
   satadina palanama gowaila tekhan.

   (tr.) When Madhavdeva was imprisoned and brought (to the capital) by the king's men, Sankaradeva became terribly afraid. Having seen that Madhava had not returned even after a number of days, he instructed his devotees to chant the name of God for his life.) See vv. 1098.
5. Ibid., vv. 1098-1100.
6. *See* Dr. P.D. Goswami, *op cit.*, p. 148.
7. Ibid., pp. 149, 155.
8. HAG, p. 169; Ibid., pp. 148f; TB, pp. 27.
9. Ibid., pp. 148f.
10. Ibid.
11. Ibid.
12. Ibid., p. 153; ASBS, p. 387.
13. ASBS, p. 388.
14. Dr. P.D. Goswami, *op cit.* p. 153.
15. Ibid.
16. Ibid., p. 156.
17. *Dakhinpat Satra*, *op cit.*, p. 73.
18. Ibid.
19. Ibid.
20. Ibid., p. 73.
21. Narayan Chandra Goswami, *op cit.*, p. 111.
22. Ibid.
23. Ibid.
24. NEIHA *Proceedings*, Imphal. *Op cit.*, pp. 63ff.
25. See L.N. Bezbaroa, *Bezbarua Rachanawali*, 2nd print, Guwahati, 1988, Vol. I, p. 390.
26. See S.N. Sarma, *op cit.*, p. 185.
27. Ibid., p. 185.
28. *Bezbarua Rachanawali*, Vol. I, *op cit.*, p. 394; also see Narayan Chandra Goswami, *op cit.*, pp. 110ff.
29. Ibid.
30. MDPH, pp. 215f.
31. Ibid.
32. TB, pp. 50f; D. Nath, 'The Rangpur Reception of king Jai Singha' in the *Proceedings of the North East India History Association*, Vol. XXI, Imphal, pp. 63ff.

33. Ibid.
34. Kunja Bihari Singh, 'Manipur Vaishnavism: A Sociological Interpretation', in R. Robinson (ed.), *Sociology of Religion in India*, Delhi, 2004, p. 128. Bhagya Chandra *alias* Jai Singh, called in the Manipuri chronicles as Chingthangkhompa ascended the throne in April, 1759. (See S.N. Abram, *The Court Chronicle of the Kings of Manipur*, London, 2005). He visited Assam in the year 1765 seeking help from the then Assam king Rajeswar Singha (1751-1769) to fight the Burmese who had invaded his kingdom and had occupied a part of it. (See TB, *op cit.*, pp. 48ff; HAG, p. 271; S.K.Bhuyan, *Swargadeo Rajeswar Singha*, Guwahati, 1975, pp. 45ff).
35. Dr. P.D. Goswami, *op cit.*, p. 123.
36. *Brahma vaivarta Puran, Krishnar Janma Khanda*, v. 6, 7, 864; Dr. P. D. Goswami, *op cit.*, p. 123.
37. Dr. P.D. Goswami, *op cit.*, p. 123.
38. Ibid., p. 126.
39. *Dakhinpat Satra*, pp. 25, 27, 73; Dr. P.D. Goswami, *op cit.*, pp. 136f.
40. Dr. P. D. Goswami, *op cit.*, p. 126.
41. Ibid., p. 127. Also interview with Indreswar Bhuyan, one of the leading inmates of the Satra.
42. Ibid., p. 125. For further details see Narayan Chandra Goswami, *op cit.*, pp. 110ff. Also information obtained from Tarun Bora, Secretary to the *Satradhikara* of Garamura Satra.
43. See Cantlie, *op cit.*, pp. 169ff; also see Kanailal Chattopadhyay (ed), *Asame Cha-Kuli Andolan O Ram Kumar Vidya Ratna*, Calcutta, 1989, pp. 96f.
44. *Op cit.*, p. 185.
45. Ibid.; *Gurulila*, p. 166; *Sri Sankaradeva aru Sri Madhavdeva Charit* by Daityari Thakur, vv. 1314-1316.
46. Dr. P.D. Goswami, *op cit.*, p. 193. *See* Appendix-XI.
47. Every such *tithi* is observed for four days at a stretch at Kamalabari Satra. *See* Appendix-XI.
48. Dr. P.D. Goswami, *op cit.*, p. 191.
49. Ibid.
50. Sankaradeva's *Bhagavata*, Book-II, v.52; Narayan Chandra Goswami, *op cit.*, p. 115.
51. Narayan Chandra Goswami, *op cit.*, p. 115.
52. Dr. P.D. Goswami, *op cit.*, p. 143.
53. Narayan Chandra Goswami, *op cit.*, p. 115; also see Appendix-XI.
54. *Guru Charit* by Ram Charan Thakur, vv.1636f; Dr. P.D. Goswami, *op cit.*, p. 143.
55. vv. 1639-1640; Narayan Chandra Goswami, *op cit.*, pp. 119f.
56. Narayan Chandra Goswami, *op cit.*, pp. 119f.
57. "The word *sabah* is derived from Sanskrit *sabha* meaning an assembly. In Assamese, the word is used only in a religious context. It means a great religious congregation where devotional functions of various nature mark the proceedings of the ceremony." Cf. S.N. Sarma, *op cit.*, p. 188.
58. This picture has been slowly undergoing changes. Today, except on specific

occasions, *bhaona*, and/ or evening practices (*akhara*) rarely mark a village atmosphere as it did in the past.

59. Every family in Majuli use to hold annual *nam-kirtan* (*nam ebhag agbarhowa*) for the welfare of all. At the *tithi* of the forefathers, at any problematic situation, men use to perform *nam* at the house.
60. A village—*Muktiyar* acts as a representative of the *Satradhikara* in settling village disputes, accounts etc.
61. A. Dutta, *Maniram Dewan and Contemporary Assamese Society*, Guwahati, 1990, p. 150; B.Sharma, *The Rebellion of 1857 vis-à-vis Assam, Guwahati*, Guwahati, 1958, p. 35; Narayan Chandra Goswami, *op cit.*, pp. 833f.
62. ASBS, p. 350; D. Nath, *Satras in Colonial Assam. etc.*, *op cit.*, p. 9; also Harinarayan Sarma, *op cit.* (Ms.); Cantlie, *op cit.*, p. 180 fn. 3.
63. During the visit to places outside the Satra the *Satradhikaras* stay in temporay camps called *bahar* with facilities of bath and toilet. Some of such *bahars* include those of Jorhat, Jhanji Garamur, Rangalu etc.
64. See *Baptist Missionary Report*; cf. H. K. Barpujari, *The American Missionaries and North-East India (1836-1900 A.D.), op cit.*, pp. 187ff; also MDPH, pp. 38ff; T.C.Pamegam, *Tarun Chandra Pamegam Rachanawali*, Vol. I, *op cit.*, p. 273.
65. They include Maniram Dutta Barbayan, Bapuram Bayan Atoi, Roseswar Saikia Bayan Mukiyar/Moktar and others. See Narayan Chandra Goswami, pp. 920ff.
66. T. C. Pamegam, *Tarun Chandra Rachanawali*, I, *op cit.*, pp. 273ff.
67. The Auniati *Satradhikara* had organized a grand *bhaona* festival/ competition in Majuli during January-February, 2006, when parties from all over state participated. *Bhaona* competition thenceforth became a regular agenda of the public life in Majuli. See Appendix-XXI.
68. It has been reported from the villages of the remote areas, often inhabited by the Mising people, that some young boys use to enjoy pornographic pictures through CD players. Such CDs when played in a solitary place like the agriculture fields away from the villages, through batteries, are attended by many young boys from the locality.
69. See also, Yogendra Singh, *Culture Change in Modern India*, New Delhi, 2000, pp. 40ff.
70. Devabrat Sarma, *Asamiya Jati Gathan Prakriya aru Jatiya Janagosthigata Anusthan Samuh*, Jorhat, 2006, pp. 328ff.
71. R.M. Nath, *op cit.*, p. 7; 'Samaj Chintamani' in P. Barkataky (ed.) *Amar Pratinidhi*, 4th year, Special Issue, pp. 1114f; Kaliram Medhi, *Studies in the Vaishnavite Literature and Culture of Assam*, Jorhat, 1978, pp. 70f. *Bihu* is a festival of almost all the Mongoloid people of South-East Asia. *See* Hastings, *Encyclopedia of Religion and Ethics*, Vol. III, p. 135.
72. *Op cit.*, p. 157.
73. *See* Gunabhiram Baruah, *Asam Buranji, op cit.*, pp. 202f. Gunabhiram Baruah, has however very clearly stated that singing, dancing and other fertility symbols of the *Bohag Bihu* are the cultures of the non-Aryan peoples. Also see Kanailal Chattopadhyay, op. cit., p. 98.

74. *See* Appendix-XI.
75. Findings of the field investigation. *Charan-kirtan* or *smaran kirtan* is a kind of congregation prayer organized and sung in group. It is popular in the Chaityanyite system of Bengal.
76. See Narayan Chandra Goswami, *op cit.*, pp. 125f
77. Ibid., pp. 127f.
78. Ibid., p. 129.
79. Ibid.
80. p. 128f.
81. See Appendix-XI; also Dr. P.D. Goswami, *op cit.*, pp. 168ff.
82. *op cit.*, p. 175.
83. *See* above fn. 64.
84. Durga Regon, "Ali Aye Lrigang: Iyar Baisista" in the *Mising Sanskritir Alekhya, ed. Bhrigumuni Kagyung,* revised edition, Guwahati, 1989, p. 120, also See Nahendra Padun, Ibid., "Ali Aye Lrigang, p. 130.
85. Ibid.
86. Cf. Ibid., p. 136. The whole prayer is: "We will give to the seeker, we will give to the beggar, we will give to our *gurus* and *bhakats*. O gods, find no fault with us. When the harvest will be gathered, we will offer *puja* to you. O ancestors, you will have to guard these plantations, otherwise your children and grandchildren won't be able to survive. Who will then give offerings to you ?" Cf. P.D. Goswami, *Festivals of Assam*, Guwahati, 1995, p. 54.
87. *See nam, guru, deo,* and *bhakat in* Narayan Chandra Goswami, *op cit.*, pp. 173ff.
88. Cf. Ibid., p. 131.
89. Illustration presenting episodes from the organized function at Ujani Majuli Kherkatiya College, Ratanpur, Nayabazar, March, 2007.
90. Indreswar Pegu, 'Murang aru P'orag', in Kagyung, *op cit.*, p. 103.
91. Ibid.
92. Ibid., p. 100.
93. P.D. Goswami, *Festivals of Assam, op cit.*, p. 54.
94. T.C. Pamegam, 'P'orag', in Kagyung, *op cit.*, p. 122.
95. Nahendra Padun, 'Dabur Puja', in Ibid., p. 415.
96. Dr. R.P. Deori, a retired teacher of Dibrugarh University, has informed the present author that he has noted significant changes in the social and cultural life-styles of the Deoris of his village. This, he says, is due mainly to the attempts at modernization of the systems.
97. P.D. Goswami, *Festivals of Assam, op cit.*, p. 57.
98. Ibid.
99. Information obtained from field investigation; also see Endle, *op cit.*, pp. 33ff.
100. Information collected from the field investigation at Sriram Deori Village.
101. Endle, *op cit.*, p. 36; Mohan Sonowal (ed.), *Sonowal Saurabh*, Dibrugarh, 2007, p. 145ff.

6

Majuli in the State Polity
Earliest Times to 20th Century

MAJULI IN TRADITION AND HISTORY: EARLIEST TIMES TO 1228

Majuli in Tradition

It has been stated earlier that the territory later covered by the Majuli island, was an extended part of the southern mainland lying between the rivers Dihing, Brahmaputra and Dikhow long before the coming of the Ahoms to the Brahmaputra Valley. It is not known for certain what sort of polity the land was associated with during this pre-Ahom period. There is no specific evidence to believe that it was a part of the old kingdom of Kamarupa as neither any epigraphic record of the early Kamarupa kings discovered so far, nor any such document speak about the land in connection with the narration of the affairs of the state. There is no doubt, however, that Majuli was a stronghold of the Bhuyans, who ruled over small territories as local chiefs over whole of the Brahmaputra Valley after the fall of the early kingdom of Kamarupa.[1] For, we have a few legends in which we find an attempt to explain the origin of the Majuli island and that of the city of Ratanpur within it in connection with some of the Bhuyans ruling over the territory. One of these legends records that a king called Ramchandra of the family of Dharmapal ruled in Majuli and established the city of Ratanpur as his capital.[2] It is said in the *Dipika Chanda*, a religious work of Purushattam Gajapati, that a king named Haravinda ruled in Kamarupa with his capital at Chandraprabha on the Lohita. He was succeeded by his son Kusaranga who ruled from Ratanpur (in Majuli).[3] The book also refers to another king called Srutasena, who ruled over Saumarapitha, and over the city of Manapura at the Brahmaputra.[4] It is observed that in the above cases the location of the capital cities are placed in the Majuli island surrounded by the Brahmaputra. In one case, the capital city is mentioned to have been located at the Lohita, while in the other case, it is stated to have been located at the Brahmaputra. In the third case, however, it is clearly called Ratanpur in Majuli. This shows that in all the cases the capital city meant the city of Ratanpur in the Majuli island in the Brahmaputra.

While this is one aspect of the legend, there is still another facet that is related in a work called *Adi Charit* or *Bhuyanr Puthi* where it is held that the city of Ratanpur in Majuli was established by one Ranga. One of his successors called Mayamatta ruled from this city of Ratanpur. It is further related therein that the latter had two sons named Arimatta and Nagamatta. The elder son Arimatta ruled over the territory of Biswanath in the west. It is said that his minister Samudra had bulit the city of Biswanath. Arimatta is alleged to have killed his father Mayamatta, and thus, earned for himself the disrespectful name of being a patricide. The rest of the story relates to the creation of the Majuli island and the city of Ratanpur as has been narrated earlier.[5]

According to the genealogy of the kings of Dimarua, a tribal chiefdom in the district of Kamrup,[6] a king called Somapala ruled over the region of Pratapapura in Biswanath. He married a wife named Harmati. She was raped by the Brahmaputra, and consequent to this Arimatta was born. Arimatta killed his father Somapala. Then in order to atone his act of committing the sin he went to the Brahmkunda and threw the ashes of his father there. The people of Pratapapura along with one of the sons of Somapala then went to Dimarua and began to live there.

There is yet another tradition which states that Mayuraddhvaja of the line of Siva ruled over the territory lying between Biswanath and Suvansiri. His grandson called Pratppuriya married Harmati, daughter of Haravinda. She was raped by the Brahmaputra. As a result of this union, Arimatta was born at Biswanath. But he killed his father and then committed suicide.[7]

Thus we see that the name Arimatta is associated with a large number of incidents taking place from Sadiya in the east to Kamarupa-Kamata in the west. P.C. Chaudhury has stated that Arimatta is associated even with some Buddhist traditions also.[8] As a matter of fact, Edward Gait has remarked that "it is quite impossible to unravel the truth from the various conflicting stories that are current among the people,"[9] But, the association of Ratanpur and Brahmaputra as recorded in these legends is significant. For, although no significant additions could be made to the understanding of the history of the island from those legends, there is no doubt that the territory of the Majuli island experienced some kind of political developments in the pre-Ahom, and pre-Chutiya periods. The association of the city of Ratanpur which is still considered as a historical place in the Majuli island, is significant in this regard.

MAJULI IN HISTORICAL TIMES: 1228-1769

Known history of the island can be traced from the time of coming of the Ahoms to Assam in the early 13th century. It is in their chronicles (called *buranji*) that frequent references to the island are to be found particularly after the mid-17th century, in connection with the establishment of the Satras, wars fought against the Koch and the Mughals, and in the expansion of the administration.

Although there is no detailed account of the political affairs in Majuli in the early middle ages, it is shown by evidence that Majuli was then ruled by the Chutiyas, then a state-forming tribe of the northeastern region. Assamese chronicles mention that Chutiya king Gaurinarayan took the name Ratnadhvajpal by conquering and occupying the neighbouring territories,[10] and by dethroning one Bhadrasen he established a city which he named as Ratanpur.[11] From the chronicles it appears that some crafts developed in Majuli during the Chutiya rule as it is recorded that the Ahom army obtained some gold and silver articles from the defeated Chutiyas and also some members of a few artisan communities.[12] That Majuli obtained some importance as a centre of polity and religious activities during the Chutiya rule can be presumed from various chronicler and legendary sources. It is stated in one of the chronicles that one of the Bhuyans who ruled over the contiguous region of Ratanpur and the surrounding areas on the north bank, had challenged the Ahom army by stating that they should not dare to occupy his territory simply because they had defeated the Chutiyas.[13] This fact proves how the Bhuyans ruled in Majuli contemporanreusly with the Chutiyas and continued to rule even after that, till at least the occupation of the Chutiya state by the Ahom king Suhungmung *alias* Dihingiya Raja in the year 1523.

Majuli had been associated with the Ahom polity almost since the beginning of their rule in the Brahmaputra valley. As has been mentioned in an earlier occasion, Sukapha spent three years in the island doing agriculture and making temporary settlement.[14] Being affected by flood, the first Ahom king, however, abandoned the place for a better site around Charaideo.[15] Majuli sheltered the unfortunate queen of king Tyaokhamthi (1380-1389 A.D.) when she was banished by her husband's first wife—the chief queen (*Bar Kunwari*) on some flimsy pretexts.[16] And it was here that king Sudangpha *alias* Bamuni Konwar was born who consequently succeeded his father to the throne in the year 1389.[17] The accession of this king to the Ahom throne was a land mark in the cultural history of Assam, as it was after his accession that Brahmanical influence entered the Ahom royal palace and the Ahom royal family came to be brahmanised.[18] Majuli, however, remained out side the direct Ahom administration till the time of king Suhungmung *alias* Dihingiya Raja (1497-1539) who defeated the Bhuyans and annexed their territories at Habung, and Panbari on the north.[19] Thus, Majuli became a part of the Ahom territory at the beginning of the 16th century.

During the rule of king Sukhampha *alias* Khora Raja, the Koch forces invaded Assam, i.e. the Ahom kingdom in the years 1546, and 1562. It has been mentioned that the Koch king Naranarayan had made his camp here at Majuli during his march against the Ahom capital in the year 1562 and received all tributes from the defeated Ahom king Sukhampha *alias* Khora Raja at this camp.[20] Even during Mir Jumla's Assam campaign one hundred years after the Koch invasion of 1562, Majuli formed a station of the Mughal forces.[21]

The administration of Majuli after it was occupied by the Ahoms, was placed at the hands of the *Bargohain,* one of the three cabinet ministers of the Ahom state, whose jurisdiction of administration included this region.[22] It is possible that after the Ahoms had established their hold over the island, they had gradually consolidated their rule over this region by introducing the *paik* system after taking a detail census of its people. Assamese chronicles have mentioned that king Pratap Singha (1603-1641) took a census of the people of Majuli by himself being present at the mouth of the Sukan Suti river in the year 1609.[23] It is also recorded that he built an embankment called *Meragarh* in Majuli by encompassing its northeastern territory.[24]

The Ahom kings made Majuli an important culture zone of their state. King Jayadhvaj Singha (1648-1663) had established three important Satras here—Auniati, Dakhinpat and Garamur, and made it an important center of Vaishnava religion.[25] Satras in Majuli, however, had to experience occasional atrocities from some of the kings due to certain political circumstances. For example, king Gadadhar Singha (1681-1696) penalysed not only the *Satra̲dhika̲ra*s of the big Satras for their aspiration to imitate the royalty in power and affluence, but also punished their inmates who accepted either celibacy or inmateship in the Satras with a view to avoiding corvee system of labour under the *paik* system, whom he engaged to build roads and embankments of the state.[26] But, against this policy of persecution, king Rudra Singha (1696-1714), son and successor of Gadadhar Singha, followed a policy of patronage and re-establishment of the *Satra̲dhika̲ras* in their original places although this mighty king had beaten the *Kamalabariya Gosain* along with his counterpart—the *Madhupuriya*—and sent them away from the capital by hanging earthen pots from their necks.[27] And since then presence of the *Satra̲dhika̲ras* was made compulsory at the capital during the time of the coronation ceremony of the kings under certain rules which governed their visits to the Ahom capital.[28] Thus the Satras once more emerged as a more powerful agency, and even Jayadhvaj Singha, who initiated the process of patronage of the Satras, died by listening to the prayer recited by the Dakhinpat *Satradhjikara* at his death bed.[29] It is interesting to note that this king died saying that he had given the responsibility of ruling the country to this *Satradhikara*.[30] Thus the power and influence of the Satras grew to such an extent that Majuli became an important centre of political and cultural activities during the later half of the Ahom rule; and by the last part of the 18th century, the kings and the Satras became united to rule the state. The unity of religion and politics created consequently what is known in history as the *Moamariya Revolt*.

MAJULI IN THE MOAMARIYA REVOLT: 1769-1805

The Moamariya Revolt of late 18th century was a significant event in the history of medieval Assam. Termed variously by historians as rebellion, popular peasant movement, insurrection, *jeehad*, intestinal commotion, uprising, the Moamariya Revolt took the shape of a civil war involving almost all sections of the society to fight against or in defence of the Ahom monarchy in the last quarter of the 18th century. As an important place of the time with the socio-political and cultural heritage shaped by the Ahom kings and the Brahman pontiffs receiving patronage from the monarchs, Majuli as a social entity was expected to stand by the royalty during those precarious days. But existing socio-religious structure of the land did not allow this to happen; in fact, people of Majuli got divided, fought amongst themselves killing and penalising their opponents leading to wide social schism in the times that followed.

In order to have a proper estimation of Majuli's role in the civil war started by the Moran tribe, understanding the historical background is unavoidable. As has been stated earlier,[31] both Sankaradeva and Madhavdeva had proselytized to the *ekasarana dharma* the common people of Majuli and its neighbourhood.[32] But, the *Mahapurushas,* as the Vaishnava leaders were called, could not continue their missionary work in the island for long, for soon they felt the wrath of the royalty whose feudal political ideal clashed with that of the *ekasarana dharma* or *Mahapurushiaism*.[33] Thus Sankaradeva and Madhavdeva had to leave the place, but it was here in Majuli that they left the imprint of Vaishnavism of monotheism, democratic social outlook and liberalism. Thus, the place inherits a puritan Vaishnava air and an outlook that has characterised its society since the 16th century.

The meeting of Sankaradeva and Madhavdeva in the land and their proselytizing mission was raising the eyebrow of the Ahom kings for another reason too. Both the religious leaders were hailing from the Bhuyan class who held much political power in the Brahmaputra valley contemporaneously with the early Ahom rulers and posed themselves as great challenge to the growing Ahom monarchy in Assam. Early Assamese chronicles maintain that the Ahom rulers had to adopt measures against the Bhuyans to defeat and disperse them to various secluded places of the valley.[34] This was how Sankaradeva's association with Madhavdeva and their missionary work in Majuli which was then within the kingdom of the Ahoms (called *Asama*), was politically intolerable to the kings.

By the beginning of the 17th century, political scenario in lower Assam had a new orientation with the Mughals occupying the region and annexing it to their empire, and to the consequent fall of the Koch power that sheltered and patronized Sankaradeva and his movement. The Mughal force now posed a threat to the very survival of the Ahom state in Upper Assam. They had now, therefore, the reason to muster their strength through creation of a Hindu unity. As a matter of fact, both internal and external factors inspired the Vaishnava movement to look and trace back to the place of its origin by the 17th century, almost hundred years after its propounder had left it.

Beginning with the 17th century itself, flow of a different kind of Vaishnavism entered Majuli from the north-west. Belonging to the *Kala Samhati* order, the sect called *Mayamara* or *Moamariya* soon spread among the lower echelons in the society, particularly amongst the Kaivartas. Several centres of the sect soon sprang up in the length and breadth of the island at the hands of the descendants of Aniruddhadeva (1553-1626), its founder, who was also a *Bhuyan* and his descendants.[35] The *Mayamara* or *Moumariya* sect resembled the puritan form of Vaishnavism developed by Sankaradeva in more than one way. The character of the sect was that it was more popular among the socially backward classes on one hand (which was not the case with the Brahmanical Vaishnava order) and, on the other, its followers were taught to practice equality of men at the socio-religious level. Its distinguishing feature was that it taught them to treat no body as superior, including the king, except their preacher—the *guru*.[36] Such sectarian features made it belligerent to the royalty as well as to the Brahmanical Vaishnava order from the very inception.

By the mid 17th century other branches of the Vaishnava sect also entered Assam as we have mentioned earlier. They had also created a strong population base for themselves. Taking advantage of this situation, the shrewd Ahom monarchs developed a policy of negating the growing Bhuyan power and the *ekasarana* influence by following a more positive policy, i.e. by encouraging the growth of a parallel form of Vaishnavism in the land which led to the growth of the largest and the most influential Satras in Majuli in the mid-17th century at the state patronage. This new creed of Vaishnavism that grew under the patronage of the kings, had a different character, different from that of Sankaradeva's Vaishnavism. Here, the Brahmanas replaced the non-Brahmanas, i.e. the Kayastha Bhuyans, as religious heads, and the puritan character of early Vaishnavism had allowed flexibility to its various theological aspects.[37] The other significant aspect of this new creed was that while Sankaradeva's Vaishnavism posed a challenge to the royalty, the Brahmanical Vaishnavism used to stand by the royalty in the times of its weal and woes. Majuli thus became one of the bastions of royal stronghold since the mid-17th century.

Thus society in Majuli witnessed the growth of two contending socio-religious formations by the first half of the 17th century; the Bhuyan-developed liberal Vaishnavism, and the state-patronised Brahmanical Vaishnavism. It now became apparent that with its more egalitarian character the *Mayamara* sect soon attracted the tribes and the lower castes almost over the entire state, and it was sometimes suspected that the *Mayamara guru* with his huge population strength formed by his disciples, would soon become a potent challenge to the existence of the Ahom monarchy as well as to the Brahmanical Vaishnava order.[38]

About the last part of the 18th century, relations of the Mayamara order with the royalty became tense and there was every possibility of an open confrontation between the royalty and the Mayamara followers. By the year 1769 the first flame of fire was opened by the Moran tribe in Upper Assam; they being organized by their *guru*—the *Mayamara Mahanta*, defied the Ahom authority to exploit their natural resources within the zone of their habitation,[38(a)] and by defeating the royal forces overthrew the reigning Ahom king Lakshmi Singha (1769–1780) at least for a short while. The rebels then made Ramakanta, a member of the Moran tribe, their king at Rangpur (Sibsagar). The new king soon justified his greed for vengeance by bringing the Brahman *Satradhikaras* of Majuli to book. The Assamese chronicle *Tungkhungia Buranji* records that after the occupation of the throne at Rangpur, Ramakanta and his men proceeded to Khutiyapota (near the Brahmaputra at Jorhat) and summoned to the place the *Satradhikaras* of Auniati, Dakhinpat, Garamur, Kuruabahi and other *Bamunia* and *Thakuria Mahantas*.[39] He confined them there for sometime and exacted fine from them in terms of money, Thus the Auniati and the Dakhinpat *Gosains* had to pay Rs. 8000.00 each, while those of Garamur and Kuruwabahi each Rs. 4000.00.[40] Here in Khutiyapota, the Morans were joined by the Kaivarta disciples of the Mayamara Satra, the other significat group that formed a part of the rebels.

Thus the movement which started as an ethnic protest against the state exploits of their material resources, had turned into a peoples' war against the exploiting machinery as a whole.

The unwise act of Ramakanta created much resentment in the social circle of Majuli. It is known that during the period of the Moamariya or the Matak rule the *Mayamara Mahanta* commanded the common villagers in Majuli and elsewhere to go to him and take initiation from him, 'each new disciple having had to pay only a bunch of betel leaves'.[41] Such forceful initiation continued for two months. As pointed out earlier, the rebels had special grudge against the big Satras. The '*Bagish Bapu*' (the *Bhagavata* reader) of Auniati Satra, an erudite scholar of the *Bhagavata*,[42] was punished by cutting his off nose, ears and eyes.[43] Others who refused to obey, or who tried to escape, were put to death by various other ways.[44]

The rule of the Moamariya or Mayamariyas was, however, short lived; the Ahom monarchy was soon restored. But the situation did not improve and social relations remained strained. The *Satradhikaras* who had already paid fine and put to physical punishment, were now subjected to the ordeal or purification by royal orders. Considering that the Moamariyas had violated the sanctity of the *Satradhikaras* and their disciples, king Lakshmi Singha ordered that the *Bamunia* and the *Thakuria Gosains* including Auniati and Dakhinpat should undergo expiation.[45] He then began a reign of suspicion and terror over the rebels so that there ensued a kind of civil war throughout the state in the period that followed almost to the close of that century. During this time various ethnic and sectarian groups clashed in open revolt and the weak monarchy became the target of attack by the followers of the Mayamara sect.

Assamese chronicles have recorded that in the year 1785 A.D. one Harihar, a weaver by caste, organized the Mayamara disciples at Japarivita, a place surrounded by the dead channel of the river Luhit (old Brahmaputra, Luit) and mastered strength by obtaining the support of the *Daphala-Bahatiyas* (*paiks* allocated to render service to the hill tribes called Daphala, i.e. Nishi) of the north.[46] It is believed that Harihar got through a Moamariya or Mayamariya fisherman a magical copper plate from the old capital site of the traditional king Arimatta, and by practising the *mantra* written therein, had mobilized a large gathering and harassed the people in the neighbourhood.[47] The reigning Ahom king Gaurinath Singha (1780-1795) who was then encamping at Garamur Satra to collect information,[48] however, paid no heed to the casual complaint lodged to him by the harassed villagers. But soon after his return to the capital Gaurinath Singha had to despatch forces from Gargaon to quell it.[49] The royal force thus despatched under the command of the great officers—

the *Marangikhowa Gohain*, the *Dihingia Phukan* and *Helimeli Solal Gohain* beat a hasty retreat at the battle that took place near the Solmari *bil*.[50] Similarly, the other generals—the *Dihingia Phukan* (of the Gauhati establishment), the *Naobaicha Phukan* and the *Barpatra Gohain* fought the victorious rebels at Garamur and on the other bank of the Sovansiri river.[51] It was at this juncture that the *Mayamara Mahanta* Pitambardev after having performed the Brahman killing ceremony (*Brahmaghna*) joined the rebels and attacked Garamur Satra, dispersed the defenders and occupied it and then defeating the royal forces at Garaimari and Pahumara, crossed the Dihing (i.e. Brahmaputra) and attacked Rangpur.[52] It is recorded that during this attack the residential inmates of Garamur Satra gave stiff resistance to the invaders, but in course of the fight, most of them perished and the invaders occupied the Satra.[53] Majuli now became the head-quarters of the northern rebels who thenceforth ruled the place by introducing their own systems.[54] It is recorded that one Hauha then took over the charge of administration of Majuli.[55]

The Moamariyas practically ruled the state till about 1794 when the British force under Captain Welsh freed the land of the rebel occupants and recaptured Rangpur. It is known from the early records that the people of Majuli like those in many other places of the state, and the *Satradhikaras* experienced every kind of hardships during this period. They had to desert their homes and the *Satras* and take refuge in the neighbouring jungles and territories which were free from the Moamariyas. The *Satradhikara* of Dakhinpat Satra Bishnudev Goswami (1780-1822), for instance, left for Rangpur and thencefrom to Nagaon, and put one Bidur *Aldhara* in charge of the Satra.[56] The Moamariya fighters who then ransacked the Satra, killed the *aldhara* and looted the store and then put the houses to fire.[57] The inmates of the Satra all took to flight to the nearby jungles.[58] The Auniatiya *Satradhikara* Lakshminathdeva (1785-1804), secretly left the Satra at night at the intelligence from the king himself with a few of his trusted disciples and reached Guwahati.[59] Records preserved in the Satra show that the disciples of the Mayamara Mahanta then put everything to destruction and ablazed its *namghar* and other buildings, and killed many of its inmates (*bhakats*).[60] Thus the three big *Satras* which were the centres of attraction of the rebels, were devastated. Similar was the suffering of the common people who left their hearth and home, family—wife and children, and cultivated fields allowing wild reeds to grow. Edward Gait has very rightly reflected the picture of the common life under the Moamariya rule as follows:

> 'in the country held by the Moamarias … the burning of villages, the looting of supplies and the wanton destruction of crops led to a terrible

> famine; rice was not obtainable and the sufferings of the people were so great that many abandoned their own children. Even persons of the highest castes, it is said, were reduced to eating the flesh of cows, buffaloes, dogs and jackals. Some roamed about in the jungle, devouring wild fruits and roots, while others fled to the Burha Gohain (Purnananda at Jorhat) or to the neighbouring hill tribes, and even to Bengal.'[61]

It is not that the Moamariyas alone killed and others remained silent. It might be possible that during the Moamariya regime Majuli as a stronghold of the Brahmanical Vaishnavism and a bastion of the royalists, the latter suffered loss of men and materials more than any other place; but after the Ahom monarchy had been restored, inverse was the case. There are records to show that the Moamariyas were then killed irrespective of sex and age at the orders of the king.[62] The *Tungkhungia Buranji* records how the royalists captured and killed the Moamariyas in all the villages with their sons and wives.[63] Maniram Dewan while recording the events of the days of Gaurinath Singha, writes as follows:

> 'The waters of the rivers could not be drunk, and people could not walk along the roads. Even the fish of the Brahmaputra became inconsumable for being tainted with the stinking smell of corpses. Half the country was depopulated. Thus was vengeance wreaked upon the Moamariyas for burning the *Singari ghar* and attempting to kill the monarch. From the period the kingdom became thinned and light.'[64]

By the close of the 18th and the beginning of the 19th century the Moamariya revolt ended leading to the division of the kingdom of *Asam* into two parts: one part around the present Tinsukia region in the extreme east extending as far west as the river Dihing under the rule of the Moamariya *alias* the Matak kings, and the rest under the reigning Ahom dynasty with its capital at Dichainagar or Jorhat.[65] This political division of the kingdom greatly weakened it making it vulnerable to any possible external threat which, of course, became a reality during the Burmese invasions of the early 19th century. It should be mentioned here that the people of Majuli equally participated in repulsing the invading Burmese forces as they did by taking part during the Moamariya revolt. Another important and almost lasting impact of the revolt was that it led to the creation of a permanent social schism and hatred between the followers of the Mayamara or Moamara sect and the others, i.e. between the Mataks and the non-Mataks. That happened particularly in Majuli where the society in general was and is still governed by the ideals laid down by the Brahman *Satra̱dhika̱ras* of the big royal Satras. It is significant that since the Moamariya rebellion the term *Matak* fell into disrepute among the non-Mataks who sometimes used it in derogatory sense to mean a cruel man from Upper Assam.[66]

Records show that majority of the people of the island and the *Satradhikaras* of the big Satras took part in the revolt out of compulsion as the supporters of the royalists. The natural hatred which the Brahmanical Vaishnavas and the Mayamara disciples bore against each other found Majuli as the most fertile place for expression of their hatred. It is for such reasons that the revolt took the form of a civil war in Majuli. The nature of involvement of both the contending groups did not differ much from that in other parts of the state. One significant point in this regard was that the big Satras were the prime target of attack of the rebels in Majuli which were considered the symbol of the royalty. Another significant point was that the celibate disciples of Garamur Satra who were otherwise free from any obligation to the state,[67] and not trained in the art of warfare, were to take up arms creating the first ever example of the *bhakats* going to warfare.[68] The role played by the Auniati *Satradhikara* Pranharideva (1760-1785) in support of his patron king was also significant. It is recorded that he adopted certain novel plans to suppress the revolt. He supported king Lakshmi Singha's plan of re-establishing the Mayamara Satra after it had been devastated by the rebels. Records further show that it was at the instance of Pranharideva's attitude of Matak appeasement that the Mayamara Satra with all its paraphernalia was rebuilt in the Agni Chapari in Majuli to the west of the Auniati Satra.[69] King Lakshmi Singha also desired that those tribes, such as the Kacharis of Bacha who had sympathised with the rebels, be brought to the royal camp by way of proselytization through this *Satradhikara*. Pranharideva, therefore, personally visited the area and converted a large number of the Kacharis to Vaishnavism.[70] It was found that during the later phase of the revolt when the centre of the rebels' activities shifted to Jorhat, the peoples of Bacha became divided into two fractions; those proselytized by Pranharideva came to the support of the royalists.[71]

From the records it appears that the Moamariya disciples in Majuli were mainly the members of the depressed castes and were numerically small in comparison to the non-Moamariyas. Their strength was raised temporarily with the addition of their brethrens from the north as much as to attack and loot the Satras. These outsider Mataks were more attracted towards the wealth of the big Brahmanical Satras than their local leaders. This was why plunder and raid marked the scenario of the revolt in Majuli. But no sooner had Mataks from out-side left Majuli than their number decreased[72] and normal conditions prevailed till the Burmese invasions that started from 1817.

MAJULI DURING THE BURMESE RULE

If the Moamariya Revolt facilitated and brought about the decline of the Ahom monarchy, Burmese invasions completed its collapse. At the close of the 18th century, the monarchy that had continued to hold for last six hundred years, having been swept away from its divine authority by the Moamariyas, witnessed a period of internal strife and external threat. While internal instabilities were due to the fractional and personal clashes among the members of the aristocracy, external threat was coming from the advancing British colonial interest and the Burmese policy of territorial aggrandizement in the early 19th century.[73] This situation of conflict of interests between the Burmese and the Company Government combined with the internal instability finally beckoned the Burmese to invade Assam and bring it under their control.[74] They started in early 1817 and defeated the reigning king of the state Chandrakanta Singha (1810-1818), made him their tributary, and put him under the tutelage of their supporting minister Badanchandra, the *Barphukan*.[75] The internal situation now became a hot bed of conflicts, each minister trying to place his own choice on the throne by dethroning the tutelary ruler Chandrakanta. The result was the accession of Purandar Singha (1818-1819), a great grandson of king Rajeswar Singha (1751-1769) with the support of the Buragohain Ruchinath.[76] This course of events being informed, the Burmese invaded Assam second time in 1819. Purandar Singha now fled from the capital and took shelter in Silmari in Bengal. The Burmese again placed Chandrakanta on the throne. But this time Chandrakanta Singha realized the nature of the Burmese rule and prepared to oppose it. This resulted in the third and the final invasion of the Burmese; and as could be imagined, they now committed all sorts of atrocities and exploitations on the people creating a reign of terror. They now put one Jogeswar Singha (1821-1824) on the throne, and began to rule the state as its authority.[77]

The Burmese brought their devastating activities to the Majuli island too across the great river Brahmaputra. The *Charit Puthis* preserved in the Satras of the island have recorded about it. It is known from these works that the Burmese encamped at Majuli and controlled its affairs through a network of administrative arrangement. Two important officers—*Nakham Phukan* and *Sek Phukan* were stationed at Garamur.[78] This camp of the Burmese on the bank of the Luhit river near Garamur was marked by four large *Simalu* trees, which could be seen till long time after. Many others were put in charge of other places.[79] It is to be noted that being Burmese-made king, the Satras of Majuli did not approve of the accession of Jogeswar Singha to the throne.[80] The biographical work of Keshabdeva (1658-1726) of Auniati Satra has mentioned that although the *Satradhikaras* of some other Satras offered best wishes to the king at least as a mark of courtesy, the Auniatiya *Satradhikara* refused even to see him when the king had paid a courtesy visit to the Satra after his assumption of power.[81] It was therefore natural that Jogeswar Singha took exception to it and encouraged the Burmese military rulers to avenge this insult. This being suspected, the *Satradhikara* deputed his *Katani Bora* from Barbam area to collect information about the plan and activities of the Burmese, and along with his inmates he left the Satra and took shelter in the jungles.[82] The search team of the Burmese force under one *Dikhowmukhiya Rajkhowa*, however, arrested the *Katani Bora* and advanced towards the Satra to capture the *Gosain*.[83] But, unable to find him out, they put the Satra to fire resulting in its complete devastation.[84] It was under this situation that the *Satradhikara* resolved to be in the Satra and came out from the hide out in the jungle. But he was not spared from paying penalty, and like any other *Satradhikara*, he too was compelled to pay an amount of Rs.15000.00, to them as fine.[85] But soon the Burmese General Mingimaha Tilwa came to know about the status and influence of the Satra on the society, and realizing that the penalty imposed on the *Satradhikara* would have a negative impact on their rule, returned him Rs.10,000.00, with honour although the rest Rs. 5000.00, he could not pay back saying that this amount was already distributed among the *Phukans* and the *Baruas*.[86] Keshabdev was then released with the instruction that he would thencefrom pray for the welfare of the Burmese.[87] It is interesting, however, that while there was attack and counter attack in the Garamur and Dakhinpat Satras,[88] Keshavdeva refused to join the coalition formed by the Moamariya Baskatiya to fight the Burmese although the two other big Satras were party to that.[89]

Burmese invasions and their rule in Assam (1817-1824) was a historically devastating time in all respects. It is said that half of the total population of the state died during the Moamariya Revolt, while the other half suffered during the Burmese invasions. And Majuli too shared the havoc equally as any other places of Assam.[90] Maniram Dewan, a native of the state and a devotee of the Dakhinpat Satra, has stated, "Some they flayed alive, others they burnt in oil, and others again they drove in crowds in village *namghars* or prayer houses, which they then set on fire... It was dangerous for a beautiful woman to meet a Burmese even on the public road. Brahmans were to carry loads of beef, pork and wine. The *Gossains* were robbed of their possessions."[91] This chaotic situation had its impact on agriculture and economy of the state. John M'Cosh, who wrote not long after the Burmese rule, has recorded that "though some centuries ago (it was) richly cultivated... is now throughout six-eighths of its extent covered with a jungle of gigantic reeds, traversed only by the wild elephant or the buffalo, where human step is unknown and the atmosphere even to the natives themselves is pregnant with febrile miasmata and death."[92] This impact of the devastation might have been equally felt in Majuli also. The fact that a thickly-populated and well cultivated tract of land became sparsely populated and full of jungles by the middle of the 19th century[93] needs no further support to justify this contention. It is still recorded in the public memory in the island how the Burmese collected people—old, infirm, women and children, and confined them to the houses which they then put on fire. Many children were pinned up with sharp and pointed bamboo sticks *(sa̱l)* and nailed them *(mara̱)* to the plantain trees. It is said that the name of the village called *Sa̱lmara̱* in the southeastern corner of the island, now eroded by the Brahmaputra, is stated to have been derived from the Burmese' act of killing the children by that way.[94] There were a few large tanks in Majuli called *ma̱nkata̱ pukhuri* (literally meaning *ma̱n* or Burmese cutting tank). It is stated that some clever men excavated those tanks as a part of their plan to kill the Burmese. There are stories still told by the village folk about how the Burmese invaders were invited to participate in grand feasts organized at the bottom of the tanks and then killed. Thus, in the oral and folk tradition the Burmese invasions and the story of their atrocities still occupy some place; although, for the new generation it has become only a chapter of the history text book.

MAJULI IN THE COLONIAL PERIOD (1826-1947)

The Burmese rule in Assam ended in the year 1824 when the British entered Assam and defeated the Burmese and chased them to their own land. And by February, 1826, by the Treaty of Yandaboo, they legalised their (British) occupation of the state by making it a part of the British Indian empire. Thus Majuli came under the colonial rule along with the other parts of the state at the close of the first quarter of the 19th century.

Administrative Development

After occupation by the British in 1826, Assam was divided into two divisions—western or Lower Assam, and eastern or Upper Assam with a Commissioner to administer each of the divisions. Accordingly, Colonel Richards was appointed as the Commissioner of Upper Assam with its headquarters at Rangpur (Sivasagar), and David Scott as the Commissioner of Lower Assam with its headquarters at Guwahati. The two divisions then came to be known as junior *khanda* and senior *khanda* respectively with David Scott having responsibility of looking after the affairs of both the divisions as the Commissioner senior. After the death of David Scott in 1831, T.C.Robertson took over the charge of Commissionership in 1832 after a brief gap. Robertson then reorganized the administration. He divided the lower and middle part of the valley into four districts—Nagaon, Darrang, Kamrup and Goalpara, while upper Assam was put under the charge of the fugitive Ahom king Purandar Singha.[95] Purandar Singha ruled the region till 1838 when he was dethroned and his territory was permanently annexed to the Company's dominion and was made a part of the Bengal Province with its centre of administration at Fort William at Calcutta.[96]

The Company Government divided the region of Upper Assam into two districts in 1839 with annexation of territories of the Matak kingdom and that of the Khamti Chief in Sadiya.[97] These two districts were Sibpur or Sibsagar and Lakhimpur.[98] Under this division Majuli was included into the Sibsagar district. It was then that the district administration was put at the hand of a Principal Assistant which designation was changed later in 1861 to Deputy Commissioner.[99] In 1874 Assam was made a separate province with a Chief Commissioner at the head of the administration. Accordingly, Leiutenant Colonel R.H.Keatings was appointed as its first Chief Commissioner who assumed his duty on 7th February, 1874.[100] In the mean time, Jorhat became a Sub-Division of the Sibsagar district in 1869, and transport and communication system also developed here. As a result, there was a proposal both from the public and the Government to transfer the district headquarters from Sibsagar to Jorhat on the ground that Sibsagar was not only far away from the railway stations and steamer *ghats,* but was also inundated during the rainy seasons.[101] It is recorded that the demand for transfer was also made by the *Satradhikara*s of Majuli.[102] So, in March, 1905, the proposal was approved by the Government, and in 1913 the headquarters was transferred to Jorhat.[103]

The British introduced *maujadary* and the *mahalwary* system in Assam immediately after consolidation of their rule.[104] Accordingly, Majuli was formed into two *maujas* called Ahataguri Batamara (or simply Ahataguri) and Salmara Kamalabari Karatigan (or simply Salmara).[105] While the first one was attached to the Golaghat Sub-Division, the latter was attached to the Jorhat Sub-Division[106] till a separate and the third *mauja* was created with Kamalabari (and Karatigaon) in 1879 seceding them out of Salmara. It was during the last quarter of the 19th and the first quarter of the 20th century that Kamalabari developed as the headquarter of the administration of Majuli with a Police Thana, a Post Office, offices of the SDC, EAC, Assistant Settlement Officer, a Block Development Office, a ferry *ghat*, and so on.[107]

Like earlier periods, during the British rule too Majuli was remaining almost outside the political ambience of the greater society although the *Satradhikaras* played significant role in the affairs of the state. British records show that all *Satradhikaras* welcomed the British rule and impressed upon the Company Government to retain their old landed properties granted by the Ahom kings.[108] The Company Government too responded to them with a diplomacy of 'withdrawal and retention' to show that they had the right to withdraw and that it were they who had renewed the grants made to them earlier by the Ahom kings. For that act of the British kindness, the *Satradhikaras* supported every act of the Company including their campaign against the neighbouring hill tribes. It is recorded that the *Satradhikaras* offered boats and other amenities to support the British forces in their campaign against the hill tribes.[109] It is even suspected that the Auniati *Satradhikara* Dattadeva Goswami, who published the Assamese news paper the *Asam Bilaseenee* in the year 1871-72, was in favour of the British policy of introducing Bengali language in the courts and schools of Assam.[110] There were, however, exceptions, such as Krishnakanta Goswami of Kamalabari Satra, who was a contemporary of Dattadeva Goswami of Auniati. Krishnakanta Goswami was an anti-British in his outlook, and he was a supporter of the Revolt of 1857 and collaborated with Maniram Dewan, the man behind the plot in Assam. It is stated that Maniram Dewan despatched several letters from Calcutta to Krishnakanta Goswami at Majuli informing him about his plan. The British, after knowing his association with Maniram Dewan, took exception to the *Satradhikara* and kept him under house-arrest.[111] Following this, Krishkanta Goswami had thrown away the land-grant records and disclaimed ownership over the landed property which the Satra had possessed since the days of the monarchy.[112] Similarly, Raghudev Goswami of Garamur Satra too, in protest against the policy of the British Government, had thrown away the copper plates into the Kalang river in Nagaon to disclaim ownership over the lands which the British pretended to have granted to the Satra.[113] This is how, Satras got divided in the matter of participation in the freedom struggle that soon took place in the country. While Pitambardeva Goswami of Garamur Satra (1885-1962) played the role of the man behind the struggle in Majuli by himself being in prison and holding the Presidentship of the District Congress, Naradeva Goswami (1895-1925) of Dakhinpat Satra refused even to contribute anything towards the Non-Cooperation fund.[114] On the contrary, this *Satradhikara* published through Rajanikanta Bardoloi and Taraprasad Chaliha a booklet advocating against the Non-Cooperation Movement.[115] At the same time, he and his counterparts in Auniati and Kuruwabahi Satra counteracted the ideals of the Garamuriya *Satradhikara*.[116] Thus, freedom struggle in Majuli was confined to the leadership of Pitambardeva Goswami and Keshabram Bora, the first ever graduate from the island.

Majuli in the Freedom Struggle

Like elsewhere in India the Brahmaputra valley too has its own share in the freedom struggle of the country beginning with the great revolt of 1857, although its role in India's national movement, particularly that of its peripheral areas, has been significantly marginalised in the standard text books of Indian history. Emphasis on the main stream could be seen even within the Brahmaputra valley itself where scholars pay more attention to the role of the urban centres than the rural areas—particularly those cut off from the mainland of the valley. One of the best examples of such marginalisation is the Majuli island, although, despite its peculiar geographical situation and consequent isolation from the mainland society, it had played its own role in this great chapter of our country's history.

The 19th century reform movements, started in Bengal, took a long time—till at least the last part of that century, to reach Assam when a few bright sons of the land, such as Gunaviram Barooah and Kamalakanta Bhattacharya tried to bring about certain reforms to the decayed Assamese society; and it was only since the beginning of the 20th century that some kind of attempts at organizational or individual levels were made to start those reform programmes in Assam as well. In fact, the *Anti-Partition and the Swadeshi Movement* in Bengal had finally opened the eyes of a section of the Assamese elites to realize the societal value of the reforms and use them as the motivating force to carry on their struggle for freedom.

The Partition of Bengal and the Swadeshi Movement, 1905

The partition of Bengal in 1905 and the creation of the state of '*Eastern Bengal and Assam*' caused much uproar in Bengal and soon it took the form of an all India movement—the *Anti Partition and the Swadeshi Movement.* Thus the initial objective of protesting against the partition finally led to an organized mass movement against the foreign rule in the country. The organizers adopted the technique of boycott, which was extended to include "apart from boycott of foreign goods, boycott of government schools and colleges, courts, titles and government services and even the organization of strikes."[117] Among those several methods, boycott of foreign goods met with much success and burning of foreign clothes became a common scene in Bengal.[118] Other significant aspects were the emphasis laid on self-reliance and self-help and the adoption of some constructive activity at the village level "as means of bringing about the social and economic regeneration of the villages and of reaching the rural masses. In actual terms this meant social reform and campaigns against evils such as caste oppression, early marriage, the dowry system, consumption of alcohol etc."[119]

The *Swadeshi Movement* had much impact on large sections of people and brought them for the first time to the nationalist politics. Naturally its impact was felt in Assam also. A few of the extremists in Bengal found their way to Assam and tried to secure a hold here where young revolutionaries like Ambikagiri Raychoudhury, Raktim Bora and Triguna Barua were induced to their ideals. It was after such contact that Ambikagiri founded the *Sewa Sangha* and wrote his drama *Bandini Bharat*. But more important was the spread of *Swadeshi* gospel of boycott, self-reliance and self-help and social reforms. This encouraged the nationalist leaders in Assam to create an anti-British attitude among the masses who, following the *Swadeshi Movement*, undertook a series of socio-economic reform programmes in the first quarter of the 20th century. Those programmes included mainly eradication of the habit of consumption of opium and intoxicating liquor among the illiterate masses, creation of a sense of self-dependence through boycott of foreign goods, such as clothes, abolition of caste prejudice and untouchability, introduction of widow remarriage and creation of communal harmony, etc.

The Government policy of encouraging opium consumption and earning revenue thereby, made opium supply, sale and consumption alarmingly high in the state during the first quarter of the 20th century although its production in and supply to the state had been regulated since at least the late 18th century. Thus, while the entire province was under the spell of opium, the Brahmaputra valley consumed the major part, and the island Majuli, the most backward territory, was almost its stronghold. Here not only among the backward, poor and the tribal communities, such as the Misings, but even among members of some of the advanced and well-to-do families too opium was popular. Therefore, even though demands for prohibition of opium had been raised since the last part of the 19th century, there was no such effective demand till about the third decade of the 20th century when the Congress and the Provincial Legislative Council adopted certain resolutions in this regard.[120]

It is not known how in Majuli attempts were made to eradicate the habit of opium consumption in the late 19th century when the Government was to form the *Royal Commission on Opium* in 1891. But there was a persistent attempt by Pitambardeva Goswami, the late *Satradhikara* of Garamur Satra, to alert the masses against opium consumption and the government policy of popularizing it as early as the first decade of the 20th century. It is known from his biography, that in the year 1908, he met A.W. Botham, Chief Secretary to the Government of Assam, and impressed upon him the need to prohibit opium. During the year 1909-1910, Pitambardeva Goswami organized meetings at the premises of his Satra and invited villagers to attend where he explained to the audience that the Law of *Dharma* does not permit intoxication.[121] While this had great impact on the opium eaters of the island, his own disciples who were still secretly addicted to the drug, had to face stern measures from him. Pitambardeva continued the mission and next met P.R.T. Gurdon, the Commissioner of Assam, in 1909, and requested him to take certain effective measures in this regard.[122] Thus, Pitambardeva Goswami successfully mobilized the masses against opium consumption and the Government policy of using it as revenue earning sources. This movement for eradication of opium led by Pitambardeva had spread far and wide beyond the borders of Majuli, in the tribal and backward areas of Lakhimpur, Sibsagar and Jorhat.

In the period following 1907, the year of Pitambardeva Goswami's assumption of the *adhikara* seat or headship of Garamur Satra, the *Satradhikara* undertook frequent tours to the remote villages of Majuli where he preached the ideals of boycott of foreign goods, especially clothes, and he himself began to use *khadi*.[123] It is interesting that long before Gandhiji undertook the *Dandi March* to break the salt law, Pitambardeva Goswami in Majuli had boycotted salt manufactured by British companies, and brought brine salt from Punjab for his use.[124] Contemporaneously, he devoted himself to the work of upliftment of the backward, eradication of untouchability and widow remarriage. In 1909, in one of his meetings he said: "The concept of high and low (in caste hierarchy), touchable and untouchable, and the sense of pride derived from the caste status, are not supported by logic; it is ignorance, it indicates one's lack of knowledge of the scriptures. The truth comes out when one peeps into the background of creation of the caste system".[125]

As means of bringing about social and economic regeneration in the villages Pitambardeva Goswami made efforts to start the Co-operative Society in Majuli, and in 1917, he established the *Majuli Co-operative Banking and Purchase Sale Society Ltd* in Garamur Satra with its branches in the far away villages.[126] The *Society* worked well till 1919, but in the following years, i.e. in 1920-21, due to heavy loss incurred by it, the *Co-operative* was finally liquidated.

Pitambardeva Goswami's programme of works did not apparently carry with them any message of revolt against the British Government. Like many other nationalist leaders of his time, he too supported the British as the ruling authority of the country, and on many occasions he attended meetings organized by the Government, or else he welcomed Government representatives visiting Majuli or his Satra. For example, he attended the great *darbar* (assembly) at Jorhat, held on 12 December, 1911, organized by Major Playfair, the then Deputy Commissioner of Sibsagar District, to mark the occasion of king George V and queen Mary's arrival in India,[127] and without caring much for traditions and customs, he boarded a train for Calcutta to have an audience with the royal couple.[128] On October, 20, 1920, he along with the Auniati *Satradhikara* received Lord Chelmsford, the Governor General of India, when the latter passed through Majuli from Jorhat to Lakhimpur.[129] Similarly, in most of his meetings he advised his audience that according to the scriptures going against the ruling authority is irreligious.[130] During the First World War, he contributed 500 rupees to the Relief fund although he could not subscribe to the War Loan Fund.[131] All these, however, did not indicate his real motive; and there is every ground to believe that behind his activities there was an attempt to mould public sentiments against the British. For example, while delivering his lecture at the great meeting held on the *darbar* occasion on 12th December, 1911, he says: "Now we are under the British; but it is not true that a country which is at present under the rule of a foreign country, would always be ruled by foreigners. For everyone wants to be independent. Even India would obtain independence at some point of time, but that is a different aspect. But at present we are under the British government and therefore everyone should show respect towards it".[132]

Such statements of Pitambardeva Goswami reflect on two facets of this intelligent and influential *Satradhikara.* It is not beyond suspicion that Pitambardeva too, like many others of his class, did not dare to go against the British initially. But that there was an element of dislike towards foreign domination in his thought and expression could be guessed from the British response to his acts. His activities like trying to infuse the people with his ideas through his various tours, meetings and lectures on boycott of foreign goods, use of *khadi,* establishment of schools, eradication of untouchability and prohibition of opium, were all taken by the British Government from the very beginning with much suspicion. It was due to his attempt that the anti-opium and boycott programmes, and eradication of untouchability became popular slogans and practice in the island long time before the congress took them seriously.

The period from 1905 to 1920 witnessed the growth of a kind of robust nationalism throughout the Brahmaputra valley under the initiative of various socio-political organizations, such as the *Assam Association*, the *Jorhat Sarbajanik Sabha*, the *Asam Sahitya Sabha* and the *Assam Chatra Sanmilan.* While petitions and representations made by those organizations towards obtaining socio-political advantages marked the nationalist activities in Assam, India experienced certain other significant developments during this period—the reforms of 1918, the *Rawlat Act* (1919), the *Khilafat Movement* (1919), the *Jalianwalabag Massacre* (1919) and the advent of Gandhiji in national politics. By this time the Congress became skeptical of the policies of the Government and possibilities of any kind of political gain. It became apparent that it had to work out certain strategies to pressurise the Government to accede to its demands for liberation. As a result, in the special session held at Calcutta that year the Congress adopted the resolution for non-cooperation which "included within its ambit surrender of titles and honours, boycott of Government affiliated schools and colleges, law courts, foreign cloth, and non-cooperation could be extended to include resignation from Government service and mass civil disobedience including non-payment of taxes. National Schools and Colleges were to be set up, *panchayats* were to be established for settling disputes, hand-spinning and weaving was to be encouraged and people were asked to maintain Hindu-Muslim unity, give up untouchability and observe strict non-violence."[133] Accordingly, a countrywide movement under the leadership of the Congress started during which students left schools and colleges, employees left their services and all boycotted foreign goods and used *khadi.*

In October 1920 the *Assam Association* in its meeting held at Guwahati endorsed the Congress proposal of non-cooperation and joined the movement. Thereafter the Association became merged with the Congress, and in 1920 the *Assam Provincial Congress Committee* was formed. The movement obtained much momentum in Assam when Gandhiji visited the state that year. The wave of the movement spread to Majuli too; and students studying in other parts of the state left schools and colleges, and came back home and propagated the non-cooperation ideals among the masses. Pitambardeva Goswami and many others undertook tours to remote villages of the island and preached non-cooperation, particularly non-violence, boycott of foreign goods and use of *khadi*. It was during his tours that the *Satradhikara* distributed certain printed leaflets and explained through them the ideals of non-cooperation to the villagers.[134] The visit of Gandhiji to Jorhat and his meeting with Pitambardeva Goswami gave him much impetus to carry on his non-cooperation works not only in Majuli but also in the rural areas of Lakhimpur, Jorhat and Sibsgar. His association with Gandhiji and his frequent tours undertaken in guise of a proselytizer, created much suspicion in the Government, and therefore, during his visit to Jorhat in November, 1923, John Henry Kerr (1922-1925), the Governor of Assam, met him in the Jorhat Circuit House and asking for certain clarifications about the objective behind his tour, enquired about his establishment of the rural schools, the number of disciples accompanying him, nature of the school syllabus, the number of pupils studying there, etc.[135] This indicates that he was under strict Government surveillance.

While Pitambardev Goswami was busy with the villagers, Keshabram Bora, a fresh graduate from Cotton College, and the beloved of the people of Majuli, was working among the students and advanced section of the citizens. He declined the Government offer of appointment as a judge and joined the movement preaching ideals of non-cooperation among the people, organizing strikes and boycott, etc. In support of his ideals, he burnt, in public, all the cloths of his newly wedded wife and organized strikes in front of the shops which sold foreign cloth. He was the leader of the nationalists during the *Non-Cooperation Movement* in Majuli. Bora was immediately arrested and sent to jail and was confined for six months.[136] Fearing, possibly, that the arrest of Pitambardeva could create much problems by affecting the religious sentiments of the Assamese people, the Government did not arrest him although his visits to villages and organization of meetings were put under restrictions and surveillance, and his name came to be enrolled in the black-list.[137]

The holding of the Congress session at Guwahati in 1926, which was attended by many national leaders of the country, including Gandhiji, created a vigorous sense of nationalism among both the Congress leaders and the common people in the state. The session was attended, among others, by Pitambardeva Goswami from Majuli who had a long discussion with Gandhiji while the session was going on.[138] After the Congress session, the annual conference of the *Hindu Mahasabha* was held. Presided over by Madanmohan Malaviya, the welcome address in the meeting was delivered by Pitambardeva Goswami as the President of the Reception Committee.[139] It is known that it was under the instructions of the *Satradhikara* that many capable persons from Majuli contributed in the form of money towards the success of the Congress.[140]

The period following the Congress session at Guwahati was one of reactions and counteractions. The *Bardali Satyagraha* and the boycott of the Simon Commission by the Congress, and the refusal of the British Government to grant full dominion status to India as demanded by the Congress,[141] and finally the Congress's rejection of the offer to hold a *Round Table Conference* at London for a solution of the problems, marked the period.[142] The consequent result was that the Congress at its Lahore session in 1929 adopted resolutions to launch civil disobedience for refusal of payment of taxes and to ensure resignation of the members from legislatures. Following this, the Congress Working Committee meeting at Sabarmati entrusted Gandhiji with the authority to launch the *Civil Disobedience* and start the famous *Dandi March* on 12 March, 1930.[143] The news of the *Dandi March* and the consequent arrest of Gandhiji and others soon reached Assam where a powerful agitation was launched by students against the infamous *Cunniagham Circular* which compelled the students and their parents to maintain law and order and keep good behaviour.[144]

The *Civil Disobedience Movement* had its impact on Majuli. During 1930-31 Pitambardeva Goswami was still busy carrying the gospel of Gandhiji to the people of the island—emphasising the boycott of the foreign goods, the production and use of *khadi,* the upliftment of Harijans and the backwards, eradication of untouchability, and prohibition of opium and intoxicating liquors.[145] During this period he, along with a few of his followers, moved from village to village explaining the meaning of *Swaraj*. In one of his meetings he explained to the villagers the meaning of *Swaraj* as follows:

> 'Most villagers today do not understand the meaning of *Swaraj.* To them it merely meant that one has to be imprisoned for *Swaraj* and one should be disobedient to the civil laws. In reality, however, this is not *Swaraj*; in order to have *Swaraj,* one has to be self-dependent.'[146]

This is how, the *Satradhikara* tried to form the social background for obtaining *Swaraj* which, as perceived by him, was certainly the precondition and the basic need for an independent nation. His emphasis on the eradication of untouchability and upliftment of Harijans was also based on his idea that caste-prejudice and untouchability had destroyed the very root of nationalism. He says:

> 'Therefore, I am obliged to say that every house of the 26 crore Hindus is now catching fire; some of them have awaken, while the others are still asleep. Those who have awaken, have tried their best to awake others.'[147]

It was found that when the leaders of the Congress were sent to jail, there was nobody to conduct its affairs and Pitambardeva Goswami had to preside over its provincial annual session at Jorhat in 1932.[148]

Till 1930 there was no High School in Majuli and Keshabram Bora was busy with his newly founded minor school (established in 1924). As a matter of fact, student participation in Majuli centering round the Cunningham Circular was minimal, and participation of other noteworthy *Satradhikaras* was also not much significant. Hemchandradeva Goswami of Auniati Satra was merely a sympathiser and contributed some money to the fund of the organizers of the movement in Majuli.[149] It is interesting that the Government tried to use the authority of this revered *Satradhikara* to keep his disciples away from joining the movement. It is recorded that when requested by Sir Michael Kin, the Governor of Assam, to use his authority to convince his disciples to maintain law and order, Hemchandradeva Goswami replied that he could not go against the will of the society of which he was simply a member.[150] This shows that he was becoming isolated from the stream of the struggle, and therefore, he had little power to exercise his authority over his nationalist disciples. As a matter of fact, he might have thought it better not to interfere with the activity of the people. Thus, it appears that the *Civil Disobedience Movement* in Majuli was primarily confined to the propagation of its ideals by Pitambardeva Goswami among its masses. While student participation was not significant, the *Satradhikaras* other than that of Garamur Satra were simply sympathisers. The only other feature of significance was that there was much enthusiasm among the nationalists who formed committees and collected funds to carry on the programmes of the movement in parallel to other parts of the state.

The thirties was a period of constitutional developments, and towards the close of the decade, the second Great War broke out. Since Britain was a major partner involved in the War, and it sought help and cooperation of India against its enemy, nationalists of the country regarded it as an advantage to pressurise the Government for conceding to their demand for independence. The Congress therefore, in its session held at Bombay, adopted in August, 1942, the historic proposal of *Quit India* which led to the legendary phase of the struggle better known as *August Revolution,* which aimed at 'nothing less than freedom'. But even before the congress passed the *Quit India Resolution*, Gandhiji who was then trying to build up the tempo for a mass revolution by way of his *Individual Civil Disobedience* of *Satyagraha*, was arrested and put in the jail. This incident suddenly flared up the situation and the entire nation jumped into the revolution.

Like any other parts of the state the *Quit India Movement* soon spread to Majuli, where Pitambardeva Goswami joined the *Individual Satyagraha* already adopted by Gandhiji.[151] He was soon followed by the people, and Majuli became one of the most important strongholds of the Congress under the leadership of Pitambardev Goswami. It is recorded that on 19 September, 1942, he organized a grand meeting at Garamur Satra where he appealed to his audience to adopt non-cooperation and to prevent supply of goods to the Government servants.[152] He also deputed some of his trustworthy followers to carry his messages to far off villages of the island which remained inaccessible during the rainy seasons wherein he instructed the people in the remote areas to organize mass movement and to disrupt the easy transport of the Government officers from one place to another by withdrawing their help.[153] Accompanied by Krishna Chandradeva Goswami, the *Deka Satradhikara* of his Satra, Pitambardeva himself visited the neighbouring villages including the tribal villages propagating non-cooperation and enrolling Congress volunteers. Towards the last part of the year when most of the Congress leaders were inside jails, Pitambardeva Goswami went to Jorhat and assumed the leadership of the Congress.[154] His movements and activities soon aroused the wrath and suspicion of the Government and it immediately imposed restrictions on his movements and confined him to the Satra. It made the *Satradhikara* "responsible for some of the most objectionable items of a new leaflet and poster spate."[155]

The confinement of Pitambardeva Goswami to the Satra premises kindled greater nationalist fervour among masses of Majuli. Finding that the *Satradhikara* was confined to the Satra, the *Deka Satradhikara* Krishna Chandradeva Goswami openly came out, perhaps at the instance of the *adhikara* Pitambardeva, to spearhead the movement. He now began to address people in big gatherings and inspired them to participate. The Government took immediate steps to prevent him from further participation; he was first put under detention on 12th November, 1942, under DIR 26, and then arrested and put in jail on the 13th November, 1942 under *Defence of India's Rules*.[156]

The arrest of the *Deka Satradhikara* was followed by the Government's preparation to arrest the *Satradhikara* on any pretext. He was alleged to have been involved in a case of theft of a gun, on the ground that the lost gun was recovered near the Satra. But suspecting that his arrest would create "profound and adverse affect upon the disciples of the Assamese Hindus,"[157] the Government dared not immediately arrest him. However, when the Government found that the entire movement was being conducted from the Satra, it arrested Pitambardeva Goswami in July, 1943, and put him in Jorhat jail where he was detained for the next two years.[158] Upon his arrival at the jail, it is recorded that Mr. Humphrey, Deputy Commissioner of Sibsagar District, asked him why being a *Satradhikara* he preferred to live with the social-outcastes in the prison. Pitambardeva Goswami promptly replied that "even life in prison is better than subordination to the foreigners."[159] The arrest of the *Satradhikara* produced an unprecedented scenario—the disciples of the *Satradhikara* and of the neighbouring villages took out long processions holding flags and singing the national song and the *Biswa Bijayee No-Jowan* of Jyoti Prasad.[160] Meetings were held at Garamur, Kamalabari, Salmara, Ahataguri and Rangachahi and protests were registered. The Government took stern measures upon those who participated, and arrested and jailed hundreds of them.[161] The disciples of the Satra had to suffer more than others—their food-supply including salt was stopped.[162] The residence of the *Satradhikara* was searched and many items suspected to be unlawful including seven guns of his own and a few manuscripts were confiscated. One interesting aspect of this movement in Majuli, as in any other parts of Assam, was that here also mass participation came from the students, particularly from the students of the *Majuli High School*, now known as the *Majuli Auniati Hem Chandra High School*. They showed unparalleled heroism which contributed greatly to the success of the movement.

The period following the *Quit India Movement* till the close of the War during which most of the nationalist leaders were in jail, was not one of stagnation and comparative peace; rather it witnessed the growth of a series of movements characterized by violence. These mainly include movements concerning the trial of INA prisoners of war and the revolt of the *Royal Indian Navy* (RIN). Although those movements were of short duration, their waves reached as far as Assam, for a number of young men from the state were members of the INA and 'distinguished themselves in their respective positions." It is not known what reactions were there in the island when the movement against the trial of the INA personnel reached Assam. But the coming of the *Cabinet Mission* in 1946 and its plan of grouping Assam with Muslim majority Bengal (Group C) was largely protested in the island too along with other parts of the state.[163]

Records show that there were sharp reactions in the Vaishnava atmosphere of Majuli when the Mission planned to put Assam in Group C. It was during this period of crisis and clash that, in order to obtain Assamese unity and oppose the plan, the *Satradhikaras* of Majuli, as the heads of the grand monasteries, were expected to play a vital role. As a matter of fact, Hem Chandradeva Goswami, the *Satradhikara* of Auniati Satra, published a pamphlet entitled *Hindu Samajalai Gohari* (an appeal to the Hindus) wherein he expressed his views on untouchability which has destroyed the vital strength of unity among the Hindus and appealed to the Hindus to remain united in this time of crisis.[164] The *Satradhikara* of Dakhinpat Satra Harideva Goswami (1938-1963) also sent his message to various newspapers published in Assamese, English and Bengali. Opinions of the *Satradhikaras* published within and outside Assam, and their appeals for the Hindu unity certainly contributed towards the ultimate nullification of the provision of the *Mission's* plan to include Assam within the province of Bengal and thus saved it from being a part of Pakistan one year after. Thus, when Independence came on the 15th August, 1947, people in Majuli celebrated the day with much enthusiasm and hope. Pitambardeva Goswami hoisted he national flag at Kamalabari, and *bhaonas* were performed at the Satras to mark the day.[165]

Despite all the physical disabilities that handicapped Majuli, the people here under their own leadership had played their role in the freedom struggle of the country. Being isolated and cut off from the mainland of the state, and characterized by an atmosphere of traditions and

(B. 1885-D. 1962)
PITAMBARDEVA GOSWAMI, THE REFORMER, FREEDOM-FIGHTER *SATRADHIKARA*

superstitions, it was but natural that the people of the island should have remained aloof from different phases of developments which took place in the 19th century in other parts of the country. Fortunately however, the enlightened ideas of one of the great *Satradhikaras* of the island Pitambardeva Goswami of Garamur Satra, who conducted the struggle in the island all through the period (1907-1947), and the spirit of sacrifice and patriotism of late Keshabram Bora, brought about its exposure to the 19th century reforms and 20th century developments in the country. Indeed, the freedom struggle in Majuli was permeated by the personality and activities of those two great figures.

Majuli thus actively participated in all the phases of the freedom struggle. It is interesting that Pitambardeva emphasized on non-violence at least for the sake of his religious beliefs from the beginning, possibly long before Gandhiji adopted it as his political ideal. It was presumably because of this fact that there were few or no incidents of terrorism or sabotage in Majuli throughout the period of the struggle. Nor were there many police atrocities and repressions as in other parts of the state except imprisonment, *lathi-charge* or imposition of punitive taxes.

Majuli's character as a centre of Hindu religion and Pitambardeva Goswami's concern over Hindu unity led him to bring the ideals of anti-partition to the island as early as 1905. Thus freedom struggle in Majuli began as a kind of movement for Hindu unity and Hindu strength. Naturally therefore, at the time of Independence when the country became divided into India and Pakistan, Pitambardeva Goswami was opposed to it. Even before that when attempts were being made to include Assam with East Bengal, the *Satradhikaras* of Majuli under his leadership gave an united stand opposing this proposal; and it may be stated that their opposition to such proposals contributed largely towards Assam remaining a part of Bharat or Hindusthan.

POST-INDEPENDENCE MAJULI

Majuli was a part of the Jorhat Sub-Division at the time of Independence consisting of three *maujas*. While Salmara and Kamalabari were attached to the Jorhat Sub-Division, Ahataguri formed a part of the Golaghat Sub-Division. In 1979 Majuli itself was formed into an independent Sub-Division of the Sibsagar district with its headquarters at Kamalabari. Three years later the headquarter was transferred from Kamalabari to Garamur. Gradually, there was expansion of administrative net-work. Majuli has now three Police *thanas*, one at Kamalabari, one at Garamur and the other at Jengraimukh; and it is divided into two development blocks—Ujani Majuli Development Block and Majuli Development Block. There are twenty Gaon Panchayats and 210 cadastral villages.

In the electoral politics of the state Majuli has its own role since inception. In 1952, in the first general election of the country, people of Majuli, along with others of the state, had participated with an open mind and with a dream of prosperity under their own Government knowing not that Pitambardeva Goswami, their dearest leader in the freedom struggle, will have to quit the Congress politics to lodge his protest against rampant corruption of the leaders who were once his dear friends.[165(a)] Majuli now had its own elected representatives: two representing the *maujas* of Kamalabari and Salmara then forming a part of the Jorhat (north-Charaibahi) constituency, and one representing the *mauja* of Ahataguri that was then forming a part of the Golaghat West Double Member assembly constituency under Golaghat Sub-Division. Thus, Nilamani Phukan (general caste) and Ramnath Das (Scheduled Caste) represented the joint *maujas* as a part of the Jorhat constituency, and the Ahataguri was represented by Mal Chandra Pegu along with Chanu Kheria.[166] This system, however, did not continue for long. In the second general election held in 1957 when all the *maujas* of Majuli—Salmara, Kamalabari and Ahataguri, were brought together to form an independent constituency reserved for the Plains Tribe communities. Majuli has since been represented at the Assam Legislative Assembly by a member of the tribal communities. However, the Mising community being the largest single tribal community in the island, no other communities, like the Deoris or the Kacharis, the two other major tribal communities of the island, could ever hold that job. The only exception was in the year 1996 when one member from the Koch community which was for the time being included in the list of the Plains Tribe of Assam pending approval in the Parliament,[166(a)] became an MLA from Majuli. So far as the Parliamentary election was concerned, Majuli was a part of the Jorhat Parliamentary Constituency till 1977 when it was tagged together with the Lakhimpur constituency.

Congress party, and later on Congress (I), has been the most powerful political party controlling the electoral politics of the island although most other national and regional political parties too, like the Communist Party of India (CPI), Bharatiya Janata Party (BJP), Asam Gana Parishad (AGP) and others have their existence in the island. Influence of Gandhiji and a few of his most trusted followers at Majuli like Pitambardeva Goswami of Garamur Satra and Keshabram Bora, is at the root of such support for the Congress. There are certain families for whom it is a tradition to support the Congress Party. Pitambardeva Goswami, being an outstanding personality as a freedom fighter, a religious preceptor and a social reformer, exerted much influence on the society; and being a District level Congress President and the first religious preceptor to be in prison for taking part in the freedom struggle, he has left a deep impression on the minds of men in the island towards supporting Congress politics. And this had been at work till a long time after his death even though he left Congress and Congress politics almost immediately after Independence. It is to be noted that like the tea-garden workers elsewhere in Assam, the Mising community in Majuli have always been a vote-bank of the Congress, at least till the emergence of the AGP in the eighties of the last century. Since then it has been a process of sharing of political power between the AGP and the Congress almost alternately. The beginning of what is known as the *Assam Movement* that aimed at detecting and deporting the foreign nationals from Assam during the late seventies and throughout the eighties of the last century,[167] led consequently to the emergence of the regional political party called *Asam Gana Parishad* (AGP) in 1985. Since then the AGP has been a parallel and powerful political party in Majuli.

The present MLA of Majuli is Rajib Lochan Pegu of Congress (I). His victory in the election in 2005 is often attributed to division of the AGP into two fractions, the AGP (*Pragatisil*) under Prafulla Kumar Mahanta (first AGP Chief Minister), and the AGP under the state president Brindaban Goswami.

ULFA is said to have been very active in the island, of course, due mainly to its topographical advantage. As a result, activities of the outfit are attracting attention of every concerned circle in the country. There are certain killings by the cadre in the island of which the most discussed and resented was, perhaps, the killing of Sanjay Ghose, a well-known social worker running the NGO called AVARD-NE in the island since 1996. On 4 July, 1997, he was kidnapped by some ULFA members and was killed in some unknown place of the island.[168] Similarly, one Gopiram Nath Gaonburha from the Phulbari village in the Lakhimpur district, who originally hailed from Majuli itself, was captured by the outfit at his residence and brought to Majuli and was killed there. Some of these killings therefore have significance beyond the local corner.

A few Satras play indirect role in the political affairs of the island as they did in the past. The big Satras known popularly as the *Rajaghariya Satra*, i.e. Satras established and patronized by the king, always played their role in support of the king and the state in the middle ages. Almost the same kind of interest the *Satradhikaras* of the large Satras of Majuli take in political affairs at present as their predecessors took in the monarchical systems in medieval times. It is to be noted that every candidate contesting in Assembly or Parliamentary elections from the Majuli Assembly and the Lakhimpur Parliamentary constituency (presently, Majuli is included in the Lakhimpur constituency), use to visits the Satras seeking blessings of the *Satradhikara* and their good wishes, and support from the inmates.[169] Indeed, all *Satradhikaras* of the large Satras maintain some political affiliation. A study of the diary notes and activities of some of the *Satradhikaras* reveals this fact.[170] It is interesting to note that although approval of the *Satradhikara* has much to do with obtaining the support of the inmates by a contesting candidate in the Parliamentary elections, this is not always the case. There are examples where the *Satradhikara* and his inmates maintain different political alliances. This aspect of the Satra institution playing role in socio-political affairs has still remained untrodden by the historians although a study of such aspects is sure to make many other interesting revelations about this religious institution.

END NOTES

1. *See* K.L. Barua, *op cit.*, pp. 184ff; HAG, p.p. 38f.
2. HAG, p. 17.
3. Cf. H.C. Goswami, *Descriptive Catalogue of Assamese Manuscripts*, Gauhati, 1930, No.42; CAM, No.42; P.C. Chaudhury, *op cit.*, pp. 118f.
4. Ibid.

5. See *supra*, Chapter 1.
6. *See* HAG, *Progress of Historical Research in Assam*, Shillong, 1897; D. Nath, *History of the Koch Kingdom c.1515-1615, op cit.*, p. 23; *Asam Buranji* by Gunabhiram Barua, *op cit.*, p. 43; KGC, p. 61.
7. Cf. P.C. Chaudhury, *op cit.*, p. 119.
8. Ibid., fn2.
9. HAG, p. 18.
10. DAB (part—*Chutiyar Katha*), p. 194.
11. Ibid.
12. Ibid.
13. ABSM, p. 11.
14. See *supra*, Chapter-I.
15. Ibid.
16. See *supra*, Chapter-II.
17. HAG, pp. 81f.
18. See HAG, p. 82; *Asam Buranji* by Harakanta Barua Sadaramin, *op cit.*, pp. 17f.
19. HAG, p. 86.
20. ABSM, p. 33.
21. Ibid.
22. S. Rajkumar, *Itihase Sonwara Chasata Bachar*, Dibrugarh edition, 2000, p. 263.
23. See Chapter-III, fn. 3.
24. *Asam Buranji* by Kasinath Tamuli Phukan, p. 27; ABSM, p. 40.
25. HAG, p. 140.
26. *See* TB, p. 23; HAG, pp. 168f.
27. Ibid., p. 31; HAG, p. 171.
28. *See* Maniram Dewan, *Buranji Vivek Ratna, op cit.*, pp. 25ff.
29. ABSM, p. 86; B. Sharma, *Dakhinpat Satra, op cit.*, p. 42.
30. Ibid.
31. Chapter-IV.
32. GCK, pp. 38, 56f; *Mahapurush Sri Sankaradeva aru Sri Madhavadeva Charit* by Daityari Thakur, vv. 266-272.
33. A. Guha, *Vaishnavvadar pora Mayamariya Bidrohaloi*, Guwahati, 1933, pp. 21ff.
34. ABSM, pp. 11,64; SAB, pp. 16f; HAG, p. 86.
35. These centres include Jagatananda's Satra at Ba-bhaga, Hridayananda's Satra at Sarjan near present Garamur Satra, and Bhabananda's at Gunakata. See *Shri Shri Aniruddhadeva Charit*, vv. 263-268, 270-271.
36. *Shri Shri Aniruddhadeva Charit*, vv. 287-288; S.Dutta, *The Mataks and Their Kingdom, op cit.*, pp. 73f; Anie Hazarika, *Asamar Itihasat Shri Shri Aniruddhadeva aru Mayamara Vaishnava Sampradaya*, Guwahati, 2000, p. 156.
37. All the Satras established by king Jayadhvaj Singha and subsequently patronized by his successors, and which have been still exercising much influence over the people, are headed by Brahmin pontiffs. Thus, Auniati,

Dakhinpat, Garamur and Kuruwabahi are headed by the lineal descendants of the founder *Satradhikaras*, unless it was necessary to adopt an alternative line. But, in that case also, he must be a Brahmin. See D.Nath, 'Satra and Social Change in Majuli', pp. 127; also Dr. P. D. Goswami, *op cit.*, pp. 51f.

38. S. Dutta, *op cit.*, p. 74. It is estimated that at the time of the Moamariya Revolt there were about eight lakh disciples of the Mayamara Satra. Cf. *Shri Shri Aniruddhadeva Charit*, v. 667.

38(a). According to the *Tungkhungia Buranji*, (p. 66), the Moran tribe in the area of Namrup had organized themselves under their leaders Naharkhora Saikia and Ragha Moran Neog, and refused entry of the Ahom *Kath-Katiyas* (wood cutters) into their forests to cut down the *dhak* tree for making drums. This refusal of the Moran tribe is significant in more than one ways. It indicates how the tribe did not like to see the upstart Ahoms exploit their environment by devastation of the valuable trees, and it also explains the ethnic aspect of the revolt.

39. TB, p. 66. Those pontiffs who belonged to the Brahmin caste and followed Brahmanical systems of Vaishnavism with the practice of rituals and offerings were called *Bamunia*, and those who did not normally belong to the caste Brahmin but belonged to the Sudras, and who did not follow much of the Brahmanical rituals, were called *Thakuriya*.

40. TB, p. 66.
41. Ibid.
42. Ibid.
43. Ibid.
44. Ibid.
45. Ibid., p. 74.
46. Ibid., p. 94; S.K. Bhuyan, *op cit.*, p. 222.
47. S.K. Bhuyan, *op cit.*, p. 223; HAG, p. m18fn.
48. TB, p. 94.
49. Ibid.
50. Ibid., pp. 94f; Bhuyan, *op cit.*, pp. 94f.
51. Ibid., pp. 96f; Ibid., pp. 224f.
52. Ibid., pp. 97f; Ibid., p. 224.
53. Ibid., p. 97; HAG, p. 196.
54. Ibid.; ASBS, p. 199.
55. HAG, p. 199.
56. B. Sharma, *Dakhinpat Satra*, *op cit.*, p. 61.
57. Ibid.
58. Ibid.
59. ASBS, pp. 200ff.
60. Ibid. The *Padmapanideva Charit* of Auniati Satra has recorded the incident in the following verses:

pache sabe paya lai
grama bhangi kare chai
Berhi dhare hate bate

Manushyaka paile bate
Grihata lagawe jui
Maha rudra rupa hui
Saputra bandhave mare
Luri nei luriyare...(cf. ASBS, p. 481)

(Tr. Taking advantage of the weakness, they devastated the villages. Wherever they found any person, in the way or in the market place, they grinded him to dust, and put the houses to fire. They were like the *maha Rudra*, the great destroyer, who instantly killed every body—children and friends together. They had looted everything.).

61. HAG, p. 199.
62. TB, pp. 70ff.
63. Ibid.
64. *Buranji Vivek Ratna* (Ms.); S.K. Bhuyan, *op cit.*, p. 221.
65. See N.Gogoi, 'Jorhat—the Last Ahom Capital', in the *Proceedings of the North East India History Association*, Jorhat, 1993, pp. 322ff.
66. The present author who hails from Majuli, had experienced that in Majuli non-Mataks, had used the word *Matak* in a derogatory sense in the past. It may be suspected that since the Mataks, who raised the banner of the revolt in Majuli, all belonged to the Kaivarta caste of (the so called) low social status, the term *Matak* came to be treated as low in the Brahmanical society. To this may be added another reason. Most people of Majuli are disciples of the royal Satras, and therefore, were naturally inimical to the Moamariyas. This fact, perhaps, led the majority to regard them (the Mataks) as untrustworthy or rebel. Also see *Hemkosh*, Reprint, Guwahati, 1985, p. 783.
67. The inmates of the Satras (*bhakat*) were classed during the Ahom rule as *Chamua*, i.e. privileged. They were therefore free from rendering manual service of any kind to the state. See HAG, pp. 239f; Jahnabi Gogoi Nath, *op cit.*, pp. 118ff.
68. TB, p. 1 12.
69. *Pranharidev Charit*, cf. Ibid., p. 187.
70. Ibid.
71. TB, p. 112.
72. At present there are altogether six Matak villages in Majuli—all proliferating from the original Sensowa village. Their total population strength shall not be more than two thousand. This shows that their strength was considerably reduced after the Revolt.
73. S.K. Bhuyan, *Anglo-Assamese Relations*, *op cit.*, pp. 459ff.
74. Ibid.
75. See HAG, p. 215.
76. Ibid., p. 218f.
77. Ibid., pp. 218f.
78. *Kushdev Charit*, cf. ASBS, p. 231.
79. Ibid.
80. As per custom prevailing in the state since at least the 17th century A.D.,

the *Satradhikaras* of the big and the royal Satras in Majuli were to bless the newly anointed king. But this did not happen in case of Jogeswar Singha as he was the Burmese-made king. See ASBS, p. 227.

81. Ibid., p. 227.
82. Ibid., pp. 228f.
83. Ibid., p. 229.
84. Ibid., p. 228.
85. Ibid., p. 231.
86. Ibid.
87. Ibid.
88. B. Sharma, *Dakhinpat Satra*, *op cit.*, p. 63; ASBS, p. 229.
89. Ibid., p. 63; Ibid., p. 229; S.L. Baruah, *op cit.*, p. 368.
90. No detail record about the havoc created by the Burmese in the island has been available. But there are certain oral traditions which still carry the story of the Burmese atrocities in Majuli. For details about the nature of the Burmese atrocities committed over the people of the state see the *Weissalisa* (ed.) M. Bora and B. Barua, Dibrugarh University, 1977, pp. 26ff.
91. *Buranji Vivek Ratna*, Vol. II (Ms.).
92. M'Cosh, *op cit.*, p. 13.
93. Ibid. Also see A.J. Muffatt Mills, *Report on the Province of Assam*, p. 503; *Gazetteer* by Allen *et al.*, p. 572.
94. Oral tradition prevalent in Majuli. The name *Salmara* may have also another derivation. The place Salmara on the bank of the Brahmaputra had stationed a large boat-making workshop during the Ahom regime where expert boat-makers (*nao-saliyas*) made and used bundles of bamboo pins to join the wooden planks in the process of making large boats. This act of making and using the bamboo pins might have also a bearing on the origin of the name *Salmara*, which the people later on associated with the Burmese attrocities of killing men by the same process of pinning them up with the plantain trees.
95. S.K. Bhuyan, *Anglo-Assamese Relations*, *op cit.*, p. 557.
96. H.K. Barpujari, *Assam in the Days of the Company*, Gauhati, 1963, p. 122.
97. Ibid., pp. 127ff.
98. HAG, p. 308f.
99. Ibid., p. 332.
100. H.K. Barpujari (ed.), *The Comprehensive History of Assam*, Vol.IV, p. 277.
101. Ibid., p. 329f.
102. Ibid.
103. Cf. *Gazetteer of Sibsagar District*, Shillong, 1967, p. 2.
104. Barpujari (ed.) *The Comprehensive History of Assam*, Vol IV, *op cit.*, pp. 30ff; ADB, p. 336.
105. Hunter, *op cit.*, pp. 278f .
106. See *Gazeetteer of Sibsagar District*, *op cit.*, p. 3f; Hunter, *op cit.*, p. 583.
107. See *supra*, Chapter-III.
108. Speech given by Lord Chelmsford at Majuli during his visit to the island on 20 October, 1920. cf. ASBS, p. 297; *Gazetteer* of Allen *et al.*, pp. 584f;

Amalendu Guha, *Medieval and Early Colonial Assam*, Calcutta, 1991, p. 221; D. Nath, 'Satras in Colonial Assam etc.', *loc cit.*, pp. 35ff.

109. Ibid.
110. Jogendranarayan Bhuyan, (ed) *Ratneswar Mahanta Rachanawalli*, Guwahati, 1977, p. 343. Ratneswar Mahanta wrote to Hem Chandra Goswami: "It is very painful for me to let you know that Auniati Gossain does not seem to like our mother tongue—he says let the Assamese be used only in our daily transactions & ordinary talks but books written in Bengali. I discussed with him several days & too freely." In still another letter addressed to Hem Chandra Goswami, dated 13thOctober, 1890, Ratneswar Mahanta expressed his suspicion about the integrity of Gunaviram Barua, another elite of 19th century Assam, in regard to the introduction of Assamese language in the schools and the Universities and its development. He wrote: "We expect all true Assamese & lover of our indigenous literature will help us in this end. I do not expect anything from Babu Gunabhiram Barua on this subject. I know his opinion on this is highly stoic, & he has a tendency towards Bengali." (See Ibid., p. 354). Ratneswar Mahanta's comment explains to a great extent the double standard maintained by most of the middle class elites of the late 19th and early 20th century Assamese society.
111. Narayan Chandra Goswami, *op cit.*, p. 989; D.Nath, 'Satras in Colonial Assam etc.', *loc cit.*, p. 38.
112. Ibid.
113. MDPH, p. 39.
114. Cf. B. Sharma, *Dakhinpat Satra, op cit.*, p. 84.
115. Ibid.
116. MDPH, pp. 128f.
117. Bipan Chandra, *India's Struggle for Independence*, Delhi, 1992, p. 129.
118. Ibid.
119. Ibid., p. 130.
120. A. C. Bhuyan, P. C. Dey *et al.*, (ed.) *Political History of Assam*, Vol. II, Gauhati, 1978, p. 202; K. N. Dutta, *Landmarks of the Freedom Struggle in Assam*, Gauhati, 1969, p. 67.
121. MDPH, *op cit.*, p. 46.
122. Ibid., p. 45.
123. Ibid., p. 137.
124. Ibid., p. 138.
125. Ibid., p. 96.
126. Ibid., p. 49.
127. Ibid., p. 113.
128. Ibid.
129. Ibid., p. 114.
130. Ibid., p. 113.
131. Ibid.
132. Ibid.
133. Bipan Chandra, *India's Struggle for Independence, op cit.*, p. 186.

134. MDPH, p. 72.
135. Ibid., p. 118.
136. *Majuli Auniati Hem Chandra High School Diamond Jubilee Volume, op cit.*, p. 12; also information collected from his wife on 20.04.1995.
137. MDPH, p. 127, n. 5.
138. Ibid.
139. Ibid.; Benudhar Sarma, *Kongressor Kanchiyali Rodat*, Guwahati, 1960, p. 246.
140. *Majuli Auniati Hem Chandra High School Diamond Jubilee Volume, op cit.*, p. 49.
141. K. N. Dutta, *Landmarks of the Freedom Struggle in Assam, op cit.*, p. 72.
142. Ibid.
143. Bipan Chandra, *India's Struggle for Independence, op cit.*, p. 171.
144. Ibid., p. 278.
145. B. C. Saikia, 'Amar Sonwarani' in *Bardoichila*, 1856 Sak, 3rd part, p. 143, 4th part, 1857 *Sak*, p. 131; MDPH, p. 181.
146. MDPH, p. 182.
147. Ibid.
148. Ibid.
149. ASBS, *op cit.*, p. 318.
150. Ibid.
151. MDPH, p. 204.
152. Ibid., p. 206; also information collected from late Umakanta Saikia of Garamur Satra who was an active worker during the Quit India Movement.
153. The present investigator obtained this information from his paternal uncle late Dehiram Nath who had already resigned from his job as a School teacher, and who was deputed by Pitambardeva Goswami to the remote villages with written leaflets wherein his secret instructions to the villagers were embodied. Dehiram Nath further informed the present author that he had to carry on the duties by organizing group meetings in the villages of the Kaivarta and the Nath peoples explaining to them that they were instructed by the *Satradhikara* not to supply boats to the officers on duty or to transport them from one place to another.
154. MDPH, p. 204.
155. Ibid.; *Home Political File No. 18/10/42*, F.R., Assam, 1st half October, 1942; and 18/4/43, F.R., Assam, 2nd half April, 1943; National Archaives of India. Pitambardeva Goswami was appealing to the people to launch a no-tax, no-rent campaign, to snatch away political prisoners from the clutch of the police, to seize and destroy official records and Government vehicles. *Appeals issued by Shri Shri Pitambar Deb Gosswami, General Director, Upper Assam Congress.* Cf. A.C. Bhuyan & S. Dey (ed) *Political History of Assam,* Vol.III, Second edition, Guwahati, 1999, p. 61.
156. Ibid., p. 205; Bhuyan, Dey *et.al.* (ed), op. cit, Vol.II, p. 64.
157. MDPH, p. 205; Home Poll File No. 18/10/42, 1st half of October, 1942, *op cit.* According to the police source Surendranath Bharali, who formed a war council at Jorhat, and Kumud Bora of Teok were frequent visitors

to the Satra. Home Poll, File No. 44/26/43, National Archives of India sources. Cf. Bhuyan and Dey, *op cit.*, p. 64.

158. MDPH, p. 209. The Chief Secretary of Assam in a letter to the Home Secretary, Government of India, wrote on 21 April, 1943 wrote: "the satra is now a focus of unlawful activities under the direction of the Goswami." Cf. Bhuyan and Dey, *op cit.*, p. 64.

159. Ibid., p. 208.

160. Ibid., p. 204.

161. Names of some of these persons arrested and jailed during this movement are given in Appendix-XIII.

162. MDPH, p. 209; *Majuli Auniati Hem Chandra High School Diamond Jubilee Volume*, *op cit.*, p. 48.

163. ASBS, pp. 320f.

164. See Chapter-IV.

165. Interestingly, except Pitambardeva Goswami and his deputy Krishna Chandradeva Goswami, no other *Satradhikara* in the island supported the freedom struggle who always stood firmly by the British. They also opposed his participation in the struggle since inception. The applause of appraisal of the *Satradhikaras* by Lord Chelmsford, who visited Majuli in the year 1920, is significant in this regard. In the great *darbar* attended by Auniati and Dakhinpat *Satradhikaras* with their disciples, Chelmsford said that "the warm reception which he received there from the *Satradhikaras* was not without reason. There is historical record of intimate relationship between the Government and the Satras since the Ahom days. The lands granted by the Ahom rulers have been retained also by the British. In exchange, the *Satradhikaras* had also helped the Government in the past by supplying the expeditionary forces with boats, provisions and other materials to fight the rebellious hill tribes."

The role of the *Satradhikaras* of Auniati and Dakhinpat may be well explained through the welcome address of the Auniati *Satradhikara* to Sir Andrew Gourlay Clow, Governor of Assam, when he visited Majuli on 14th February, 1945, where Hemchandradeva Goswami called himself as " Your Excellency's most loyal subject" The same was the case with Dakhinpat Satra. Benudhar Sarma has stated that " opposing the Government is not the religion of the *Satriyas*; that is why Naradeva Goswami totally disliked the Non-Cooperation Movement led by Mahatma Gandhi....Anything that had the remotest connection with the anti-Government agitation never enjoyed any sympathy with the *adhikar*"(*Dakhinpat Satra*, *op cit.*, p. 84). It is interesting that Naradeva Goswami of Dakhinpat Satra refused to contribute anything to the freedom movement although he gave Rs. 8,000/- for the British war fund (Ibid.). This refusal to participate in the struggle for freedom by the Auniati and Dakhinpat *Satradhikaras*, and following them by many others, had impact on the people of Majuli in particular, and those under their spheres of influence all over the state in general.

165(a). PDGH, pp. 232f.

166. Interview with Mal Chandra Pegu at his Jorhat residence on 19/8/07 over telephone.

166(a). Vide Ordinance No. 9, 1996, dated 27 January; Re-promulgated vide Ordinance No. 19, 1996 and Ordinance No. 30, 1996, and Ordinance No. 3, 1997. The Ordinances, however, were not enacted into a bill.

167. See for details M. Husain, *Assam Movement—Clan, Ideology and Identity*, Delhi, 1993.

168. Sumita Ghose, *op cit.*, preface, p. VII.

169. From Dr. Pitambardeva Goswami's diary (Ms.). In discussing the process of changing value systems in Indian societies in the post-Independence period, M.N. Srinivas has remarked: "A recent and significant development is the coming together of the politician and the 'renouncer', or man in ochre robes. (The politician is indeed versatile: he moves from the company of criminals of all kinds at one end to that of 'godmen' and sanyasis at the other.) .... Politicians know that it is good for their image to be seen close to renouncers, and there is always the hope that at some point closeness might yield votes. 'Godmen' command large followings and their support is not only politically beneficial, it also provides a shield against the insecurities of the high-risk profession of politics. Finally, the reclusive renouncer is contacted only rarely, for his 'blessings.' It is in the Indian tradition that the temporal realm acknowledges, though only rarely, the supremacy of the spiritual." Cf. Social Change in *Modern India*, Indian edition (1972) Reprint, pp. 186f.

170. From Dr. P. D. Goswami's diary (Ms.).

Epilogue
Majuli—Past and Present

Majuli is considered as the largest river island in the world. It is situated in the Brahmaputra river in Assam approximately a little above the middle part of that great river that falls within the territorial area of the state. Administratively, the island is within the territorial jurisdiction of Jorhat District of Assam; and it forms a sub-division with more than one and a half lakh population according to the last census enumeration. Cut off from the mainland of Assam all around by river channels, Majuli forms a distinct geographical, social and cultural entity with its own norms and value systems. The present investigation is a systematic study of its society, economy and culture in historical perspective. Sources for the work have been derived from both historical and empirical data based on investigation and the author's own observation. Attempts have been made to interpret things as objectively as possible.

Majuli's standing as the largest river-made island in the world has now been questioned in some quarters. Two questions are raised: (a) whether Majuli is yet the largest island of its kind in the world, as there are evidences to the effect that its territorial extent has been increasingly reduced due to erosions; and the island which was once 160 miles in length (perhaps, may have been more than that at other times) and about 60 miles in breadth (in the maximum), now stands at 75-80 kilometers in length, and, at the maximum, 10 kilometers only in breadth; and (b) whether Majuli can be considered an island at all as its northeastern boundary formed by the Kherkatiya suti, a channel of the old Brahmaputra, has been spanned by an embankment that connects Majuli with the northern mainland making it look like a peninsular extension of a landmass from the northeast. While both the arguments have some justification, the present investigation has led to the conclusion that (i) there is no contrary evidence to prove that there are such other fresh water river-islands which not only embrace large chunks of landmass, but also shelter more than one and a half lakh population as Majuli does today, and

(ii) despite its man-made artificial connection with the northern mainland,[1] Majuli has been essentially an island with perfect island-features in all aspects of its society and culture. It is not unlikely that this man-made embankment connecting Majuli with the northern landmass will some time fall a victim to the roaring flow of the great river. At least, evidence of its creation and existence of numerous dead river channels inside the greater landmass point to its possibility.

Antiquity of the island still remains obscure. There are varying presumptions about the time of its creation, although as to its formation process, there are not much variations in ideas. On the basis of a tradition, of unknown origin, it is still believed that the island was created not long ago, may be in 1735, or half a century before that date, as Captain Wilcox has mentioned.[2] The present investigation, however, comes to a different conclusion. On the basis of the existing literary and other evidences and their re-interpretations, it has been found that the island was sufficiently older than it was thought to be. It took its island shape in an unknown past, at least before the 13th century A.D. The only question was: what volume of water formed its four boundaries at the initial stage—big or small, seasonal or regular. It is also found that the name *Majuli* was used to stand for this island at least as early as the mid-16th century A.D; before that the territory was perhaps called *Habung* which is a Bodo word, meaning low-lying flood affected but extensive landmass, or, was a part of it.

As most parts of the island are comprised of the *chaporis* and the beds of the dead river channels—large and small—Majuli had always been a marshy zone in the past with innumerable ponds, rivers, swamps, jungles, forests, fishes and varieties of wild animals. This topographical situation is, of course, not there at present; at least there are no jungles or wild animals, and many ponds and river channels have dried up and died; more so in the second half of the last century when not only number of its inhabitants increased leading to reduction of agricultural lands, but also because of growing administrative and semi-urban centres at few places of the island. To an outsider, however, Majuli still presents a topographical zone with nature's gift of green landscape and varieties of flora and fauna,[3] although to a native it is a dismal picture of what it was half a century ago. The rate of change has been swift and sweeping in the post-Independence periods. The factor behind this change is the human activity.

Society in Majuli consists of both castes and tribes. Of the known indigenous castes are the Brahmin, Kayastha, Kalita, Keot, Koch, Nath-Yogi or Katani, Kaivarta (including Matak), Hadi and Sut. While the tribes include the Mising, the Deori and the Kachari, among the non-indigenous communities are the Bengali, Bihari or Deswali, Marwari, Nepali and a few Muslim families. All the people live in well-demarcated villages distinguished mostly by caste and topography. Located on higher sites with high housing plinths to avoid submersion by flood, villages in Majuli look like an embankment covered with bamboo bushes and other jungle vegetation. All Mising villages are located on the river banks or on low-lying lands in the vicinity of swamps. They live in platform houses (*chang-ghar*) except otherwise necessary, such as those living in the semi-urban or township areas who have their *kecha̠* houses. On the basis of distinction maintained in selection of sites and the designs followed in building respective houses, tribal and non-tribal villages can be distinguished from a distance.[4] Formed with inhabitants of specific caste or tribe, all villages in Majuli have their individual characteristics stamping individual identifiers.[5] Thus, we find independent culture cells under the cover of a greater cultural identity.

Caste system prevails in the society as do the caste distinctions; and although it has gradually lost its earlier hold among the elite sections, caste prejudice is still inherent in men's mind.[5(a)] But, there is no untouchability as it exists in societies of some other parts of the country. The late 19th and early 20th century social mobility movements started by some of the depressed castes contributed to this on a large scale. The system of initiation to Vaishnavism of one form or the other of the members of the lower social echelons by some of the Satras, and the provision of allowing entrance of all to the common prayer hall—the *na̠mghar*, have perhaps contributed a share to that end. The role of the late *Garamuriya Satra̠dhika̠ra* Pitambaradeva Goswami boosted up the emerging social values.[6] But, there are social classes based both on caste and economy. Affluent section here generally belongs to the higher castes except a microscopic minority who comes from among the lower stratum. To this group may be added the ecclesiastical section—the *Satra̠dhika̠ras*—who enjoy both economic and social power. Thus, caste and class in Majuli are related and reciprocal to each other.

Geography and economy are complimentary to each other in Majuli. Mainly based on agriculture, economy of the island was, and still is to a certain degree, a subsistence economy. In medieval times when land was sufficient in proportion to population, shifting was the system of cultivation here.[7] But along with the growth of population and consequent scarcity of agricultural lands shifting became limited, and at present, it has become almost obsolete. Constant clearing of jungle lands and their conversion to agricultural fields to meet the growing demands, and the necessity to convert the otherwise *cha̠poris* and the riverine belts into agriculture fields, slowly extending the plough up to the river banks, not only have reduced the number of ponds, *bils* and river channels, but have also affected its economy in other ways, such as reduction of cattle farming and fish and milk sources. Thus Majuli is bound to borrow from outside to feed its people today. Markets of Majuli today are alive with *chalani mach* (imported fish), *rechanar chaul* (subsidized rice), *Shillongiya alu* (Shillong patato), *Punjab piyaj* (Onion from Paunjab), Bombay textiles, and so forth.

About 80 per cent of the total labour force in Majuli is engaged in agriculture.[8] Rice, different varieties of pulses, sugarcane, potato, mustard and vegetables are the major crops grown in the island. But, the volume of production does not tally with the need of the growing population. Rice is the staple food, and wheat has been lately introduced. But it is not at all popular. Mustard is the only considerable cash crop. In the past, neither there was need nor there was knowledge of using chemical fertilizer. Soil was naturally rich with fertility due to annual inundation. But it has slowly lost its earlier fertility due mainly to the prevention of flood by building of high embankments all around the island. Thus, unless fertilizer is used, production is bound to be nominal per unit of land under cultivation. But not many people can afford to purchase it. Loss of the *chaporis* has affected the cattle rearing farms; and most cultivators have now no bullocks to plough, nor even the ability to use tractors or power tillers. As a result, although both fertilizer and machinery have entered the system of agriculture, their use is bound to be limited in Majuli.

As there are limited avenues for other vocation than agriculture, most educated and professionally trained persons here form the valued emigrant group of the people. It is to be noted that a good number of scientists, intellectuals and writers in Assam who have earned names in their respective fields, earlier hailed from Majuli. The rest seek jobs in the schools and colleges. As there is not much scope to absorb them in the few colleges and the schools, mushroom growth of schools can be seen in the island, one at least in almost every two/three villages so that the graduates of the village could be accommodated in those schools. But due to lack of adequate school fund, these self-employed teachers have to spend most part of their life without earning sufficient money and at the same time, losing some valuable time of their life.[9]

In the medieval times people had their own professions; some used to trade in fish, some in weaving and production of silk, some in pottery, some others in building boats, making of fans, working on ivory, and so forth. And life was one of contentment and self-sufficiency. With whatever was produced they maintained their life, and there was little or no trade.[9(a)]

Milk and fish, and vegetable and herbs were abundant. Now, topography has changed leading to significant change in the life-styles. Growing consumerism and modernization of the life styles have also increased the needs of men. This fact has compelled its inhabitants to search for other means of livelihood. As a result, trade and market system has been slowly growing during the colonial and post-colonial periods; and a few places have emerged as semi-urban centers and townships. Towards the close of the Ahom rule, and more particularly, during the colonial period money economy entered Majuli. Slowly along with the growth of township and markets, have emerged administrative set up. Things earlier gifted or exchanged for another, are now sold in the bazaars; and poor cultivators having no source of income, live a wretched life. Thus there is sharp stratification among the inhabitants with salaried teachers and service holders, officers and contractors on one side, and the marginal cultivators on the other, forming the two distinct groups. Economically therefore, Majuli witnessed emergence of two opposite classes—the poor class having neither enough cultivable land nor enough resources to earn, and the affluent class having both land as well as resources to earn. With comparatively less cost of living, therefore, service holders and the contractors are the most affluent class in Majuli. They have social status in the villages on one hand, and on the other, they find enough time to participate in and control rural politics.

Majuli has a strong cultural heritage of its own in its Satras. Sankaradeva, the founder of Assam Vaishnavism, had been here for more than two decades (1522-1546) establishing the centre of his religion and proselytizing people to it. It was here that he discovered his great disciple Madhavadeva who was initiated to non-violence and monism by the saint in about the year 1522. Recorded as *mani-kanchan yog*,[10] their combined effort left a permanent legacy to its society; and Majuli still takes pride in the *dujana-guru*'s[11] activity in the island. It was against that background that one has to understand the establishment of numerous Vaishnava monasteries or religious colleges (Satras) in the island in the subsequent centuries.

There were once numerous Satras in Majuli numbering nearly a hundred as a matter of patronage and policy of the Ahom kings for which it has earned the name *etaka̲ mahantar tha̲n,* i.e. a place of the religious men. Hundreds and thousands of pilgrims are visiting the island annually only for attaining religious merit. The Satras are the repositories and practising centres of all Assamese classical dance and musical forms, tagged together as 'Satriya culture' (*Satriya Sanskriti*) consisting of all forms of performing arts-*bha̲ona̲* (*na̲taka*, *ankiya̲ na̲t*), *bargeet* and other religious songs, and dance forms. These are at the root of what is often called by the social scientists as Assamese identity and nationality formation.[12] As a derivative from the all India Bhakti movement, Sankaradeva's Vaishnavism stressed on social equality in the religious plane and enlightenment of the commoners in religious scriptures.[13] Satras being a legacy of this movement, have contributed significantly towards social uplift and public edification here. It is therefore not at all surprising to learn that almost all men and women in the island irrespective of being literate or otherwise, are acquainted with the stories and teachings of the *Puranas*, the *Bhagavata*, and more particularly, of the epics. Indeed, children in Majuli learn the *Mahabharata* and the *Ramayana* when they are in their mothers' laps! This uplift is however confined to the religious life alone, for, according to the proselytizers, poverty or low birth does not prevent one to worship Hari (God).[14] It is interesting to note that by two of the forms of *bhakti*, Sankaradeva taught complete submission of the self to the *guru* (*dasya*), and services to his feet (*pada-sevana*).[15] Hiren Gohain has therefore pointed out that by these forms of *bhakti*, God Hari is made all powerful, shelter of the helpless, and a symbol of patriarchy in the form of a feudal lord.[16] Here poverty is considered as a qualification to become a beloved of the God, and low-birth disqualification of a man is rejected for his devotion to Him.[17] Interestingly, as against this, the Satras of Majuli often advocate that rules for maintenance of caste as laid down by the ancient law givers cannot be broken or disrespected by them.[17(a)] For both the above reasons, Satras as the guardian of controlling men's religious and moral life have slowly lost their popularity in modern times in the elite circle.[18]

Despite decline in popularity among the elites, Satras are still the practising centres of moral values and social norms among a large section of the people in Majuli, particularly among the villagers. Their impact is felt to a large extent on men's daily and social life, food and dress habit, their behaviour and speeches. As a consequence, despite differences between various culture and caste groups, and caste distinctions, there is one common bond, the bond created by the Vaishnavite systems, that binds its society into an integrated whole; and it is here that the island derives its identity.

Number of the Satras in Majuli has slowly been decreasing, mostly due to erosion and consequent reduction of territories leading to shifting of many of them to other places out side Majuli. Even the large Satras still having foothold in the island are making alternative arrangements elsewhere. The present languishing condition of the Auniati and the Dakhinpat Satras, the two largest Satras in Majuli, speaks much about their future in the island.[18(a)]

Satra systems of life style, particularly monasticism and celibacy, have lost popularity in the face of the growing consumerism creating gradually a need for the Satras to adopt a more liberal attitude towards the traditional systems, and the movement and activities of their inmates. Today, the place of traditional education for the pontiff as well as for their inmates has been taken by growing desire for modern education and learning; and the art forms which were once confined to the limited number of inmates in the Satras alone or to the members of specific castes and communities in their vicinity, have now become consumers' commodity being out of the closet of their traditional boundaries. No able parents today, therefore, desire to send their sons to the Satras simply to learn those art forms and culture by adopting a celibate and a restricted life completely devoted to the *guru* in the form of the *adhikara*. Under the circumstances, number of celibate inmates in the Satras today were bound to decrease. Thus, Dakhinpat Satra which once sheltered some hundreds of them have now hardly fifty; and Auniati which had in the past thousands of them, now possesses just above three hundred.[19] Thus, the Satras are now a continuum of a medieval institution in its bare essentials only; it is languishing for survival in a modern setting. There is enough scope to further investigate into the Satra system, and the place of the Satras in the social formation process of the island in particular, and that of the state in general.

Like any other place of the state cultural life in Majuli consists mainly of festivals and celebrations, a peculiar mix of secular and religious ones. Secular festivals and celebrations are to be seen mainly in the villages while religious ones in the Satras. One interesting aspect of such observances is that in Majuli even the secular festivals have been Vaishnavised to a certain extent, so much so that they have become part of the overall cultural agenda of the Satras. Thus, all secular festivals celebrated in the villages are observed in the Satras. For example, although *Bihu* is a secular and a village festival, it is also occupying an important place in the agenda of the cultural festivals in the Satras. Similarly, we find here how religious festivals celebrated normally in the Satras are also observed in the villages, or, at least, participated in by the villagers. Thus while the *Ras Lila* is mainly a festival of the Satras, it is also performed in the village public halls as a secular festival. The only distinction is in their agenda. Even in the villages secular festivals are accompanied by some religious resonance. The only significant aspect in this regard is that no tribal festival—religious or secular, has yet entered the Satra circle with either modification or purification, although a few religious festivals celebrated in the Satras, like the *Ras Lila* or *bhaona* have slowly entered the tribal villages. It therefore appears that major festivals of the greater Assamese society have been slowly entering the tribal agenda in an increasing process of marginalising them; but at the same time, the growing fear psychosis of the ethnic communities has inspired them to retain and cultivate their own systems in more vigorous ways. Thus the Mising in Majuli celebrate their ethnic festivals in the same manner and extent as they celebrate the non-tribal festivals. Similarly, the Kacharis celebrate both the Brahmanical and their own tribal festivals. Even among the Deoris, best known for their orthodox attitude, are fond of celebrating *Ras* festival and *bhaonas*.[20] It appears that the ethnic tribes have not only imitated the life styles and culture of the non-tribal societies, but they have also maintained with equal vigour their own ethnic cultures. As a matter of fact, tribal society in Majuli today maintains a common bond with the other parts of the society. While one is necessary for their uplift, the other is essential for protection of their identity. This recent trend in cultural reconfiguration is interesting to understand the inherent force that has been working beneath the emergence of resituating a maze of value systems in a recognizably heritage site in rural India.

As a part of the mainland Assam, Majuli has always been in the political scenario of the land. Although there is no specific record to ascertain, Majuli was perhaps within the sphere of the ancient kingdom of Kamarupa Pragjyotisha; but there is no doubt that Majuli, like most other places of Assam, was under the politico-cultural domination of the Bodo speakers at an early time. The picture becomes more clear as we approach the early middle ages when the Bhuyans had their hold over this region in the post-Kamarupa times.[21] There is no doubt that many legends and myths connecting Majuli were created at this stage of the Bhuyan rule attempting to sanskritise, or more properly, brahmanise, the old Bodo names and to legitimize their rule.[22] It was perhaps, at the same time, that a part of the island in its northeast was brought under the Chutiya territory which was then emerging on the north across the Luit (old Brahmaputra). Thus when the Ahom king Sukapha entered the Brahmaputra Valley, mainland Majuli was under the Bhuyan-Chutiya rule, and Sukapha was bound to spend three years in its flood affected riverine belt on the bank of the great river. Traces of the Bhuyan-Chutiya rule could still be found in the island's social complex.

Majuli formed a part of the Ahom state in the year 1512 when Suhungmung Dihingiya Raja conquered Panbari and Habung, the two places on the north. In the 17th century, king Jayadhvaj Singha established the three big Satras here—Auniati, Garamur and Dakhinpat. Since then Satras of Majuli were the ardent supporter of the state; and with this dignity of being established by the king along with enormous grant of landed and other properties, they still support the Government of whichever party it is formed. As a matter of fact, the Satras supported the state in the late 18th century when the Moamariya Revolt took place. During the Burmese wars too, Majuli was not spared mainly because of its Satras which used to direct the society in support of the state. The Burmese too planned to obtain the support of the Satras in their favour. Thus the big Satras in Majuli became the target of the invaders till they okayed their invasion.[23] Similarly, the British too tried and succeeded in obtaining the support of the Satras in their colonising period.

During the freedom struggle, Majuli under the leadership of Keshabram Borah and Pitambardeva Goswami took part in the various phases of the struggle beginning with the Partition. Even after Independence, Majuli has been always a part of the political system of the state. Thus, despite geographical isolation and natural barrier, Majuli has always been associated with the mainland politics of the state. This fact indicates that there was always a minority elite class which was concerned with the current politico-cultural developments elsewhere. At least the presence of Sankaradeva, Madhavdeva, Aniruddhadeva, Vamsigopaldeva in the island is significant. The middle age was also noted for regular visits of the Ahom kings to the island. In the modern times too, we find how Dattadeva Goswami introduced Majuli to the 19th century technological renaissance of Bengal; and, Pitambardeva and Keshabram Bora made it a force behind the freedom struggle in rural Assam.[24] It is to be noted that Pitambardeva Goswami had played a significant role in protesting against Assam's merger proposal with East Bengal (Pakistan), and in bringing to light the foreign-national influx problem into the state as early as the 1960s.[25] Thus, despite its geographical isolation, Majuli has always been politically and culturally vibrant and connected with the mainland systems.

Majuli is both geographically and culturally a heritage site of India; at least it has maintained that character for the past centuries since the middle ages. But, there are forces of changes that have been at work since at least the close of the middle ages; and more significantly, since the second half of the 19th century. The trend of changes are apparent in both moral and material life. Colonial rule and post colonial conditions—both man-made and natural, have acted upon the life styles of the people and on the system of its culture.

Although not much is known about its ancient systems, there is no doubt that during the Ahom rule (1228-1826) an established system of society governed mainly by the political system of the state and the moral ethics of the Satras was coming into being which lasted with the same strength and weakness till the later half of the 18th century when the Moamariya Revolt first gave it a jerk and opened the initial crisis for its breakdown. The Revolt subsided by the beginning of the 19th century; but it led to a more serious crisis in the form of the Burmese invasions and the British responses. Thus the later half of the 18th and the early part of the 19th century were a periods of crisis in the island as it was all over Assam. In the year 1838, Upper Assam was annexed to the British Indian empire and Majuli became a part of this integrated system. But this did not immediately uproot its old systems for the colonial Government retained the old ones, specially the Satras, with all sorts of power and status they had enjoyed during the monarchy. Majuli therefore still remained an ecclesiastical state with the same kind of 'old world air' till at least the close of the 19th century. For, the new regime was certainly dependent on the old regime of the island for maintenance of its economy and society, peace and stability; and in most cases, for information and advice of the *Satradhikaras* who formed a part of the elites of contemporary Assam. Thus the Auniati *Satradhikara* Dattadeva Goswami met the British Commissioner Jenkins and explained and acquainted him with the prevailing customs and systems of the society. Similarly, *Satradhikaras* of the other large Satras were also taken into confidence by the British.

This is, however, only one aspect of the developments. The British soon introduced new revenue policy and began to assess even the island which was once, more or less, a revenue-free zone. Mills in his *Report* (1853) has noted that although it was a very large island, its revenue collection was considerably small. Mills report was soon taken into account when much of the revenue-free lands were reclaimed by the British and converted into revenue-paying or half-revenue paying lands, and amount of charge was also raised. In the meantime, ferry *ghats*, roads and other means of communications began to develop and they could gather more information about the island of their own through investigations and surveys. Building of road and ferry *ghats* slowly replaced the old communication hazards, and by the post independence period, Majuli had a new system of travel and communication inside and outside. Thus, economically, this was a period of transition from medieval system to a modern setting.

Towards the close of the 19th century the British introduced new education system through the establishment of the L.P. and M.V. schools although the island had to wait till 1924 to have its first English school. Consequently, the British had no longer any necessity to request the *Satradhikaras* for advice, information and help. They could now call upon the *Satradhikaras* to their courts to discuss anything of their liking, and even imprison some of them for reason of their participation in the freedom struggle. Thus, politically, while the late 18th and early 19th century witnessed a crisis in the form of Moamariya Revolt and the Burmese invasions in both of which Majuli had played its role, the rest of the century twitnessed a period of consolidation of the British colonial rule compromising with some of the old but strong traditions, such as the Satras and the caste systems, but at the same time, introducing certain new systems for their own advantage.

Socio-culturally, this period for Majuli was both a continuum, and an evolution. It is interesting to note that the Satras have remained as an institution till now as they were in the 17th and the 18th centuries; but they had undergone internal and external evolutions at least since the second half of the last century. There were now Satras and *namghars*; but neither the *namghars* were the village courts as it were earlier, nor the comment of the *Satradhikaras* on the criminal cases were abiding on the people. Neither all of their lands were revenue-free nor they were empowered to possess so much of lands received from the Ahom kings as gifts, nor they are confined to the old system of caste and religion based education. Even the system of culture which they advocated, is now no longer confined to the Satras alone; it has an open space to spread now—thanks to the system of open economy and commercialization. In the society everywhere—inside and out side the Satras, old systems and customs have given way to the new which could perhaps be called *modern.* Thus, despite continuity in many aspects, in the second half of the 19th and in the entire 20th century, a stream of change, continuous but uneven, marked the life and culture of the island creating a break with the continuities of the 18th and the early 19th century. If, however, one looks at these changes that have occurred in the mid-20th century, they seem to be the last phase of an evolution, but when looked at the close of the century, they appear to constitute a revolution.[26]

END NOTES

1. *See Illustration*, and Chapter Introduction.
2. *See* Chapter-I, fn.85.
3. M. Islam, *The Flora of Majuli*, Dehra Dun, 1990, for details.
4. *See* Illustrations. The Kalitapar Mising Village (in the illustrated sketch) is located on the bank of a swamp. It is a cluster of platform houses built in lines. The Dhapak Gaon (illustrated) is situated in a part of a *chapori* on the bank of the Brahmaputra.
5. This difference is noted in their food and dress habit, housing and living systems, thoughts and ideas, and even in some cases, in languages, tones and speeches. Thus, while the inhabitants of the Kalitapar and Phutuki Chapori Mising villages go to the bed early in the evening, those of

Gopalpur, Madhupur and Meruwabari in the immediate neighbourhood go sufficiently late. Similarly, when both old and young use to consume rice beer (*apong*) in a tribal village, smoking is largely treated as a matter of shamefulness in a non-tribal village. Even in dress and housing systems distinct features can be noted for different villages on the basis of economy which is largely based on caste or tribe affiliation. Thus, although the Vaishnava culture forms the surface of the culture systems of Majuli giving it a greater identity, beneath the surface can be traced different independent cells represented by villages, castes and communities.

5(a) Sanjay Ghose has noted that an unknown person visiting a family in any village of Majuli, is sure to face certain questions at the time of his/her introduction. The normal question in greeting is: "we don't recognize the new guest, where is he from? And when they would get a little more familiar, they would ask, *Das manuh*? Scheduled caste?" Cf. Sumita Ghose, *op cit.*, p. 105. There is no doubt that untouchability has largely been eradicated in the society; but that constitutional and colonial term 'Scheduled Caste' still carries some element of that social evil in the traditional and orthodox caste-based society of the island.

6. Pitambaradeva Goswami of Garamur Satra undertook certain socio-religious reform agenda beginning with 1908, the year of his assumption of the *adhikarship*. These agenda included movements for widow remarriage, temple entry and uplift of the low-castes, reform of the religious sect of which his class is the upholder, and against child marriage. Being the *Satradhikara* of a royal Satra, Pitambardeva Goswami and his class had the recognized authority to shape and change things in any rural society of Assam. Pitambardeva Goswami's stamp of reform can still be felt in Majuli, particularly in the Garamur Satra and its neighbourhood. About Pitambardeva Goswami's refom movements and consequent impacts on the society, see D. Nath, 'Social Change in Rural Assam in the 20th Century: A Study of the Majuli Island', *Proceedings of the Indian History Congress*, 66th Session, Visva Bharati, Santiniketan, Calcutta, 2006, pp. 706ff.

7. Hunter, *op cit.*, p. 251; also see chapter-III.

8. K.C. Bora, *loc cit.*, (Ms.).

9. *See* Sumita Ghose, *op cit.*, p. 108.

9(a). Gunabhiram Baruah, *op cit.*, pp. 185f.

10. See Chapter-II.

11. Sankaradeva and Madhavdeva together called *dujana guru* by the Vaishnavas of Assam. On any occasion of religious or ritual function of a family the officiating person—*pathek/patheki/pathak/ namlagowa* while chanting the *asirvad* offers salutation to the *dujana guru*.

12. Manorama Sharma, *Social and Economic Change in Assam: Middle Class Hegemony*, Delhi, 1990, pp. 130ff; also see for opposite view R. Saikia, *Social and Economic History of Assam 1853-1921*, Delhi, 2000, p. 136; D. Sarma, *op cit.*, pp. 54ff.

13. SHTN, pp. 360ff.

14. The Neo-Vaishnavite Movement of Sankaradeva advocated equality for all irrespective of caste or birth status; and affluence is treated as detrimental to *bhakti*. See the *Nam-Ghosha* by Madhavdeva, vv.130, 482, 610, 671, 686; SHTN, p. 328 (fn.40); S. N. Barman, *Srimanta Sankaradeva—Kriti aru Krititva, op cit.*, pp. 91ff.
15. SHTN, pp. 218f
16. Hiren Gohain, *Kirtan Puthir Rash Bichar*, Guwahati, 1981.pp. 26f.
17. See the *Nam-Ghosha* of Madhavdeva, *op cit.*, vv. 130, 482,686; Barman, *op cit.*, pp. 109ff.

17(a). Cf. ASBS, pp. 321f.

18. This is also the finding of an investigation among selected members of elite section of the island. Arati Bora of the History Department, Majuli College, for instance, told us that the Satras being centres of traditionalism and orthodoxy, have gradualy lost their early popularity among the elite classes.

18(a). The differences between the newly built *namghar* of the Auniati Satra at Teok, and the old one at Majuli can be cited as examples. *See* Illustration.

19. Findings from our field Investigation.
20. Ibid.
21. D. Nath, 'The Bhuyan Land-Lords and Their Role in the Economy of Medieval Assm', *India Past and Present*, Vol. IV, Bombay, pp. 243ff.
22. See Chapter-VI.
23. For the interaction between the Auniati *adhikara* and the Burmese general details are recorded in the biographical works of the Satra, See *Padmapanidev Charit* (Ms.); cf. ASBA, pp. 481ff.
24. D. Nath, *Proceedings of the Indian History Congress, loc cit*, pp. 706ff.
25. Pitambardeva Goswami wrote letters to the then Prime Minister Jawaharlal Nehru explaining to him about the Pakistani (now Bangladesh) influx problem and about possible consequence in the politico-economic and socio-cultural life of the people of Assam. *See* Appendix-XIV.

Appendix - I

Gaon Panchayatwise Village List and Population Figure of Majuli, 2001

Census of 2001:

Total Population	**1,53,400**
Male	79,481
Female	73,919
M-F Ratio	1000:930
Scheduled Caste	**21,479**
Male	11,237
Female	10,242
Scheduled Tribe	**68,198**
Male	34,676
Female	33,522

A. Ujani Majuli Development Block

Sl. No	Name of the Village	Population			Scheduled Caste			Scheduled Tribe		
		M	F	Total	M	F	Total	M	F	Total
1. Ratanpur Gaon Panchayat:										
1	Ratanpur Gabharumelia	326	309	635	0	0	0	0	0	0
2	Lahan Gaon	421	396	817	180	184	364	0	0	0
3	Baghar Gaon	979	953	1932	303	285	588	0	0	0
4	Gayan Gaon	305	255	560	86	71	157	0	0	0
5	Gayanchuk	327	346	673	0	0	0	0	0	0
6	Kathalkhowa Kathaniya	228	235	463	0	0	0	0	0	0
7	Owguri Baghpam	276	249	525	155	132	287	43	57	100
8	Kathalkhowapam	51	58	109	0	0	0	51	58	109
9	Banariyachapori NC	171	160	331	0	0	0	171	160	331
10	Chinatoli Chapori N/C	58	8	66	0	0	0	0	0	0
11	Phulani Chapori	1	1	0	0	0	0	0	0	0
	Total	**3143**	**2969**	**6112**	**724**	**672**	**1396**	**268**	**276**	**544**
2. Jengrai Gaon Panchayat:										
1	Barpamua No. 1	1094	1038	2132	6	6	12	903	918	1818
2	Barpamua No. 2	959	904	1863	8	7	15	950	896	1846
3	Gobarchuk	219	218	437	0	0	0	187	194	381

Sl. No	Name of the Village	Population			Scheduled Caste			Scheduled Tribe		
		M	F	Total	M	F	Total	M	F	Total
4	Maghuwachuk	650	654	1304	3	2	5	636	642	1278
5	Jengrai Chapori	797	760	1557	0	0	0	778	743	1521
6	Jengrai Mirigaon	319	307	626	0	0	0	314	301	615
	Total	4038	3881	7919	—	—	—	3768	3691	7459
3. Phulani Gaon Panchayat:										
1	Kaliagaon	822	809	1631	0	0	0	599	602	1201
2	Jamut chuk	435	408	843	0	0	0	434	408	842
3	Nagan chuk	198	191	389	2	1	3	196	190	386
4	Phulani No.1	399	338	677	15	14	29	118	118	236
5	Phulani No.2	998	944	1942	6	3	9	270	236	506
6	Karkichuk	231	248	479	0	0	0	231	248	479
7	Karkichuk Lahan	286	277	563	0	0	0	282	271	533
8	Polongani	500	428	928	0	0	0	0	0	0
	Total	**3809**	**3643**	**7452**	**23**	**18**	**41**	**2130**	**2073**	**4203**
4. Luhitpariya Gaon Panchayat:										
1	Kuhiarbari	234	199	433	0	0	0	0	0	0
2	Kandhulimari	206	186	392	0	0	0	135	109	244
3	Panikhati	578	586	1164	0	0	0	250	277	527
4	Phutchang	364	364	728	0	0	0	0	0	0
5	Mayangiya	273	246	519	0	0	0	178	159	337
6	Baligaon	589	549	1138	0	0	0	584	544	1128
7	Chikari Gaon	375	294	669	0	0	0	366	284	650
8	Kachari Gaon	561	510	1071	0	0	0	541	491	1062
9	Tantibari	214	202	416	0	0	0	156	149	305
10	Apechipathar	295	264	559	0	0	0	295	264	559
11	Puria Satra Gaon	267	205	472	0	0	0	165	150	315
12	Moamari Chapori	10	10	0	0	0	0	1	1	1
	Total	**3966**	**3605**	**7571**	—	—	—	**2671**	**2427**	**5098**
5. Rangachahi Gaon Panchayat:										
1	Rangachahi	1354	1268	2627	0	0	0	321	278	599
2	Pahumora	570	546	1116	76	65	141	0	0	0
3	Sukansuti Pathar	11	15	26	0	0	0	0	0	0
4	Guwalbari No.1	464	455	919	49	57	106	88	91	179
5	Guwalbari No.2	235	212	447	0	0	0	229	211	440
6	Gosaibari	291	251	542	38	38	76	0	0	0
7	Jorbil	275	243	518	236	207	443	36	31	67
8	Barnalani No.1	424	379	803	0	0	0	286	256	542
9	Barnalani No.2	71	67	138	0	0	0	0	0	0
10	Bhuramara No.1	284	266	550	0	4	4	201	196	397
11	Bhuramara No.2	262	253	515	208	206	414	0	0	0
12	Thakur Suti	253	251	504	0	0	0	252	251	503
	Total	**4499**	**4206**	**8705**	**607**	**577**	**1184**	**1413**	**1314**	**2727**

Sl. No	Name of the Village	Population			Scheduled Caste			Scheduled Tribe		
		M	F	Total	M	F	Total	M	F	Total
6. Chiram Gaon Panchayat:										
1.	Rangalibahar	389	353	742	42	34	76	0	0	—
2.	Abhaipuriya	322	276	598	—	—	—	0	0	—
3.	Sriram chapori	1485	1373	2858	48	38	86	158	161	889
4.	Bokajan Miri	664	633	1297	208	195	403	453	436	705
5.	Hawli	362	348	710	—	—	—	360	345	363
6.	Deoripam	197	174	371	—	—	—	192	171	363
7.	Bokajanpam	12	16	28	—	—	—	—	—	—
	Total	**4248**	**3915**	**8163**	**866**	**454**	**3915**	**1411**	**1341**	**2752**
7. Cherpai Gaon Panchayat:										
1	Bhewchuk Kumarbari	186	178	364	0	0	0	169	161	330
2	Bhewchuk	871	925	1796	9	9	18	826	886	1712
3	Namani Chapori No.1	211	231	442	0	0	0	211	231	442
4	Namani Chapori No.2	280	293	573	0	0	0	245	256	501
5	Ujani Chapori No.1	133	141	274	0	0	0	131	138	269
6	Ujani Chapori No.2	192	206	398	1	1	2	191	205	396
7	Barbil Bebejia	466	449	915	0	0	0	—	—	0
8	Manbhalchuk	396	382	778	0	0	0	396	382	778
9	Major Deori	794	784	1578	0	0	0	672	671	1343
10	Namani Chapori No.3	197	223	420	0	0	0	175	202	377
	Total	**3726**	**3812**	**7538**	**10**	**10**	**20**	**3016**	**3132**	**6148**
8. Ratanpur (Miri) Gaon Panchayat:										
1	Jabarchuk Kathani	138	139	227	1	0	1	138	138	276
2	Jabarchuk Basa Gaon	174	177	351	4	10	14	166	165	331
3	Jabarchuk Gaon	Uninhabited			—	—	0	—	—	0
4	Takarchuk Chapori N/C.	81	79	160	1	—	1	80	79	159
5	Haladhibari	42	45	87	—	—	0	—	—	0
6	Gejera	371	370	741	—	—	0	367	364	731
7	Chowrukia	261	271	532	—	—	0	88	98	186
8	Ratanpur Miri Gaon	2027	1922	3940	92	92	184	1571	1561	3132
9	Anaichuk No.1	198	101	198	3	1	4	98	96	194
10	Anaichuk No.2	124	132	256	—	—	0	124	132	256
11	Ratanpur Miri pam	35	28	63	—	—	0	35	28	63

Sl. No	Name of the Village	Population			Scheduled Caste			Scheduled Tribe		
		M	F	Total	M	F	Total	M	F	Total
12	Dhankhowa Chapori N/C	Un-inhabited			—	—	0	—	—	—
13	Mayengiya Chapori N/C	208	190	398	—	—	0	166	169	335
14	Dabli Chapori N/C	172	113	285	—	—	0	—	—	0
15	Gunasing Chuk	Un-inhabited			—	—	0	—	—	—
16	Kaling Chuk	—	—	-do-	—	—	0	—	—	—
17	Latum Chuk	—	—	-do-	—	—	0	—	—	—
18	Kalakutum Chapori N/C	—	—	-do-	—	—	0	—	—	—
19	Kathalkhowa Chapori N/C	—	—	-do-	—	—	0	—	—	—
20	Ratanpur Chapori N/C	—	—	-do-	—	—	0	—	—	—
21	Ratanpur Miri pathar	183	186	369	—	—	0	136	135	271
22	Barghuli No. 1	Un-inhabited			—	—	0	—	—	—
23	Barghuli No. 2	—	—	-do-	—	—	0	—	—	—
	Total	**3917**	**3749**	**7666**	**100**	**104**	**204**	**2969**	**2965**	**5934**
	Grand Total of all GP	***31346***	***29780***	***61126***	***1945***	***1808***	***3743***	***17646***	***17219***	***34865***

B. Majuli Development Block:

9. Kamalabari Gaon Panchayat: Majuli Development Block:

Sl. No	Name of the Village	M	F	Total	M	F	Total	M	F	Total
1	Dariya Gaon			1113			10	1	—	1
2	Opar Katani			2308			462	84	84	148
3	Phutuka Pathar			179			0	83	83	166
4	Pohardia			422			0	119	102	221
5	Mohkhuti No. 2			479			0	252	224	476
6	Motiabari			547			4	70	47	117
7	Bhogpur Miri			450			20	183	160	343
8	Bhogpur Pathar			236			0	2	5	7
9	Bhogpur Satra			1330			164	52	36	88
10	Kerelagaon			592			0	—	—	0
	Total			**7656**			**660**	**846**	**714**	**1567**

10. Dakhin Kamalabari Gaon Panchayat:

Sl. No	Name of the Village	M	F	Total	M	F	Total	M	F	Total
1	Kamalabari Satra	2026	1870	3896	266	274	540	1494	1350	2844
2	Lahalial	610	599	1209	224	199	423	11	8	19
3	Namkatani	536	398	934	58	54	112	—	—	0
4	Katanigaon Na Satra	140	150	290	130	127	257	—	—	0

Sl. No	Name of the Village	Population			Scheduled Caste			Scheduled Tribe		
		M	F	Total	M	F	Total	M	F	Total
5	Namkatani Chapori N/C	—	—	UI		—	—	—	—	—
6	Kartik Chapori	131	129	260	—	—	0	129	130	259
7	Auniati Chapori Satra	279	275	554	—	—	0	150	130	289
8	Burah Kalita N/C	—	—	UI	—	—	0	—	—	0
9	Darbar Chapori N/C	—	—	-do-	—	—	0	—	—	0
10	Bhakat Chapori	54	49	103	—	—	0	—	—	0
11	Jugunidhari	626	250	876	35	28	63	—	—	0
	Total	**4401**	**3720**	**8122**	**713**	**682**	**1395**	**1763**	**1618**	**3381**
11. Karatipar Gaon Panchayat:										
1	Chengelisuti	153	136	289	0	0	0	153	136	289
2	Missamora	340	361	701	0	0	0	333	358	691
3	Auniati jungle	243	237	480	0	0	0	242	237	479
4	Eri Chapori	716	650	1366	289	272	561	187	182	369
5	Okhalchuk	122	95	217	0	0	0	122	95	217
6	Molual Kalita	724	726	1450	150	142	292	444	466	910
7	Molual Kaibarta Miri	238	219	457	65	40	105	173	179	352
8	Molual Miri	491	512	1003	0	0	0	480	502	982
9	Major Chapori N/C	465	454	919	0	0	0	464	454	918
10	Karati Gaon				Uninhabited					
11	Karati Pathar	134	129	263	0	0	0	100	95	195
12	Sankopara No. 1				Uninhabited					
13	Bebejiya	31	32	63	0	0	0	31	32	63
	Total	**3657**	**3551**	**7208**	**504**	**454**	**958**	**2729**	**2736**	**5465**
12. Sri Luhit Gaon Panchayat:										
1	Guwal Gaon	1040	1015	2055	522	515	1037	0	0	0
2	Kalia Gaon	165	163	328	0	0	0	0	0	0
3	Malapindha Chilakala Miri	1525	1462	2987	1	0	1	1513	1452	2965
4	Biralipara	370	354	724	0	0	0	365	352	717
5	Bengenaati Purani Satra	85	76	161	0	0	0	85	76	161
6	Birinabari				Uninhabited					
7	Alengi Gaon	443	414	857	181	158	339	0	0	0
8	Auniati Lakheraj	81	55	136	38	22	60	0	0	0
9	Bar Alengi Satra	47	38	85	0	0	0	0	0	0
10	Bardowar Chapori	697	680	1377	25	19	44	672	661	1333
11	Barbam Pathar				Uninhabited					
12	Pakhimari Chapori				Uninhabited					
13	Bengenaati Chapori N/C				Uninhabited					
14	Chorachori Bil	175	180	355	32	32	64	3	4	7
	Total	**4628**	**4437**	**9065**	**799**	**746**	**1545**	**2638**	**2545**	**5183**
13. Garamur Gaon Panchayat:										
1	Garamur Satra	1276	1066	2342	58	30	88	64	41	105
2	Garamur Phutukichapori	1545	1358	2903	16	11	27	1054	962	2116
3	Garamur Pathar	1098	956	2054	626	590	1216	174	147	321

Sl. No	Name of the Village	Population			Scheduled Caste			Scheduled Tribe		
		M	F	Total	M	F	Total	M	F	Total
4	Mohkina Gaon	622	561	1183	311	267	578	0	0	0
5	Manika Pathar	354	326	680	180	167	347	0	0	0
	Total	**4895**	**4267**	**9162**	**1191**	**1065**	**2256**	**1292**	**1150**	**2542**
14. Chilakala Gaon Panchayat:										
1	Bargaya No. 1	585	572	1157	0	0	0	570	560	1130
2	Bargaya No. 2	876	831	1707	490	471	961	273	276	549
3	Borachuk	72	60	132	0	0	0	0	0	0
4	Chilakala Kaibarta	992	919	1912	786	713	1499	3	1	4
5	Chilakala Chapori	316	303	619	1	0	1	313	303	616
6	Singariya Bil	55	58	113	0	0	0	39	39	78
7	Kakarikata	196	171	367	105	88	193	0	0	0
8	Kaibarta Gaon	85	110	195	0	0	0	82	107	189
	Total	**4326**	**4074**	**8405**	**1630**	**1482**	**3112**	**1757**	**1758**	**3515**
15. Dakhinpat Gaon Panchayat:										
1	Dakhinpat Satra	1897	1668	3565	591	557	1148	133	120	253
2	Barbaka Pathar	621	538	1159	0	0	0	0	0	0
3	Karhal Gaon	411	381	792	0	0	0	0	0	0
4	Goroimari Dalani	459	402	861	99	101	200	59	56	115
5	Bessamara				Uninhabited					
6	Gagal Doba	30	31	61	0	0	0	0	0	0
7	Radha Chapori				Uninhabited					
	Total	**3418**	**3020**	**6438**	**690**	**658**	**1348**	**192**	**176**	**368**
16. Bangaon Gaon Panchayat:										
1	Jogi gaon	402	342	744	280	221	501	0	0	0
2	Bangaon	775	734	1509	221	211	432	0	0	0
3	Atoichuk	445	419	864	22	24	46	0	0	0
4	Kamjan Alengi	451	441	892	44	42	86	7	5	12
5	Chakuli Pathar				Uninhabited					
6	Dhowa Chela Gaon	483	445	928	0	0	0	11	10	21
7	Sukansuti Pathar	11	15	26	0	0	0	0	0	0
8	Chamaguri Satra	423	397	820	0	0	0	1	00	1
9	Meragarh	165	175	340	70	56	126	0	0	0
10	Mudoi tanti	276	258	534	0	0	0	0	0	0
11	Charala (Chaala) Pathar				Uninhabited					
12	Manikbil Pathar	46	33	79	0	0	0	46	33	79
13	Keturi bil Khal bam	9	9	18	6	7	13	0	0	0
	Total	**3486**	**3268**	**6754**	**643**	**561**	**1204**	**65**	**48**	**113**
17. Pakajara Gaon Panchayat:										
1	Ujani Jakaibowa	558	451	1009	0	0	0	450	454	904
2	Namoni Jakaibowa	322	344	666	0	0	0	317	339	656
3	Pakajara	448	446	894	176	160	336	157	165	322
4	Jogi Gaon	308	277	585	0	0	0	0	0	0
5	Kakatibari	258	217	475	0	0	0	76	69	145

Sl. No	Name of the Village	Population			Scheduled Caste			Scheduled Tribe		
		M	F	Total	M	F	Total	M	F	Total
6	Mohkhuti No. 1	187	139	326	0	0	0	21	17	38
7	Mohkhuti No. 3	436	459	895	0	0	0	266	273	539
8	Bengena Kalia	120	122	242	0	0	0	82	82	164
9	Bhuramara No.3	1246	1109	2355	466	399	865	273	280	553
10	Pakajara Miri	500	494	994	0	0	0	450	454	904
11	Natun Kulamua Chapori	319	319	638	0	0	0	82	82	164
	Total	**4702**	**4377**	**9079**	**642**	**559**	**1201**	**2174**	**2115**	**4389**
18. Rawanapar Chamaguri Gaon Panchayat:										
1	Mekheli Gaon	527	466	993	0	0	0	0	0	0
2	Bankhowachuk	657	611	1268	356	318	674	0	0	0
3	Burasensowa	581	544	1125	342	325	667	125	119	244
4	Deka Sensowa	563	506	1069	563	506	1069	0	0	0
5	Patia Gaon	355	352	707	0	0	0	82	69	151
6	Kamar Gaon	706	669	1375	0	0	0	0	0	0
7	Tataya Gaon	766	745	1511	0	0	0	0	0	0
8	Sumaimari	653	629	1282	0	0	0	653	628	1281
	Total	**4808**	**4522**	**9330**	**1261**	**1149**	**2410**	**860**	**816**	**1676**
19. Ahataguri Gaon Panchayat:										
1	Jamuguri	143	127	270	0	0	0	98	92	190
2	Kachikata	74	66	140	0	0	0	74	66	140
3	Kachikata natun	124	124	248	0	0	0	124	124	248
4	Saru Phakuwa	126	113	239	1	0	1	0	0	0
5	Doloi Jarani					Uninhabited				
6	Bakara					Uninhabited				
7	Gatanga	56	60	116	0	0	0	0	0	0
8	Hutter	262	231	483	223	194	417	0	0	0
9	Lakhan pathar					Uninhabited				
10	Missamara Chapori NC	147	151	298	0	0	0	142	149	291
11	Cheyani	46	44	90	0	0	0	0	0	0
12	Tenga Chapori	26	40	66	0	0	0	26	40	66
13	Cheyani Miri	205	177	382	0	0	0	155	153	308
14	Cheyani Chapori NC	222	191	413	0	0	0	222	191	413
15	Param Chapori	208	224	432	0	0	0	206	224	430
16	Kakola Gaon	94	98	192	0	0	0	94	98	192
17	Barphakuwa	85	84	169	0	0	0	0	0	0
18	Pagbandha Miri					Uninhabited				
19	Haladhiati					Uninhabited				
20	Solmari	74	60	134	0	0	0	0	0	0
21	Rowmari	161	201	462	0	0	0	146	101	247
22	Phelengi	59	61	120	1	2	3	0	0	0
23	Chakala Satra					Uninhabited				
24	Loklangiya	—	—	—	—	—	—	—	—	—
25	Barchapori	—	—	—	—	—	—	—	—	—

Sl. No	Name of the Village	Population			Scheduled Caste			Scheduled Tribe		
		M	F	Total	M	F	Total	M	F	Total
26	Bura Chapori NC	—	—	—	—	—	—	—	—	—
27	Bura Tikirai	—		—	—	—	—	—	—	—
28	Tapatolo	—	—	—	—	—	—	—	—	—
29	Ghoriya	—	—	—	—	—	—	—	—	—
30	Dakua	—	—	—	—	—	—	—	—	—
31	Bakani Pathar	—	—	—	—	—		—	—	—
32	Kashingati	—	—	—	—	—	—	—	—	—
33	Karaiguri	—	—	—	—	—	—	—	—	—
34	Charai Chapori	1363	1261	2624	169	134	303	343	345	688
35	Garu Chapori	88	89	177	0	0	0	52	51	103
36	Bura Chapori	279	267	546	8	6	14	75	74	149
37	Kumalia Chapori	119	117	236	0	0	0	118	117	235
38	Garu Chapori NC				Uninhabited					
	Total	**3961**	**3887**	**7848**	**402**	**336**	**738**	**1875**	**1825**	**3700**
20. Dakhin Ahataguri Gaon Panchayat:										
1	Dhodang Chapori	1222	617	1838	446	432	878	256	259	515
2	Dalkhowa*				Uninhabited					
3	Namghariya				Uninhabited					
4	Baghmora				Uninhabited					
5	Dadhara*				Uninhabited					
6	Roumora*				Uninhabited					
7	Roumora Suti				Uninhabited					
8	Pohumara Bhekeli	423	402	825	0	0	0	421	401	822
9	Ujir Ati*				Uninhabited					
10	Charai Koroka *No. 1				Uninhabited					
11	Charai Koroka No. 2				Uninhabited					
12	Na-Mati	24	22	46	0	0	0	0	0	0
13	Abani Chapori	171	125	296	9	3	12	0	0	0
14	Cheuni Chapori				Uninhabited					
15	Sagun para Chapori	110	92	202	11	8	19	51	46	97
	Total	**1949**	**1258**	**3207**	**466**	**443**	**909**	**728**	**706**	**1434**

* The villages with star mark are in fact found to be inhabited when the two Research Assistants—Sri Biman Bora and Sri Debajit Khataniar working under the present project had visited in June, 2005, and surveyed them. It therefore appears that the field investigators under the Census operation, for the year 2001, who have recorded them to be uninhabited, perhaps did not visit the villages.

GAON PANCHAYATSWISE POPULATION FIGURE, 1991
(SUMMARY SHEET)

Census of 1991:

Total Population	1,35,378
Male	70,410
Female	64,968
M-F Ratio	1000:922
Scheduled Caste	**19,278**
Male	10,133
Female	9,145
Scheduled Tribe-	**57,195**
Male	29,075
Female	28,120

A. Majuli Development Block

Sl. No.	Name of the Gaon Panchayat	Population			Scheduled Caste			Scheduled Tribe		
		M	F	Total	M	F	Total	M	F	Total
1	Kamalabari	3850	3350	7200	311	311	622	785	732	1517
2	Dakhin Kamalabari	4299	3583	7382	640	588	1228	1904	1780	3684
3	Sri Luhit	3424	3140	6564	688	663	1351	1677	1610	3287
4	Karatipar	3646	3534	7180	513	492	1005	2426	2402	4828
5	Garamur	4096	3541	7637	977	840	1317	839	773	1612
6	Silakala	3717	3450	7167	1418	1256	2674	1527	1462	2989
7	Dakhinpat	3454	3221	6675	615	600	1215	237	243	480
8	Rawanapar Chamaguri	3217	2961	6178	1030	915	1945	90	83	173
9	Bangaon	4415	4054	8469	1163	1009	2172	645	607	1252
10	Pakajara	3976	3690	7666	601	530	1131	1971	1931	3902
11	Ahataguri	2603	2414	5017	205	176	381	1324	1283	2607
12	Dakhin Ahataguri	2343	2006	4349	101	110	211	612	616	1228
	Total	**43040**	**38944**	**81484**	**8262**	**7490**	**15252**	**14037**	**13522**	**27559**

B. Ujani Majuli Development Block:

Sl. No.	Name of the Gaon Panchayat	Population			Scheduled Caste			Scheduled Tribe		
		M	F	T	M	F	T	M	F	T
1	Ratanpur Gyan	3083	2883	5966	595	525	1120	426	422	848
2	Jengrai	3589	3426	7015	60	47	107	3260	3244	6504
3	Luhitpariya	3762	3537	7299	36	29	65	3264	2254	4618
4	Rangachahi	3620	3416	7036	564	500	1064	896	861	1757
5	Phulani	3386	3206	6592	21	27	48	2074	1984	4058
6	Sriram	3389	3209	6598	422	396	818	1064	1057	2121
7	Cherepai	3204	3210	6414	57	50	101	2466	2525	4991
8	Ratanpur	3337	3137	6474	122	81	203	2468	2436	4904
	Total	**2770**	**2624**	**33394**	**171**	**155**	**326**	**1538**	**1498**	**29636**
	Grand Total (A+B)	**135378**	**70410**	**64968**	**10133**	**9145**	**19278**	**29079**	**28120**	**57199**

Appendix – II

Decennial Growth of Population in Majuli, 1901-2001

Sl. No.	Year	Majuli Sub-Division		Growth Rate	
		Population	Growth Rate		
1	1901	31,219	—	—	—
2	1911	40,420	+29.47	+16.90	+16.99
3	1921	47,960	+18.65	+17.26	+20.48
4	1931	56,461	+15.06	+8.88	+19.91
5	1941	75,040	+32.90	+15.27	+20.40
6	1951	81,001	+7.94	+14.84	+19.93
7	1961	93,541	+15.48	+24.17	+34.98
8	1971	99,369	+5.87	+17.47	+34.95
9	1981	—	—	—	—
10	1991	1,35,378	+36.23	+33.10	+53.26
11	2001	1,53,362	+13.28	+15.84	+18.85

Sources: (a) *A Statistical Account of Assam*, Vol. I, W. W. Hunter

(b) Gazetteer of Eastern Bengal And Assam, B. C. Allen, 1905

(c) K.C. Bora - Income, Expenditure and Saving in Rural India, Doctoral Thesis, Dibrugarh University, Published from Mittal, Delhi, 1985 (p.21)

(d) Provisional Population table, 2001 census of India Series, Assam part, p.17.

Appendix – III

List of Revenue *Bils* in Majuli

***Bils* Under Majuli Development Block**

Sl. No.	Name of Bils	Land area in *bigha*	Govt. value (2005-2006)
1.	Gondhowa bil	22 - 2 - 15	1000.00
2.	Misamora bahir bil	15 - 4 - 2	5000.00
3.	Misamora Chapori bil	12 - 0 - 0	3000.00
4.	Joljolia dubi	4 - 0 - 0	2500.00
5.	Bhomoraguri bil	2 - 0 - 0	2500.00
6.	Chiram Chapori	20 - 0 - 10	3000.00
7.	Konkur Chapori	10 - 3 - 0	800.00
8.	Balidora bil	57 - 4- 5	1000.00
9.	Jonai bil	10 - 0 - 0	5000.00
10.	Geladora bil	23 - 4 - 2	1500.00
11.	Bordora bil	73 - 3 - 1	1000.00
12.	Kathchapori bil	15 - 0 - 0	2000.00
13.	Godhowa bil	6 - 4- 0	2000.00
14.	Misamora bahir ghuli	26 - 0 - 0	1000.00
15.	Laliti balidoar bil	26 - 0 - 0	1000.00
16.	Molapindha alichiga khanda dubi	26 - 0 - 0	1000.00
17.	Mori Kharjan bil	30 - 8 - 4	2500.00
18.	Garamur Phutuki	3 - 4 - 0	1500.00
19.	Kharjan Morisuti	57 - 3 - 1	1000.00
20.	Garmur Jogi Pathar	1 - 4- 0	800.00
21.	Borachuk Nadua bil	30 - 8 - 4	2500.00
22.	Mayasuti dubi	1 - 0 - 10	500.00
23.	1 No. Borgaya dubi	9 - 4- 10	2000.00
24.	Pithakhowa bil		
25.	Totoya bil	15 - 0 - 0	2000.00
26.	Tataya Khanidubi	10 - 0 - 0	2500.00
27.	Potia Kachariboka	36 - 2 - 2	2500.00
28.	Rawanapara dubi	11 - 0 - 16	1500.00
29.	Potia Noidoh	11 - 4 - 0	1000.00
30.	Deka Sensowa bil	37 - 3 - 5	1500.00
31.	Mekheligaon bil	51 - 3 - 6	1000.00
32.	Bihdia bil		
33.	Jugunidhari bil	8 - 0 - 8	2500.00
34.	Lahalial Chakuli	31 - 1 - 7	4000.00

(*Contd.*)

Sl. No.	Name of Bils	Land area in *bigha*	Govt. value (2005-2006)
35.	Pohardia Gergeri bil	5 - 2 - 3	5000.00
36.	Bhogpur bil	39 - 10 - 0	1000.00
37.	Poharadia dighali	14 - 15 - 10	1000.00
38.	Doria Alichiga		
39.	Motiabari bil	7 - 2 - 10	700.00
40.	Kerelagaon Alichiga	2 - 4 - 0	5000.00
41.	Bherek bil		
42.	2 No. Mohkhuti (Khohuli)	6 - 3 - 8	2000.00
43.	Kerelagaon bil	10 - 0 - 2	2500.00
44.	Pokajora bil	49 - 0 - 8	3500.00
45.	3 No. Mohkhuti	20 - 2 - 11	3500.00
46.	38 No. Pokajora	12 - 0 - 0	1500.00
47.	Balidubi	12 - 0 - 0	500.00
48.	32 No. Pokajora	8 - 2 - 0	1000.00
49.	Gorubat dubi	7 - 2 - 2	700.00
50.	Pokajora Charala	22 - 0 - 0	5000.00
51.	161 No. Jakaiboa	5 - 0 - 0	5000.00
52.	3 No. Bhuramora	53 - 0 - 1	2000.00
53.	Kalia-Jakaibowa	10 - 9 - 2	5000.00
54.	Charala bil	43 - 0 - 0	5000.00
55.	Kapordhowa	52 - 4 - 19	2000.00
56.	Tuninodi Balichot	23 - 2 - 3	3000.00
57.	Dhowachala Param	79 - 2 - 3	2500.00
58.	Baghedhara bil	50 - 0 - 0	1000.00
59.	Gayangaon Nikinikhowa chiga bil	2 - 4 - 0	2000.00
60.	Boka bil	10 - 0 - 0	2000.00
61.	Moran bil	12 - 0 - 17	1000.00
62.	Goroimari	50 - 0 - 0	3000.00
63.	Ga-khojua bil	52 - 4 - 19	1000.00
64.	Ghotahola bil	7 - 2 - 10	5000.00

***Bils* Under Ujani Majuli Development Block**

Sl. No.	Name of *Bil*	Land area in *bigha*	Govt. value (2005-06)
1.	Tura *bil*	15 - 0 - 0	1000.00
2.	Morisuti Khomkha doba	1 - 4 - 0	1000.00
3.	Morisuti P.W.D. Chiga	1 - 0 - 0	1000.00
4.	Morisuri Boria doba	5 - 4 - 0	1000.00
5.	Panikhati bil	8 - 2 - 12	1000.00
6.	Kandhulimari dyke chiga	5 - 0 - 0	1000.00
7.	Chiga near Kacharigaon	5 - 0 - 0	1000.00
8.	Kachari Bhagania bil	1 - 4 - 8	2000.00
9.	Tenga Pania bil	8 - 1 - 1	4548.00
10.	Kandhulimari Bahir Bhitar bil	4 - 10 - 0	3997.00
11.	Miligaon Tiniali dyke Chiga (Breach)	5 - 1 - 0	5700.00
12.	Miligaon Haldhibari 1 No. dyke chiga breach	4 - 2 - 0	9800.00

(*Contd.*)

Sl. No.	Name of *Bil*	Land area in *bigha*	Govt. value (2005-06)
13.	E & D Gejera dyke (breach)	6 - 1 - 1	9000.00
14.	Chowrekia dyke breach	7 - 7 - 17	3300.00
15.	E & D Haldhibari Dyke Chiga	23 - 0 - 1	5000.00
16.	Haldibari PWD Chiga	9 - 4 - 8	2500.00
17.	Bhalukaguri breach	5 - 0 - 1	2500.00
18.	Kachudubi breach	23 - 0 - 6	1000.00
19.	Kachamari	4 - 2 - 0	1000.00
20.	Bogolipora bil	1 - 4 - 0	1000.00
21.	Borpomua Alichiga	9 - 2 - 18	1000.00
22.	Alichiga Balidoba	5 - 0 - 0	1370.00
23.	Dhunia Suti bil	13 - 4 - 4	1000.00
24.	Kasu dubi	17 - 0 - 0	5500.00
25.	Alichiga diba	2 - 0 - 0	1000.00
26.	P.D.G. 9km. Near dubi	70 - 0 - 0	3500.00
27.	Alengmari bil	4 - 4 - 0	1665.00
28.	Boka bil	14 - 2 - 4	1665.00
29.	Bokajan bil	15 - 4 - 0	1680.00
30.	Kotia Naharani bil		1650.00
31.	Kathalkhowa Kathamia bil	8 - 3 - 0	8620.00
32.	Kherkota Arasuti bil	26 - 18 - 0	4000.00
33.	Kumarbari Alidubi	9 - 4 - 8	1000.00
34.	Salmari bil	17 - 2 - 3	3000.00
35.	Cherepai Majordubi	26 - 18 - 0	4000.00
36.	Gotonga Pulmukh duba	2 - 0 - 0	1000.00
37.	Phulani Dolong	1 - 3 - 0	1000.00
38.	Gatiola Alichiga	2 - 0 - 0	1250.00
39.	Phulani Alichiga dubi	4 - 4 - 4	1450.00
40.	Naganchuk Alichiga	4 - 0 - 0	1000.00
41.	Mudoi bil	48 - 0 - 2	1000.00
42.	Hatighuria bil	68 - 0 - 1	1100.00
43.	Bokajan bil	125 - 3 - 0	1000.00
44.	Siram Deori	15 - 2 - 5	1000.00
45.	Chengamari dubi	35 - 4 - 5	1500.00
46.	Hokaidubi	25 - 4 - 2	1500.00
47.	Bokajan dubi	13 - 4 - 1	4500.00
48.	Deori bil	22 - 0 - 0	5000.00
49.	Boraguri Alichiga 1 No., 2 No. dubi	10 - 3 - 0	1110.00
50.	Pohumora Sowla doba	2 - 0 - 0	1000.00
51.	Sonariati Alichiga doba	3 - 0 - 0	1145.00
52.	Rahgachahi doba	17 - 3 - 1	1000.00
53.	Batamari bil	50 - 0 - 0	5800.00
54.	Nalani bil	20 - 0 - 0	5000.00
55.	Borbam Chapori Major dubi	6 - 3 - 19	300.00
56.	Pahumora Nabhanga doba	14 - 0 - 10	500.00
57.	Kherkati bil	6 - 0 - 0	1000.00
58.	Pohumora Alichiga	1 - 0 - 0	1000.00
59.	Thakursuti bil	10 - 0 - 0	3330.00
60.	Chandmari bil	48 - 2 - 18	1749.00
61.	30 No. Bhuramora bil	17 - 4 - 6	6810.00

***Bils* under AFDC**

Sl. No.	Name of bil	Land area in *bigha*	Govt. Value
1.	Sawal Gotanga		34,000.00
2.	Kakarikota	55	2,15,000.00
3.	Buruk	38	50,000.00
4.	Jorbil	7	15,000.00
5.	Howli	35	40,000.00
6.	Vereki	3	29,000.00

Revenue *Bils*

Sl. No.	Name & Number of Fishery	Current Revenue 2005-06
1.	No. 17 Luhit Erasuti	63,974/-
2.	No. 31/32 Rupohi Molong	14,194/-
3.	No. 18 Sukansuti Borbil	14,687/-
4.	No. 23 Garmur Pathar Dubi	36,383/-
5.	No. 23 Doria dubi	27,589/-
6.	No 21 Kharkhori	68,182/-
7.	No. 13 Dakhinpat Borbil	27,866/-
8.	No. 12 Tuni fishery	50,000/-
9.	Magurmara	17,142/-

N.B.: Brahmaputra II and III part.

Source: Majuli Development Block
Ujanj Majuli Development Block
S.D.O. (C), Sub-Division
Fishery Development Office
AFDC – Guwahati

(The author is indebted to Shri Rajen Bora of Economics Department, Majuli College, for collecting the above data on his behalf.)

Appendix – IV

Medical and Health Facilities in Majuli

1. Total population — 1,53,400 as per 2001 Census
2. PHE — 1 (Kamalabari PHE)
3. Mini PHE- 4
   - — Karatipar (established in 1986)
   - — Jengraimukh PHC
   - — Ratanpur Lahan PHC (established in 1996)
   - — Ratanpur Miri (established in 1986)
4. Dispensary: 4 nos.
   - — Ahataguri State Dispensary
   - — Bangaon State Dispensary
   - — Dakhinpat State Dispensary
   - — Rangachahi State Dispensary
5. C.H.C-1 — Kamalabari30 bed Rural Hospital (established in 1985, June)
   - — Sub-divisional Hospital-1
   - — Garamur 100 bed Hospital (May, 2003)
6. Sub Centres-34 nos.
   - — Madhya Ahataguri Sub Centre
   - — Sikali Chapori
   - Funtaniya S/C
   - Dhodang Uzuwaati
   - Malapindha
   - Kardaiguri
   - Silakala
   - Balichapori
   - Pahumara Kaivarta
   - Bokura
   - Auniati Satra
   - Potia Sumoimari
   - Uriampara
   - Laimanika
   - Mohkhuti
   - Namani Jakaibowa
   - Phulani
   - Natun Bechamara
   - Siram Devattor
   - Majardeori
   - Phulani
   - Jengrai Balichapori

Majardeuri
Nayabazar
Banariyachapori
Rawanapar
Salmara
Na-pamuwa
Salmara
Bhakatiduar
Gezera Dighalagaon
Namani Gezera
Baghgaon
Kuhiarbari

Source: Information supplied by the Office of the Kamalabari PHE.

LIST OF INSTITUTIONS
(As per estimate prepared on 31st march, 2003)

1. Primary School-436
2. Middle School-95
3. High School-76
4. HS School-4
5. Junior College-2
6. Degree College-4
7. Basic Training Centre-1
8. PHE-1
9. Mini PHC-4
10. Sub Centre-34
11. Family Welfare Centre-42
12. State Dispensary-3
13. Community Health Cemtre (CHC)-1
14. Villages having water supply facilities-244
15. Villages having ecectrcity connections-79

Appendix – V

Road and Bridge Records of Majuli

LIST OF ROADS UNDER MAJULI SUB-DIVISION (PWD)

Sl. No.	*Name of the Road*	*Length in kms.*
1.	Pahumara-Garamur-Jengrai-Haladhibari	48.00
2.	Lachan Gaon Ratanpur Road	2.60
3.	Merbil Ratanpur Road	7.32
4.	Kapahtoli-Majdeori	4.43
5.	Opar Chapori Kathaniya Road	4.00
6.	Mayengiya Phulani Road	6.50
7.	Nikinikhowa Kalia Gaon Road	5.50
8.	Bangaon Barpamua Road	12.50
9.	Bali Barpamua Road	2.80
10.	Majuli Road	24.00
11.	Bangaon Dakhinpat Road	5.5
12.	Chamaguri Satra Approach Road	1.62
13.	Bhogpur Satra Approach Road	0.80
14.	Deodiaati Pakajara Road	5.38
15.	Dariya Guwalabari	9.08
16.	Majuli College Approach Road	1.00
17.	N.L.K. Road	9.00
18.	Bengena Ati Approach Road	0.30
19.	Dhapak Gaon-Patiya Gaon Road	2.80
20.	Luhitghat Approach Road	0.50
21.	Jengrai-Dhakuakhana Road	3.70
22.	Garamur Approach Road	1.88
23.	Mohkina Road	3.50
24.	Auniati Satra Approach Road	0.60
25.	Gualgaon-Baghgaon road	13.36
26.	Gualgaon Approach Road	1.22
27.	Balibheti Chirampuriya Road	1.60
28.	Badatighat Approach Road	2.11
29.	Sakupara Mohaidubi Road	12.00
30.	Narasingha Bhakatiduar Road	1.00
31.	Gaharighat Sital Dubi Road	1.00
32.	Link Road from PGJH to GB Road	1.00
33.	Uttar Kamalabari Satra Approach Road	0.50
34.	Rangachahi State Dispensary Approach Road	0.74
35.	Jorbil Mirigaon Road	1.00
36.	Molapindha Chelekchapori Road	0.74
37.	Molapindha Molual Road	1.40
38.	Dumichuk Road	0.24
39.	Jengrai Chapori to Phulani Bazar Road	0.75
40.	Jamudchuk-Karkichuk Road	3.24

(*Contd.*)

Sl. No.	Name of the Road	Length in kms.
41.	Patia Gaon-Sumoimari Road	1.65
42.	35th km. Majuli Road to BB Road	0.70
43.	Kerela Gaon-Mohkina Road	2.40
44.	Chamaguri-Bakura Road	2.00
45.	Chitadarchuk Road	0.50
46.	Kamalabari to Circle Office Road	0.50
47.	Kamalpur to SDC Office	0.60
48.	Ghunuchabari to Natun Bechamara Road	4.48
49.	Silikhaguri to Natun Dhowachela Road	1.53
50.	Road from 6th km of BB Road to Kharkati Road	0.30
51.	Ratanpur-Silikhaguri Road	0.73
52.	Garamur Satra Approach Road to 11th km. of PGJH Road	0.20
53.	Garamur-Kakatibari Road	3.40
54.	Gopalpur-Madhupur Road	2.50
55.	Circuit House Road	2.91
56.	Baraguri Dispensary Approach Road	2.00
57.	Khonachuk Road	0.50
58.	Garamur Circuit House to Gualabari Road *via* Phutukichapori	0.63
59.	Puranibari Road	0.63
60.	Kamalpur Road	0.20
61.	28th km. of the Majuli Road to Daria Gualabari Road *via* Bhukakalita	0.32
62.	25th km. of Majuli Road to Mohkhuti Road	1.27
63.	33rd km. of Majuli Road to Deka Sensua Road	0.40
64.	Santipur to Civil Tini Ali	3.00
65.	Rawanapar-Dakhinpat Road	0.80
66.	Gejera Gaon to 48th km of PGJH Road	2.40
67.	Nayabazar-Kekuri Road	1.84
68.	Phulani-Nichalachuk Road	1.34
69.	Lakhimi-Barpamua Road	1.60
70.	Kumarbari to Lakhimi Road	0.50
71.	Road from 35th km. of PGJH Road to Jengrai Dhakuakhana	0.40
72.	Bhakatibari-Mayengiya Road	2.00
73.	Natun Kamalabari Satra Approach Road	2.18
74.	Mudoibil to Phulanibazar Mayengiya Road	0.85
75.	Mayengiya Phulanibazar to Dhowachela Road	1.40
	Total Travel Road	**262.368**
	Surfaced Road	**13.993**

(B) LIST OF TIMBER BRIDGES UNDER MAJULI ROAD SUB-DIVISION: (PWD)

Sl. No.	Name of the Road	Breach Number	Length in rm.	Remark
1.	Majuli Road	33/1	55.00	Running condition
2.	NLK Road	39/1	97.60	-do-
3.	Auniati Satra Approach	1/1	45.00	-do-
4.	Bangaon Barpamua	10/1	33.00	-do-

(*Contd.*)

Sl. No.	Name of the Road	Breach Number	Length in rm.	Remark
5.	Phulani-Mayengiya	1/1	65.00	-do-
6.	Chamaguri Satra Approach	1/1	33.00	-do-
7.	Nikinikhowa kaliagaon Road	2/1 & 3/1	20+20=40	-do-
8.	Opar Chapori Kathani	1/1	21.00	-do-
9.	Jengrai-Dhakuakhana	1/1	132.00	-do-
10.	Uttar Kamalabari Satra Approach Road	1/1	32.00	Running Condition (newly constructed)
	TOTAL	11	553.60 rms.	

Source: Office of the PWD, Garamur, Majuli, on 11.6.004.

Appendix – VI

Market Growth in the Ratanpur Nayabazar Area, 2005 (A Survey)

Sl. No.	Owners Name	Type of Business	Caste/ Community	Opening Year	Educational Qualification
1.	Sri Subash Dey	Shoe & Stationary	OBC (Bengali)	1997	M.A.
2.	Sri Bimal Bhatta	Book Stall	Gen (Brahmin)	1996	H.S. Pass
3.	Sri Bijoy Kr. Dey	Homeo-Pharmacy	OBC (Bengali)	1965	Diploma in Homeopathy
4.	Sri Sanku Dey	Cloth shop	OBC (Bengali)	2003	B.A.
5.	Sri Bitul Borah	Bakery	OBC (Assamese, Koch)	1998	H.S. Pass
6.	Sri Satya Dey	Tailoring	OBC (Bengali)	1998	Below HSLC
7.	Sri Jagnnath Prasad Gupta		-do-	2003	-do-
8.	Sri Rajindar Gupta	Electrical	-do-	2000	H.S. Passed
9.	Sri Rajindar Gupta	Stationery	-do-	-do-	-do-
10.	Sri Anil Bhatta	Stationary	Gen (Brahmin)	2003	H.S.L.C
11.	Sri Ajit Borah	Pan shop Gumti	M.O.B.C (Chutia)	2000	Below H.S.L.C
12.	Sri Ganesh Gupta	Stationery	O.B.C	1980	-do-
13.	Sri Ganesh Gupta	Book Stall	-do-	2003	-do-
14.	Sri Subut Choudhury	Bicycle shop	OBC	1995	-do-
15.	Sri Uma Mala	Vegetable shop	SC(Bengali)	2000	HSLC
16.	Sri Kiran Pegu	Tailoring	SC (Mising)	1985	HSLC
17.	Sri Swami Nath Mala	Repairing of Bicycle	SC (Bengali)	1997	H.S. Pass
18	Sri Baneswar Doley	PCO	ST Mishing)	2003	B.A.
19.	Sri Dinanath Mala	Hotel keeping	SC (Bengali)	2002	Below HSLC
20.	Sri Dipen Hazarika	Printing works	General (Ass. Kalita)	2000	B.A.
21.	Sri Muhidhar Pegu	Vegetable	ST(Mising)	2000	B.A.
22.	Sri Ranjit Dey	Jewellery	OBC (Bengali)	1976	Below HSLC
23.	Mrs. Ashru Lodh	Medicine Store	SC (Bengali)	1985	HSLC
24.	Sri Sunil Doley	Motor Garrage	ST (Mishing)	1985	HSLC
25.	Sri Beznath Barma	Grocery	SC	2003	Below HSLC
26.	Sri Mintu Kr. Dey	Bicycle Repairing	OBC (Bengali)	1985	-do-
27.	Dipak Mala	Jewelry	SC (Bengali)	2004	-Do-
28.	Sri Gopal Gupta	Grocery	OBC	2001	HSLC
29.	Sri Ranji Choudhury	Tailoring	OBC (Bengali)	1986	HS
30.	Sri Subut Ghosh	Hotel keeping	OBC (Bengali)	1986	Below HSLC
	Sri Subut Ghosh	Grocery	-do-	-do-	-do-

(*Contd.*)

Sl. No.	Owners Name	Type of Business	Caste/ Community	Opening Year	Educational Qualification
31.	Sri Ganesh Dey	Jewelry	OBC (Bengali)	1997	HSLC
32.	Bishnu Prashad	Pottery Shop & Grocery shop	OBC	1965	Below HSLC
33.	Sri Tarun Borah	Stationery	OBC (Chutia)	1995	HSLC
34.	Sri Safi Ali	Stationaery	OBC (Muslim)	1998	HSLC
35.	Sri Lalbahadur Gupta	Monehary	OBC (Bengali)	1990	Below HSLC
36.	Sri Sujit Prasad Gupta	Grocery	OBC	2000	-do-
37.	Sri Nandalal Gupta	Stationery, Spoon Shop	OBC	1977	-do-
38.	Sri Dharmendra Sarah	PCO	ST (Bengali Muslim)	2003	HS
39.	Sri Chandan Gupta	Stationery	OBC	2003	-do-
40.	Sri Rajesh Mondal	Ayurvedic Pharmacy	OBC (Bengali)	1998	HS (BAMS)
41.	Sri Sonjoy Gupta	Repairing of Bicycle	OBC	1999	HSLC
42.	Sri Gopal Sil	Barber	SC (Bengali)	1980	Below HSLC
43.	Sri Dilip Sil	Hotel keeping	-do-	1985	-do-
44.	Sri Suresh Singh	Hotel keeping	OBC (Rajput Hindi speaking)	2002	-do-
45.	Sri Ramkrishna Thakur	Barber	OBC	1999	-do-
46.	Sri Ayodhra Sahu	Stationery	SC	2004	-do-
47.	Sri Jitul Senapati	Vegetable shop	OBC (Chutia)	1997	HS
48.	Sri Dipu Borah	Agricultural	MOBC (Chutia)	1995	BA
49.	Sri Dharmendra Dey	Watch Repairing	OBC (Bengali)	1976	HSLC
50.	Sri Subhas Sarma	Cloth shop	Gen (Brahmin)	1970	HSLC
51.	Sri Mongra Gupta	Grocery	OBC (Bengali)	2003	HSLC
52.	Sri Umesh Doley	PCO	ST (Mising)	2004	B.A.
53.	Sri Gokulkishore Josi	Cloth	Gen (Bihari Brahmin)	1997	HS Passed
54.	Sri Ganesh Gupta	Cloth	OBC (Bengali)	1998	Below HSLC
55.	Sri Bhabalal Josi	Cloth	Gen (Bihari Brahmin)	1987	HSLC
56.	Sri Omprakash Jain	Cloth	Gen (Marwari Brahmin)	1985	-do-
57.	Sri Kailash Gupta	Grocery	OBC	1975	-do-
58.	Sri Nonda Sarma	Cloth	Gen (Brahmin)	1995	M.Com.
59.	Sri Omprakash Gupta	Grocery	OBC(Bengali)	1997	Below HSLC
60.	Sri Ganesh Prashad Gupta	Grocery + Hardware	OBC(Bengali)	1975	-do-
61.	Sri Tarakeswar Gupta	Grocery	OBC (Bengali)	1975	-do-

(*Contd.*)

Sl. No.	Owners Name	Type of Business	Caste/ Community	Opening Year	Educational Qualification
62.	Sri Ramsarkar Gupta	-do-	OBC(Bengali)	1975	-do-
63.	Sri Amarnath Gupta	-do-	OBC (Bengali)	1970	-do-
64.	Sri Umesh Saikia	-do-	MOBC (Chutia)	1996	BA
65.	Sri Deben Ghosh	Hotel keeping	SC (Bengali)	1992	Below HSLC
66.	Md. Mustak Monsuri	Cloth	OBC (Bengali Muslim)	1992	HS
67.	Sri Sriram Gupta	Monehary	OBC	1992	-do-
68.	Sri Mohendra Jain	-do-	Gen (Marowari)	1980	-d0-
69.	Sri Paresh Senapati	Vegetable	MOBC	2001	BA
70.	Sri Berigeanarayan Gupta	Grocery	OBC (Bengali)	2001	Below HSLC
71.	Sri Sontosh Choudhury	-do-	SC (Bengali)	2003	MA
72.	Babul Choudhury	Bicycle Reparing	-do-	1980	B. Com.
73.	Sri Ananta Dev	Fine Art	OBC	1991	HS
74.	Sri Ajoy Choudhury	Cloth	OBC (Bengali)	1985	HS
75.	Sri Mohan Singha	Grocery	OBC (Rajput)	1998	HSLC
76.	Sri Ashok Pareek	Cloth	Gen (Bihari Brahmin)	2002	-do-
77.	Sri Atul Baruah	-do-	OBC (Konch)	1999	HSLC
78.	Sri Prafulla Baruah	-do-	-do-	1975/77	HSLC
79.	Sri Bakul Baruah	Pan shop Gumti	-do-	1998	HS
80.	Sri Anil Mili	Studio	ST (Mising)	1999	BA
81.	Sri Sushil Doley	Stationery & Photocopying	ST (Mising)	1999	HS
82.	Sri Norean Boruah	Stationary	MOBC (Chutia)	2001	Hs
83.	Sri Rajib Dutta	Motor Parts & Steel furniture	OBC (Koch)	2004	MA
84.	Sri Rajnesh Barman	Hardware shop	OBC (Bengali)	2003	B. Com
85.	Sri Ramastrey Barman	Jewelry	-do-	1968	HSLC
86.	Sri Kamala Saikia & Sri Poresh Bordoloi	Computer education center & Printing	Gen (Kalita) -do-	2003	BA BA
87.	Sri Prodip Gupta	Ghani	OBC (Bengali)	1970	Below HSLC
88.	Sri Nitya Saikia	Welding center	OBC (Chutia)	2001	BA
89.	Sri Sundar Saikia	Pan Shop, Gumti	-do-	2002	BA
90.	Sri Luhit Saikia	-do-	-do-	2004	HSLC
91.	Sri Dilip Saikia	Vegetable	-do-	2004	HSLC

(*Contd.*)

Sl. No.	Owners Name	Type of Business	Caste/ Community	Opening Year	Educational Qualification
92.	Sri Prashanta Saikia	Bakery	-do-	2003	HS
93.	Sri Swaton Agarwala	Garage	Gen (Marwari)	2000	Below HSLC
94.	Sri Bipul Bhatta	Stationery	Gen (Brahmin)	2002	HS
95.	Sri Prodip Choudhury	Tailoring	OBC (Bengali)	2001	-do-
96.	Sri Harichandra Senapati	Bicycle Repairing	MOBC (Chutia)	2001	-do-
97.	Sri Sujit Dey	Stationery & Pan shop	OBC (Bengali)	2001	-do-
98.	Sri Sanjib Sil	Hotel Keeping	SC	2002	HSLC
99.	Sri Ganesh Sahu	Garage	SC	2004	HS
100.	Sri Sarat Senapati	Vegetable	MOBC	2000	HS
101.	Sri Manik Saikia	Pan Shop gumti & Embroidery	OBC	1990	HSLC
102.	Miss Binita Kuli	Embroidery	ST	1998	Below HSLC
103.	Sri Kamala Begam	Laundry	OBC (Bengali Muslim)	1986	Illiterate
104.	Sri Omprakash Gupta	Pan Shop Gumti	OBC (Bengali)	1998	Below HSLC
105.	Sri Lama Kuli	Gumti	ST (Mising)	1998	-do-
106.	Sri Bakul Khanikar	Pharmacy	MOBC (Chutiya)	1994	BA
107.	Sri Dul Samua	Furniture	OBC (Chutiya)	1998	HSLC
108.	Sri Debananda Doley	Video Hall	ST (Mising)	2000	BA
109.	Sri Bisturam Lagasu	-do-	ST (Mising)	2000	HS
110.	Sri Debiram Pegu	-do-	ST (Mising)	2000	HS
111.	Sri Bhim Kuli	Small-scalePetrol/Diesel Depot	ST (Mising)	1995	HSLC
112.	Sri Ratneswar Khanikar	Small scale Petrol Depot & supply of Sound system	MOBC (Chutiya)	1990	HSLC
113.	Sri Rai Sing Doley	Co-operative	ST (Mising)	1985	HS
114.	Sri Makhan Dey	Soft rice (Komal Chaul)	OBC (Bengali)	1965	Below HSLC
115.	Sri Ranjit Doley	Fish selling in the daily market	ST (Mishing)	1989	BA
116.	Sri Lafiram Patir	-do-	-do-	1995	HSLC
117.	Sri Paramesh Pegu	-do-	-do-	1996	Below HSLC
118.	Sri Monuj Doley	-do-	-do-	2001	HSLC
119.	Sri Ranjit Doley	-do-	-do-	2001	Below HSLC
120.	Sri Premadhar Doley	-do-	-do-	1994	-do-

Appendix – VII

List of the Satras of Majuli (Past and Present)

1. Auniati Satra: (Earlier established in the Salmara Mauja), its first Satradhikara was Niranjandev who was established as such in the *Saka* year1575-76 (1653-54 A.D.). It has branches almost over the entire state among which the one at Teok within Jorhat District on the south of the Brahmaputra, and the other at North Guwahati are most well known. It was at the branch at Teok that the Satra celebrated its 350th year jubilee in 2004.

2. Adhar Satra: It was established earlier in the Salmara Mauja.

3. Ulutalia Satra: It was established earlier in the Salmara Mauja.

4. Elengi Satra: It was extended from the branch of Purushottam Thakur (Purush sanghati), earlier established in the Salmara mauja. It has few branches, e.g. Kakarikata Bar Elengi, Adi/Porabheti Elengi, kamja nia/bagi Ai Elengi, Dikhowmukhiya Elengi, Balichapari Elengi, barachuk saru Elengi (Kamalabari Mauja)

5. Owa satra: It was within the Kamalabari Mauja, Kerelagaon. It has a branch at Garakhiya Dol, Baligaon, Jorhat.

6. Kalakata Satra: It was earlier established on the bank of the river called Kalakata established by one Daivakinandan, grandson of Bhavanipuriya Gopal Ata.

7. Kamalabari Satra: It was established earlier within the Salmara Mauja by one Badala Padma Ata in the year 1673. It has been divided into three Satras now-Purani (or original) Kamalabari Satra, Natun Kamalabari Satra and Uttar Kamalabari Satra.

8. Karatipar Satra: It was earlier established in the Salmara Mauja, then shifted to Kamalabari Mauja to the west of Auniati and Bengena Ati. It has branched off from Barjadumanidev through Ramananda Dvija of Ahataguri satra.

9. Kakarikata Satra: See above Elengi satra

10. Katanipar Satra:	It was established in the Salmara Mauja. Now dead
11. Kamjaniya El:	See as above Elengi Satra
12. Kaupatiya Satra:	Established earlier in the Salmara Mauja, affiliated to Kanaklata Ai (Bar Bara-Janiya Satra)
13. Kherkatiya Satra:	Established earlier in the Salmara Mauja on the bank of the Kherkatiya Suti. It belongs to the Saru Barajaniya group.
14. Gajala Satra:	Established by one Saru Jadumanidev on the bank of the Gajala river in Majuli within Salmara Mauja. This Satra was affiliated to the sect of Bhavanipuriya Gopal Ata. During the Burmese invasions the Satra left Majuli and shifted to the southern bank. It has branches now at Amguri and Simaluguri within Sivasagar District. Within Jorhat District also there are a few branches of the Satra.
15. Garamur Satra:	It was earlier established in the Salmara Mauja, but now within the Kamalabari Mauja. Its founder *Satradhikara* was Lakshminarayanadev (some wrongly believe that it was Jaiharidev, nephew of Vamsigopaldeva), grandson of Paramai, uncle of Vamsigupaldeva. It was established in the year 1657-58.
16. Garamur Saru Satra:	During the time of Jayramdev of Garamur Satra (1704-1719) when the line of descendants of Vamsigopaldev were no more, one member of his ancestors was brought and established near Garamur Satra. The Satra is still there; but without an *adhikara*. (In the Pavitra Asam, M.Neog writes that this Stara is no longer there. P. 83)
17. Chamaguri Satra (Purani):	It is in Bangaon within the Salmara Mauja. Chakrapanideva, son of Keshavpriya, daughter of Purushottam Thakur, and Niranjan Gabharugiri *alias* Petphala Ata (her husband), established this Satra in the year 1585 *Saka* (1663 A.D.)
18. Natun Chamaguri:	It is a branch of the Purani Chamaguri Satra. It was established in the year 1824 *Saka* (1902 A.D.)
19. Chupaha/ Chipaha Satra:	Established in the Salmara Mauja. It has branches elsewhere in Jorhat, such as Hamdoi Chupaha near Titabar, Kakajan or Kola Chupaha, Ranga and Baga Chupaha in Sivasagar.

20. Doukachapari Satra: It was established in the Majuli island by Jadavananda, grandson of Gopaldeva of Bhavanipur.

21. Dakhinpat Satra: It is within the Salmara Mauja of Majuli. Its founder *Satradhikara* was Banamalideva. It was established in the year 1660.

22. Dihing Satra: It was established in the Salmara Mauja. This Satra is not existing.

23. Dighali Satra: It was established in the Salmara Mauja. One Sarangapani, son of Keshavpriya, daughter of Purushattam Thakur, established this Satra on the bank of a *bil* called Dighali.

24. Narasingha Satra: It was established in the Salmara Mauja. It is affiliated to the Bar Bara-Janiya branch of Bapuramdev family.

25. Nachanipar Satra: It was at Ahataguri Mauja in the Majuli island; now shifted to Lakhimpur.

26. Nepali Satra: It is now at Teok. It is stated that earlier it was in Majuli Jengraimukh.

27. Porabheti Elengi: As stated in the case of Elengi Satra.

28. Phulbari (Puniya): There were four Puniya Satras in Majuli in the Salmara Mauja. They were Motiyabariya Puniya Satra, Puniyar Bar Satra, Puniya Maju Satra, Puniya Saru Satra.

29. Batargayan Satra: There were two Batargayan Satras in Majuli within the Salmara Mauja. It was established by Chaturbhujbapu and was affiliated to the branch established by Vamsigopaldev.

30. Bar Sankopara Satra: Earlier it was within the Salmara Mauja. Now it is within the Kamalabari Mauja. It belongs to the Kal Sanghati order.

31. Baghargaya Satra: One Purushattam of the Chaitanya cult established in the Majuli island. It later on shifted to Nagaon.

32. Bihimpur Satra: There were two Bihimpur Satras- one within the Salmara Mauja and the other within Kamalabari Mauja. It was established by one Govinda Ata and affiliated to the Saru Barajaniya fold.

33. Bengenaati Satra: It was originally within the Salmara Mauja, now within Kamalabari. According to the *Gazetteer of India*, its revenue-free lands amount to 2500 acres.

34. Belasidhiya Satra: It was originally within the Salmara Mauja, now within Kamalabari. One Nityanandabapu of the sect of Vamsigopaldeva had established this Satra.

35. Bhagati Satra:	It was established to the east of Meragarh in the Salmara Mauja. It was affiliated to the Bar Bara-Janiya fold established by one Paramananda Brahman Mahanta.
36. Matiyabariya Satra:	It was earlier in the Salmara Mauja, now within the Kamalabari Mauja. Related to Bihimpur.
37. Madarguri Satra:	There were three madarguri Satras, one at Kaliyani, another at Karanga, both within Jorhat, and the third in Majuli within the Ahataguri area. It was affiliated to the Bar Bara-Janiya group and established by Sahajananda and Ramananda, the second and the third sons of Bapuramdev respectively.
38. Letugram Satra:	It was established by one Bapuramdev, under the instruction of Purushottam Thakur at a place called Kodobahi lying between Auniati and Bengenaati. This Satra is now not in Majuli. There are four Letugram Satras now within the Jorhat subdivision.
39. Saru Sankopara :	Established within Salmara Mauja, now within Kamalabari Mauja.
40. Saudkuchi Satra:	There are four Saudkuchi Satras in Jorhat subdivision. The Satra was originally in Kamrup, but for some years it was also in Majuli.

Appendix – VIII

Annual Cultural Programme of the Satras

Sl. No.	Name of the Function	Description
	Sri Sri Natun Kamalabari Satra: P.O. Kamalabari, Majul	
1.	*Tinijana Gurur Tithi*	In the month of *Bhadra* death anniversary (*tithi*) of Sankardeva, Madhavdeva and Badula Padma Ata, the founder of the Satra, are observed each for four days. Chief features of those *tithis* are performance of *nam-rasanga* (congregation prayer) in the *Kirtanghar,* gayan-bayan, jhumura, chalinach, ojapali, barpetia dhemali, bahanach,* and music, *bhaona* (both *ankiya* and *asamiya matribhashar natak*), recitation of *charit puthis* etc.
2.	*Sri Krishna Janmotsav*	On the 8th day of the dark fortnight of the month of *Bhadra Janmastami* is observed. On that day *nam prasanga* is held at day time, and in the evening, music relating to Lord Krishna and *gayan-bayan* are performed. Inmates observe fasting and will not go to the field for work on that day. Often drama called *Janmayatra* is performed, and drama in Assamese depicting the birth stories of Krishna are performed.
3.	*Rās Lilā*	In the month of *Kartik* or *Aghon* on the full moon day the *Rās* festival is performed. In the morning on that day *nam-prasanga* is held. Monks also perform *gayan bayan*, music and dance; and in the evening, they perform the drama of *Ras-Lila* at the *kirtan ghar.* *Remarks:* Now a days the system is modernized; the *Ras-Lila* is performed not in the open or at the *kirtan-ghar* of the Satra, but in the stage built for that purpose.
4.	*Phalgutsav*	In the full moon day of *Phalguna* or *Chaitra* this function is performed. In the previous day in the *Daul mandir* or *kirtan-ghar* the image of Lord Krishna is placed and songs called *holi-igeet* are sung. On the next day in the morning *nām-prasanga* is held and powder called *phaku* with *chandan* are distributed among the monks for use on the fore-head.. In the afternoon *holi* songs are sung and *bhaona* is performed. The next day monks sing *holi-geet* and carrying the image of Lord Vishnu organize a procession to the neighbouring villages where families come out to the road and prostrate before the image taken out by the procession by offering money and betel nut and leaf. After that the image is placed at sanctum called *manikut.*

Sl. No.	Name of the Function	Description
5.	***Bahag Bihu* or *Rangali Bihu*	The *Bahag Bihu* is celebrated in the Satra for three days at a stretch beginning with the last day of the month of *Chaitra* (13/14 April). The first day is called *Uruka*, the second day is called *Garu Bihu*. All aspects ascribed to the *Garu Bihu* are the same as done by the common people. The distinctions that the Satra maintains from the villagers are in the field of the cultural programmes of the day. In the morning the young *bhakats* take bath and pay homage to the *Satradhikara* and the senior *bhakats* of the Satra. Then they do *nām-prasanga* at the *nāmghar/ kirtanghar*, recite the *charit puthis* and play on the *khol* and *tal*. They will not go to plough that day, and fast. The next day is called *Manuhar Bihu*. On that day they all put on new dress and give new dress to the image of the worshipful deity in the sanctum. The day is marked by dance and music, drama, *gyan bayan, chalinach, ojapali, bhaona* at night. The *bhakats* will not perform *huchari* like the common people. The third day is also marked by *nāmkirtan**** and *prasad* distribution. *Remarks*: The Bihu is performed on the day as celebrated by other peoples, but in the Satra it is celebrated as a religious function rather than as a social function.
6.	*Bhogali Bihu*	This is celebrated for two days beginning with the last day of the month of *Pausha* (*Puh*). The first day is called *Uruka* and the second day is called *Bihu*. This is also known as *Magh Bihu*. The inmates build *meji* like the villagers and burn it after performing certain rituals. In the morning of the Bihu day, that being the first day of the month of *Magh* (January 14/15), all the inmates along with the *Satradhikara* burn the *meji* in the morning and then at noon assemble together at the *kirtan ghar* and offer new dress to the sanctum (*guru asan*). Then they perform *nam-prasanga*, recite the *Bhagavata* and the *charit puthi*, perform *gyan bayan* and other religious songs and dances. Thus the whole day is passed.
7.	*Palnam*	Organized in the month of Jeth for three days on certain convenient condition specified after due astrological calculation. Congregation prayer called *nam daka* is done from the *Nam-Ghokha* of Madhavdeva. Thousands of people grader of that day.

Sl. No.	Name of the Function	Description
8.	*Kati Bihu* or *Kangali Bihu*	This Bihu is celebrated on the last day of the month of *Ahin* (October 14/15). It is not celebrated as elaborately as the two other Bihus. On this occasion new dress is given to the sanctum (*guru-asan*). It is marked by *nam-prasanga*, offering of *naivedya*, and recitation of the *Bhagavata* and the *charit puthis*.
9.	*Sankardevar Janmotsav*	It is the birth anniversary of Sankardeva celebrated on the 10th day of the bright fortnight (*sukladasami*) in the month of *Ahin*. It is celebrated for one day. New cloth is offered to the sanctum, congregation of prayer, distribution of *prasad*, recitation of the *Bhagavata*, and *charit path* are done. Meetings are also held and lectures are delivered. *Remarks*: It is interesting that while the birth anniversary of the great Vaishnava reformer is celebrated all over Assam with elaborate agenda and cultural programmes, the Satra that claims ideological origin from him, celebrates this in most minimal extent. The organization of meeting in imitation of the public of Assam is a new development.
10.	*Ata sakalar Tithi*	*Tithis* (death anniversary) of Mathuradas Burha Ata, Narayandas Thakur Ata, Bar Bishnu Ata and Bhataukuchiya Keshavcharan Ata are observed in the months of *Ahin, Puh* and *Phagun* respectively. These are celebrated with performance of *nam-prasanga*, *Bhagavata* recitation, *charit path*, *gayan-bayan* etc.
11.	*Palnam*	*Palnam is a heritage festival in the Kamalabari Satra. Earlier it was a seven-day festival organized in imitation of what Sankaradeva had organized at Belaguri Dhwahat for safety and welbeing of Madhavadeva. Organized in the month of Jeth, it is npw held for three days only.*

Uttar Kamalabari Satra: P.O.Kamalabari, Majuli

Sl. No.	Name of the Function	Description
1.	*Rangali Bihu* or Bahag Bihu	Celebrated for three days. On the last day of the month of *Chaitra* (*Sankranti* day) the Bihu begins. Nature of celebration is like that of the Natun Kamalabari Satra
2.	*Sriram Guru, Haricharan Atai and Chakrapani Atair Tithi*	Sriram Guru was the first *Satradhikara* of the Satra. The *tithis* are celebrated on the 11th day of the bright fortnight in the month of *Baisakh*, with *nama-prasanga*, performance of dance and music and distribution of *prasad*. Celebrated for one day.
3.	*Sri Sri Vishnudev Adhikar Tithi*	11th day of the bright fortnight in the month of *Jeth*. Celebrated for one day.

Sl. No.	Name of the Function	Description
4.	*Bhataukuchiya Kesabcharan Atar Tithi*	On the last day of *Ambubachi* in the month of *Ahar*. Celebrated for one day.
5.	*Sri Sri Biswanathdevar Tithi*	In the month of *Sravana* in the 1st day of the dark fortnight. Celebrated for one day.
6.	*Sri Sri Muhikanta devar Tithi*	In the month of *Ahin* on the 4th day of the bright fortnight. Celebrated for one day.
7.	*Sankardevar Janmotsav*	In the month of *Ahin* on the 10th day of the bright fortnight. Celebrated for one day.
8.	*Mathuradas Burha Atar Tithi*	On the 4th day of the dark fortnight in the month of *Ahin*. Celebrated for one day.
9.	*Kati Bihu*	On the last day of the month of *Ahin*. Celebrated for one day.
10.	*Sri Sri Gaurikantadevar Tithi*	12th day of the Krishnapakshya of the month of Kati. Celebrated for one day.
11.	*Rās Utsav/Ras Lila*	On the full moon day of *Kati/Aghon*. It is celebrated for 2-3 days performing Lord Krishna's childhood, and *Ras-kriya* with the *gopa balakas* and *gopis* on the Yamuna. It is performed at the *kirtan-ghar* and the role of women are played by the young chaps of the monks. The first day of the festival is marked by *gayan-bayan*, *natuwa-nach* and other activities pertaining to the *Satriya* culture. At night *natakas* are performed. *Remarks:* Unlike the Natun Kamalabari Satra where the function of the *Ras Lila* is done in a separate stage built for that purpose, *Ras Lila* here is performed in the traditional way at the *Kirtan-Ghar*. But it appears that the *Satradhikara* will go for the stage performance had he enough economic support to do that. Many visitors, particularly from outside, go to the Satra to see this traditional system of performance.
12.	*Narayandas Thakur Atar Tithi*	In the month of *Puh* on the 5th day of the dark fortnight of the month. Celebrated for one day.
13.	*Magh Bihu*	On the *Sankranti* day of the month of *Puh*. *Magh Bihu* is celebrated here in the same manner as in the Natun Kamalabari Satra. Celebrated for three days.
14.	*Dakhinkulia Bar Vishnu Atar Tithi*	On the 13th day of the bright fortnight in the month of *Chaitra*. Celebrated for one day.

Sl. No.	Name of the Function	Description
15.	*Phakua* or *Phalgutsav*	On the full moon day of *Phalgun/ Chaitra*. This festival is celebrated. It is celebrated for one day. *Remarks:* The custom of taking out the image of Vishnu by the *bhakats* and moving around in the neighbouring villages, like the Natun Kamalabari Satra, has now been stopped.
16.	*Mahapurush Srimanta Sankardevar Tithi*	Celebrated on the 2nd day of the bright fortnight in the month of *Bhadra*. It is performed for four days at a stretch. Monks perform *namkirtan*, *gayan-bayan*, and various forms of dances. They sing *ojapali, ghosha* and *kirtan* day and night. On this occasion every monk is given a plate of rice by the *Satradhikara* on the first day. This is called *chaul bhojani.* On the second day they establish the *Bhagavata* called *thapani* in the *Kirtan-ghar*; on the third day, they recite from the original *Kirtan* written by the *Mahapurusha*; and on the 4th day they explain the book to the gathering inmates and public. On all the *tithis* of the *gurus Ankiya* dramas are invariably performed. *Remarks:* The *tithis* of Sankardeva, Madhavdeva and Badula Padma Ata are performed with elaborate agenda in this Satra and in the most dignified way. It is celebrated for four days.
17.	*Mahapurush Sri Sri Madhavdevar Tithi*	On the 5th day of the month of *Bhadra* the *tithi* of Madhavdeva is performed. It is performed for 4 days. *Remarks:* As above in 16
18.	*Sri Sri Badula Padma Atar Tithi*	It is performed on the 11th day of the bright fortnight in the month of *Bhadra*. Performed for 4 days at a stretch. *Remarks:* As above in 16
19.	*Sri Sri Krishnar Janmastami*	On the 8th day of the dark fortnight of the month of *Bhadra.* *Remarks:* As above in 16
20.	*Guru Atai and Paramananda Bhagawati Atair Tithi*	Performed on the 5th day of the dark fortnight of the month of *Bahag.* *Remarks:* As above in 16
21	*Aldhara Govinda Atai Tithi*	On the full moon day of the month of *Bhadra.* *Remarks:* As above in 16
22	*Dakhinkulia Krishna Atair Tithi*	On the 11th day of the dark fortnight in the month of *Bahag.* *Remarks:* As above in 16
23	*Dhemali Jora*	This is a cultural programme annually organized in the Satra. It begins in the last part of the month of *Sravana* at

Sl. No.	Name of the Function	Description
		least 7 days earlier to the beginning of the monthly congregational prayer held in the month of *Bhadra* (*Bhadamahiya nam*), and continue for the whole month thereafter. On a day considered as auspicious this function is closed after one month by performing a *bhaona*.
24	*Nitya Prasanga* (daily Schedule of work)	Daily cultural agenda of the Satra. It begins with biting of the drum (*daba)* in the morning in the *kirtan-ghar*, washing of the sanctum (*asana*), recitation of *puwar bar geet* in the *raga* of *ahira, lalita, kalyan, syam*, and then recitation of the *nama*. It is followed by the recitation of two chapters from the *Kirtan Ghosha* of Sankaradeva. After that congregational prayer is held. Then the *Bhagavata* is recited, then the *charit puthis* of the two *gurus* are read. Then the morning session becomes over. The second session starts at 2 p.m. During this session more other scriptures are recited, such as, the *Namghosha*, *Ratnawali*. On that occasion *bhatima* and *upadesh* are also recited. The evening session begins with the beating of the drum and recitatin of *bhatima,* and reading of the book *Gunamala*, and the *Lilamala*. After that the *gayan-bayan* team comes and perform. One *bargeet* is also sung. Then follows the congregational prayer. After the prayer is over *oja-pali* is performed, or the *Ghosha* is recited. With the beating of the drum the evening session closes. Besides, the special feature of the evening schedule is that every day the *charit puthis* preserved in the *Satradhikara*s house are recited at his residence at the presence of the inmates. *Remarks:* It is stated that the library of the *Satradhikara* contains the manuscripts written by the two *Mahapurushas*.

Garamur Satra: P.O. Garamur Satra, Majuli

Sl. No.	Name of the Function	Description
1.		Celebrated in the Satra beginning with the *Sankranti* day of the months of *Chaitra* and *Baisakh* as in the Natun Kamalabari Satra. Significant aspects of celebration include *nam-prasanga, gayan-bayan*, recitation of the *Bhagavata*, organization of the cowri games, *pasa* etc.
2.	*Barsik Sabah-Bhaona (Mahanam Utsav)*	*Rangali Bihu*
3.	*Palnam*	*Palnam* is organized here for one day. Its starts on the closing day of the *Palnam* at Auniati Satra, and ends next day. The *Nam-Ghokha* of Madhavdeva is recited continuously as congregation payer.

Sl. No.	Name of the Function	Description
4.	*Nitya-naimittik nām Prasanga*	Held in *A̲har* and *Sa̲on* (June-July-August) during which period recitation and explanation of the *Bhagavata* consists of the main progarmme.
5.	*Sri Sri Krishnar Janmāstami*	As in the other Satras. Special feature includes women-programme. In the evening that day women of the Satra perform a drama the story of which is based on religious themes of the *Purans* or the epics. The next day women of the Satra along with their counterparts of the neighbouring villages perform a cultural show called *pa̲chati saba̲h* when they perform the *Sisu Lilā* (i.e. dramatise the childhood days of Sri Krishna). The children of the Satra participate in this '*din bha̲ona̲*'. *Remarks:* The role of the women of the Satra and the neighbouring villages in the cultural activities, particularly, in the *Janma̲stami*, is interesting. Some women artists of the Satra are well known for their performance. Pitambardeva Goswami had established the *Vamsigopaldev Natya Mandir*, the stage of the Satra, and was opened on the *Janmāstami* day of the year 1920.
6.	*Sankardevar Tithi*	Performed on the 2nd day of the bright fortnight of the month of *Bha̲dra*. The inmates perform *na̲mprasanga.*
7.	*Madhavdevar Tithi*	Performed on the 5th day of the dark fortnight of the month of *Bha̲dra*. *Remarks:* Since the month of *Bha̲dra* is significant for the *tithis* of both the *gurus*-Sankardeva and Madhavdeva, the whole month is devoted to *na̲mkirtana* by the women of the Satra.
8.	*Ma̲gh Bihu*	As in the other Satras. It is celebrated with *na̲mprasanga*, fire worship in form of burning of the *Meji*. *Remarks:* It is on this day that the inmates of the Satra adopt resolutions to do certain works for the welfare of the Satra during the coming year.
9.	*Sripanchami Tithi*	*Saraswati puja̲* is performed in the Satra. This day being the day of the death anniversary of late *Satradhikara* Sri Sri Krishna Chandradeva Goswami, it has certain other programmes also. Major features include *na̲m-prasanga*, organization of seminars and discussions, and cultural activities. *Remarks:* It is noted by organization of meetings and cultural shows than by mere *na̲m kirtan* and other religious activities.
10	*Phalgutsav*	On the full moon day in the month of *Pha̲lgun/Chaitra*. It is characterized by '*mesha da̲ha*', *maha̲ puja̲*, *maha̲prabhu* organize peocession and visit the neighbouring villages, playing of *rang* (colour), singing of *holi geet*, and performing music and dance. Then in the *Vamsigopal Natya Mandir* a drama is performed.

Sl. No.	Name of the Function	Description
11	*Chaiddhya Prasanga*	It is not a festival. As per tradition, a day in the Satra is featured by the performance of the 14 *prasangas* called *Chaiddhya Prasanga*. The inmates perform *puja-sewa, nāmkirtan, gayan-bayan, oja-pali, arati*, and *nam-prasanga* in the evening.
12	*Satradhikar Sakalar Tithi*	Death anniversaries of all the *Satradhikaras* beginning with Vamsigopaldeva, the founder of the Kuruwabahi Satra, down to Krishna Chandradeva Goswami, are performed on a specified day in a specified month. The *tithi* days are marked by *pindadidan, nama-prasang, gayan-bayan*, dance and music and so on. Besides meetings are also held to discuss religious and spiritual aspects, and women too perform *nam* or congregation prayer.
Bengena Ati Satra: P.O. Bengenaati, *Majuli*		
1.	*Bahag/Rangali Bihu*	Celebrated as in other Satras, the *Bahag* or *Rangali Bihu* is one of the festivals celebrated in the Bengenaati Satra under religious cover. Inmates of the Satra take bath in the morning on the first day of the Bihu and go to the *Satradhikara* and other senior members of the community and offer their salutation (*sewa*). At noon they perform the *nitya prasanga*, and then perform prayer - *nam*, such as *thiya nam, gayan-bayan, natuwa, ojapali nam mangal* etc. On the third day of this festival, the inmates perform specially *nam mangal* and *Krishna mangal*. They also play *cowri, pasa* and other games.
2.	*Phalgutsav*	The best celebrated of all the festivals and cultural functions in the Satra. As in other Satras it is celebrated in the month of *Phagun* or *Chaitra* on the full moon day. It is stated that this festival used to be celebrated in the Satra since the time of the Ahom king Lakshmi Singa (1769-1781) who with a view to obtaining religious merit and welfare to himself, his mother (*rajmao*), and his subject population, had gifted the Satra with the image of the *Govinda Mahaprabhu* in the year *Saka* 1699 (1777 A.D) and instructed the Satra to regularly celebrate the *Phalgutsav*. For that matter he also donated to the Satra revenue-free lands, *paiks* and *sisyas*. This festival is celebrated for four days at a stretch. In the first day the *Mahaprabhu* is bathed and worshipped through *hom-yajna*. After the *hom* is over, the image is established in a separate pendal called *puja mandap* made for that purpose. Then the priest performs the *hom* and take oath to do the *mesdah* ritual i.e. putting a goat to fire. The goat is washed, ornamented, and then worshipped. Then it is put inside a small cottage made for that purpose and put to fire to the extent of burning a few of its hair. The next day the image is put aside from the *asana*, and washed (*mahasnana*). Then it is put in the *asana* again and

Sl No.	Name of the Function	Description
		adorned with new dress and ornaments. The mesdah is followed by eight forms of worship during the next eight *praharas*. Every time the image is worshipped by performing *hom* and reading incantation (*mantra*). After that the *paiks* granted originally by the king to the Satra will play on *dhol, mridang*, and band. Women of the Satra then sing the *Phalgutsav geets* as composed by Sankardeva, and continue for the whole day and night. In the evening the inmates perform *bhaona*. The third day is called *bisarjan puja* or *jirani*. In the morning *puja* starts as usual. Then follows the *hom, bhujotsarga, brahmadakhina*. Then the inmates and other visitors will put the *bhasma* (ashes) of the *hom* as *tilak* and thereby seek God's blessings. It is followed by *thiya nam, natuwa nach, ojapali* etc. and take the *nirmali*. Then the disciples will perform varieties of religious songs and dances. At night the inmates perform *bhaona*. The fourth day is called *phurani* or *Mahaprabhu bhraman*. In the morning after *nam-prasanga*, the image is taken out all around the Satra in presence of the inmates, believers, visitors. During this visit the inmates of the Satra perform various agenda, and other attendants perform dance and music as they like. This procession called *ghunuchabari bhraman* is thus finally ended. Then the image is brought to the main gate of the temple (*manikut*) when suddenly the door is made to collapse before the image is put inside. Then follows the debate between Govinda and Lakshmidevi (through recitation of scriptures.) At last goddess Lakshmidevi apologises and the door suddenly opens and the *Mahaprabhu* enters. Thus ends the festival. In the evening the inmates perform *bhaona*. *Remarks:* It is very interesting that in a Satra of *Purush Sanghati* order sacrifice is so enormously performed, and a poor goat is symbolically burnt in the name of worshiping God *Govinda Mahaprabhu*. The Guru Charit (in prose) records how Sankardeva prevented Madhavdeva from sacrificing a goat before the goddess Durga and accept the ideal of non-violence as the only way of attaining salvation. There are criticism about the information recorded in the *Guru Charit* by Ramcharan Thakur. (See Chapter-V)
3.	*Janmāstami*	It is celebrated like any other Satras in the island dominated by cultural agenda and *nām*-prasanga. A drama called "*Sri Sri Krishnar Janma Lilā.*"is performed on that day.
4.	*Sankardeva aru MadhavdevarTithi*	In the month of *Bhadra* the death anniversary of both Sankardeva and Madhavdeva are performed. The days are marked by performance of *nam-prasanga*, recitation of *charit puthis*, reading from the *Bhagavata*, and performance of different cultural agenda. In the evening the inmates perform an *Ankiya natak* (drama)

Sl No.	Name of the Function	Description
		composed by the *guru* whose *tithi* is this. *Remarks:* In order to make a difference between the *tithis* of the two saints, three *Kirtans* are presented in the *tithi* of Madhavdeva while four *Kirtanas* are presented in the *tithi* of Sankaradeva.
5.	*Rasotsav*	In the morning the image of the *Govinda Mahaprabhu* is washed (*mahasnan*) and worshipped. Then follow the *Nitya Prasanga*. At noon the inmates perform *thiya nam, gayan-bayan, natuwa nach, ojapali* etc. In the evening inmates perform a *bhaona* called '*Sri Krishnar Raslila*' in a stage which is but an annexie of the *kirtan-ghar* only. *Remarks:* It has tried to modernize the theatres at least in the technique of performance.
6.	*Satradhikar sakalar Tithi*	Death anniversaries of the late *Satradhikaras* are performed as usual- with performance of different forms of prayer and cultural agenda.
7.	*Palnam*	In the month of *Bhadra* the *palnam* is performed for the whole month. In the evening women (*ayati*) of the Satra perform *arati*. It is also a custom of the Satra to recite a few of the religious scriptures, such as *Gunamala, Lilamala* etc. Various cultural agenda feature the occasion including recitation of the *charit* of the *Mahapurusha*.
8.	Occasional Performance	As a Satra that received royal patronage, a class of song called *rajaghariya* song is sung here. Other songs performed on such occasions include folk songs,such as, boat plying songs called *nauka khelar geet* in which the inmates of the Satra once had major role to play during the monarchy. This custom has now been almost dead.

Natun Chamaguri Satra: P.O. Rawanapar, *Majuli*

Sl No.	Name of the Function	Description
1.	*Janmastami*	As in other Satras *Janmastami* is celebrated in Chamaguri Satra with performance of *nam-kirtan* both in the day and at night. On that day a *bhaona* depicting the life of Lord Krishna is performed. In the next day inmates celebrate what is called '*Nandotsav*'. The day begins with playing of mud (*boka*) inside the *kirtanghar* by the inmates. The *boka* play is closed with a congregation prayer.
2.	*Palnam*	*Palnam*, organized in the month of *Bhadra*, is an important function of the Satra. Besides congregation prayer the inmates also perform *bhaona*. *Palnam* is sometimes organized by individual persons as a mark of devotion to *bhakti* and with an objective of attaining religious merit, and often wishing recovery of some one who suffers from serious diseases.

Sl No.	Name of the Function	Description
3.	*Sankardeva aru Madhavdeva*	The death anniversary of Sankardeva is performed in the month of *Bhadra* with performance of various cultural agenda and *ankiya bhaona*.
4.	*Chakrapanir Tithi*	The death anniversary of Chakrapani Ata, the founder of the Satra, is celebrated in the month of *Phaguna* on the 6th day of dark fortnight of the month with *nāmkirtan* and *bhaona*.
5.	Rasutsav	*Ras Yatra* is the most important festival celebrated in the Satra. In fact the Satra is well known for its traditional form of presentation of the *Ras* festival. It is performed for two days at a stretch with elaborate agenda. On the previous day the inmates organize a kind of *nam* called *awahan nam kirtan.* The next day, i.e. the day of the *Ras* starts with morning prayer called *pratah kirtan manjira.* Then follow *nam* performed by women, and then by men in which, besides the inmates of the Satra, people from all around take part. The *nam* is followed by the *ojapali* dance through which the entire story of the *Ras-Lila* is presented to the audience. Then the *natuwa nach* is organized as the last item of the day. The night function begins with *gayan-bayan*. Then the drama called *Keli Gopal* of Sankardeva is presented in *Brajawali* language. The drama continues till the next morning. A large fair is held in front of the *kirtan-ghar* on the two days of the festival. On the second day also the same kind of celebrations are done. *Remarks: Rasutsav* in the Chamaguri Satra is significant in more than one way. First, the drama is performed in the *kirtan-ghar* itself as it was done earlier. The language of the drama is still carried on in *Brajawali* as composed by Sankardeva. Thus while other Satras perform the drama in *matribhasha* i.e. in Assamese, this Satra has maintained the old tradition by doing it in *Brajawali.* Use of mask carries another distinction to the performance of the Satra.
6.	*Phalgutsav*	*Phalgutsav*, also called *Phakuwa,* is another important festival of the Satra. It is organized on the full moon day of *Phalgun* or *Chaitra*. It is also called *Daul Yatra* or *Daul Utsav*. One significant aspect of this festival celebrated in this Satra is that besides various cultural agenda, women of the Satra sing *biya nam* (marriage songs) to mark the marriage between Ghunucha and Lord Krishna.

Bhogpur Satra P.O. Bengenaati Satra, *Majuli*

Sl No.	Name of the Function	Description
1.	*Guru Tithi*	Death anniversary of Sankardeva is celebrated in the moth of *Bhadra* for 4 days at a stretch. The first day is called '*thapani*', the second day is called '*chaul bhojani*', the third day is called '*kirtan*' while the 4th day is called '*samarani*' which ends with the recitation of the *guru*

Sl No.	Name of the Function	Description
		charit (the biography of the saint). Along with the *tithi* of Sankardeva, the *tithi* of Madhavdeva is also performed in the same manner. *Remarks:* Since the Satra is a monastic Satra, women participa-tion in any pro-gramme does not arise. But they can go to the Satra during the day time and enjoy the progra-mmes.
2.	*Satradhikalar Tithi*	The founder *Satradhikara* was one Burha Damodar. His and those of other *Satradhikaras* are celebrated annually with *nam-kirtan,* dance and music. Performing of the *ankiya bhaona* is the special feature of the *tithis.*
3.	*Ras Purnima*	The Satra like other Satras of the island, celebrate the *Ras* festival for two consecutive days. This festival was not held earlier; it is a new entrant in the cultural agenda of the Satra.

Auniati Satra P.O.Auniati (Kamalabari), *Majuli*

1.	*Bahag Bihu*	Celebrated in the same days as in other Satras. The Satra celebrates the *Bahag Bihu* for three days- (a) *Garu Bihu* (*Bihu* celebrated for the cows),(b) *Manuhar Bihu* (*Bihu* celebrated for men and (c) *Chera Bihu* (*Bihu* to say good bye to itself). On the last day of the month of *Chaitra* (April 13/14) the *Garu Bihu* is celebrated with which the *Bihu* starts. The Satra has a custom that on that day its inmates write the prayer of Lord Siva on the leaf of the *nahar* tree and hang on the lintel of the house praying the God for protection of the inmates from wind and storm. On that day besides the usual prayer (*prasanga*) the inmates hold a special prayer called *barman* to be followed by another prayer from the *Nam Ghosha* of Madhavdeva (*barhaghosha*).*** Performance include *gayan-bayan, natuwa nach, ojapali* dance etc. On the close of the *barha ghosha**** the *Satradhikara* accompanied by the junior ones (*Deka Adhikar* and the *Govindapuriya*) enter the *Kirtanghar* and offer salutation first to the worshipful deity (*Govinda Mahaprabhu*) and then to the *bhakats* who perform the prayer. He then takes his seat in the middle of the *Kirtanghar* by the side of the main pillar called *lai khuta*. After the congregation all go to their respective residences and take light food consisting of varieties of cakes and soft rice (*jalpan*). The next day, called *Manuhar Bihu,* is celebrated in the same manner as the *Garu Bihu* so far religious activities are concerned. But on that day the inmates engage in various games such as the *pasa, gudu, bagh-garu, mangalpat, dhop* etc. In the morning the inmates play a mud-game called *boka-khel* in which substance prepared from mud and cow-dung mix are the object of play among the younger generation of inmates. *Remarks: Bihu* celebrated as a folk festival, and the *Bihu*

Sl No.	Name of the Function	Description
		celebrated in the Satras, are different in essence although not in apparent form. It is observed in the Satra under a religious cover, and is distingui-shed with spiritual character. The dance and song characterized by love and desire in the folk dances and music is absent in the celebration of the Satras.
2.	*Kati Bihu*	Celebrated on the *sankranti* day of the months of *Ashin* and *Kartik.* It is believed in the Satra that the month of *Kartik* (*Kati*) is the most celebrated month, and if Lord Vishnu is worshipped with *tulasi* in that month, it gives more religious merit than any other form of worship. The inmates plant *tulasi* plant in the courtyard and worship it. The most significant aspect of this *Bihu* in the Satra is the custom of lighting lamps in the sky. These lamps are called *akash banti*. The inmates prepare for the *akash banti* long before the *Bihu* and a few office bearers of the Satra are given the duty of organizing that. Three bamboo poles of the height of 20/9/5 cubits long are prepared, coloured with lime, and then posted in the middle of the campus. The place is cleansed by the *paiks* of the Kaivarta caste, granted to the Satra by the kings of Assam in middle ages. The potter *paiks* excavate the hole to put the bamboo poles into the earth. Twenty one pairs of lamps are lighted, and they are refilled with oil every morning and new cotton threads (*salita*)are put into the lamps. This continue for the whole *Kati* month. Besides this *akash-banti* system, the day is observed with congregation prayer, performance of dance and music consisting of *hiyanam*, *dihanam*, *ojapali* etc. *Remarks:* The inmates refrain from taking fish for the whole *Kati* month. The system of erecting bamboo poles and burning lamp in the sky is interesting. It involves a long process of labour and preparation characterized by a religious fervour. Thus the Satra has picked up folk culture and has Brahmanised it with a religious tone. It appears that this elaborate agenda was a kind of discovery on part of the Satra to make its festival more gorgeous than that of others.
3.	*Magh Bihu*	Celebrated on the last day of the month of *Magh* as done in other Satras. As celebrated by the villagers the inmates of the Satra also erect *meji* and burn them both in the night of the *uruka* (the previous day of the actual *Bihu*) and in the following morning. It is a kind of fire worship carried on by people as a part of their culture possibly since the days of their primitive civilization. The Satra has, however, a special method of worshipping the fire on the day of the *Bihu*. On that day the inmates worship fire in the prayer hall itself as per Vedic procedure. It is interesting that both *nam-prasanga* and *hom* are done at the same time; while the *vagish* perform the *hom*, the inmates perform the *nam*. Both run in parallel. During the

Sl No.	Name of the Function	Description
		day inmates perform *hiya nam, diha nam, gayan-bayan, natuwa, oja-pali* etc. *Remarks:* It is interesting that unlike many other Satras the *Brahma Sanghati Satras* do not per-form *bhaona* on such occasions.
4.	Palnam	The *Palnam* is the most celebrated of all the functions of the Auniati Satra. This is a purely religious function held in the last five days of the month of *Kati*. The objective of *Palnam* is seeking welfare of all living and non-living beings. It is indispensable in the Auniati and Garamur Satra, but optional in other Satras. In the Garamur Satra it is celebrated for one day only. (See the text in Chapter-V for details)
5	*Ras Purnima*	As in other Satras, Auniati Satra also observe *Ras Purnima* as a form of sacrifice (*puja*) following the manner of the Dakhinpat Satra where it was first introduced in the *Saka* year 1762 (1840 A.D.)
6	*Janmastami:*	*Janmastami* too is held as a kind of *puja*; but *nam-prasanga* is the way to perform it. The inmates recite the *Janma Khanda* from the *Kirtan-Ghosha* of Sankardeva. The day is observed with dances of various forms except, however, *natuwa* dance, *gayan-bayan, oja-pali, hiyanam* etc.
7	*Guru Tithis:*	The following *tithis* of the Vaishnava saints are celebrated in the Satra: *tithi* of Sankardeva, Madhavdeva, Damodardeva, Vamsigopaldeva, Bhavanipuriya Gopal Ata *alias* Gopaldeva and the *tithis* of the late *Satradhikaras* of the Satra. On that day the inmates organize *annadan, nam-kirtan, natuwa nach, oja-pali* dance etc.

Dakhinpat Satra :P.O. Dakhinpat, Majuli

Sl No.	Name of the Function	Description
1.	*Mahaprabhu Puja*	On the 1st day of the Assamese new Year- 1st *Bahag* *Remarks: Puja* (worship by sacrifice)
2.	*Shri Shri Damodardevar Tithi*	*Sukla Pratipad* (1st day of the bright fortnight), *Bahag* *Remarks:* Death anniversary
3.	*Satradhikar Shri Shri Krishnadevar Tithi*	*Krishna Chaturthi* (4th day of the dark fortnight), *Bahag* *Remarks:* Death anniversary
4.	*Sayan Ekadasi*	Month of *Aha* *Remarks:* Death anniversary
5.	*Shri Shri Bishnudevar Tithi*	*Krishna Panchami, Aha* *Remarks:* Death anniversary
6.	*Parsva parivartan Ekadasi*	*Ahin*

Sl No.	Name of the Function	Description
7.	*Durga Puja Chandi Path*	*Ahin/Kat* *Remarks: Puja* (recitation of the *Devi strota*)
8.	*Shri Shri Balodevar Tithi*	*Sukla Panchami, Ahin* *Remarks:* Death anniversary
9.	*Shri Shri Banamalidevar Tithi*	*Sukla Saptami, Ahin* *Remarks:* Death anniversary
10.	*Shri Shri Paramanandadevar Tithi*	*Sukla dasami, Ahin* *Remarks:* Death anniversary
11.	*Utthan Ekadasi*	*Kati/Aghon*
12.	*Shri Shri Lakshmi Puja*	*Purnima, Kati* *Remarks: Puja* (worship by sacrifice)
13.	*Dvipandita, Kalipuja, Mahalaya Sraddha*	*Ahin/Kati* *Remarks: Puja* (worship by sacrifice).
14.	*Rās puja Festival*	*Kati/Aghon* *Remarks: Puja* (worship by sacrifice)
15.	*Shri Shri Ramdevar Tithi*	*Sukla Ekadasi, Kati* *Remarks:* annual *sraddha* (Death anniversary)
16.	*Shri Shri Basudevar Tithi*	*Krishna Sasthi, Kati* *Remarks:* annual *sraddha* (Death anniversary)
15.	*Navanna Sraddha*	*Aghon* *Remarks:* Sacrifice with new rice
16.	*Shri Shri Kamdevar Tithi*	*Krisnastami, Aghon* *Remarks:* Annual sraddha
17.	*Shri Shri Narayandevar Tithi*	*Suklastami, Puh* *Remarks:* Annual sraddha
18.	*Shri Panchami*	*Magh* *Remarks: Saraswati Puja*
19.	*Brahma Bhojan*	*Magh* *Remarks:* Feeding of the Brahmans
20.	*Shri Shri Atmadevar Tithi*	*Krishna Pratipad, Magh* *Remarks:* Annual *Sraddha*
21.	*Shri Shri Sahadevar Tithi*	*Krishna Ekadasi, Magh* *Remarks:* Annual *Sraddha*

Sl No.	Name of the Function	Description
22.	*Shri Shri Bantidevar Tithi*	*Purnima, Magh* *Remarks:* Annual *Sraddha*
23.	*Shri Shri Subhadevar Tithi*	*Sukla Dvitiya, Magh* *Remarks:* Annual *Sraddha*
24.	*Phalgutsav*	*Purnima, Phagun*
25.	*Shri Shri Sivaratri*	*Phagun* *Remarks:* Worship of Siva
26.	*Shri Shri Bibhudevar Tithi*	*Sukla saptami, Phagun* *Remarks:* Annual *Sraddha*
27.	*Shri Shri Haridevar Tithi*	Krishna Pratipad, Phagun
28.	*Shri Shri Naradevar Tithi*	Krishna Ekadasi, Chot

Source: List of annual functions of the Dakhinpat Satra has been taken from the *Souvenir* of the Conference of the Disciples (*sisya samaroh*) of the Dakhinpat Satra, held on 19-21 February, 1997, Jorhat)

* There is an indistinct difference, not noted by ordinary observers, between the names of the prayer halls of a Satra and those of the common people in the villages. While the one in a Satra is usually called *Kirtanghar*, the one in a village is called *Namghar* although both carry the same meaning- house for congregation prayer. It is interesting to note that while the term *Kirtan* is a word of dignified Sanskrit, *nam* belongs to the common language of the people. It is more interesting to note that in the *charit puthis* the *Kirtanghar* is called *Kirtan-griha* (complete Sanskrit). We find here a sense of maintaining a difference between the ordinary commoners and sanskritised society of the Satras.

** It is not known when did the *Bihu* started to be celebrated in the Satras. The *Charit Puthis* have no reference to the celebration of the *Bihu* in the Satra. It appears that *Bihu* formed a part of their functions since inception

Appendix – IX

List of Select Manuscripts Preserved in a few Satras of Majuli

A. List of Manuscripts Preserved in the Uttar Kamalabari Satra

1. *Mahabharatar Yuddha*
2. *Mahabhagavata*
3. *Bhagavata Gita*
4. *Dasam Scandha Bhagavata (copied 1696 Sak) (Bhagavata X)*
5. *Rukmini Harana (from the Hari Vamsa)*
6. *Janma rahasya*
7. *Bargeet*
8. *Dvadas Scandha Bhagavata (Bhagavata XII)*
9. *Kirtan Ghosha*
10. *Sloka Bhagavata*
11. *Karna Badh (Natak)*
12. *Brahmabrata Prayachitta*
13. *Guru Charit*
14. *Padma Puran*
15. *Sruti Gayatri*
16. *Hari Chandra Upakhyan*
17. *Nam malika*
18. *Sankara Madhava Charitra*
19. *Rajasuya Yajna*
20. *Ramayana*
21. *Katha Bhagavata*
22. *Dasam*
23. *Ratnawali*
24. *Ghosha*
25. *Sanskrit Bhagavata*
26. *Nam Ghosha*
27. *Ankar Barachowa Geet*
28. *Guru Sakalar Charitra (composed 1807 sak)*
29. *Gunmala*
30. *Bhakti Pradip*
31. *Ghosha Kirtan Ratnawali*
32. *Arjun sangvad*
33. *Bali Chalan*
34. *Ghosha nam*
35. *Sapar mantra*
36. *Bishar mantra*
37. *Baghe Kamurile jarar mantra*
38. *Nam Chandra*
39. *Kulupia Ghosha*
40. *Gunmala*
41. *Prarthana*
42. *Kawach*
43. *Syamanta Haran*
44. *Ghosha (composed 1707 Sak)*
45. *Kodo barale jara mantra*
46. *Bhuyan Vansar Utpatti Charitra Puthi*
47. *Karna Badh*
48. *Siva Parvati*
49. *Rajasuya*

B. List of Manuscripts Preserved in the Auniati Satra (Sanskrit and Assamese Mixed):

1. *Bhagavata*, IXth Canto
2. *Kumar sambhav*
3. *Sri Chandogra Sulapani Bajra Raja Pratyengika Strota*
4. *Mahapuja Bidhi*
5. *Jyotish Muktawali*
6. *Gopa Sahasra Nam*
7. *Bhatti Kavya*
8. *Sri Hasta Muktawali*
9. *Ripunjay Smriti*
10. *Bhagavata* (complete)
11. Bhagavata (Illustrated)/ *Chitra Bhagavata*
12. *Bhagavata*, VII, VIII, IXth Canto
13. *Dasam* (illustrated)

14. *Bhagavata* (Rajasuya Yajna)
15. *Bhagavata,* XIth Canto *Katha Bhagavata*
16. *Sundara Kanda Ramayana*
17. *Adbhuta Ramayana*
18. *Ramayana* (Kiskindha Kanda)
19. *Kirtan-Ghosha*
20. *Kirtan Ghosha and Lilamala* (combined)
21. *Kirtan Ghosha, Gunamàla, Nam Ghosha* (combined)
22. *Hari Chandra Akhyan*
23. *Anadi Patan*
24. *Bhakti Ratnawali*
25. *Vaishnavi Kirtan*
26. *Mahabharat- Udyug Parva*
27. *Mahabharata- Drona Parva*
28. *Babrubahanar Yuddha*
29. *Mahabharata-Sailya Parva*
30. *Mahabharata –Manichandra Ghosh Parva*
31. *Mahabharata-Bhishma Parva*
32. *Devajit Kavya*
33. *Brahma Vaivarta Puran*
34. *Satrunjay*
35. *Srimad Bhagavata Gita*
36. *Mahamoha Kavya*
37. *Kumar Sambhav*
38. *Hasti Vidyarnava/ Gajendra Chintamani/ Hati Puthi*
39. *Katha Gita*
40. *Govinda Charit*
41. *Yugal Mangal Gan* (manuscript on songs)
42. *Gajendra Chintamani / Hati Puthi*
43. *Sankaradeva Charit by Bhushan Dvija*
44. *Damodardeva Charit*
45. *Gopaldeva Charit*
46. *Keshavdeva Charit*
47. *Kushdeva Charit*
48. *Harideva Charit*
49. *Harideva Charit*
50. *Pranharideva Charit*
51. *Lakshminathdev Charit*
52. *Padmapanidev Charit*
53. *Lakshiramdev Charit*
54. *Dattadev Charit and Lilakantadeva Charit (combined)*
55. *Sarisrip Jara Mantra*
56. *Nidra Jara Mantra*
57. *Nara Singha Mantra*
58. *Bhut Pisach Kheda Mantra*

C. List of Manuscripts Preserved in the Chamaguri Satra:

1. *Anadi Patan* (complete but one leaf; total 18; illustrated)
2. *Sri Charit* (*Guru Charit Puthi,* 1675 *Sak*- 1753 A.D.)
3. *Namghosha* (entirely written on a single piece of *muga* cloth, total 70 pages and different illustrations; See Illustration)
4. *Kirtan Ghosha* (complete, copied by Chidananda Mahanta, 1852 *Sak*)
5. *Namghosha* (copied by Chidananda Mahanta)
6. *Guru Charit* by Ramcharan Thakur
7. *Nam Malika* (date of copying could not be traced; too old a manuscript)
8. *Bhakti Ratnakar* (dated 1905 *Sak,* copied by Mukheswar Mahanta)
9. *Janma Rahasya* (1900 *Sak,* copied by Chidananda Mahanta)
10. *Hari Chandra Upakhyan* (1700 Sak, copied by Mahendra Ata)
11. *Brihad naradiya Puran* (1931 *Sak,* copied by Chidananda Mahanta)
12. *Jyotisha* (titled not found; it is a book on astrology)
13. *Bhakti Ratnawali* (of Sridhar Swami)
14. *Hamdoi Mantra* (2 number of manuscripts preserved)
15. *Sarbaroga Mantra* Nidan (a work of *Ayurveda*)

16. *Adikanda Ramayan* (by Madhavdeva, copied by Roseswar Ata, 1800 *Sak*)
17. *Uttarakanda Ramayan* (by Sankaradeva)
18. *Bhagavata* (Sanskrit, 300 years old)
19. *Kiskindhakanda Ramayan*
20. *Srimad Bhagavata* (VIth canto, copied by Maheswar Ata in 1884 *Sak*)
21. *Rukmini Haran Kavya* (200 years old)
22. *Udyog Parva* of the Mahabharata (copied in 1804 *Sak*)
23. *Amarakosha* (copied in 1830 *Sak*; Sanskrit)
24. *Bhagavata* Xth canta (copied by Krishna Charan Das)
25. *Bhagavata* (Sanskrit)
26. *Sri Ram Kirtan* (written in *tulapat*)
27. *Namghosha* (dated 1870 *Sak*)
28. *Srimad Bgagavata* XIIth canta (dated 1815 *Sak*)
29. *Kirtan-Ghosha*
30. *Srimad Bhagavata* Xth canta (total 105 folios)

* The Purani Chamaguri Satra preserves many more manuscripts than those listed herewith. At least when I, along with my friend Golap Chandra Nath of Majuli College, visited the Satra in December 2004 (16/12/2004), I could count as many as 120 usable manuscripts on various subjects. These usable manuscripts may be classified into two categories in terms of dates : some are very old, as old as 300-400 years, while some others are quite new, as new as to be dated 1905 *Saka*. This shows that the art and culture of manuscript writing in this Satra continued since the beginning and till the last part of the 20th century. One of the manuscripts – the *Namghosha* of Madhavadeva (Sl.No.3 above) is a novel piece of art work being written in a single piece of *muga* cloth, about 8 inches broad. From the point of illustration, the *Anadipatan* (under Sl.No.1) is outstanding. The Satra claims to have possessed the *p<u>a</u>duk<u>a</u>/kharam* (shoe/foot-wear) of Sankaradeva made of brass; and a folio from the *Bhagavata*, Xth Canto (*Dasam*) translated by the *Mahapurusha* with his own handwriting. (Also see M. Neog, *Pabitra Asam*, op.cit, p. 74) The *p<u>a</u>duk<u>a</u>*, as shown to me, was preserved in a box wrapped up with a piece of *g<u>a</u>moch<u>a</u>* (Assamese towel) and kept with utmost care and devotion. It is made of brass in the Mughal style, and is as dazzling as a show room piece. There is no doubt that it was made by some one later and preserved at the name of the *guru*. So far the *Bhagavata* folio was concerned, on my persistent request the *Satradhikara* agreed to open a wooden box put inside the sanctum on condition of performing some rituals. We did accordingly. The process and preparation of opening it up was, of course, heart-beating as it was said that only once in a year the box is opened to the public, that too after performing certain rituals. To all our surprise, when the box was opened, it was found that there was a ball of powder created by the white ants (See Illustration), which had eaten up the material that was kept hidden inside the box for years together. I felt sorry to understand that my persistent request had ended the source of the belief and that of the interest that visitors used to put on the box since long past. From the volume of the powder ball I however believe that there was not a single folio, as publicized, but a complete manuscript; and when some one visited the Satra to have the fortune of looking at the hand writings of the *Mahapurusha*, the officiating priest used to show one page from the lot from inside the box from a safe distance stating that it was that

historical and heritage page; and the devoted man looked at it with gratifying satisfaction.

D. List of Manuscripts preserved in the Garamur Satra

1. *Bhagavata*, IXth Canto
2. *Bhagavata* Xth canto (8 copies)
3. *Bhagavata*, canto-I (3 copies)
4. *Bhagavata* (Sanskrit)
5. *Bhagavata* (12 copies)
6. *Bhagavata* Xith canto
7. *Dasam* (6 copies)
8. *Bhagavata* VIIth canto
9. *Bhagavata* Vth canto (2 copies)
10. *Bhagavata*, Ivth canto
11. *Bhagavata* II canto
12. *Ramayana* (2 copies)
13. *Ramayana*, Lanka Kanda
14. *Ramayana*, *Ayodhya Kanda*
15. *Mahabharata* (8 copies)
16. *Mahabharata*, *Swarga Khanda*
17. *Mahabharata*, *Bana Parva*
18. *Mahabharata*, *Adi Parva*
19. *Bhishma Parva* (2 copies)
20. *Bhishma Parva* (of the *Mahabharata*) Nataka
21. *Bhakti Pradip*
22. *Krishna-Uddhava Samvad*
23. *Kirtan Ghosha* of Sankaradeva (5 copies)
24. *Nam Ghosha* of Madhavadeva
25. *Bargit*
26. *Ratnawali* (2 copies)
27. *Gita*
28. *Lila Mala*
29. *Kaliya Daman Nat*
30. *Krishna Lila Nat*
31. *Git* (2 copies)
32. *Ayurveda*
33. *Brahman Bidhi*
34. *Puja Bidhi*
35. *Kriya Bidhi*
36. *Sraddha Bidhi*
37. *Sruti*
38. *Brahman Bhairavi Mantra*
39. *Hara Gauri Samvad*
40. *Mantra*
41. *Tantra Sar*
42. *Jyotish Sastra*
43. *Brahman Kriya Mantra*
44. *Prayacchitta Bidhi*

Appendix – X

List of Freedom Fighters in Majuli

(AS RECORDED IN THE REPORT OF THE ENQUIRY COMMITTEE OF THE FREEDOM FIGHTERS, GOVERNMENT OF ASSAM, 1979)

Sl. No.	Name and Address of the Fighter	Nature of Participation	Remark
1.	Keshabram Bora S/O Ramcharan Bora Salmara Gaon, Majuli	Actively participated in the 1921 movement. Had 3 months R/I u/r 17(1) CLA, and 17(2) respectively. Put in 1 year R/I on 30/3/1922 u/r 17(2) CLA. Released on 31/3/1923	
2.	Badar Baishya Bhakatiduar, Ratanpur	Active worker during the movements of 1939-1945	
3.	Khagendranath Bhuyan S/O Rupram Bhuyan, Garamur Saru Satra, Majuli	Participated in the movement of 1942-43. Imprisonment for 3 years 2 months and 24 days, and 5 months and 14 days in 1943, and 2 years imprisonment in 1943-1944	Not clear
4.	Bharat Chandra Bora, Garamur Saru Satra	Actively participated (in the 1942 movement)	Not clear
5.	Madhab Chandra Bora, S/O Kanak, Garamur Saru Satra	Put in prison on 24/9/43 for 9 months and put under R/I u/r 56 (4) DIR. Released on 1/6/44	
6.	Jibeswar Bora, S/O Rupali, Garamur Saru Satra	Put in prison on 24/9/43 for 9 months and put under R/I u/r 56 (4) DIR. Released on 1/6/44	
7.	Kamal Chandra Bhagawati, S/O Lakshmi-nath, Garamur Saru Satra (now in Lakhimpur)	Put in prison on 24/9/43 for 9 months and put under R/I u/r 56 (4) DIR. Released on 1/6/44	
8.	Bidyadhar Barua, Garamur (now Teok)	Actively participated in the movements of 1942-1945	Not clear
9 .	Jayram Bharali, Vill-Lagua Ali, P.O.Phulanibari	Actively participated in the movements of 1942-1945	-do-
10.	Phanidhar Barua, S/O Krishnakanta Barua, Garamur satra	Offered Satyagraha in 1942 uttering anti-war slogan. He was arrested thrice, but was released outside prison. His name was struck off from the School roll.	Lone example of offering Satyagraha in Majuli as recorded

Sl. No.	Name and Address of the Fighter	Nature of Participation	Remark
11.	Khageswar Barua, S/O Loknath Barua. (Garamur Satra)	Participated in the 1932 movement and worked among the student. He joined the group going to hoist the national flag in the Thana building. He was made to pay a punitive tax of Rs.257/-	Lone example of paying punitive tax
12.	Indeswar Bhuyan, S/O Aturam, Garamur Satra	Active participant in the movements of 1942-1945 period. Arrested on four occasions; and on one occasion he was put in jail where he stayed with Rajanikanta Chakravarty and others.	Not clear
13.	Nabin Chandra Bora, Garamur Satra	Active Congress worker	Vague
14.	Beenda Barua, Garamur Satra	Active Congress worker during 1942-1945	-do-
15.	Surama Bora, Kamalpur	Active Congress worker during 1942-1945	-do-
16.	Golapi Bora, Garamur Satra (now Japi Sajia, Panigaon, Lakhimpur)	Actively participated in the 1942 movement	-do-
17.	Gopiram Bora, Deodia Ati (now Tipling path)	Actively participated in the 1942 movement	-do-
18.	Bhaben Bhagawati	Actively participated in the 1942 movement	-do-
19.	Kosada Bhuyan, Garamur	Actively participated in the 1942 movement	-do-
20.	Krishnakanta Barua, Garamur	-do-	-do-
21.	Nayada Bhuyan, Garamur	-do-	-do-
22.	Kanmai Bora, Garamur	-do-	-do-
23.	Rupram Bara, Karatipar	-do-	-do-
24.	Betharam Bora, Ratanpur	-do-	-do-
25.	Golapi Bharali, Garamur	-do-	-do-
26.	Gunaram Barchetia, Moran Gaon, O.O. Gohain bari	-do-	-do-
27.	Gangadhar Barua, Chinatoli Gaion	-do-	-do-
28.	Someswar Bora, S/O Sona, Auniati	Detained on 15/2/1943. Released on 17/3/1943	
29.	Narayan Chandra (Bharali) Bordoloi, S/O	Arrested at Majuli on 26/1/1943 for leading a procession for flag hoisting	

Sl. No.	Name and Address of the Fighter	Nature of Participation	Remark
	Tankeswar, Garamur Satra,	ceremony. Was arrested on 6/2/43 and put in jail for two years R/I u/r 56 DIR. Released on 7/10/194 on remission of 118 days.	
30.	Bharat Chandra Bora, S/O Bapuram Bora, Majuli Satra	Arrested at Majuli in 26/1/1943 for leading a procession for flag hoisting ceremony. Was arrested on 6/2/43 and put in jail for two years R/I u/r 56 DIR. Released on 7/10/194 on remission of 118 days.	
31.	Sunanda Bhuyan, S/O Sabharam, Majuli Kamalabari Ferry Ghat	Detained on 8/1/43 by order 48, dated 24/1/42 u/r 26. Released on 28/5/1943	
32.	Dimba Barua, Garamur satra	Active participant	vague
33.	Jayram Bora, S/O Daya Bora, Garamur Satra	-do-	-do-
34.	Purnakanta Bharali, S/O Muhiram, Garamur Satra	Active participant in the movements of 1935-1945	-do-
35.	Rebat Chandra Bora, S/O manuram, Vill- Kar-doiguri, P.O. Balicha-pori,	Participated during 1936-1945	-do-
36.	Punya Bora, W/O Loknath Bora	Active participant of 1942	-do-
37.	Loknath Bora, S/O Bapu-ram Bara, Gualgaon,	Participated in the 1936-1945 movements	-do-
38.	Jayram Bora, Garamur Satra	Participated in the 1936-1945 movements	-do-
39.	Dimbeswar Barua, Garamur Satra	Participated in the 1936-1945 movements	-do-
40.	Purnakanta Bharali, Garamur Satra	-do-	-do-
41.	Rewat Chandra Bora, Kardoiguri	-do-	-do-
42.	Mahesh Chandra Bora, Garamur Satra	-do-	-do-
43.	Gangadhar Chamua, Bangaon	Active participant in the 1942 movement	-do-
44.	Manik Chandra Chutiya, Garamur Satra	Detained on 8/1/1943 u/r 26 by order 46 dated 24/12/42. Released on 16/6/1943	A Chutiya cannot be a member of the bhakat community

Sl. No.	Name and Address of the Fighter	Nature of Participation	Remark
			of a Satra. He might have been associated with the activities of Pitambardeva Goswami of the Garamur Satra
45.	Kanak (Koch) Dutta, S/O Puram, Majuli	Offered Satyagraha in 1941 at Charing. He was arrested and detained for 15 days by order 45 dated 24/12/1942 u/r 26 (1) (b) DIR. He was again arrested on 8/1/1943 and then released on 2/7/1943. Again he was arrested and convicted on 23/7/1943 and put in jail for 1 year and 3 months of R/I to be released on 15/8/1944.	
46.	Dhiren Dutta, Garamur	Active participant in the 1942-1945 movement. Arrested and let off. Name struck off from the school registrar	
47.	Golap Dutta, Garamur Saru Satra	Joined Congress in 1939, and actively participated in the 1942 movement	vague
48.	Sarupahi Dutta, Garamur Satra	-do-	-do-
49.	Lakhikanta Das, S/O Mahiram, Opar Katani Gaon	Arrested at Majuli on 20/11/1942 for preventing supply to Government servants. Released on 3/3/43, but detained under order 120. And then released on 14/7/43	
50.	Ashradha Dutta, S/O Somnath	Participated in 1932 movement. Actively participated in 1942 movement hampering military supplies and joined flag hoisting campaign in the Thana building	Not clear what form of participation he had during 1932
51.	Madhab Dutta, S/O Dinai, garamur Satra	Participated in the 1932-1945 period	Vague
52.	Bholanath Dutta Kakati, Garamur Satra, S/O Cheni Chandra	Actively participated in 1932, 1942 and 1945 movements	-do-
53.	Hemada Goswami, Garamur Satra	Actively participated in 1939, 1945 movement	It is not clear in which movement he participated in 1939

Sl. No.	Name and Address of the Fighter	Nature of Participation	Remark
54.	Narayan Goswami, Garamur Satra, S/O Paniram	Participated during 1933-1945 movements	No 'clear information
55.	Muluk Gam, S/O Dhani Gam	Participated in 1922-1942 movements	-do-
56.	Manik Chandra Hazarika, majuli	6 months R/I during 1942 movements	No clear record
57.	Bodheswari Hazarika, Baghar Gaon	Participated in the 1942 movement	vague
58.	Bagaram Kakati, S/O Rangagara, Kerela gaon, Majuli	Arrested on 24/9/1942 and put in jail for 9 months R/I u/r 56 (4). Released on 1/6/1944	
59.	Charu Chandra Kakati, S/O Bholanath Dutta Kakati, Garamur Satra	Actively participated in 1942 movement. Arrested and freed from Kamalabari Thana. Again arrested along with the Garamuriya Satradhikar Pitambardeva Goswami and set free next day. Again arrested for leading a procession on three occasions and set free.	Not clear about arrest and nature of participation. Not clear for what period he was put in jail, nor clear as to the dates on which he was arrested.
60.	Suren Kakati, S/O Mahesh, Garamur Satra	Participated in 1932 movement and picketed. Actively participated during 1942-1945 movements and helped underground freedom fighters with food and shelter. Arrested but set free.	Not clear
61.	Kamal Kakati	Participated in the Non-Cooperation in 1921. Suffered imprisonment	Not clear as the kind of imprisonment
62.	Phuleswari Dutta Kakati, Garamur Satra	Actively participated in the 1942-1945 movements	Vague
63.	Dharmeswar Kakati, Garamur Satra	Actively participated in the movements of the period 1942-1945	-do-
64.	Narendranath Kakati, S/O Mahesh Chandra	Joined Congress in 1936, actively participated in 1942. Arrested and set free. Again arrested on 9/8/1943 in connection with (Gandhi's) Poona Yatra	
65.	Bideshi kaibarta, S/O Keroman, Baghar Gaon, P.O. Ratanpur	Participated in 1922-1942 movement	vague

Sl. No.	Name and Address of the Fighter	Nature of Participation	Remark
66.	Bodhbar Pamegam, S/O Latum Pamegam, 1 No. Bargaya Gaon	Participated in the 1922-1942 movements	-do-
67.	Bapuram Na-Pamua, P.O. Ratanpur	Participated in 1942 movement	-do-
68.	Manaram Saikia, S/O haripad	Participated in the 1942 movement, and arrested on 30/10/1942 for one of his prejudicial (public) speeches delivered in Majuli (probably in Kamalabari where the movement took place) 17/9/1942. He was put in jail for 6 months under R/I u/r 38 (5)	
69.	Deoram Saikia, S/O Baloram, Deodia Ati	Participated in the1942 movement. Was detained on 8/1/1943 by order 49, dated 24/12/1942. Was released on 2/7/1943	
70.	Kosha Saikia, Deodia Ati	Participated in 1932 and 1942 movements. Arrested on 9/8/1942 (?, 3) in connection with the Poonayatra campaign.	Not clear about his role in 1932, nor the date of his arrest is correct.
71.	Sarada Saikia, Garamur Satra	Actively participated in 1942 movement	vague
72.	Dimba Saikia, Garamur Satra, Santipur	-do-	-do-
73.	Pavai saikia, Garamur Satra	-do-	-do-
74.	Gajen Tamuli, S/O Tileswar, Garamur Satra	Participated in the 1932 and 1942 movements. Arrested in 1942 and set free. His bicycle was seized.	It is doubtful if he had a bicycle at that point of time
75.	Loknath Tamuli, S/O Milaram, Garamur	Participated in 1942 movement. First time arrested but set free. Second time arrested on 26/1/1943 for leading a procession but was released next day. Again arrested on 9/8/1943 on the Poona Yatra campaign, but was released next day.	No clear record
76.	Krishna Chandra Deva Goswami, S/O Jadav Chandra Goswami, Garamur Satra	Arrested on 12/11/1942 u/r 26(1) (6). Detained by order 11, dated 20/11/1942, but released on 16/6/1943. His detention order was cancelled on 18/12/1944. Was interned in (the Satra) Garamur	

Sl. No.	Name and Address of the Fighter	Nature of Participation	Remark
77.	Pitambardeva Goswami, Garamur Satra	Detention order dated 14/7/1944. Continued by order dated 20/12/1944	Very brief record on a personality who created the freedom movement not only in the Majuli island, but also created his personality wave all over the state, is interesting

* In the above proforma the head termed 'remark' is ours. There is no doubt that some of the names put in the above list are later additions added by interested corners when the list was prepared later on by orders of the national Government. This may be known from the nature of the records themselves indicated by their vagueness and incorrect dating. On the other hand, a large number of fighters who were indirect participants, but who largely added to the strength of the movements, or who came forward to participate in the struggle in its various phases and in different individual capacities, but who did not come forward to put their role in record, or who were not given that opportunity, or who did not realize that their names would be important for their descendents, were not included in the list. Nor did they have official records in their personal possession to prove their participation except local memories of the old generation or stories narrated by those noble souls to their descendents.

Appendix – XI

Memorandum submitted by the Auniatiya Satradhikara to His Excellency Andrew Gourlay Clow, the Commissioner of Assam

To
His Excellency Sir Andrew Gourlay Clow
K.C.S.I.,C.I.E.,I.C.S
GOVERNOR OF ASSAM

May it please your Excellency,
May your Excellency's august visit to Majuli, an island of Vaishnavite Satras, augur well for the land and its people.

Bereft of worldly grandeur though Majuli has failed to accord a fitting reception to your Excellency, may the spiritual influence of the place however benedictions on your lofty head.

Your excellency has graciously set your foot on the sacred soil of Majuli, hallowed by the sanctity of Satras like Auniati and Dakhinpat, famous in the annals of the lands patronized by kings of yore and ever upheld by the British Raj. On this auspicious occasion, our words of greetings go forth to welcome such a high souled guest.

As an appendage to the Satras, Majuli, in process of time, has grown into three Mauzas.The natural disadvantages of the inhabitants are now crying for possible redress.

Even this solitary cloistered nook has not been free from the effects of the devastating War. We are constantly in prayful mood for the glorious Victory of the Allies, so that, in international Peace and Freedom may reign supreme soon over the distressed world.

May your Excellency enjoy a long life and happiness and the Province peace and prosperity, under your wise guidance. With a prayerful heart.

Camp- Kamalabari
The 14th Feb, 1945

We remain,
Your Excellency's most loyal subject,
The Adhikar Goswami of the Auniati Satra

Appendix– XII

A. Women's Literacy Rate in Majuli: 2004-2005

Name of the Village	Total Household	Surveyed Household	Total Population Surveyed	Women population surveyed	Literate Women	Literacy P.C.
Mohkhuti Bania	36	12	70	29	20	
Natun Pohardiya	40	15	92	38	32	
Phutchang Gaon	105	15	89	47	33	
Gopalpur Gaon	50	11	82	39	32	
Barpamua	650	35	299	158	81	
Namani Jakaibowa	83	15	99	44	11	
Kalitapar Mising	50	20	176	87	8	
Kaniajan Gaon	70	20	137	63	35	
Kumarbari Lakhimi	55	20	145	74	49	
Dhapak Gaon	142	20	140	68	51	
Sriram Devottar Nepalibari (Nepali)	26	10	68	29	21	
Milanpur Gaon, Garamur (Bengali)	97	15	88	39	27	
Sonowal Kachari Gaon (Kachari tribe)	167	25	166	75	50	
Dakhinpat Kaivarta Gaon(SC)	250	25	163	81	51	
Kamalpur Gaon (General Caste)	60	15	110	57	40	
Sonari ati Gaon	80	20	120	57	42	
Barbam Gaon	60	15	90	44	33	
Rangachahi Gaon	81	20	119	58	48	
Baraguri Gaon	85	21	124	60	43	
Nagaon	94	22	132	67	41	
Pahumara	70	18	106	51	32	
Tataya Gaon	113	20	114	50	36	
Sakopara Gaon	85	15	74	34	28	
Ahataguri Seraati Gaon	26	10	56	24	18	
Khalihamari	45	13	82	40	31	
Na-Mati Gaon (Sut Caste)	15	06	36	18	11	
Chamaguri Karatipar	110	22	143	70	25	

(Contd.)

Name of the Village	Total Household	Surveyed Household	Total Population Surveyed	Women population surveyed	Literate Women	Literacy P.C.
Chaorekia	70	20	130	60	40	
Purani Mati	8	6	44	18	12	
Salmara Kumar Gaon	517	38	262	127	79	
Ujir Ati	80	15	76	35	28	
Ghuriya (Sut)	63	12	50	23	17	
Thakurbari (Matak Kaivarta)	140	20	115	53	31	
Puranibari	58	12	61	30	24	
Natun Deodia Ati	45	12	77	34	29	
Barhola Muslim Gaon	12	12	96	46	35	
Sriram Deori	80	23	163	81	55	
Roumara (Koch) gaon	45	8	47	25	19	
Dolkhowa (Kalita) Gaon	20	10	59	27	22	
Majar Deori	200	21	178	89	46	
TOTAL				**2147**	**1366**	**63.56**

B. Women's Employment Ratio in Majuli: 2004-2005

Name of the Village	Women Population Surveyed	Literacy Rate	Number of women employed	Percentage of Employment
Mohkhuti Bania	29	86.20	nil	00
Natun Pohardiya	38	97.36	1	2.63
Phutchang	47	93.61	nil	00
Gopalpur	39	97.43	1	2.25
Barpamua	158	68.35	4	2.53
Namani Jakaibowa	44	50.00	nil	00
Kalitapar Mising	87	22.98	nil	00
Kaniajan	63	82.53	1	1.58
Kumrbari Lakhimi	74	77.02	3	4.05
Dhapak	68	82.35	2	2.94
Sriram Devottar Nepal	29	86.20	1	3.44
Milanpur Bengali Gaon	39	84.61	1	2.56
Sonowal Kachari	75	89.33	nil	00
Dakhinpat Kaivarta	81	76.54	nil	00
Kamalpur Kamalabari	57	94.73	7	12.28
Sonariati gaon	57	84.21	2	3.50
Barbam gaon	44	81.81	1	2.27
Rangachahi	58	96.55	3	5.17
Baraguri	60	88.33	2	3.33
Nagaon	67	77.61	2	2.98

(*Contd.*)

Name of the Village	Women Population Surveyed	Literacy Rate	Number of women employed	Percentage of Employment
Pahumara	51	86.27	1	1.96
Tataya Gaon	50	94.11	1	2.00
Sakopara	34	95.11	nil	00
Ahataguri Seraati	24	83.33	nil	00
Khalihamari	40	92.50	nil	00
Namati	18	77.77	nil	00
Chamaguri Bhati Karatipar	70	50.00	1	1.42
Chaorekia	60	80.00	2	3.33
Puranimati	18	88.8	nil	00
Salmara Kumar	127	79.52	3	2.36
Ujir Ati	35	91.30	5	14.28
Ghuriya (Sut)	23	95	nil	00
Thakur bari Sensowa (Matak Kaivarta)	53	75.47	nil	00
Puranibari	28	93.33	1	3.57
Natun Deodia Ati	34	97.05	nil	00
Sriram Deori	81	85.18	4	4.93
Raumara	45	88.00	nil	00
Majar Deori	89	69.66	2	2.24
Dolkhowa	27	88.88	1	3.70
Barhola Muslim	46	93.47	nil	00
Total	**2169**	**78.77**	**52**	**2.39**

Appendix – XIII

Photo Copy of the Letter of Pitambardeva Goswami to Dehiram Nath (Ms.), dated 13 Kartik, 1883 Saka

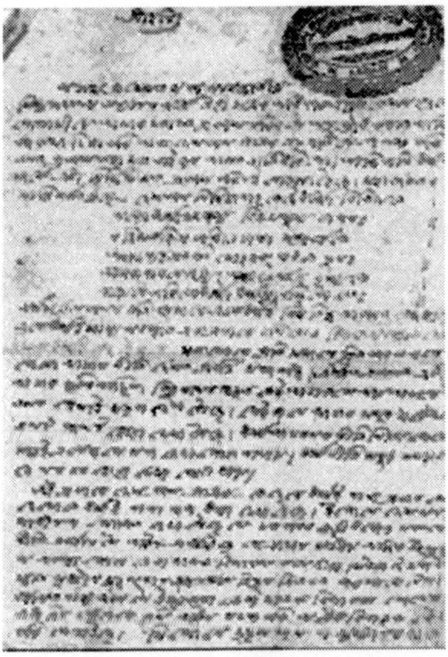

Page No. 1

Page No. 2

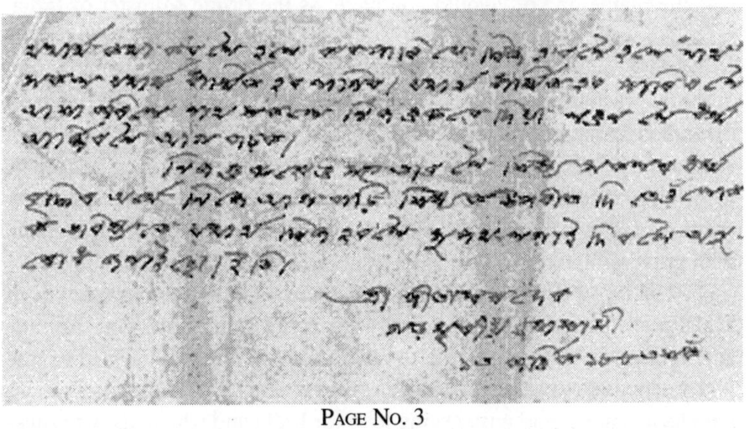

Page No. 3

Appendix – XIV

Open Letter to Sri Jawaharlal Nehru, Prime Minister of India, from Pitambardeva Goswami

26 Jan. 1962

Respected Prime Minister, Panditji,

I feel urgent necessity to submit the following to you. If there be any short coming herein, I beg to be excused considering my good intentions.

Before this, on 27-8-61 I addressed a letter to you indicating how unchecked and extensive Pakistani infiltration into Assam is going to endanger her security, economy and culture. But from your reply dated 30-9-61, it does not appear that the internal situation in this northeastern frontier state received adequate attention from you.

Due to (defective) policy and inefficiency of Assam Congress and leaders in the Government, basking under the sunshine of your favour, Assam is demonstrably slipping into the bosom of Pakistan by a gradual process. Although you know what is happening, you do not appear to be anxious about it. If, noticing this state of affairs, the people of Assam lays the blame on you, would you have, as the Prime Minister of India, reasons for feeling sorry for it?

Panditji, although India is a democratic country by its constitution but in actual practice, one may say, the country is run autocratically. Because, the Indian leaders, particularly the Congress leaders, dare not tell you what is right and proper out of fear for incurring your displeasure. In consequence, leadership of India has in actual practice vested in one person. Yet, forty crores of Indians are going ahead today quietly accepting your leadership with great faith, treating you as the successor of Mahatma Gandhi.

In 1947 you agreed to partition of India against the express will of Mahatmaji. Since then, particularly for some years now, your attitude and behaviour have given rise to doubts in the mind of many of us that you are inclined towards disregarding the earnest feelings of those Indians who have sincere and unswerving love for India and who consider you as a Superman or Mahatma.

Countless Pakistanis with the sinister purpose of converting this North Eastern State of Assam into a wing of Pakistan, are spreading all over the State. Seeing the people of unfriendly Pakistan seeking to bring about ruin to the State in this way, the people of Assam have repeatedly drawing the attention of Assam Government to this danger. But the Government have expressed the opinion that the Pakistani infiltration is not to that extent. You might also have been similarly informed. Yet, at the public meeting in Gauhati towards the end of December last, you admitted in a way considerable Pakistani Infiltration into Assam. A little before that, the Central Home Minister, Sri Lal Bahadur Sastri also made statement admitting indirectly substantial infiltration of the Pakistanis into Assam. Considering all facts and circumstances, it may be said without any manner of doubt that although the Government of Assam may not admit, it is a true fact that there has been extensive Pakistani infiltration into Assam. You may not attach importance to this problem now; but you will realize the situation when the Pakistanis will assert having numerical majority in Assam. But at that time even though you will appreciate the gravity of the situation, we doubt whether you will have the power to rectify the position then. As an illustration, it will suffice to point at your once dear friend Sheikh Abdulla and Kashmir. Assam's Sheikh Abdulla appears to bc no less dear to you.

Panditji, pray, do not think that I am troubling you with this matter for fear of death or any other (personal) fear. But I am making these submissions apprehending that Assam, for that matter Bharat, may be in great danger in no distance future and also in the hope of alerting the Government of India under your leadership and the Government of Assam at your command so that they may proceed along the correct path of their duty in this matter.

Since India is a secular state, it was expected of you to have accorded equal treatment to different religious faiths. But instead of that, while you have shown great liberality, comparatively speaking, to other religions, you have helped to repress by various legislations and other ways that Religion, on the foundation of which Indian Culture and Statehood grew up, and this is creating handicap in the way of fuller development of the Indian civilization and culture (in its true line) It is needless for me to go into details in this matter.

Being the Prime Minister of secular and democratic India, do you place "Dharma" (in ethical sense) and "Adharma" on the same plane? If that be so, opinion of the majority of the masses will not agree with yours. In which case, I humbly leave it to you for considering as to what should be your duty.

Let me pray, cite few instances of how you are helping the spread of "Adharma" in the country. Once you said that black marketers would be severely punished when the country would attain Independence. But under your regime, particularly during last 4 or 5 years, corruption has greatly increased. Can you say that you have not given shelter to this corruption. Today the ruling group in India is dancing like puppets at your will and pleasure. If, then, corruption has not decreased but is increasing in the country, who is responsible for this? What justification can you advance for giving nomination to some characterless self-seekers, disregarding persons known for integrity and having faith in the Congress. Has not the great Congress organization directly encouraged corruption by giving nomination to those M. L. A's and ministers against whom grave charges of corruption were being openly leveled? If the Congress raises funds for election from the black marketers, does it not amount to encouraging corruption? Let me cite another instance of gross exploitation coupled with corruption. Paddy was purchased from the cultivators at Rs 9/- per md. under State Trading monopoly by Legislation. Rice out of this paddy is being sold in the market at the rate of round about Rs. 37/- per maund. Does this not amount to squeezing the people (paddy growers and rice consumers) and making the rich mill owners and capitalist traders richer still?

Panditji, although you are constantly declaring crusade against casteism and communalism in India, which you are seeking to build up in socialistic pattern, yet in actions, you and the Congress under your leadership are sheltering casteism and communalism and contributing towards the increase of these. To substantiate it, one needs point only to the policy of giving nominations to the general election by the Congress. In selection of candidates, giving a go-by to integrity, efficiency and public service, even an unfit candidate belonging to a particular community has been given nomination, without any other consideration, for a constituency in which that community is in majority or in substantial number. By splitting up the double-member constituencies into single only for scheduled tribes and castes, communal mentality has been lawfully strengthened. Formerly there was no feeling of enmity between different communities although they remained separate. Now, owing to policy and action taken, there is a growing feeling of fearful enmity, besides increase of bitter communalism. Pray, can you deny all these?

I earnestly appeal, through you, to the Hindus, Muslims, Christians and other people of Assam to consider this matter coolly, dispassionately and without any bias. If there has been no extensive Pakistani infiltration into Assam, how could the last Census register an increase of population by 44 per cent whereas, in the two previous Census, the increase was only by about 20 per cent. It appears that in certain sub-divisions, the minority community is becoming majority or near majority. Considering the natural rate of increase of population in Assam, and also taking into account at least 50 thousand newcomers in connection with new industry and trade, still the presence of several lakhs of people, exceeding 6 lakhs, cannot be accounted for. And if these are not Pakistani infiltrators, there is no other explanation for their presence. There has been great shortage of arable lands for settlement of landless Hindus, Muslims, Christians, Buddhists and other local people in Assam. In such a situation, will not the infiltration of lakhs of Pakistanis into Assam create a dangerous crisis in the economy of this State?

Panditji, you will be pleased to agree with us that danger to Assam means danger to the whole of India. If Assam is involved in a dangerous situation, security of India will be affected, political integrity and independence of India cannot remain unaffected. I humbly beseech you not to be influenced by self-seeking sychophants and fail in your duty.

May God lead you along the correct path of "Dharma".

Humble Selfless Servant
Of the Country
Shri Pitambardeva Garmuriya Goswami,
Garamur: Assam

Appendix – XV

A Cover Page from the Asam Bilasinee
(*12th Issue, 5th Year, March, 1876*)

Appendix – XVI

A Part from the Leaflet titled *Kartipakshya, Janasadharan aru Eke Pathar Pathik Guru Sakalar Ocharat Mor Antarar Bhav Nivedan*, 28 *Bohag*, 1878 *Sak* (used in the present work as *Confession*) by Pitambardeva Goswami, Satradhikara of Garamura Satra.

মোক প্ৰায় পাঁচ বছৰ বয়সত মোৰ পিতৃ মাতৃৰ লগৰ পৰা একেবাৰে গড়মূৰ সত্ৰলৈ অনা হৈছিল আৰু মাৰপিট কৰিও কঠোৰ শাসনেৰে ধেমালীৰ পৰা একেবাৰে বঞ্চিত বৰ্ণমালা-শিক্ষা দি অৰলে বান্ধি পঢ়োৱা হৈছিল। বৰ্ণপৰিচয় হোৱা মাত্ৰে সংস্কৃত মুগ্ধবোধ ব্যাকৰণ পঢ়িবলৈ বাধ্য কৰা হৈছিল। এইবিলাক কাৰ্য্যৰ দ্বাৰা মোৰ বিশেষ অনিষ্ট হোৱা নাছিল, কিন্তু অভিপাত ৰূপে মোৰ অনিষ্ট হৈছিল উদাসীন প্ৰথাৰ মাজত উদাৰ গতিৰে প্ৰবৃত্তি থকা অবৈধ আৰু অত্যন্ত ঘৃণাজনক ইন্দ্ৰিয় সেৱাৰ প্ৰতি লালসা বঢ়াই দিয়া নীতি সমূহৰ পৰাহে। পূৰ্ব্ব কালত উদাসীন প্ৰথাৰ মাজত কি নীতি প্ৰবৰ্ত্তিছিল মই নেজানো, কিন্তু মোৰ ৬-৭ বছৰ বয়সত যি দেখা পাইছিলোঁ তাত মাত্ৰ দুৰ্নীতিৰ চুড়ান্ত অত্যাচাৰ চলি থকা দেখা পোৱা হৈছিল। অতি দুখৰ কথা যে উদাসীন প্ৰথাৰ দুঃ চৰিত্ৰৰ মাজত লালিত পালিত হোৱা বাবে মোৰ নিজৰো চৰিত্ৰগত অৱনতি ভীষণভাৱে হৈছিল। যাৰ ফলত মোৰ চৰিত্ৰ নষ্ট হৈছিল, উদাসীন প্ৰথাৰ দুনীতিবোৰ মনত পৰিলে আজিও মোৰ অন্তৰত হৃৎকম্প উপস্থিত হয়। তেনে বিধৰ অসৎ সঙ্গৰ মাজত পৰি মোৰ ভীষণ অৱনতি ঘটিছিল। উদাসীনৰ অসৎ সঙ্গত পৰি মোৰ পঢ়া শুনা ভাল নহল। তথাপি সামান্য ৰূপে সংস্কৃত ভাষাৰ জ্ঞান উপাৰ্জিছিলোঁ। সেই জ্ঞানৰ সহায়তাৰেই মই জীৱনত কিছু কিছু সংজ্ঞান আহৰণ কৰিব পাৰিছিলোঁ। কিন্তু মোৰ সেই কালৰ পৰা যি মতে উদাসীন প্ৰথাৰ ওপৰত ঘৃণা উপজিছিল, সেই ভাবৰ আৰু সলনি নহল। আজিও মই অতীত স্মৃতিলৈ মনত পেলাই কওঁ যে উদাসীন প্ৰথাই অসমীয়াৰ সনাতন ধৰ্ম্মী সকলৰ আধ্যাত্মিক জীৱনৰ ওপৰত যেনেকৈ আঘাত কৰিছে তেনে আঘাত আন কোনো সামাজিক ৰীতি নীতিয়ে কৰিব পাৰিছে বুলি মই বিশ্বাস নকৰোঁ। কিন্তু আমালোকে বিশ্বাস কৰোৱেই বা নকৰোৱেই, তথাপি আমালোকে তথাকথিত গুৰুৱে-গোঁ সাইবে থোৱা মাথীয়ে মোক পৰি মৰাৰ দৰে আজিলৈকো এই প্ৰকাৰৰ ফাঁকি দিয়া উদাসীন প্ৰথাৰ এটাতে লাগি মৰিব লাগিছোইক। মোৰ নিজৰ ওপৰতেই নিজৰ দৃঢ় সন্দেহ হয় যে মোৰ জীৱনটো এনেদৰে উদাসীন প্ৰথাৰ মাজত সোমাই কলুষিত নোহোৱাহেতেন মোৰ জীৱটো আপোনামনলৈ আন পুথিদহে যোৱা দেখা পালেহেতেন। দুৰ্ভাগ্য গতিকে মই উদাসীনৰ জালত সোমাই নষ্ট প্ৰায় হলো আৰু সেই অৱস্থাতে পৰি মই পঢ়ি-শুনি জ্ঞানী হব নোৱাৰিলো।

Bibliography

PRIMARY SOURCES

A. Chronicles

(i) Assamese Chronicles:

Asam Buranji by Harakanta Sadaramin: (ed.) S. K.Bhuyan, 3rd ed., Guwahati, 1990.

Asam Buranji Sar by Kasinath Tamuli Phukan: (ed.) P.C.Chaudhury, 4th Print, Guwahati, 1991.

Asam Buranji obtained from the family of Sukumar Mahanta: (ed). S. K. Bhuyan, 3rd edn, Guwahati, 1988.

Asamar Padya Buranji: (ed). S.K.Bhuyan, 2nd edn, Guwahati, 1964.

Asam Buranji (1884): Gunabhiram Baruah, Reprint, Guwahati, 1972.

Assam Buranji: P. N. Gohain Barua, 19th edn, Guwahati, 1976.

Buranji Vivek Ratna by Maniram Dewan: (ed) N. Saikia, Dibrugarh, 2002.

Buranji Vivek Ratna (Ms.), Vol. II: DHAS, Transcript No.

Deodhai Asam Buranji: (ed). S. K. Bhuyan, 3rd edn, Reprint, Guwahati, 1962.

Kamrupar Buranji: (ed.) S.K.Bhuyan, 2nd edn., Guwahati, 1958.

Purani Asam Buranji: (ed). H.C.Goswami, Reprint, Guwahati, 1977.

Satsari Asam Buranji: (ed). S.K.Bhuyan, 2nd edn., Guwahati, 1964.

(ii) Chronicles in English

Ahom Buranji: (tr.) G. C. Barua (1930), Reprint, Guwahati, 1985.

An Account of Assam: (tr.) Dr. J .P. Wade, (ed) B. Sharma, North Lakhimpur, 1927.

Fathiya-I-Ibriya by Shihabuddin Talish: (tr.) Sir J. N. Sarkar, JBORS, 1915, Vol. I, Pt. II; also in E. A.Gait's A History of Assam.

Alamgirnamah by Muhammed Cazim: (tr.) Henry Vansittart, Reprinted in Asiatic Researches, Vol. II, 2nd edn., Delhi, 1979.

(iii) Bengali

Asam Buranji: Haliram Dhekial Phukan, (ed.) Jatindra Mohan Bhattacharaya, Guwahati, 1962.

B. Biographical and Genealogical Works (Charit Puthis and Vamsavalis)

Darrang Raj Vamsavali by Suryyakhari Daivajna: (ed) N. C. Sarma, Pathsala, 1973.

Guru Charit by Ramcharan Thakur: (ed) H. N. Duttabarua, Nalbari, 506 Sankarabda.

Sri Sankaradeva aru Sri Madhavadeva Charit: (ed) H. N. Duttabarua, Nalbari, 509 Sankarabda (1978 A.D.).

Guru Charit Katha: (ed) M.Neog, Guwahati, 1986.

Katha Guru Charit: (ed) U.C.Lakharu, Nalbari, 1952.

Guru Lila by Ramray: (ed) S.C.Goswami, Barpeta,1869 Sak.

Santa Samprada Katha by Govinda Dasa (Ms.): DHAS, Ms. 315.

Sri Sri Gopaldeva Charitra: (ed) M.Mahanta & N.C.Bardoloi, Jorhat, 1978

Sri Sri Badala Padma Atar Charit: (ed.) B. K. Goswami Adhikar, Jorhat, 1888 Sak.

Sri Sri Mathuradas, Burha Atar Jivan Charitra: by Jagannath Mahanta, Barpeta, 1349 Sak.

Sri Dattadeva Charitra by Sridhar Chandra Barua: (ed) N. Saikia, Auniati, 2004

Sri Sri Aniruddhadeva Charitra aru Mayamara, Satrar Gosai Sakalar Vamsavali by Chidanandadev and Krishnadas Dvij: (ed) Hridayananda Chandra Adhikar, Chabua,1853 Sak (1931).

Sri Sri Vamsigopaldevar Charitra: (ed) M. Neog, Guwahati, 1872 Sak.

Sri Vanamalidev Charit, Asam Sahitya Sabha, Jorhat, 1955.

Niranjandev Charit (Ms.): Preserved in the Auniati Satra, Majuli.

Pranharideva Charit (Ms.): -do-

Keshavdev Charit (Ms.): -do-

Kushdev Charit (Ms.): -do-

Hati Puthi (Ms.): -do-

Dattadeva Charit (Ms.): -do-

Bar Charit: Dinanath Bezbarua, Guwahati, 1987.

C. Religious Works

Bhagavata by Sankaradeva and others: (ed) H.N.Dattabarua, 8th edn., Nalbari, 1976.

Kirtan Ghosha aru Namghosha by Sankaradeva and Madhavadeva respectively: (ed) H.N.Dattabarua, 12th Reprint, Nalbari, 1975.

Kalika Puran: (ed) P.Tarkaratna, Calcutta, B.S., 1384.

Kalika Purane Murtivinirddesah: B. N. Shastry, Delhi, 1994.

Manu's Code of Law: A Critical Edition and Translation of the Manava-Dharma Sastra: Olivelle, P., OUP, second impression, New Delhi, 2006.

Rukmini Haran Kavya by Sankaradeva: (ed) H.N.Dutta Barua, Nalbari, 498 Sankarabda.

Sri Hastamuktawali: (ed) M.Neog, Reprint, Guwahati, 2003.

Yogini Tantra: Calcutta, B. S. 1333.

D. English Records, Reports, Accounts and Documents:

A Descriptive Account of Assam (1841): William Robinson, Reprint, Delhi, 1975.

A Statistical Account of Assam (1879), Vol.I: W. W. Hunter, Reprint, Delhi, 1990.

An Account of Assam: Francis (Buchanon) Hamilton, Guwahati, 1963.

A Report on the Province of Assam: A. J. Muffatt Mills (Calcutta, 1854), Reprint, Guwahati, 1984.

Gazetteer of Eastern Bengal and Assam (renamed as Gazetteer of Bengal and North East India): B. C. Allen, E.A.Gait et. al., Reprint, Delhi, 2001.

A Geographical Sketch of Assam by Dr. J. P. Wade (incorporated in B. Sharma (ed.): An Account of Assam (op.cit)), North-Lakhimpur, 1927.

Topography of Assam: John M'Cosh, Reprint, Delhi, 1986.

Travels and Adventures in Assam: John Butler, (1855), 2nd Reprint, Delhi, 1988

Sketch of Assam: -do-, London, 1847.

Report on the Eastern Frontier of British India, 1835: R. B. Pemberton, 2nd Print, Gauhati, 1966.

Memoir of a Survey of Assam and the Neighbouring Countries, Executed in 1825-6-7-8: In Asiatic Researches, Vol.XVII, Reprint, Delhi, 1980.

Asiaric Researches, Vols. XVII, containing Lieutenant R. Wilcox's 'Survey of Asam and the Neighbouring Countries': (ed) Sir William Jones, Reprint, Delhi, 1980.

Asiatic Researches, Vol. II containing translation of the *Alamgirnamah*: Reprint, Delhi, 1979.

The North East Frontier of India: Alexander Mackenzie (1884), Reprint, Delhi, 1999.

E. Miscellaneous (Assamese and English): Goswami, H. C.: Descriptive Catalogue of Assamese: Manuscripts, Calcutta, 1930.

Goswami, Pitambardeva: Leaflet titled Kartipakhya, Janasadharan aru Eke Pathar Pathik Guru Sakalar Ocharat Mor Antarar Bhav Nivedan, 28 Bohag, 1878 Sak (used here as Confession): Brahmanar Vidhava Bivah, Halakarshan aru Puspita Kanyar Bivah, Jorhat, 1846 Sak.

Asam Sarkar (Government of Assam): Bharat Tyag Andolanar Sonali Jayanti Barsha Udjapan, Asamar Mukti Yujaruloi Sambardhana, 1993.

Hzarika Gangadhar: Mahapurush Sri Srimat Dharmacharyya Pitambar Deva Goswami, 2 vols, Titabar, 1924, 1964.

Neog, M.: Prachya Sasanawali, Guwahati, 1974.

Neog, M. (comp. & ed.): Orunodoi (ed. Rev. Nathan Brown).

Pamegam, Tarun Chandra: Tarun Chandra Pamegam Rachanawali, Vol. I & II, (ed) B. Kagyung, Jorhat, 2005.

Phukan, Dilip Kumar: Auniati Satrat Sanrakshita Prachin Grantha samuhar Bibarantmak Talika, Auniati, 2004.

Saikia, N. (comp. & ed.): Asam Bandhu(ed.Gunabhiram Baruah), Guwahati, 1992.

Sarma, M. M.: Inscriptions of Ancient Assam, Guwahati, 1978.

Sarma, K.: Krishna Sarmar Diary, Guwahati, 1972.

Sadaramin Sarma Barua, H. K.: Sadaraminar Atma Jivani, Guwahati, 1999.

Orunodoi (ed. Rev. Nathan Brown): (comp. & ed.) M. Neog, Guwahati, 1083.

Banhi (ed. L.N.Bezbaroa): (Comp.) L. N. Tamuli, Guwahati, 2005.
Jorhat-200 (bicentenary volume): (ed.) P. C. Sabhapandit, Jorhat, 1997.

SECONDARY SOURCES

A. Assamese

Barbaruah, H.: Ahomar Din, Guwahati, 1981.
Bargohain, Homen (ed): Asamiya Sahityar Buranji, Vol.VI, Guwahati, 1993.
Barman, S. N.: Sankaradeva- Kriti aru Krititva, Gowahati, 1986.
Barman, S. N.: Oitihya aru Itihash (Prof. Amalendu Guha felicitation Volume), Guwahati, 2005.
Barua, B. K.: Asamar Loka Sanskriti, Guwahati, 1961.
Barua, Hem Chandra: Hemkosh, 6th edition, Guwahati, 1985.
Baruah, Gunabhiram: Anandaram Dhekial Phukanar Jivan Charitra, Reprint, Guwahati, 1971.
Baruah, S.L & Nath, D. (ed): Chutiya Jatir Buranji, Guwahati, 2007.
Bezbaroa, L. N.: Bezbaroa Granthavalee, 2 Vols, Reprint, Guwahati, 1988.
Bhattacharyya, S. K.: Asamar Satra Parichay, Auniati, 2004.
Bhuyan, N. C.: Bara Bhuyanr Chamu Buranji, Jorhat, 1961.
Bhuyan, S. K.: Swargadeo Rajeswar Singha, Guwahati, 1975.
Borah, Karuna: Satriya Nrittyar Rup Darshan, Kamalabari, 2006.
Choudhury, P.: Orunodoi, Guwahati, 1995.
Das, Taranath: Tribedika, Revised edn., Sibsagar, 1991.
Dattabarua, H. N.: Prachin Kamrupiya Kayastha Samajar Itivritta, Nalbari, 1941
Deori, I.: Asamar Janagosthiya Samasya, Guwahati, 2001.
Gohain, H.: Asamiya Jatiya Jibanat Mahapurushiya Parampara, 2 Vols., Guwahati, 1991.
————: Kirtan Puthir Ras Bichar, Guwahati, 1981.
Goswami, H. C.: (ed) Asamiya Sahityar Chaneki (1929), 7 Vols., Reprint, Dibrugarh, 2002.
Goswami, Narayan Chandea: Satriya Sanskritir Swarna Rekha, Revised And enlarged edition, Guwahati, 2005.
Goswami Dr. Sri Sri Pitambardeva: Satriya Utsavar Paricoy aru Tatparyya, Dibrugarh, 2002.
Guha Amalendu: Vaishnav Badar para Moamariya Bidrohaloi, Guwahati, 1993
Handique, B. C.: Purani Asamar Silpa, Jaysagar, 1959.
Hazarika, A. & Goswami, J. (ed): Asam sahitya Sabhar Bhashanawali, Part-III, Jorhat, 1961.
Kagyung, B. M.: Mising Sanskritir Alekhya, Revised and enlarged edition, Guwahati, 1989.
Kakati, B.: Purani Kamrupar Dharmar Dhara, Pathsala, 1955.
Kakati, K. C. (ed): Majuli, Guwahati, 2001.
Mahanta, P. K. (ed): Majuli, Jorhat, 2001.
Mahanta, Dr. P. K.: Asamiya Madhyavritta Srenir Itihas, Guwahati, 1971.
Mahanta, R. (ed. J.N.Bhuyan): Ratneswar Mahanta Rachanawali, Guwahati, 1977.
Mahanta, B. C.: Mahapurushiya Paramparat Satra aru Sangit, Jorhat, 2003.

Neog, M.: Pabitra Asam, 2nd print, Guwahati, 1969.
——: Asamar Sanskritik Aitihya, Dibrugarh, 2002.
——: Maheswar Neog Rachanawali, Dibrugarh, 1986.
Nath, D.: Adhunikatar Unmeshat Shri Shri Auniati.
——: Satra, Auniati, 2004.
Padun, Nahendra: Asamiya Sanskritiloi Janajatiya Barangani,Sivasagar, 1988.
Prastab Gosthi (comp.): Sankaradevar Chintat Pragatisilata, Dibrugarh, 1982.
Roychoudhury Anil: Asomar Samaj Itihasot Nava-Vaishnavbad, Guwahati, 2000.
Sarma, D. B.: Asamiya Jati Gathan Prakriya aru Jatiya Janagosthigata Anusthan Samuh, Jorhat, 2006.
Sarma, Tirthanath: Auniati Satrar Buranji, Auniati, 1975.
Sarma, J. N.: Asamar Nad-Nadi, Guwahati, 1993.
Sharma, Benudhar: Dakhinpat Satra, Guwahati, 1977.
Saikia, D & Saikia, K. (ed): Jyotirgamaya (a commemorative volume published on the occasion of the 350th anniversary of Garamur Satra, Majuli, 2007.
Sonowal Mohan (ed.): Sonowal Saurabh, Dibrugarh, 2007.
Tamuli, L. N.: Bharatar Swadhinata Sangramat Asamar Bhumika, Guwahati, 1988.

B. English

Alavi, Seema: The Eighteenth Century India- Debates In Indian Society, OUP, 2007.
Beteille Andre: Caste, Class and Power, OUP Paperback, 2007.
——: *Studies in Agiarian Social Structure,* OUP Paperback, 3rd Print, 1979.
Borah, K. C.: Income Expenditure and Saving in Rural India, Delhi, 1985.
Baden Powel, B. H.: Indian Village Community, Reprint, Delhi, 1972.
Barpujari, H. K.: Assam in the Days in the Company, Guwahati, 1963.
——: The American Missionaries and North-East India (1836-1900), Delhi, 1986.
Barua, B. K.: A Cultural History of Assam, Vol.I, 2nd edition, Gauhati, 1969.
Barua, K. L.: Early History of Kamarupa, 2nd edn., Guwahati, 1966.
Barua, S. L.: A Comprehensive History of Assam, Delhi, 1985.
Bhattacharji, R.: Lands of Early Dawn, Delhi, 2002.
Bhattacharyya, N. N.: Medieval Bhakti Movements in India, Delhi, 1989.
——: History of the Tantric Religion, Reprint, Delhi, 1999.
Bhuyan, S. K.: Anglo-Assamese Relations, Guwahati, 1949.
Cantlie, A.: The Assamese, London, 1984.
Chatterjee, S. K.: Kirata Jana Kriti, 2nd edition, Calcutta, 1974.
Chandra Satish: *Essays on Medieval Indian History,* OUP Paperback, New York, 2005.
Dalton, E. T.: Tribal History of Eastern India (originally Descriptive Ethnology of Bengal,1872), Reprint, Delhi, 1978.
Dasgupta, S. B.: Obscure Religious Cults, Calcutta, Reprint, 1995.
Desai, Neera & Thakkar, Usha: Women in Indian Society, NBT, Reprint, 2005.
Dumont, Louis: Homo Hierarchicus—The Caste System and Its Implications, Complete revised English Edition, OUP, 5th impression, 2006.
Dutta, S.: The Mataks and Their Kingdom, Allahabad, 1985.

Endle, S.: The Kacharis, Reprint, Delhi, 1975.

Elwin, V.: A Philosophy for Nefa, 4th Reprint, Delhi, 1999.

Forbes, Geraldine: The new Cambridge History of India (IV.2)Women in Modern India, 3rd South Asian Reprint, 2004.

Gait, E .A.: A History of Assam, 2nd edn. Reprint, Gauhati, 1981.

Ghurye, G. S.: Caste and Race in India, 5th edition, Bombay, 1969.

Gohain, U. N.: Assam under the Ahoms, 2nd edn. Reprint, Guwahati, 1992.

Gogoi Nath, Jahnabi: Agrarian System of Medieval Assam, Delhi, 2002.

Gogoi, P.: Tai Ahom Religion and Customs, Guwahati, 1976.

Goswami, P. D.: Festivals of Assam, Guwahati, 1995.

Guha, Amalendu: Planter-Raj to Swaraj- Freedom Struggle And Electoral Politics in Assam 1826-1947, Reprint, Delhi, 1988.

————————: Medieval and Early Colonial Assam, Calcutta, 1991.

Jones, W. Kenneth: Socio-Religious Reforms Movements in British India, 1st Paperback Indian end., Reprint, New Delhi, 2003.

Kakati, B. (ed): Aspects of Early Assamese Literature, Gauhati University, 1959.

Kuli, J. J.: (ed) The Misings- Their History and Culture, Guwahati, 1998.

Dutta, A. K.: Maniram Dewan and the Contemporary Assamese Society, Guwahati, 1990.

Majumdar, R. C.: History of Bengal, Vol.I, Patna, 1971.

Marshall, P. J. (ed): The Eighteenth Century in Indian History, OUP, Paperback, 2005.

Nath, D.: History of the Koch Kingdom, Delhi, 1989.

————————: Satras in Colonial Assam, ICHR,Guwahati, 2007.

Nath, R. M.: The Back-Ground of Assamese Culture, Shillong, 1948.

Neog, M.: Sankaradeva and His Times, Gauhati, 1965.

————————: Socio-Political Events in Assam Leading to the Militancy of the Mayamariya Vaishnavas, Calcutta, 1982.

Robinson Rowena: Sociology of Religion in India, New Delhi, 2004.

Risley, H. H.: Tribes and Castes of Bengal, 2 Vols.,Reprint, Calcutta, 1998.

Robinson Rowen and Clarke Sathianathan (ed): Religious Conversion in India, OUP, Paperback, 2007.

Saikia, R.: Social and Economic History of Assam 1853-1921, Delhi, 2000.

Sharma, R. S.: Perspective in Social and Economic History of Early India, New-Delhi, 1983.

Sarma, S. N.: The Neo-Vaisnavite Movement and the Satra Institution of Assam, Reprint, Guwahati, 1999.

Sarma, S. N.: A Socio-Economic and Cultural History of Medieval Assam (1200-1800 A.D.), Gauhati, 1989.

Singh, Y.: Cultural Change in India, New Delhi, 2000.

Sharma, Manorama: Social and Economic Change in Assam: Middle Class Hegemony, Delhi, 1990.

Singh, K. S.: People of India, Assam, Vol. XV, Pts. I & II, Calcutta, 2003.

Srinivas, M. N.: Social Change in Modern India, Calcutta, 1972, Indian edition Reprint, Delhi, 2002.

Tajguru, S.: Medieval Assamese Society, Nagaon, 1988.

Terwiel, B. J.: Tai of Assam and Ancient Tai Ritual, Vol.I, Gaya, 1980.
T. N. Madan (ed.): Religion in India, OUP, 10th impression, New Delhi, 2006.
Vansina, J.: Oral Tradition—A Study in Historical Methodology (tr.) H.M. Wright, Routledge, London, Reprint, 1969.

C. Bengali

N. N. Bhattacharyya: Bharatiya Dharmer Itihas, Calcutta, 1977.
Kanailal Chatoosadhyaya: (ed.) *Asame Cha-Kuli Andolan O Ramkumar Vidyaratna*, Calcutta, 1989.

Journals/Periodicals/News papers

Dainik Janambhumi
Amar Asam
Pratidin
Prantik
Gariyashi
Purbachal (Amar Asam group)
Dipa Lok (all volumes, 1997 (monthly journal published from Majuli by the NGO AVERD-NE).
Majuli Jila Mahila Samity Smriti Grantha (Silver Jubilee Volume of the Majuli District Women's Association, 2007.
Majulian (Majuli College Magazine).
Majuli Dvipika (published on the occasion of the 3rd annual conference of the Jorhat District Sahitya sabha, 1996).
Swarnasri (Souvenir, Lakhimpur District Silver Jubilee Volume, 1996).Sowansiri (Souvenir published on the occasion of the 67th annual Conference of the Asam Sahity Sabha, Lakhimpur, 2003).
Souvenir (published on the occasion of the Silver Jubilee year of Sri Sri Pitambardeva High School, 2002).
Souvenir (Dakhinpat Satra Sisya Sanmilan, 1997).
Souvenir (published on the occasion of the abhishek utsav of Sri Sri Pitambardeva Goswami of Auniati satra, 1998).
Smriti Grantha (Majuli Auniati Hem Chandra High School, Kamalabari, Majuli, Diamond Jubilee Volume) (ed) B.Saikia, Kamalabari, 1998.

English

Asiatic Researches

Beacon (Vol.III, No. III, Jan-June, 2004, Moridhal College Study Circle.
India Past and Present, Bombay.
Journal of the Asiatic Society of Bengal (JASB).
Journal of Historical Research, Dibrugarh University.
Proceedings of the North East India History Association Annual Conferences.
Proceedings of the Indian History Congress.

Glossary

Adhikara : Head of a Satra, a *Satradhikara.*

Ata : A senior and prepectable devotee residing in a Satra.

Atai/Atoi : A celebate devotee residing in a Satra.

Ali : Road

Ankiya-nat : One-act devotional plays written by Sankaradeva and Madhavdeva.

Baha : House of an inmate of a Satra.

Bhakat : Celibate inmate of a Satra.

Bata : A kind of traditional Assamese tray.

Bil : Pond, also see *doba*, *dubi.*

Bihu : Assamese national festival.

Banaraja : Literally king of the forest, the tiger.

Bargeet : Devotional songs in classical tunes composed by Sankardeva and Madhavadeva.

Bar-sabah : Big congregation prayer, large religious assembly.

Bayan : Leader or member of an instrumental musical party.

Bepari : Small trader.

Bhaona : Religious dramatical performance.

Bigha : Measure of land forming 1/4 of a *pura,* 7,200 sq.ft.

Bhawariya : Actors of Assamese religious drama.

Buranji : Assamese chronicle; written and preserved by the orders of the Ahom state. Some chronicles were also written by private individuals.

Chapori : River island.

Charit Puthi : A biography of a Vaishnava saint.

Chali nach : A type of *Satriya* dance resenbling the spreading out of the tail of a peacock.

Churiya : Men's waist cloth.

Chadar (Cheleng) : upper garment of both men and women.

Daba : A large drum.

Dalang : Bridge

Devottar : Revenue free lands granted for the purpose of erection and maintenance of temples.

Dhuti : Garment used by men in the lower part of their body.

Dharmottar : Revenue free land granted for religious purposes.

Dola : The Assamese littre; sedan or palanquin.

Dhol : A drum used by the Assamese people during *Bihu* dance.

Dhenki : Wooden machine for husking rice

Din-bhaona : Drama performed during the day time

Duli : Bamboo made appliance for preserving grain

Ekasarana : *eak*=one; *sarana*= initiation; the supreme surrender to one God.

Ga-dhan : Bride-price.

Gamocha : An Assamese towel

Gaon : Village

Gayan-bayan : Singing of religious song and biting of *khol* and cymbal

Ghat : River or ferry station

Guru-asan : Sanctum for the Assamese Vaishnavas

Gosain : A spiritual guide; the head of a Satra. Initially only the Brahmin *Satradhikaras* were called *Gosains*, but subsequently all *Satradhikaras*, Brahmins or non-Brahmins, were called so.

Guru : Preacher

Guru-Charita : A biography of a Vaishnava saint.

Hat : A market place.

Hati : Cloister of houses of the celibate inmates

Hola : Marshy low-lying swamp.

Jalpan : Assamese breakfast

Kathā : Measure of land forming 1/5th of a *bigha*, 1440 sq.ft.

Kharâhi : Small bamboo basket

Kirtan-ghar : Prayer hall, see *namghar*

Komal-chaul : Soft rice that can be taken as breakfast

Kalah : Pot—earthen or matetic

Kewalia : Celibate (inmate)

Kharani : A kind of alkalin prepared from the ash of plantain plant, specially from the rhizoms.

Kirtana : A devotional work by Sankaradeva; an act of chanting Prayers.

Kumar : Potter

Khol : A kind of musical instrument made of wood and skin

Mah-prasad : Offerings made in a religious function by an Assamese Vaishnava.

Maha-purushiya : Another name of Sankardeva's sect.

Manikut : Sanctum sanctorum of the Assamese Vaishnavas

Mantra : Incantations

Mauja : Collection of villages, a revenue division

Mahanta : *Satradhikar* belong to the Kayastha group. They were classified as *Bamuniya* and *Thakuriya* according to their affiliation.

Mathauri : Embankment.

Merduli : Bamboo encloser in the form of a large basket to contain grain.

Mithoi : A kind of Assamese sweet made of rice powder and jaggery.

Nach : Assamese classical dance.

Naimittika : Occasional agenda of a Satra.

Namghar : Prayer hall.

Nam-kirtan/ Nam-prasanga : Congregation prayer.

Nitya : Daily agenda of a Satra.

Nata/Nataka : Assamese drama.

Oja-pali : A choral performance with dance and music where Puranic tales are recited.

Pachati : A drama depicting childhood days of Lord Krishna.

Pâchi : bamboo basket

Palnam : Performance of congregation prayer by inmates in group by turn/ in succession.

Phoura : A jackal that use to cry when he sees a tiger in search of haunt.

Paka mithoi : A kind of Assamese sweet made of dry rice powder and boiled jaggery.

Pohari : Women trader who exchange articles going from house to house, invariably from the Kaivarta caste.

Paik : An adult male having had to render specific services to the state.

Prahara : One of the eight time divisions of the day (approximately three hours).

Prasad/mah-prasad : Offering made by an Assamese Vaishnava, made of pulses, gram, rice, ginger, coconut and rice.

Puja : Worship of idol.

Pura : Measure of land consisting of 4 *bigha* of land.

Raga : One of the six primary modes of music.

Sabah : A congregation of people for religious or semi-religious purposes.

Sanchipat : A sheet prepared from the sanchi-tree *(aqnilaria agallocha*) used for writting the manuscripts.

Sanghati : A Sectarian division of Vaishnavism of Assam.

Satradhikara : Head of a Satra.

Satra : A Vaishnava monastery of Assam.

Sarai : A traditional Assamese tray made of brass or bell metal, sometimes even of wood.

Tal : Cymbal, rhythm

Than : A sacred place; a place of worship at the cremation ground of a religious man.

Thapana : Sanctum where the Assamese Vaishnavas keep the *Bhagavata;* also called *thagi.*

Tola : A school for Sanskrit learning kept by a Brahmin scholar.

Tithi : Death anniversary of the Vaishnava saints.

Udasin : Celibate inmate of a Satra.

Ural : A kind of husking machine made of wood and used by the Misings.

Uthanam : Chanting of prayers with rhythmic movements in standing posture.

Vamsavali : A genealogical table; a history of a royal or a noble family or a Satra.

Index